NEWCOMER'S
HANDBOOK®

FOR

New York City

FIRST BOOKS

P. O. Box 578147
Chicago, IL 60657
773-276-5911
www.firstbooks.com

Editor: Belden Merims.
Publisher: Jeremy Solomon.
Cover/Interior Design, Production: Miles & Gale DeCoster, Art Machine.
Maps: Hung Nguyen.
Contributors: Jennifer Cecil, Ronen Glimmer, Martha Hanson, Chris Hornsby, Patty Moosbrugger

ISBN 0-912301-37-6   ISSN 1086-8887

Manufactured in the United States of America.

Published by First Books, Inc., P. O. Box 578147, Chicago, IL 60657, 773-276-5911.

THIS book is dedicated to the proposition that it is as rewarding to live in New York City as it is to work here. However, the transition from newcomer to New Yorker isn't necessarily achieved without some discomfort. To minimize the difficulties involved in moving to New York, we have written the *Newcomer's Handbook™ for New York City.*

The *Newcomer's Handbook™ for New York City* has been continually updated since its 1980 inception in order to keep up with change in this fastest-paced of cities.

Whether you are looking for the right neighborhood or the right health club, the right synagogue or merely the right radio station, these chapters will guide you, the newcomer, in your search.

In the late 1980s and early 1990s, New York City seemed sick and its long term prognosis even worse. But the 1990s brought a boom in two pillars of the New York economy: the stock market and tourism. These resurgent industries, plus a lower crime rate and a vague but real feeling that the city is no longer out of control, have turned the real estate market around. Once again the rental market is tight, especially in the more desirable neighborhoods, and rents are up roughly 30% over 1993. The quest for an affordable good apartment is more difficult. Wherever you settle, now more than ever, it is important to know your neighborhood: establishing a sense of community where you live will make your life in New York more rewarding.

In addition to regular updating and detailed descriptions of neighborhoods in the city and New Jersey, this 17th edition includes timely information on buying a home, as well as a chapter discussing the options in **Child Care and Schools** in the city. Keeping pets and finding a physician are addressed in the chapter on **Getting Settled**, and we've surveyed resources and services for people with disabilities in the chapter on **Helpful Services**.

As usual, we welcome readers' suggestions and comments on the tear-out page at the back of the book.

We hope that the information presented on the following pages will help you establish a New York City residence smoothly and speedily.

We also hope that once you select your neighborhood and settle in, the book will help you get on with the pleasure part: enjoyment of the city's myriad and unrivaled resources.

FROM the wind-whipped corner of East End Avenue and 86th Street on an icy January evening, Greenwich Village seems as accessible as Alaska. So you cancel plans to meet a Village acquaintance downtown, call a friend on East 85th and get together at an uptown bistro instead. There is no question but that the neighborhood in which you live affects what you do and who you see in New York City. Like attracts like and most newcomers tend to pay more attention to where they live than to how they live there. The determination of I-want-to-be-aloners wilts when faced with the choice between a nicely renovated one-bedroom apartment in Brooklyn's Park Slope for $1,000 a month (30 minutes from Manhattan by F train) and a two-person share in a one-bedroom apartment in Yorkville for $1,500, or more. The cachet of the Upper East Side (or another of Manhattan's established communities) usually has more allure for the neophyte than privacy in the boroughs or a newly gentrified enclave. It takes time, familiarity with the city and a certain street-honed sophistication to be totally at ease in distant or just-emerging districts. Still, unless money is no object, Manhattan's rental market often requires compromises, not only in the way you live but also in the neighborhood you choose. But wherever you land, once established, you'll probably become a booster of your own special area.

Not for nothing are New Yorkers neighborhood proud. More than just an address or a source of necessary services, neighborhoods provide residents with identification and a sense of belonging, which in turn gives the individual sufficient sustenance and heart for daily confrontations with the city's size and pace. Most New Yorkers feel profoundly chauvinistic about their area and delight in extolling its virtues—and its faults as well.

Manhattan neighborhoods are listed clockwise (picture an exceedingly elongated clock) starting with Yorkville, continuing south along the East River downtown around the tip of the island and then uptown along the Hudson ending with Washington Heights/Inwood. Descriptions of communities in The Bronx, Brooklyn, Queens, and Staten Island, as well as five in New Jersey follow Manhattan. No description, however, can substitute for your own experience. You are strongly encouraged to visit the neighborhoods that interest you and talk to residents before signing a lease. (Among other things, it is an excellent way to get leads on apartments that might otherwise escape your attention.) Resources and city services within each neighborhood are included in order to facilitate orientation once you're settled.

For newcomers who might wish to look further afield, to the suburbs for example, we have listed additional communities worth investigating in Brooklyn, Queens and Staten Island, as well as suburban towns in New Jersey, Connecticut, Westchester County, NY, and Long Island, none more than an hour's commute from Manhattan.

Suggestions on how to go about finding an apartment and how best to enjoy the city come after **Neighborhoods** in **Looking for A Place to Live** and in other sections.

Manhattan Address Locator

Formulas for finding street and avenue addresses above 14th Street are described below. Crosstown street numbers follow a more-or-less set pattern; not so, avenue street numbers. In a town where 950 Amsterdam Avenue is at 107th Street, 950 Broadway at 23rd, 950 5th at 76th and 950 Third at 57th, the somewhat elaborate system used to discover the llocation of an Avenue address is worth knowing.

East and West Side Avenues

To detemine the cross street for an address on an avenue, proceed as follows: first, take off the last digit of the building number; second, divide the remainder by two; third, add or subtract the number given in the column below.*

Avenues A, B, C, D	+ 3
1st Ave.	+ 3
2nd Ave.	+ 3
3rd Ave.	+ 10
4th Ave.	+ 8
5th Ave.	
Up to 200	+ 13
Up to 400	+ 16
Up to 600	+ 18
Up to 775	+ 20
From 775 to 1286 (Cancel last figure)	– 18
6th Ave. (Ave. of the Americas)	– 12
7th Ave.	
Below 110th St.	+ 12
Above 110th St.	+ 20
8th Ave.	+ 10
9th Ave.	+ 13
10th Ave.	+ 14
Amsterdam Ave.	+ 60
Broadway	
Above 23rd St.	– 30
Columbus Ave.	+ 60
Convent Ave.	+127
Lenox Ave.	+110
Lexington Ave.	+ 22
Madison Ave.	+ 26
Manhattan Ave.	+ 100
Park Ave.	+ 35
West End Ave.	+ 60

East Side Crosstown Streets

5th to Madison & Park	1-99
Park to Lexington	100-140
Lexington to 3rd	140-199
3rd to 2nd	200-299
2nd to 1st	300-399
1st to York	400-499

West Side Crosstown below 58th

5th to Ave. of Americas	1-99
Ave. of Americas to 7th	100-199
7th to 8th	200-299
8th to 9th	300-399
9th to 10th	400-4499
10th-11th	500-599

West Side Crosstown above 58th

Central Park West to Columbus	100-199
Columbus to Amsterdam	200-299
Amsterdam to West End	300-399
West End to Riverside	400-499

* Central Park West and Riverside Drive do not fit into this formula. Divide the house number by 10 and add 60 to find the cross street on Central Park West; for Riverside Drive, divide the house number by 10 and add 72.

MANHATTAN

Yorkville

Boundaries and Contiguous Areas: North: East 96th Street and East Harlem; **East:** East River; **South:** East 79th Street and Upper East Side; **West:** Lexington Avenue and Upper East Side.

What distinguished Yorkville from its Upper East Side surroundings until recently was the character imbued by immigrants from Germany and Eastern Europe. Now, however, you'll find more co-op signs and health clubs than residents of Hungarian or Czechoslovakian ancestry. In the 1980s, a co-op, condo and rental apartment boom finished off what World War II started: the erosion of Yorkville's old-world ethnicity. Old walkups were first leveled in the late 1940s to make way for new apartment buildings attractive to professionals—white-collar types who, once drawn to the neighborhood, began replacing the immigrants in the remaining railroad flats. Only traces of Yorkville's European heritage remain, and while Yorkville is still the most accessible part of the Upper East Side, what began as a scattering of stolid brick apartment buildings in mid-century is now an area that overflows with living space unlike any other part of the city. From the East 90s south is a forest of ever-more-fanciful towers and fortresses.

86th Street from Lexington to First Avenues has been attempting to redefine itself into a pricier shopping strip. However, the hoped for stability has not entirely materialized. Large residential projects such as the 17-story Park Avenue Court (really on Lexington) and the Colorado luxury apartment building are offering prime retail space (and lots of it) that has been attracting upscale, international stores.

Yorkville was a pleasant rural community when the first wave of German and Irish immigrants arrived on these shores in the 1850s. Tranquil pastures surrounded river estates owned by wealthy merchants, many of whom—John Jacob Astor, the Rhinelanders and the Schermerhorns—were of German origin. In the 1880s the completion of the Second and Third Avenue elevated lines opened the area to settlement, and German immigrants, many attracted by jobs in the developing breweries, moved north from the Lower East Side. Irish immigrants followed and then, as they grew more prosperous, Hungarians, Czechs and Slovaks. Today, the second and third generations are more likely to be found in Queens and Westchester than in Yorkville, and it is a dwindling, elderly Middle European population that patronizes the few remaining ethnic bakeries, butcher shops and restaurants. Not that these stores are empty; customer ranks have been swelled by appreciative young professionals lately come to dominate the area.

The inviting mix of buildings, old and new, that characterizes Yorkville, as well as the community's relatively low crime rate and good public schools, makes it an attractive destination for the determined apartment seeker. Housing construction, co-ops and rentals, spurred by development of the former Ruppert Brewery site between 90th and 93rd Streets, still booms south of 96th Street. Those bulky red brick blocks and columns east of Second Avenue are part of the Ruppert project, a complex that contains subsidized low income housing and middle income rentals, for which New York State residency is one of the qualifications. The Sunday *Times* Real Estate Section is thick with ads drumming those amenity-laden new Yorkville buildings as well as shareable one-bedroom apartments in newly renovated brownstones and tenements.

For a refreshing pause, explore Carl Schurz Park bordering the East River at 86th Street, where you can also spy the mayor's residence, graceful Gracie Mansion built in 1799. Jutting over F.D.R. Drive, this semi-sylvan oasis recalls Yorkville of yore and affords a spectacular view of the East River, its islands, boats and barges.

Upscale new apartment towers have attracted a tide of young professionals to the upper northeast reaches of Yorkville, and with them food and convenience stores, not to mention coffee bars which have lately Seattlized Manhattan. Streets once sparsely peopled are now alive with baby strollers and dogs.

Area Code: 212

Post Offices: Yorkville Station, 1619 Third Avenue, NYC 10028, at 91st Street, 369-2230; Gracie Station, 229 East 85th Street, NYC 10028, 988-6682.

Zip Codes: 10128, 10028, 10021

Police Precinct: Nineteenth, 153 East 67th Street, NYC 10021, 452-0600.

Emergency Hospitals: Mt. Sinai Hospital, Fifth Avenue at 100th Street, NYC 10029, 241-6500; Metropolitan Hospital, 1901 First Avenue, NYC 10029, 423-6262; Doctors Hospital, 170 East End Avenue, NYC 10128, 870-9000.

Library: Yorkville Branch, 222 East 79th Street, NYC 10021, 744-5824.

Public School Education: School District #2 (see **Chelsea**).

Cultural Resources: 92nd Street Y, Young Men's and Young Women's Hebrew Association, 1395 Lexington Avenue, NYC 10128, 427-6000.

Transportation—Subway: #4, #5, #6 Lexington Avenue at 96th Street, 86th Street (Exp), 77th Street, 68th Street, 59th Street (Exp).

Transportation—Bus: Crosstown *96th Street* (#19); Crosstown *86th Street* (#86); Crosstown *79th Street* (#79); Crosstown *72nd Street* (#72); Crosstown *66th/67th Street* (#66); Crosstown *57th Street* (#57, #58); Uptown *First Avenue*-Downtown *Second Avenue* (#15); Uptown *Third Avenue*-Downtown *Lexington Avenue* (#98, #101, #102).

The Upper East Side

Boundaries and Contiguous Areas: North: East 96th Street to Lexington Avenue and Yorkville, East Harlem: **East:** Lexington Avenue to 79th Street and the East River; **South:** 59th Street and the East Forties and Fifties; **West:** Fifth Avenue.

The affluent heart of the Upper East Side—that quadrant caught between Fifth, 79th, Lexington and 60th Street and the panhandle stretching from 79th along Fifth to 86th Street—has landmark status and as a result may remain ever thus. But this does not mean that Manhattan's most popular neighborhood for the wealthy and the upwardly mobile is completely homogeneous. Each avenue that traverses the area, from Fifth east to York, has a distinctive character all its own.

Fifth Avenue, flanking Central Park, glitters with some of the city's most magnificent museums, most exclusive cooperatives and some of its most glamorous relics, those wonderfully ornate mansions which so clearly reflect the tastes and fortunes of our turn-of-the-century millionaires. Fricks, Dukes, Carnegies, Whitneys—their copies of palaces, chateaux and Gothic castles established the avenue as highly fashionable. Dominating Fifth in the East 80s, the Metropolitan Museum, not content with being the major physical and artistic presence on the Upper East Side, is also the site of one of the liveliest street scenes in town. Its sprawling stone steps, while providing access to the museum, offer seats and a meeting place from which to watch the mimes, musicians and street vendors who use the sidewalk around the entrance as performing space.

Madison Avenue between 60th and 86th Streets is a veritable gauntlet of classy international boutiques and fine arts galleries. This solid wall of chic has been pepped up some with the addition of The Limited, Ralph Lauren, Timberland and the latest arrival: a Barneys. Around 81st Street and P.S. 6 (Public School #6), the premier elementary school on the Upper East Side, as well as a number of trendy designers have set up shop. Above 86th Street, where Andrew Carnegie built the elaborate mansion that now houses the Cooper-Hewitt Museum, most of the other palatial Beaux Arts residences constructed in the early 1900s have been acquired by schools, consulates and cultural institutions. Today these grand buildings, interspersed with bow-fronted, brick Georgian homes and solid pre-World War II apartment buildings, form an exceedingly harmonious neighborhood.

On Park, the handsome center strip of year-round greenery and seasonal plantings make the stately square cooperative buildings that proceed shoulder to elegant shoulder up the avenue more gracious still.

Lexington Avenue has largely taken over from Madison as purveyor of quality produce to Upper East Siders. Immaculate, and imaginative, shops harboring fishmongers and florists, greengrocers and bakers are crowded into the ruddy, rustic brick buildings that line the street.

The area from Third Avenue east to the river, once the province of the "el" and tenements, has been Trumped up. Today, sleek glass and granite shafts intersperse postwar brick apartment blocks that loom over the once characteristic, and now fast disappearing, five-story walkups. And turnover is a constant among the clubs, bars and restaurants catering to east-of-Third singles.

Area Code: 212

Post Office: Lenox Hill Station, 217 East 70th Street, NYC 10021, 879-4401. Nearby: Gracie Station, 229 East 85th Street, NYC 10028, 988-6682.

Zip Codes: 10128, 10028, 10021, 10022

Police Precinct: Nineteenth, 153 East 67th Street, NYC 10021, 452-0600.

Emergency Hospitals: Lenox Hill Hospital, 100 East 77th Street, NYC 10021, 434-2000; New York Hospital-Cornell Medical Center, 525 East 68th Street, NYC 10021, 746-5454; Manhattan Eye, Ear and Throat Hospital, 210 East 64th Street, NYC 10021, 838-9200. Nearby: Mt. Sinai Hospital, Fifth Avenue at 100th Street, NYC 10029, 241-6500.

Libraries: 96th Street Branch, 112 East 96th Street, NYC 10128, 289-0908; Webster, 1465 York Avenue between 77th and 78th Streets, NYC 10021, 288-5049. The New York Society Library, 288-6900, a private institution with membership dues $135 per year) and 250,000 volumes, is an outstanding resource located at 53 East 79th Street, NYC 10021.

Public School Education: School District #2 (see **Chelsea**).

Adult Education: Marymount Manhattan College, 221 East 71st Street, NYC 10021, 517-0400; Hunter College, 695 Park Avenue at 68th Street, NYC 10021, 772-4000.

Cultural Resources: 92nd Street Y (Young Men's and Young Women's Hebrew Association) 1395 Lexington Avenue, NYC 10128, 427-6000; the Cooper-Hewitt Museum, 2 East 91st Street, 860-6898; the International Center of Photography (ICP), 1130 Fifth Avenue at 94th Street, 860-1777; the Jewish Museum, 1109 Fifth Avenue at 92nd Street, 423-3200; the Solomon Guggenheim Museum, 1071 Fifth Avenue at 89th Street, 423-3500; the Whitney Museum of American Art, 945 Madison Avenue at 75th Street, 570-3600; the Metropolitan Museum of Art, Fifth Avenue at 82nd Street, 535-7710; the Frick Collection, 1 East 70th Street, 288-0700; The Asia Society, 725 Park Avenue (at 70th Street) 288-6400; the Center for Inter-American Relations, Park Avenue and 68th Street; the China Institute, 125 East 65th Street, 744-8181; Society of Illustrators, 128 East 63rd Street, 838-2560, and numerous other societies, museums, galleries and auction houses.

Transportation—Subway: #4, #5, #6 Lexington Avenue at 96th Street, 86th Street (Exp), 77th Street, 68th Street, 59th Street (Exp).

Transportation—Bus: Crosstown *96th Street* (#19); Crosstown *86th Street* (#86); Crosstown *79th Street* (#79); Crosstown *72nd Street* (#72); Crosstown *66th/67th Street* (#66); Crosstown *57th Street* (#28); Uptown *Madison Avenue* (#1, #2, #3, #4); Downtown *Fifth Avenue* (#1, #2, #3, #4).

Roosevelt Island

Located off 59th Street in the East River.

Roosevelt Islanders have always had an unusual commute: a silent aerial float to and from 59th Street—Second Avenue in Manhattan (every 5 to 15 minutes for $1.50) up and over the East River with the city's skyline first at eye level and then, incredibly, beneath your feet. Small wonder that the trams find favor with tourists and day-trippers. Residents used to be reduced to taking cabs or a roundabout bus ride through Queens to Manhattan when the funicular occasionally faltered. Now, however, the city's Transit Authority has a subway line (the Q train) connecting the island with Queens (at 21st Street and 41st Avenue) and Manhattan (at 63rd and Lex).

An appealing small-town quality pervades this island community of modern apartment buildings. It's quiet. Automobile access is limited, and a minibus (10¢) provides regular service between the tram terminal and high rises lining relatively spotless streets where strolls with baby carriages and street corner chats are ritual—a sort of time zip to the 1940s. Sunbathers crowd the greensward on a warm afternoon, joggers pad silently along the Promenade, and the contemplative sit observing sailboats and barges parading Manhattan's skyline. Roosevelt Island has extensive recreational facilities and stores supplying the basic needs, if not the exotic or ethnic ones. Built by early farmers in 1796, the Manor House is preserved at the foot of Main Street. The Octagon Lighthouse has recently been restored. Superior schools go up to the eighth grade and are part of District #2 (information in the **Chelsea** section).

Inauguration of the long-awaited subway line came not a moment too soon: the red brick five-building Manhattan Park development on an eight-acre site just north of the original concrete buildings added 1,100 units to the housing stock and some 2,500 inhabitants to the island's existing population of 5,200. Manhattan Park, unlike Roosevelt Island's rent-subsidized housing, is attracting upper middle class families (no studios) with stunning views and concierges at prices about 25% below comparable Manhattan rents. Residents hope these changes and the future development of the island's south point will do nothing to disturb the peaceful, low-crime character of the island.

Manhattan Park buildings are managed by Grenadier Realty Corp., 308-4040, with a rental office in Building 2 at 30 River Road. The

Roosevelt Island Housing Management Corp., 838-4747, at 552 Main Street manages the rental units and subsidized apartments (for which there are specified income limits) in the original buildings; co-ops are managed by Rose Assoc. Inc., 308-7271. NB: If you own a dog, Roosevelt Island isn't for you; dogs are *verboten* on the narrow 2 1/2-mile-long island.

Area Code: 212

Post Office: Island Post Office, 694 Main Street, 752-5564.

Zip Code: 10044

Police Precinct: One Hundred and Fourteenth, 34-16 Astoria Boulevard, Astoria, New York 11103, (718) 626-9311.

Emergency Hospital: Goldwater Memorial Hospital, Roosevelt Island, 318-8000.

Library: Roosevelt Island Community Library, 524 Main Street, NYC 10044, 308-3423.

Transportation: *Tramway* (59th Street and Second Avenue). *Bus*: Queens (Q32). *Subway:* 63rd Street (B, Q).

East Forties and Fifties

Boundaries and Contiguous Areas: North: 59th Street and the Upper East Side; **East:** East River; **South:** 42nd Street and Murray Hill; **West:** Lexington Avenue.

In the 18th century, this urbane neighborhood was known as Turtle Bay Farm, a charming name that still applies to the tree-shaded community lying in the shadow of the United Nations. The mid-19th century brought industrialization and the "el" rumbling over tenements built along the East River. A construction boom in the 1920s left the heart of Turtle Bay much as you see it today; handsome blocks of carefully maintained brownstones interspersed with relatively small apartment buildings. But not until the 1940s, when the squalid slaughterhouses that had replaced the riverside slums were razed to make room for the United Nations, and the 1950s, when the "el" came tumbling down, did Turtle Bay become eminently respectable from Lexington Avenue clear to the East River. Now the area is one of the most prestigious—and one of the safest—in town, a self-assured place with tony restaurants and charming cul de sacs like Amster Yard on 49th Street, Greenacre Park on 51st and the private, somewhat secret, garden enclosed by twenty Italianate townhouses in which Katharine Hepburn and E.B. White once lived.

Apartment prices, as befits a neighborhood embracing exclusive Sutton Place, Beekman Place and the two glass towers at United Nations Plaza, are among the highest around. For the least rarefied rates look along First and Second Avenues and the side streets in between.

Tudor City lies southwest of Sutton Place and somewhat downscale. Bounded by 40th and 43rd Streets, this huge complex of Tudor-style buildings between First and Second Avenues includes a hotel, church and private parking area. Unfortunately for would-be tenants, eleven of the twelve buildings completed in 1930 have been converted to cooperatives.

Area Code: 212

Post Office: Tudor City Station, 5 Tudor City Place, NYC 10017, 697-8656.

Zip Codes: 10022, 10017, 10016

Police Precinct: Seventeenth, 167 East 51st Street, NYC 10022, 826-3211.

Emergency Hospital (nearest): New York Hospital-Cornell Medical Center, 525 East 68th Street, NYC 10021, 746-5454; New York University Hospital and Medical Center, 560 First Avenue, NYC 10016, 263-7300.

Libraries (nearest): 58th Street Branch, 127 East 58th Street, NYC 10022, 759-7358; Mid-Manhattan, 455 Fifth Avenue, NYC 10016, 340-0849.

Public School Education: School District #2 (see **Chelsea**).

Adult Education: Turtle Bay Music School, 244 East 52nd Street, NYC 10022, 753-8811.

Cultural Resources: Young Men's Christian Association of Greater New York, Vanderbilt Branch, 224 East 47th Street, NYC 10017, 756-9600; YWCA of the City of New York, 610 Lexington Avenue, NYC 10022, 755-2700; Japan Society, 333 East 47th Street, NYC 10017, 832-1155; Phillip Morris branch of the Whitney Museum of American Art, 120 Park Avenue, NYC 10017, 878-2550.

Transportation—Subway: #7 Crosstown 42nd Street Shuttle (S), Lexington Avenue; Crosstown (#7) Lexington/Third Avenues; #4, #5, #6 Lexington Avenue at 59th Street (Exp), 51st Street, 42nd Street (Exp).

Transportation—Bus: Crosstown *49th/50th Streets* (#27, #50); Crosstown 42nd Street (#42); Uptown *Madison Avenue* (#1, #2, #3, #4); Uptown *Third Avenue*—Downtown *Lexington Avenue* (#98, #101, #102); Uptown *First Avenue*—Downtown *Second Avenue* (#15).

Murray Hill

Boundaries and Contiguous Areas: **North:** 42nd Street and the East Forties and Fifties; **East:** East River; **South:** 34th Street and the Gramercy Park Area; **West:** Fifth Avenue.

Murray Hill is the kind of neighborhood where you can walk into a compact ground floor apartment, open a back door and have access to a garden larger than the flat. Time was when the great mansions of Fifth and Madison Avenues—lastingly elegant buildings like J.P. Morgan's magnificent McKim, Mead and White-designed library—conferred social status on the houses highest on the hill. Below these were the stables and carriage houses serving them, and in the shadow of the old Third Avenue "el," tenements. The tenements are gone now and as Fifth Avenue became more commercial, residential Murray Hill shifted east and the carriage houses proved to be fashionable—indeed, charming—homes. The streets are a mix of tranquil landmarks such as Sniffen Court, a private mews at 150-158 East 36th Street, nondescript brick apartment buildings and postmodern fantasies like the undulating, 57-story Corinthian. And brownstones: these solid and unpretentious turn-of-the-century buildings are nonetheless elegant and lend a particularly substantial quality to the crest of Murray Hill.

This popular area is made more attractive still by the vitality of its early evening street life. The doctors, nurses and other young professionals employed by University and Bellevue Hospitals and related New York University medical facilities are a major presence on the scene, and the casual, inviting shops and restaurants crowding Second and Third Avenues play to a youthful audience. Housing possibilities include proliferating high rises on the flatlands east of Third as well as brownstones and carriage houses on Murray Hill itself.

Area Code: 212

Post Office: Murray Hill Station, 115 East 34th Street, NYC 10016, 679-9127.

Zip Code: 10016

Police Precinct: Seventeenth, 167 East 51st Street, NYC 10022, 826-3211.

Emergency Hospitals (nearest): New York University Medical Center, 560 First Avenue (and 33rd Street), NYC 10016, 263-7300; Bellevue Hospital Center, 462 First Avenue (and 27th Street), NYC 10016, 562-4141.

Library: Kips Bay, 446 Third Avenue, NYC 10016, 683-2520.

Public School Education: School District #2 (see **Chelsea**).

Adult Education: American Academy of Dramatic Arts, 120 Madison Avenue, NYC 10016, 686-9244.

Cultural Resources: J. Pierpont Morgan Library, 29 East 36th Street, NYC 10016, 685-0008.

Transportation—Subway: Crosstown *42nd Street Shuttle* (S), Lexington Avenue; Crosstown(*#7*) Lexington/Third Avenues; #4, #5,

#6 Lexington Avenue at 42nd Street (Exp), 33rd Street.

Transportation—Bus: Crosstown *34th Street* (#16, #34); Uptown *Madison Avenue* (#1, #2, #3, #4); Uptown *Third Avenue*—Downtown *Lexington Avenue* (#101, #102); Downtown *Second Avenue* (#15).

Gramercy Park Area

Boundaries and Contiguous Areas: **North:** 34th Street and Murray Hill; **East:** Second Avenue and Stuyvesant Area; **South:** East 14th Street; **West:** Park Avenue South/Chelsea and the Flatiron District.

The Gramercy Park is a verdant, block-square, fenced and locked enclave to which only residents of the surrounding buildings hold keys. With its lovely old trees, squirrels, flowering spring plantings and the occasional nanny, the park is reminiscent of a quiet London square. But it wasn't the work of a homesick Brit; a real estate developer, to increase the value of 66 lots he owned nearby, laid out the private park in 1831. That this strategy was successful is evidenced by the quality of the ornate later-19th century buildings that still surround the square—elaborate structures like The Players Club (Edwin Booth's former home) and the National Arts Club (designed by Calvert Vaux in a Gothic Revival style).

The air of dignified elegance which permeates Gramercy Park and sets such a pleasant tone for the neighborhood as a whole is reinforced by historic Stuyvesant Square (located four blocks to the southeast at 15th Street) with its lovely white clapboard Friends Meeting House and brownstone St. George's Church, where J.P. Morgan once worshiped. In general, this is an enclave of small townhouses and rows of trim brick-fronts dappled with upgraded tenements, modest apartment houses and an occasional highrise.

And, propelled by emergence of the East 20s and of the Union Square area as a major publishing and public relations neighborhood, more are on their way. On Park Avenue and on Second Avenue, and in the 20s and low 30s, new condos have sprouted like field mushrooms after a warm fall rain. Pricey rentals are available at the Rutherford Place apartments overlooking Stuyvesant Square and in the older and highly desirable Waterside complex between 23rd and 28th Streets overlooking the East River.

Gramercy Park is a desirable place to live, but you probably have a better chance of finding an apartment in one of the newer high rises that ring the neighborhood than in one of the townhouses adjacent to the park itself. In any event, the Gramercy area is relaxed and neighborly, and it pays to walk through the community talking with doormen and building superintendents when searching for an apartment here.

Area Code: 212

Post Offices: Murray Hill Station, 115 East 34th Street, NYC 10016, 679-9127; Madison Square Station, 149 East 23rd Street, NYC 10010, 673-3771.

Zip Codes: 10016, 10010, 10003

Police Precincts: Seventeenth (above 30th Street), 167 East 51st Street, NYC 10022, 826-3211; Thirteenth, 230 East 21st Street, NYC 10010, 477-7411.

Emergency Hospitals (nearest): New York University Hospital Medical Center, 560 First Avenue at 33rd Street, NYC 10016, 263-7300; Bellevue Hospital Center, First Avenue and 27th Street, NYC 10016, 562-4141; Cabrini Medical Center, 227 East 19th Street, NYC 10003, 995-6000; Beth Israel Medical Center, 16th Street at First Avenue, NYC 10003, 420-2000; New York Eye and Ear Infirmary, 310 East 14th Street, NYC 10003, 979-4000.

Library: Kips Bay Branch, 446 Third Avenue, NYC 10016, 683-2520.

Public School Education: School District #2 (see **Chelsea**).

Adult Education: School of Visual Arts, 209 East 23rd Street, NYC 10010, 679-7350; Baruch College of Adult and Continuing Education, 48 East 26th Street, NYC 10010, 447-3020, general information 802-2000.

Cultural Resources: The Players, 16 Gramercy Park South between Irving Place and Park Avenue South, NYC 10003, 228-7610, contains important collections of letters, playbills, prompt books, plays and materials relating to 19th century British and American theater which can be seen by appointment. Theodore Roosevelt House, 28 East 20th Street, NYC 10003, between Broadway and Park Avenue South, 260-1616; Roosevelt's exuberantly Victorian birthplace contains letters, books and objects collected from his many trips.

Transportation—Subway: Crosstown 14th Street (L) at Union Square, Third Avenue; #4, #5, #6 Lexington Avenue at 33rd Street, 28th Street, 23rd Street, 14th Street/Union Square (Exp).

Transportation—Bus: Crosstown *34th Street* (#16, #34); Crosstown *23rd Street* (#23); Crosstown *14th Street* (#14); Uptown *Madison Avenue* (#1, #2, #3, #4); Uptown *Third Avenue*—Downtown *Lexington Avenue* (#101, #102); Downtown *Second Avenue* (#15).

Stuyvesant Town and Peter Cooper Village

Boundaries and Contiguous Areas: North: 23rd Street; **East:** FDR Drive; **South:** 14th Street and the East Village; **West:** First Avenue and Gramercy Park Area.

Two of the oldest and best known housing developments in New York City, Stuyvesant Town, 14th Street to 20th Street, and its upscale (larger apartments and rents) big brother, Peter Cooper Village, 20th Street to 23rd Street, are difficult to penetrate. In addition to income requirements, there is a long waiting list where time is meted out in years, not weeks or months. What makes these developments so desirable, besides the relatively reasonable rents, is their resolutely middle-class, family-oriented population, relative safety and—after twenty-five years' growth of trees, flowers, ivy and climbing hydrangea against the otherwise unrelieved brick walls—unpretentious attractiveness. So, if you care to pursue the matter, apply at the renting office for both developments, which are owned by Metropolitan Life Insurance Co., at 629 East 14th Street, NYC 10009, 780-1300, and get in line, or "on line," as we say in New York.

The community surrounding Peter Cooper and Stuyvesant includes luxury buildings as well as owner-occupied brownstones and upgraded tenements. When scouting the area (First Avenue west to Lexington), try the side streets. The neighborhood is a comparison shopper's dream, with major supermarkets and many ethnic food stores (especially south on First Avenue), clothing shops and decorating showrooms along First and Second Avenues vying for your dollars. There are large, quiet tree-shaded parks for breaks between apartment visits, and in warm weather the renovated public swimming pool at 23rd Street and Asser Levy Place is available for a cooling few laps. (In fact, look for this turn-of-the-century stone Roman bath even if you can't swim; it's a beauty.) And if you're beset by hypochondria, this neighborhood, with five top hospitals within walking distance, merits serious consideration.

Area Code: 212

Post Office: Peter Stuyvesant Station, 432 East 14th Street, NYC 10009, 677-2112.

Zip Codes: 10010, 10009

Police Precinct: Thirteenth, 230 East 21st Street, NYC 10010, 477-7411.

Emergency Hospitals: New York University Hospital Medical Center, 560 First Avenue at 33rd Street, NYC 10016; 263-7300; Bellevue Hospital Center, First Avenue and 27th Street, NYC 10016, 562-4141; Cabrini Medical Center, 227 East 19th Street, NYC 10003, 995-6000; Beth Israel Hospital Medical Center, 16th Street and First Avenue, NYC 10009, 420-2000; New York Eye and Ear Infirmary, 310 East 14th Street, NYC 10003, 979-4000.

Libraries: Epiphany Branch, 228 East 23rd Street, NYC 10010, 679-2645; Kips Bay, 446 Third Avenue, NYC 10016, 683-2520.

Public School Education: School District #2 (see **Chelsea**).

Adult Education: School of Visual Arts, 209 East 23rd Street, NYC 10010, 679-7350; Baruch College of Adult and Continuing Education, 48 East 26th Street, NYC 10010, 725-7172.

Transportation—Subway: Crosstown 14th Street (L) at Lexington Avenue, Third Avenue, First Avenue; #4,#5, #6 Lexington Avenue at 23rd Street, 14th Street/Union Square (Exp).

Transportation—Bus: Crosstown *34th Street* (#16) goes across 34th Street and down Second Avenue, then east across 23rd Street and uptown to 34th Street along F.D.R. Drive; Crosstown *23rd Street* (#26); Crosstown *14th Street* (#14); Uptown *First Avenue—*Downtown *Second Avenue* (#15).

East Village

Boundaries and Contiguous Areas: North: 14th Street and the Stuyvesant Area; **East:** East River; **South:** Houston Street and the Lower East Side; **West:** Broadway and Greenwich Village.

Once again this colorful neighborhood is in the process of reinventing itself. Time was when it was best described as the upper Lower East Side, both geographically and socio-economically. Indeed, some long-time residents still consider themselves Lower East Siders, but sometime in the 1960s, perhaps in an attempt to bestow a bit of cachet, this largely immigrant neighborhood with an emerging avant-garde colony was dubbed the East Village. The name stuck, and while the East lacks the charm of Greenwich to the west, this Village no longer has the depressing poverty and crime of much of the Lower East Side to the south.

What this up-beat but slightly off-center community of homesteaded tenements does have is a combination of ingredients that makes it one of the most desirable alternative neighborhoods in town: an abundant and often eye-popping street life, antique shops, boutiques on the cutting edge of fashion, a burgeoning restaurant and club life, and beauticians expert in the latest hairstyle. The East Village also boasts an influential ethnic population. Italians, Poles, Ukrainians and Latinos, and the bakeries, butcher shops, restaurants and various cultural institutions they have nurtured for decades, add not only diversity but depth to the neighborhood.

The retaking of Alphabet City, the A, B, C and D Avenues east of First Avenue, from the control of drug dealers and junkies has been a major factor in the redevelopment of the East Village since the 1980s. Projects along Avenue D still render that area dicey, but now Avenues A and B boast co-ops, and the stunning renovation of Tompkins Square saved the park from Calcutta-like squalor and brought back the East Village's leafy back yard. Consequently rents, while still more affordable than in other areas, have been rising here.

To the west, the Astor Place area bubbles with student life centered around Cooper Union and nearby NYU, the ever-lively Joseph Papp Public Theater, and good buys in books, booze and latest-look clothing along a revivified Broadway. Connecting Astor Place with the Second Avenue heart of the East Village is St. Mark's Place, actually part of 8th Street, where hippies and flower children frolicked, the Electric Circus drew limousines from uptown and W. H. Auden lived. That's gone now and St. Mark's is a bit quieter, visually and audibly, but little changed. To the south the area between the Bowery and Broadway, where once Vanderbilts and Astors lived, has re-acquired a bit of its old chic—if not its elegance—and the tag Noho (for **No**rth of **Ho**uston Street). Lofts in the brick and cast-iron industrial buildings fetch lofty prices, but much of Noho is legally reserved for certified artists. Prospective residents should check with the City Loft Board (212-788-7610) to determine their eligibility and to be sure the particular building is in compliance with the Loft Law.

Throughout the East Village, pocket-sized boutiques offering chic and exotic clothing coexist nonchalantly with The Boys Club of New York, Hell's Angels' NYC headquarters and the "Indian Block" curry parlors on Sixth Street. In these surroundings, briefcase-toting law associates and young Wall Street trainees look somewhat out of place but they, no less than trendily dressed students, are attracted by the neighborhood's decidedly lively pace and comparatively reasonable rents. Although condo conversions are multiplying, be prepared for walk-ups; most of the housing stock consists of improved tenements. Start your apartment search by studying ads in *The Village Voice*, then check Cooper Union and NYU bulletin boards, walk the streets and talk to people who live here.

Area Code: 212

Post Offices: Cooper Station, 93 Fourth Avenue, NYC 10003, 254-1389; Peter Stuyvesant Station, 432 East 14th Street, NYC 10009, 677-2112; Tompkins Square Station, 244 East Third Street, NYC 10009, 673-6415.

Zip Codes: 10003, 10009

Police Precinct: Ninth, 321 East Fifth Street, NYC 10003, 477-7811.

Emergency Hospitals: Beth Israel Hospital Medical Center, 16th Street and First Avenue, NYC 10009, 420-2000; New York Eye and Ear Infirmary, 310 East 14th Street, NYC 10003, 979-4000.

Libraries: Ottendorfer Branch, 135 Second Avenue, NYC 10003, 674-0947; Tompkins Square Branch, 331 East 10th Street, NYC 10009, 228-4747.

Public School Education: School District #1: Community School Board, 80 Montgomery Street, NYC 10002, 602-9700.

Adult Education: Third Street Music School Settlement, 235 East 11th Street, NYC 10003, 777-3240; Stuyvesant Adult Center, 345 East 15th Street, NYC 10003, 254-2890, offers a wide variety of inexpensive evening adult education courses, from languages to sewing.

Cultural Resources: La Mama Experimental Theater Club, 74A East Fourth Street, 475-7710, on the cutting edge of avant-garde theater for over two decades, and PS (Performing Space) 122, 150 First Avenue, 477-5288, a reclaimed public school, to say nothing of the Joseph Papp Public Theater, 425 Lafayette Street, 598-7100, indicate the lively state of this neighborhood's arts. Second Avenue was the Yiddish rialto until 1940. Now the Theater for the New City performs new plays in a converted city market building at 155 First Avenue, 254-1109, and CSC Repertory Theater has been successfully producing classics at 136 East 13th Street, 677-4210, for nearly 20 years. The Third Street Music School (see above) also offers concerts and recitals, and Cooper Union at Third Avenue and 7th Street, 353-4195, has frequent exhibits, concerts and lectures. Theater and opera thrive even on the Bowery: classics at the Jean Cocteau Repertory, at 330 Bowery, 677-0060, and Italian opera at The Amato Opera Theater at 319 Bowery, 228-8200.

Transportation—Subway: Crosstown 14th Street*(*(L) at Third Avenue, First Avenue; #6 at Lexington Avenue and Astor Place, Bleecker Street; F at Houston Street/Second Avenue.

Transportation—Bus: Crosstown *14th Street* (#14); going East: Crosstown *West 10th Street/West Eighth Street* (#13); going West: Crosstown *West Ninth Street/Christopher Street* (#13); Uptown *Third Avenue/Lexington*—Downtown *Lexington/Third Avenue* (#101, #102); Uptown *First Avenue*—Downtown *Second Avenue* (#15).

Lower East Side, Little Italy and Chinatown

Boundaries and Contiguous Areas: **North:** Houston Street and the East Village; **East:** East River; **South:** Downtown; **West:** Broadway and SoHo.

"Give me your tired, your poor…" wrote Emma Lazarus, and when they arrived, many of them, it was to the Lower East Side. Between 1870 and 1920, wave upon wave of immigrants from Italy, Bohemia, China and the ghettos of eastern Europe poured into the warren of fetid tenements on Mulberry, Elizabeth, Hester and Division Streets, where they lived and worked until able to move up and out to the suburbs, or at least The Bronx, leaving room for the next wave.

Although public housing, especially along the easternmost strip of the Lower East Side, has alleviated crowding and let in some light and air, much of the area remains unchanged from the turn of the century. Whole chunks of the neighborhood are rat-, roach-and drug-infested—and dangerous. Along the fringes, however, there are enclaves where the young and impecunious—artists, students and the like—have established beachheads. Even grungy Ludlow Street is showing unmistakable signs of gentrification: among the grim tenements, a thriving cafe in the basement of a newly renovated building with an incredible *trompe l'oeil* facade.

Actually, at least three Lower East Sides exist, with imprecise and constantly changing borders: (1) the old Jewish Lower East Side, now largely Puerto Rican, to the east; (2) Chinatown in the southwest portion, which continues to expand inexorably northward into (3) Little Italy. Colorful Orchard Street is still chockablock with little stores and Yiddish-speaking shopkeepers, many of them bearded, black-hat-wearing Hasidim. On Sunday in particular, crowds flock in from New Jersey, Long Island and uptown in search of bargains and Jewish food specialties. But shop owners live elsewhere, most of them, and at night all that remains of a once vibrant Jewish community are forlorn old synagogues, deserted or converted to Pentecostal churches.

Thousands upon thousands of recent arrivals have burst Chinatown's traditional seams past East Broadway into the old Jewish enclave and north over Canal Street into Little Italy, which is now two-thirds Asian. Continuing immigration via Hong Kong has also severely split the once stable social and political fabric of the Chinese community. Housing is impossibly crowded, and sweatshops are said to be increasing. But walking the almost impassable sidewalks of Chinatown on a Saturday, one would think this area existed solely to satisfy the city's insatiable appetite for Chinese food. Like bounty hunters, mavens stalk the crowded streets, pouncing on new restaurants with cries of delight. On Saturdays, there are numerous street vendors.

Little Italy, between Canal and Houston Streets, has a declining Italian population and an expanding selection of Italian restaurants and cafes. Along Mulberry Street on a warm spring evening the combined hisses of uncountable cappuccino machines sound like a locomotive gathering steam. The neighborhood seems destined to become a restaurant district operated increasingly from Long Island, Staten Island and New Jersey. And although bean sprouts have replaced fagioli and frozen dim sum take the place of frozen ravioli in innumerable small stores, a bit of the old Southern Italian character still remains, as does the community's reputation as a don't-mess-with-us, low-crime neighborhood with strong ethnic ties around the old, original St. Patrick's. Infiltration of the Lower East Side by the middle class has begun. In fact, it's old news. In 1984, intrepid souls brave enough to sign leases on The Bowery, Rivington or Pitt Streets were featured in *The New York Times*. Now bright banners advertising slick co-ops flutter in Little Italy and Chinatown. Most notably the refurbished Police Building at 240 Centre Street, a granite Renaissance Revival palazzo built in 1909, reopened with crystal chandeliers and 54 luxury condos behind a statuary-cluttered facade in the heart of Little Italy. Rents in the neighborhood move ever upward, and the unmonied and creative have moved to Queens. Still, apartment listings are sparse. Best to talk to someone who lives in the neighborhood, and do walk around, exercising caution and looking (carefully) block by block.

Area Code: 212

Post Offices: Knickerbocker Station, 128 East Broadway, NYC 10002, 227-0089; Chinatown Station, 6 Doyers Street, NYC 10013, 267-3510.

Zip Codes: 10012, 10013, 10002

Police Precincts: Fifth, 19 Elizabeth Street, NYC 10013, 334-0711; Seventh, 191/2 Pitt Street, NYC 10002, 477-7311.

Emergency Hospital (nearest): New York Downtown Hospital, 170 William Street, NYC 10038, 312-5000.

Libraries: Hamilton Fish Park Branch, 415 East Houston Street, NYC 10002, 673-2290; Seward Park Branch, 192 East Broadway, NYC 10002, 477-6770.

Public School Education: School District #1: Community School Board, 80 Montgomery Street, NYC 10002, 602-9700; School District #2 (see **Chelsea**).

Cultural Resources: The Henry Street Settlement is actually a variety of resources, with its Arts for Living Center, Settlement Playhouse and New Federal Theater at 466 Grand Street, NYC 10002, 598-0400. The Lower East Side Tenement Museum, 97 Orchard Street, NYC 10002, 431-0233, includes exhibits in three buildings (one of which has been "unrestored" to illustrate life as it was) as well as neighborhood walking tours. The recently renovated and renamed Museum of Chinese in the Americas, 70 Mulberry Street, NYC 10013, 619-4785, offers historical walking tours as well as exhibits and video documentaries.

Transportation—Subway: #6 Lafayette Street at Spring Street, Canal Street (Exp); F Houston/Second Avenue, Delancey Street; B and D at Grand Street (Exp); N and R at Broadway and Canal; J, M, Z Canal, Bowery and Essex Street.

Transportation—Bus: Crosstown *West-East Houston* (#21); Uptown *First Avenue*—Downtown *Second Avenue* (#15); Uptown *Bowery/Third Avenue* —Downtown *Third Avenue/ Bowery* (#101, #102).

Downtown

Boundaries and Contiguous Areas: North: Chambers Street and Tribeca; **East:** East River; **South:** Upper New York Bay; **West:** Hudson River.

The streets of downtown New York are so convoluted and irrational in design that even natives sensibly carry maps. It is an area which encourages the visitor to look up—to the top of the World Trade Center, where television airwave receptors hover like rocket launchers; up at the four limestone sculptures (of Asia, America, Europe and Africa) emerging from the granite palace which was once the US Customs House at Bowling Green and Bridge Street; up at the delicate spire of Trinity Church (Broadway and the beginning of Wall Street), where lunchtime crowds gather for concerts at noon and munch sandwiches while walking among the historic tombstones; up at the masts of ships docked at the South Street Seaport Museum alongside the Fulton Fish Market and the Rouse Development Corporation's South Street Seaport renewal.

Consisting of renovated Schermerhorn Row, museum shops, a new Fulton Market and a shopping Mecca on Pier 17, the Seaport edges the East River at Fulton Street and, just like sister developments in Boston and Baltimore, is a pleaser. Crowds browse craft stands and upscale boutiques, stroll and nosh their way through a tantalizing assortment of ethnic snack bars, queue for the multimedia show at the Trans-Lux Theater, and dine in the glamorous glass-enclosed pavilion shimmering over East River waters.

Visitors downtown also look up at old wholesale houses, offices and bank buildings in the process of conversion to residential use and new structures going up expressly for that purpose. Downtown is slowly adjusting to the fact that people live (as opposed to work) there, 24 hours a day, seven days a week. The 1970 census showed only 7,000 residents in the oldest part of Manhattan; you could take tea in the middle of Wall Street on a Sunday afternoon—if you could find some tea to take. An estimated 25,000 people live here now, serviced by dry cleaners where there were none, day care centers, supermarkets, and food specialty shops (stocked with tea). Indeed, the community is on its way to becoming a full-fledged neighborhood, with its own handsome, new Public School 234, several hotels, and plans for a Downtown branch library.

Battery Park City, built between West Street and the Hudson River on landfill excavated from the World Trade Center site, is the largest development ever constructed in Manhattan. The recently created 92 acres is made up of a collection of architecturally diverse residential and financial complexes managed by the Battery Park City Authority. The World Financial Center—four stunning, copper-topped buildings fastidiously designed by Cesar Pelli—faces the World Trade Center and forms Battery Park City's hub.

At its center like an imperial gateway to the city, the soaring, glass and polished-steel Winter Garden with sixteen California palms set in gleaming marble provides an elegant site for free concerts edging the North Cove Yacht Harbor. Surrounding the Winter Garden throughout the ground floor of the World Financial Center, upscale shops and restaurants beckon. The beautifully landscaped Esplanade—connecting the Winter Garden with South Gardens and North Park—constitutes the spine of the development as it stretches over a mile along the Hudson River.

With two residential complexes occupied and more to come, along with a huge fifth office building, public parks and gardens, a floating skating rink, and a museum of the Holocaust, Battery Park City is a work in progress. Gateway Plaza consists of 1,712 apartments in six (three tall, three short) buildings, which are fully rented. All ten of the mostly-Deco, brick and limestone mid-rises that form Rector Place are now in place, with a total of 2,200 rental apartments and condominiums. Three new upscale condo buildings have opened in Battery Place to the south with 630 units.

Battery Park City residents tend to be young professionals who work in Lower Manhattan. Some 25,000 people will live, another 35,000 will work, within sight of the Statue of Liberty when the mammoth project is completed. The whole is even now surrounded by parks and sculpture-filled plazas and connected by ferry service to New Jersey and by climate-controlled walkways to the World Trade Center, public transportation and the Financial District.

The size and splendor of this mega-project should not, however, obscure the presence in Lower Manhattan of other residential possibilities. For example, small, architecturally distinguished condominiums such as Greenwich Court have sprung up on the West Side below Chambers Street, and conversions are rife throughout lower Manhattan. New tax incentives have quickened the pace of conversion from commercial to residential use, and today many of the handsome turn-of-the-century office towers near Wall Street contain nary a brokerage firm but, rather, families in rentals and co-ops, lofts even. And in a tight real estate market these pioneers are paying less than they would pay for comparable space uptown.

Area Code: 212

Post Offices: Church Street Station, 90 Church Street, NYC 10007, 330-5247; Peck Slip Station, 1-19 Peck Slip, NYC 10038, 964-1055; Bowling Green Station, 25 Broadway, NYC 10004, 363-9490.

Zip Codes: 10007, 10038, 10047/48 (World Trade Center), 10006, 10004, 10005, 10041, 10280, 10281, 10282

Police Precinct: First, 16 Ericsson Place, NYC 10013, 334-0611.

Emergency Hospital: New York Downtown Hospital, 170 William Street, NYC 10038, 312-5000.

Library (nearest): Chatham Square Branch (Chinatown), 33 East Broadway, NYC 10002, 964-6598.

Public School Education: School District #2 (see **Chelsea**).

Adult Education: Pace University, 1 Pace Plaza, NYC 10038, 346-1200; New York Institute of Finance, 2 Broadway, 5th Floor, NYC 10004 344-2900.

Cultural Resources: South Street Seaport Museum, Fulton and Water Streets, NYC 10038, 748-8600 National Museum of the American Indian, Alexander Hamilton U.S. Customs House, I Bowling Green, NYC 10004, 825-6700; Trinity Church, Broadway at Trinity Place, 10006, 602-0800, houses a museum and offers mid-day concerts on weekdays, as does St. Paul's Chapel up Broadway at Fulton. Concert information is available at 602-0747; also see **Tribeca**.

Transportation—Subway: #1/#9, #2, #3 Varick/Greenwich Streets at Chambers (Exp), Cortlandt, Rector, South Ferry/Battery Park, Park Place/Broadway, Fulton (Exp), Wall(Exp); A, C, E at the World

Trade Center, N and R at Broadway/Nassau (Exp); City Hall, Cortlandt, Rector, Whitehall; #4, #5, #6 Brooklyn Bridge, Fulton (Exp), Wall(Exp), Bowling Green (Exp); J, M Fulton (Exp); Broad (Exp) PATH (to New Jersey) World Trade Center.

Transportation—Bus: Crosstown *Chambers/West/Vesey/Park Row to Madison Street* (#22); Uptown *Church/Hudson/Eighth Avenue—*Downtown *Seventh Avenue/Varick/West Broadway* (#10); Uptown *Church/Sixth Avenue—*Downtown *Broadway* (#6); Uptown and Downtown *Grand Central Terminal—Wall Street Express* (#X25) weekdays only.

Tribeca

Boundaries and Contiguous Areas: North: Canal Street and SoHo; **East:** Broadway; **South:** Chambers Street and Downtown; **West:** Hudson River.

South of Canal Street, where the island of Manhattan narrows toward its tip, Greenwich Street angles to intersect West Broadway, leaving in its wake not only the loft district dubbed Tribeca (**tri**angle **be**low **Ca**nal) but triangular blocks and crossroad parks unique in the city. Felicitous little Duane Park, the most charming of the lot, breathes into an area composed of 19th century brick and cast iron structures, sprawling warehouses and commercial space, an air of peace and tranquillity rare in the Big Apple.

Before becoming Tribeca-ized, the area consisted of a warren of scruffy walkups that housed the city's wholesale fruit, vegetable and flower district, the Washington Market, as well as the butter and egg district. Most of the market was razed and sent packing to The Bronx in the late 1960s, to be replaced in part by the ponderous brick Independence Plaza project at 40 Harrison Street, but a few vestiges of the produce district remain. A row of Federal houses has been tucked under Independence Plaza's angular wing, and the satisfying scents of roasting coffee beans and nuts, ground spices, chocolate and an occasional wheel of aging cheese perfume air already salted by breezes blowing off the Hudson.

Tribeca is also home to a number of elegantly sculptural cast iron buildings—the first built not far from Duane Park by James Bogardus in 1849. The noticeably cleaner of the arched and colonnaded facades front residential lofts and cooperatives skillfully adapted from commercial space, as well as the galleries and offices of the avant-garde establishment (the pioneering fringe has moved to the Lower East Side and across the East River into Queens and Brooklyn). Loft living is now an accepted urban lifestyle, and Tribeca has changed radically from the quiet backwater it remained throughout the 1970s. It is a prime destination for those who like their buildings wide and their spaces open.

The vaunted, often vaulted warehouses just south of the Holland Tunnel sheltered the clubs responsible for Tribeca's dominant position on the late-night-life scene during the 1980s. Long after midnight, limos, cabs and private cars from New Jersey jostled for curb space, much as their passengers, confined behind red velvet ropes, angled for positions at the head of the waiting line. The restaurants that the disco devotees haunted remain, catering these days to a more staid clientele. Tribeca hosts a kaleidoscopic range of restaurants—Ethiopian, streamlined hangouts, trattorias and French cafes—for the young, the chic and the up-and-coming; middays they nourish neatly pressed Wall Streeters and rumpled denizens of City Hall.

Competing pressures—southbound from booming SoHo, from 10,000 students at Manhattan Community College in its midst, and most insistently from affluent, ever-expanding Battery Park City to the South—are transforming Tribeca into a thriving, cohesive mixed-use community. Conversion of commercial buildings to handsome residential lofts proceeds; service businesses spring up among the faded signs of the vanished butter, egg and cheese trade. A growing population of children where once there were none, an attractive neighborhood school (P.S. 234) and now a small-town newspaper, *The Tribeca Trib,* all contribute to the fine community feeling which, along with unimpeded bike-riding on weekends, the architecture and night life, is one of the great attractions of living in Tribeca.

Area Code: 212

Post Office: Canal Street Station, 350 Canal Street, NYC 10013, 925-3378.

Zip Code: 10013

Police Precinct: First, 16 Ericsson Place, NYC 10013, 334-0611.

Emergency Hospital (nearest): New York Downtown Hospital, 170 William Street, NYC 10038, 312-5000; St. Vincent's Hospital and Medical Center, 153 West 11th Street (at Seventh Avenue), NYC 10011, 604-7000.

Library (nearest): Hudson Park Branch, 66 Leroy Street, NYC 10014, 243-6876, has an excellent film program for children.

Public School Education: School District #2 (see **Chelsea**).

Adult Education: Borough of Manhattan Community College, Office of Continuing Education, Room S763, 199 Chambers Street, NYC 10007, 346-8000, offers a variety of inexpensive evening and weekend courses ranging from computer to business to self-improvement. Concerts and theater are also presented regularly in the College's Triplex Theater.

Cultural Resources: Tribeca quarters alternative spaces displaying works for and by the avant-garde much as Madison Avenue in the 70s houses deluxe galleries catering to the establishment. These include Artists Space, 38 Greene Street, 3rd Floor, NYC 10013, 226-3970; Franklin Furnace, 112 Franklin Street at West Broadway,

NYC 10013, 925-4671; and The Clocktower (Institute for Art and Urban Resources), 108 Leonard Street, 13th floor, NYC 10013, 233-1096. Also, Borough of Manhattan Community College, 199 Chambers Street, NYC 10007, 346-8000; and the New York City Fire Museum, 278 Spring Street, NYC, 10013, 691-1303.

Transportation—Subway: A, C, E Canal Street (Exp), Chambers Street (Exp); #1/#9, #2, #3 Varick Street at Canal Street, Franklin Street, Chambers Street (Exp).

Transportation—Bus: Crosstown *Madison & Chambers Street/West Street & Grand Street* (#22); Uptown *Hudson Street/Eighth Avenue*—Downtown *Seventh Avenue/Varick Street* (#10); Uptown *Sixth Avenue* (#6); Uptown and Downtown *Grand Central Terminal—Wall Street Express* (X25) weekdays only.

SoHo

Boundaries and Contiguous Areas: North: West Houston Street and Greenwich Village; **East:** Broadway and Lower East Side; **South:** Canal Street and Tribeca; **West:** Sixth Avenue.

SoHo's cast iron buildings are justifiably famous and a visual delight. Look up to appreciate the beauty of the patterns—columnar shapes, Greek Revival capitals and other architectural embellishments—pressed into the cast iron facades. Windowsill house plants, paintings and some of the city's most colorful walls reveal the loft residences which now occupy most of what was manufacturing space. Behind these slightly grimy fronts live some of New York's trendiest setters, often in 4,000-square-foot spreads.

The structures are based on a technique perfected by James Bogardus around 1850. Forerunners of today's "curtain wall" skyscrapers, these cast iron buildings are supported by interior columns, obviating the need for thick walls and allowing the use of much more glass than was previously possible. As a result, the graceful windows, many of them arched, nicely complement the strong, solid buildings, and the whole is extremely harmonious. The buildings are also exceedingly attractive to the city's artists, ever on the lookout for good light and space. In the early 1960s they began to move into the area, just as industry had moved into what had been the city's red light district a century before; loft living became legal in 1971. With the subsequent discovery of SoHo by the affluent, high prices have driven many of the original artists to less costly neighborhoods. But art galleries and audacious boutiques remain to prosper and proliferate.

The popularity of SoHo has in no way diminished. On the contrary, monied *arrivistes* commingle with painters and sculptors on the upper floors of the converted cast iron structures while at street level, hard-edged, minimalist (whatever the fashion-of-the-moment) showrooms spread their plate glass windows far and wide. "An international marketplace for style and design," *The New York Times* calls it, attracting shoppers from Jersey to Germany. "This feels like the world's greatest shopping mall," exclaims a merchant of upscale linens. Just so. You can buy the latest in wearable art, Japanese designer clothes, French *pret-a-porter*, exquisite antique blouses and accessories, antique or art deco furniture, and more. Take a shopping break in a chic eatery along West Broadway's restaurant row. Bring money. And if you live here, don't venture out on the weekend. It's packed.

What has changed in recent years is the eastern edge of SoHo. Galleries, clothing shops, and even offices, have spread east from West Broadway past Wooster, Greene and Mercer to Broadway and beyond. Once drab and lifeless, Broadway is undergoing a personality change as faux marble and hand-grained surfaces replace the tatty showrooms of fabric wholesalers. The relocation of Dean and DeLuca's extraordinary food emporium to a vast, white space resembling an edible art gallery was a sure sign of the Broadway revival. Then along came Armani, The Nature Store, Eddie Bauer, William-Sonoma. As SoHo crawls ever eastward, the boundary between SoHo and Little Italy is blurring.

While loft living is legal in many buildings, and you need not necessarily qualify as an artist to rent or sublet SoHo space, caution is advised in taking over a lease or paying key money for a loft or apartment. Checking with a local tenants' association is a good idea; the Housing Clinic, 280 Broadway, Room 412 (no phone), can inform about legal rents and living situations (see **Lofts**). Many artists teach and sublet when they go on sabbatical or receive grants which take them to other parts of the country. If you're not in the market for a condo, the best line on housing availability down here is by word-of-mouth (and conversation is lively at the local art galleries and show openings, which anyone can attend) and bulletin boards. Try the one at the Broome Street Bar.

Area Code: 212

Post Office: Prince Street Station, 103 Prince Street, NYC 10012, 226-7868.

Zip Codes: 10012, 10013

Police Precinct: First, 16 Ericsson Place, NYC 10013, 334-0611.

Emergency Hospitals (nearest): St. Vincent's Hospital and Medical Center, Seventh Avenue and 11th Street, NYC 10011, 604-7000; New York Downtown Hospital, 170 William Street, NYC 10038, 312-5110.

Libraries (nearest): Jefferson Market Branch, 425 Avenue of the Americas, NYC 10011, 243-4334; Hudson Park Branch, 66 Leroy Street, NYC 10014, 243-6876.

Public School Education: School District #2 (see **Chelsea**).

Adult Education: The French Culinary Institute, 462 Broadway,

NYC 10013, 219-8890, offers a variety of professional and non-professional cooking courses (lunch and dinner too at their restaurant, L'Ecole, 219-3300 for reservations); Pratt Manhattan, the local branch of Brooklyn's Pratt Institute, 295 Lafayette Street, NYC 10012, 925-8481, has extensive evening and weekend course offerings in the arts and professional areas.

Cultural Resources: New Museum of Contemporary Art, 583 Broadway, NYC 10012, 219-1355; Guggenheim SoHo, 575 Broadway, NYC 10012, 423-3500; Museum for African Art, 593 Broadway, NYC 10012, 966-1313. The district is crammed with great and small gallery spaces—investigate them at leisure. Most are closed Sunday and Monday. A scan of Art Now's *Gallery Guide*, available in galleries throughout the city, gives a total picture of the area's resources and current shows. For weekly guides to arts events in SoHo see *The Village Voice*, the Weekend section on Friday and the Arts and Leisure section on Sunday in *The New York Times* and *The New Yorker* magazine's "Goings on About Town" section, *New York* magazine's "Cue" section, as well as the *N.Y. Press*, a free weekly covering and available mainly downtown. Nearby Tribeca also offers opportunities to explore the more avant-garde side of the arts, as does the East Village, from which, amoeba-like, galleries have spread throughout the Lower East Side.

Transportation—Subway: A, C, E Sixth Avenue at Spring Street, Canal Street (Exp); B, D, F, Q at Broadway/Lafayette; N, R Prince Street, Canal Street; #4, #6 at Bleecker Street, Spring Street, Canal Street.

Transportation—Bus: Crosstown *West-East Houston* (#21); Uptown *Sixth Avenue*—Downtown *Fifth Avenue* (#5); Downtown *Seventh Avenue/Broadway* (#10); Uptown *Sixth Avenue*—Downtown *Broadway* (#6).

Greenwich Village

Boundaries and Contiguous Areas: North: 14th Street, Chelsea and Flatiron District; **East:** Broadway and the East Village; **South:** West Houston Street and SoHo; **West:** Hudson River.

Greenwich Village is the kind of community where neighbors look after each other's plants and pets and where people *do* call the police or fire department if they notice something amiss. Residents still tend to be arts-oriented and more liberal and politically active than most, particularly when it comes to incursions, real or threatened, on the free-wheeling life style adopted by some or on the hallowed six-story maximum building limit. It was the Village's great good fortune to have its streets laid out along the original 18th century farm lanes and property lines before city planners superimposed the grid pattern on most of Manhattan. The crooked streets that intersect major arteries at ungainly angles prevent the standardization, through traffic, and large buildings (not to mention urban boredom) that mar other neighborhoods.

Since the 19th century, the brick, Federal-style structures along these crooked streets have housed more than their share of the city's talented and creative. Writers came first: Edgar Allan Poe in 1837, later Mark Twain, Henry James and Walt Whitman. Artists and intellectuals followed. A handful of people and institutions played key roles in the evolution of the Village as a magnet for those in the vanguard of the arts and letters. Gertrude Vanderbilt Whitney opened her first studio here, exhibiting and encouraging the artists who subsequently became the nucleus of the "Ashcan School" of social realist painters. Mabel Dodge's famed literary salon was on Washington Square, and the Provincetown Players established an early experimental theater on MacDougal Street in 1916. New York University was founded on Washington Square in the 1830s, the New School on West 12th Street in the 1920s. By then the local populace included John Dos Passos, e.e. cummings, Willa Cather, Henry Miller and Edna St. Vincent Millay, and the Village was the avant-garde capital of the nation.

After World War II, abstract expressionists, method actors, controversial novelists and muckraking journalists all coexisted, bringing creative vitality to the area. The early 1960s may have changed the surface look of things, with its beaded and feathered hippies garlanding the streets, but the foment and ferment of past decades continued unchecked. Only as recently as the early 1970s and the advent of spiraling rents has the Village's appeal lessened as a haven for artists and writers. These days there are probably more appreciators around than doers, but the charm of the Village, with its pleasing proportions and special kind of peacefulness, remains.

Greenwich Village contains a balanced mix of high rise elevator buildings, older rent stabilized apartments, lofts, renovated tenements and brownstones (a harmonious ensemble threatened, in the West Village at least, by the emergence of several buildings above the prescribed height limit to obtain remunerative Hudson River views). New, pricey rental apartments and condos in now-fashionable converted warehouses lining West and Washington Streets and in the handsome conversions found in the wholesale antiques district bordering University Place are widely advertised.

A relatively recent addition to Village housing stock is The Archive, a handsome, landmarked Romanesque Revival monolith which was originally a waterfront customs warehouse and later a post office. It has been cleaned and refitted into 479 upscale duplex rentals by Rockrose (212-691-9800), the largest rental outfit in the Village.

Because the area is essentially an assembly of small communities—the predominantly Italian South Village, the central Washington Square neighborhood, and the West Village bounded by Seventh Avenue and the Hudson River—searching for rentals is best done on foot and through reliable real estate agents.

Area Code: 212

Post Offices: Patchin Station, 70 West 10th Street, NYC 10011, 475-2534; West Village Station, 527 Hudson Street, NYC 10014, 989-5084; Cooper Station, 93 Fourth Avenue, NYC 10003, 254-1389; Village Station, 201 Varick Street, NYC 10014, 989-9741.

Zip Codes: 10014, 10011, 10012, 10003

Police Precinct: Sixth, 233 West 10th Street, NYC 10014, 741-4811.

Emergency Hospital: St. Vincent's Hospital and Medical Center, Seventh Avenue and 11th Street, NYC 10011, 604-7000.

Libraries: Jefferson Market Branch, 425 Avenue of the Americas, NYC 10011, 243-4334; Hudson Park Branch, 66 Leroy Street, NYC 10014, 243-6876.

Public School Education: School District #2 (see Chelsea). Greenwich Village has two elementary schools. P.S. 41 offers "traditional" public school education, while P.S. 3 with an "open corridor" program is more experimental.

Adult Education: Parsons School of Design, 66 Fifth Avenue, NYC 10011, 229-8955; The New School for Social Research, 66 West 12th Street, NYC 10011, 229-5600; The Cooper Union for the Advancement of Science and Art, Third Avenue and 7th Street, NYC 10003, 353-4195; Greenwich House Music School, 46 Barrow Street, NYC 10014, 242-4770; Greenwich House Pottery, 16 Jones Street, 242-4106; New York University, 50 West 4th Street, NYC 10003, 998-1212.

Cultural Resources: The District Office of Community Planning Board No. 2 has a resource directory of all Greenwich Village associations, service organizations and cultural agencies. The directory is up-to-date and free (3 Washington Square Village, Suite 1A, NY 10012, 979-2272).

Transportation—Subway: Crosstown L at Eighth Avenue, Sixth Avenue, Broadway/Union Square; A, C, E at Eighth Avenue and 14th Street (Exp), West 4th/8th Street (Exp); #1, #2, #3 at Seventh Avenue and 14th Street (Exp), Christopher Street/Sheridan Square, Houston Street; F, D, B, Q at 14th Street, West 4th/8th Street (Exp); #4, #5, #6 at 14th Street/Union Square (Exp), Astor Place, Bleecker Street at Lafayette; N, R at 14th Street/Union Square (Exp), 8th Street/NYU; PATH (between New Jersey and 33rd Street) Christopher Street at Hudson, 9th and 14th Streets at Sixth Avenue.

Transportation—Bus: Crosstown *14th Street* (#14); Going east: Crosstown *West 10th Street/West 8th Street* (#13); Going west: Crosstown *West 9th Street/Christopher Street* (#13); Uptown

Greenwich Street/Tenth Avenue—Downtown *Ninth Avenue/Hudson Street* (#11); Uptown *Hudson Street/Eighth Avenue*—Downtown *Seventh Avenue* (#10); Uptown *Sixth Avenue* (#5, #6, #7); Uptown *University Place*—Downtown *Fifth Avenue* (#2, #3).

Flatiron District

Boundaries and Contiguous Areas: **North:** 23rd Street and Madison Square; **East:** Park Avenue South and **Gramercy Park Area**; **South:** 14th Street and **Greenwich Village**; **West:** Sixth Avenue and **Chelsea**.

Thanks to the famous wintry photograph by Edward Steichen, the thrusting nose of the Flatiron Building is familiar, even to out-of-towners. The triangular structure at the convergence of Broadway and Fifth Avenue at 23rd Street was a wonder, a skyscraper, when completed in 1902. The 21-story steel-frame structure was also at the apex of the Ladies' Mile, New York's elegant shopping district. Macy's, Altman's, Lord & Taylor, W & J Sloane and other luxurious emporiums now forgotten cut a fashionable swath down Broadway, Fifth and Sixth Avenues in the late 19th century.

But just as the rumbling Sixth Avenue elevated had stimulated the development of the Ladies' Mile, so the city's booming economy caused the great stores to move uptown. The elegant buildings with rhythmic cast iron fronts, elaborate mansard roofs, Byzantine columns and Gothic finials were abandoned to a dim and sooty half-life as manufacturing lofts and warehouses.

Today, there's a reawakening south of 23rd Street, and the wedge-shaped Flatiron Building has lent its name to New York's newest neighborhood. Andy Warhol was, perhaps, the first to set up in the Flatiron District when he established his notorious Factory on Union Square. Professional photographers began moving bed-and-tripod into the neighborhood's vast manufacturing lofts in the 1970s. Photo supply houses and model agencies came next, followed by publishing houses, advertising agencies and, most recently, internet and multi-media startups. Now Lower Fifth Avenue is experiencing a retail renaissance, led by such fashion heavyweights as Armani, Paul Smith and Matsuda. The abandoned palaces of the Ladies Mile on Sixth Avenue have re-opened as mega-stores selling books, housewares, office supplies and clothes. Young cyber whizzes working in hi-tech computer studios have earned a new name for the area: Silicon Alley. On and off the avenues, trendy restaurants have proliferated like chanterelles after a rain, as have fitness clubs of every persuasion. So you can lunch among the literati and leggy lovelies in sprawling theme restaurants, furnish your kitchen at Williams-Sonoma and outfit yourself in the latest Italian threads at Barneys (both on Seventh Avenue), work up a sweat, shoot billiards till dawn, and boogie the night away, all in the Flatiron District.

There are some rentals available in the handsome Zeckendorf Towers set back from Union Square with airy, teal pyramid points atop the brick towers and a 24-hour super-A&P downstairs. Madison Green, overlooking restful Madison Square Park, is among the notable modern condominiums. More typical of the Flatiron District, however, are the elegant, converted living lofts hidden away in the stolid manufacturing buildings which darken the side streets. Consult a real estate broker for the occasional sublet that comes on the market when the owner's away shooting photos in Crete. Besides a prime location with good public transportation, you'll have the graceful, green breathing space that is now Union Square for a front yard. The four-day-a-week greenmarket (see **Greenmarkets** in the **Shopping for the Home** chapter) is the Square's *piece de resistance*. Manhattanites trek year round to the northwest corner at East 16th and Broadway for fresh produce, fish, sausages, cheese, pretzels, breads, honey...oh, endless edibles.

Area Code: 212

Post Offices (nearest): Cooper Station, 93 Fourth Avenue, NYC 10003, 254-1389; Madison Square Station, 149 East 23rd Street, NYC 10010, 673-3771.

Zip Codes: 10003, 10010, 10011

Police Precinct: Thirteenth, 230 East 21st Street, NYC 10010, 477-7411.

Emergency Hospitals (nearest): Cabrini Medical Center, 227 East 19th Street, NYC 10003, 995-6000; St. Vincent's Hospital and Medical Center, Seventh Avenue and 11th Street, NYC 10011, 790-7000.

Libraries (nearest): Muhlenberg Library, 209 West 23rd Street, NYC 10011, 924-1585; Epiphany, 228 East 23rd Street, NYC 10010, 679-2645.

Public School Education: School District #2 (see **Chelsea**).

Adult Education: School of Visual Arts, 209 East 23rd Street, NYC 10010, 679-7350; Baruch College of Adult and Continuing Education, 48 East 26th Street, NYC 10010, 447-3020.

Transportation—Subway: Crosstown *L* 14th Street, Sixth Avenue, Union Square; #4, #5, #6, 23rd Street, 14th Street/Union Square (Exp); *N, Q, R* 14th Street/Union Square (Exp).

Transportation—Bus: Crosstown *23rd Street* (#23); Crosstown 14th Street (#14); Uptown *Park Avenue South/Madison Avenue* (#1, #2, #3); Uptown *Sixth Avenue* (#5, #6, #7); Downtown *Park Avenue South* (#1); Downtown *Fifth Avenue* (#2, #3, #5); Downtown *Broadway* (#6, #7).

Chelsea

Boundaries and Contiguous Areas: **North:** 34th Street and Clinton; **East:** Sixth Avenue and Flatiron District; **South:** 14th Street and Greenwich Village; **West:** Hudson River.

Residential Chelsea is a sunny community renowned for peace, quiet and four and five-story brownstone row houses, but its origins date back to 1750, when Capt. Thomas Clarke's farm encompassed the area. In the 1830s, Clarke's grandson, Clement Clarke Moore, began developing Chelsea as a highly desirable suburb and donating land for the block-square General Theological Seminary just down the street from the Gothic Revival style St. Peter's Episcopal Church, where Moore read his "A Visit from Saint Nicholas" to family and parishioners. The tree-shaded Seminary Close is still a neighborhood oasis.

To the west, the Hudson River Railroad attracted slaughterhouses, breweries and shanties, and in 1871 Chelsea was darkened by the city's first elevated railroad on Ninth Avenue. Successive decades saw the brief emergence of 23rd Street as the city's theater district; the raising of vast cast iron structures on Sixth Avenue to house fashionable emporiums such as the original B. Altman's, and in the 1920s and 1930s a thriving vice district; the beginning of the nation's movie industry; and the opening of one of the city's first cooperative apartment houses, now the Chelsea Hotel, home over the years to artists and writers and still a fascinating building. Urban renewal in the 1950s and 1960s removed chunks of slums from the district, spurring the restoration of many fine townhouses and making way for two low-income housing projects and the middle-income International Ladies Garment Workers cooperative extending from 23rd to 27th Streets between Eighth and Ninth Avenues.

Sharing the side streets with restored one-and two-family houses are the occasional apartment house and tenement, not to mention formidable London Terrace, 405 West 23rd Street, with 14 buildings, four of which are co-op. The lofts in the photography, flower, fur and fashion districts (roughly 15th to 30th Streets between Fifth and Eighth Avenues, which includes the Flatiron District) were discovered by artists in the 1950s and increasingly now attract young families and professionals.

In 1982 the down-at-the-heels Elgin, a 1930s movie house on Eighth Avenue, was transformed into the exuberantly deco Joyce, the first theater in the dance capital of the world to be specifically designed for small and medium-sized dance troupes. Since then, Chelsea has become something of a dance and performance district. The Dance Theater Workshop is a block east of the Joyce on 19th Street. The relatively avant-garde Kitchen lies west near the Hudson River. Way west several nightclubs have nestled in between auto-repair shops and factories, usurping Tribeca's reign over the night club scene. A proliferation of new art galleries, led by the Dia Center for the Arts, marks Chelsea's bid for a share of Soho's corner on the art market.

Eighth Avenue, between 15th and 23rd Streets, has become Main

Street, Chelsea. With a lively restaurant scene and trendy boutiques punctuating the relatively unobtrusive condos and co-ops, Eighth Avenue has taken on the youthful character of Columbus Avenue in the West 70s and 80s. The latest wave to hit Chelsea is the art scene, galleries, some of which have moved up from Soho and clustered near the Dia Center for the Arts on 22nd Street near 10th Avenue.

Simultaneously anchoring the neighborhood is the extraordinary new 1.7 million square foot Chelsea Piers Sports and Entertainment complex, which opened in 1995 in four piers over the Hudson River stretching between 17th and 23rd Streets. The movie industry returns to Chelsea in the new film and television studios housed in the pier-head, through which once streamed passengers from some of the world's great ocean liners. In the handsome complex stretched out behind the studios, work-out devotees strain and sweat on state-of-the-art equipment while others run, ice skate, in-line pirouette, play league hockey, soccer, lacrosse and basketball, scale a climbing wall, refine gymnastic skills or drive balls to target greens on a 200-foot Astroturf fairway under nightlights. Others watch and hang out at one of several large restaurants. This $100 million entry into Chelsea's westernmost, hitherto industrial neighborhood is transforming it into a destination once again.

Area Code: 212

Post Offices: General Post Office, Eighth Avenue at 33rd Street, NYC 10001, 967-8585, open 24 hours; London Terrace Station, 234 Tenth Avenue, near 24th Street, NYC 10011, 242-8248; Old Chelsea Station, 217 West 18th Street, NYC 10011, 675-2415; Port Authority Station, 76 Ninth Avenue, NYC 10011, 929-9296.

Zip Codes: 10001, 10011

Police Precincts: Midtown South, 357 West 35th Street, NYC 10001, 239-9811; Tenth, 230 West 20th Street, NYC 10011, 741-8211.

Emergency Hospitals (nearest): St. Clare's Hospital and Health Center, 415 West 51st Street, NYC 10019, 586-1500; St. Vincent's Hospital and Medical Center, Seventh Avenue and 11th Street, NYC 10011, 604-7000.

Library: Muhlenberg Branch, 209 West 23rd Street, NYC 10011, 924-1585; Library for the Blind and Physically Handicapped, 40 West 20th Street, NYC 10011, 206-5400.

Public School Education: Chelsea is in the NYC Board of Education's School District #2, one of the best in Manhattan. School Superintendent, 330 West 18th Street, NYC 10011, 330-9400; Committee on the Handicapped, District Manager, P.S. 33, 281 Ninth Avenue, NYC 10011, 244-6426. Bayard Rustin High School for the Humanities, 351 West 18th Street, 675-5350, is the city's newest college preparatory high school.

Adult Education: Fashion Institute of Technology, 227 West 27th Street, NYC 10001, 760-7650, classes plus art gallery open to the public.

Cultural Resources: McBurney YMCA, 215 West 23rd Street, NYC 10011, 741-9210; the Joyce Theater, 175 Eighth Avenue at 19th Street, 212-242-0800; Dance Theatre Workshop, 219 West 19th Street, NYC 924-0077; Dia Center for the Arts, 548 West 22nd Street, NYC 989-5912; Atlantic Theater Company, 336 West 20th Street, NYC 645-1242.

Transportation—Subway: Crosstown (L) at Eighth Avenue and 14th Street (crosses 14th Street and continues into Brooklyn); #1, #2, #3 at 34th Street/Penn Station (Exp), 28th Street, 23rd Street, 18th Street, 14th Street (Exp); A, C, E at Sixth Avenue and 34th Street (Exp), 23rd Street, 14th Street (Exp); PATH (between New Jersey and 33rd Street) 14th, 23rd and 33rd streets on Sixth Avenue.

Transportation—Bus: Crosstown *34th Street/Ninth Avenue* (#16); Crosstown *23rd Street* (#23); Crosstown *14th Street* (#14) also down Avenue A and Avenue D; Uptown *Tenth Avenue*—Downtown *Ninth Avenue* (#11); Uptown *Eighth Avenue*—Downtown *Seventh Avenue* (#10).

Midtown

Boundaries and Contiguous Areas: North: 59th Street (Central Park South) and Central Park; **East:** Lexington Avenue and East 40s and 50s, Fifth Avenue (south of 42nd Street) and Murray Hill; **South:** 34th Street and Chelsea; **West:** Eighth Avenue and Clinton.

For all that it contains within its bounds, Midtown is not a neighborhood. Some 700,000 people work here, but few call it home. Not since the mansions of the mighty—the Rockefellers, the Havemeyers, the Vanderbilts—were left to the wrecker's ball and commercial development around the turn of the century has Midtown felt like a neighborhood. This core of the core of the city throbs and bustles daily with industry in the garment district, commerce between Lexington and Sixth Avenue (or Avenue of the Americas, officially speaking but rarely spoken), with shoppers from Macy's to Bergdorf Goodman to Bloomingdale's, and with tourists everywhere. Except in the theater district, the 40s and 50s west of Sixth Avenue, Midtown is quiet at night, all but deserted in some areas.

There are no supermarkets here, no children's playgrounds (or children to speak of either) and but one city park, the elegantly renovated Bryant Park, one block square and a little bit of Europe, behind the New York Public Library at 42nd Street. What there *is* is almost all of the city's legitimate theater, ballet at City Center, music at Carnegie Hall and smaller venues, museums, restaurants of every conceivable persuasion, Rockefeller Center, major art galleries along 57th Street, and shopping till you're dropping from Woolworth's to Tiffany's. Not to mention that perhaps your job is here.

You *can* live in Midtown. On the high side in Trump and other glassy towers along Fifth and Park Avenues and Central Park South, in some fine pre-war (WW II, that is) apartment buildings between Sixth and Eighth Avenues in the 50s, and just a bit more modestly in modern doorman buildings. The occasional brownstone is a side-street surprise west of Fifth. Affordable apartments may be found in the 40s between Broadway and Eighth Avenue; explore the area first and talk to residents in order to be sure about location. Until West 42nd Street is finally cleaned up, perhaps by 2000, this will continue to be a spotty area. The search is best made with the help of reliable real estate agents. Watch the ads in the Sunday *New York Times* and the *Village Voice* to find agents handling properties in the area. You may also find the list of brokers under **Apartment Hunting** in this book helpful.

Area Code: 212

Post Offices: Grand Central Station, 450 Lexington Avenue, NYC 10017, 330-5768; Midtown Station, 221 and 223 West 38th Street, NYC 10018, 967-8585 and 944-6597; Rockefeller Center Station, 610 Fifth Avenue, NYC 10020, 265-3854; Bryant Station, 23 West 43rd Street, NYC 10036, 279-5960; Murray Hill Station, 115 East 34th Street, NYC 10016, 679-9127; Station #138 Macy's, 151 West 34th Street, NYC 10001, 695-4400, ext. 2688.

Zip Codes: 10001,10016,10017,10018, 10019, 10020, 10022, 10036

Police Precincts: Midtown North, 306 West 54th Street, NYC 10019, 767-8400; Midtown South, 357 West 35th Street, NYC 10001, 239-9811.

Emergency Hospital (nearest): St. Luke's-Roosevelt Hospital Center, 1000 Tenth Avenue, NYC 10023, 523-6800.

Libraries: The Mercantile Library, 17 East 47th Street, NYC 10017, 755-6710, a membership library; General Society Library, 20 West 44th Street, NYC 10036, 921-1767, a membership library; Donnell Library Center, New York Public Library, 20 West 53rd Street, NYC 10019, 621-0618; Fifty-Eighth Street Branch, 127 East 58th Street, NYC 10022, 759-7358; Mid-Manhattan Branch, 455 Fifth Avenue, NYC 10016, 340-0863; New York Public Library, Fifth Avenue and 42nd Street, NYC 10018, 869-8089; the new Science, Industry and Business Branch (SIBL) in the former B. Altman building, 188 Madison Avenue at 34th Street, NYC 10016, 592-7000.

Public School Education: School District #2 (see **Chelsea**).

Adult Education: Graduate School and University Center, City

University of New York (CUNY), 33 West 42nd Street 10018, 642-1600.

Cultural Resources: International Center of Photography (ICP) Midtown, 1133 Avenue of the Americas at 43rd Street, NYC 10036; Museum of Modern Art, 11 West 53rd Street, NYC 10019, 708-9480; Museum of Television and Radio, 25 West 52nd Street, NYC 10019, 631-6600; American Craft Museum, 40 West 53rd, NYC 10019, 956-6047; City Center Theater, 131 West 55th Street, NYC 10019, 903-9600; Carnegie Hall and Weill Recital Hall, 154 West 57th Street, NYC 10019, 903-9600.

Transportation—Subway: S train (shuttle), 42nd Street from Times Square to Grand Central; #7, 42nd Street at Times Square, Fifth Avenue, Grand Central; A, C, E, Eighth Avenue at 34th Street (Exp), 42nd Street (Exp), 50th Street, 59th Street (A, C), 50th Street at Seventh, Fifth and Lexington Avenues (E); #I, #2, #3, #9, Seventh Avenue at 34th Street (Exp), 42nd Street (Exp), 50th Street and Broadway, 59th Street and Broadway; B, D, F, Q, Sixth Avenue at 34th Street (Exp), 42nd Street (Exp), 47-50th Street (Exp), 57th Street (B, Q), 53rd Street at Fifth Avenue and Lexington Avenue (F); #4, #5, #6, Lexington at 42nd Street (Exp), 51st Street, 59th Street.

Transportation—Bus: Crosstown *34th Street* (#34); Crosstown *42nd Street* (#42, #104); Crosstown *49/50th Street*s (#50); Crosstown *57th Street* (#57, #31); Uptown *Eighth Avenue*—Downtown *Seventh Avenue* (#I0); Uptown *Sixth Avenue*—Downtown *Fifth Avenue* (#5); Uptown *Sixth Avenue*—Downtown/*Seventh Avenue and Broadway* (#6, #7); Uptown *Madison Avenue*—Downtown *Fifth Avenue* (#2,#3, #4, #18); Uptown *Madison Avenue*—Downtown *Fifth Avenue and Park Avenue* (#1); Uptown *Lexington Avenue*—Downtown *Third Avenue* (#101, #102, #98).

Clinton

Boundaries and Contiguous Areas: North: 59th Street and Lincoln Center; **East:** Eighth Avenue and the Theater District; **South:** 34th Street and Chelsea; **West:** Hudson River.

Not so long ago Clinton was "Hell's Kitchen," the neighborhood—and it *is* a real neighborhood—that produced gangster Owney Madden and inspired *West Side Story*. Traditionally a poor workingman's district with often squalid tenements and rooming houses, Clinton still has a few Irish and Puerto Rican gangs and raunchy blocks catering to transients. Reason enough to explain why this area, so close to midtown that developers are calling it "Midtown West," has remained something of a backwater until the incursion of desirable living space brought semi-respectability.

Upgrading began in the 1970s when Manhattan Plaza, 400 West

43rd Street, with its two towers, pool and tennis courts, was built. People with enough money to pay the high rents originally charged for the apartments were disinclined to live in the neighborhood, so the buildings were converted to subsidized housing for long-time residents displaced by the complex and for people in the performing arts. This new population helped found and now supports the thriving off-Broadway Theater Row on the south side of 42nd Street, a bonanza for New York's theater-going public, not to mention the theater world. The new respectability is firmly anchored on West 42nd Street (albeit with entrances on quieter 43rd Street) by The Strand condo tower and the Riverbank West rental complex near Eleventh Avenue. Now, in an area noted for sleaze and depression, there are good restaurants catering to the theater trade, a few blocks of spiffed-up townhouses, and handsome co-op renovations like the Piano Factory. The gentrification of Clinton is in full swing, and the gentry are mostly young, mostly gutsy.

Two mammoth projects that have had a profound effect on Clinton are the 1,800-room Marriott Marquis Hotel on West 46th Street and the Jacob K. Javits Convention Center, 655 West 34th Street.

One Worldwide Plaza, a 49-story tower capped by an ever-so-fashionable nouveau mansard roof, is both a symbol and a powerful instrument of change in Clinton. Prestigious law firms and ad agencies now serve a classy clientele at Eighth Avenue and 50th Street, where the shabby, old Madison Square Garden once squatted and winos, hookers and pushers roamed. A plaza separates the office spire in the mixed-use Zeckendorf development from the residential area, which is located to the west in the block-square complex. There a 39-story high rise and a series of attractive brick low rises contain some 650 condo units. Eighth and Ninth Avenues and the adjoining side streets are moving up.

The transformation of neighboring West 42nd Street from the tawdry "Deuce" that it has been for years to a safe, family-oriented entertainment/business center is in progress, especially now that the Disney organization is firmly committed to the location. The giant stock-market ticker at 47th Street in Times Square proclaims Morgan Stanley's confidence in this redevelopment, which is also driving change in Clinton. Because the neighborhood is in the midst of a radical transformation, any apartment hunting here should be done block by block on foot. Besides the possibility of lucking into a reasonable rental on a decent block, Ninth Avenue in the 30s and 40s offers foods of every ethnic variety and outdoor stands heaped with tantalizing fresh fruits and vegetables. Consult the weekly *Chelsea Clinton News* as an informative neighborhood reference, 268-3087.

Area Code: 212

Post Offices: Midtown Station, 223 West 38th Street, NYC 10018, 944-6597; Times Square Station, 340 West 42nd Street, NYC 10036, 244-0111.

Zip Codes: 10019, 10036, 10018

Police Precincts: Midtown North, 306 West 54th Street, NYC 10019, 760-8400; Midtown South, 357 West 35th Street, NYC 10001, 239-9811.

Emergency Hospitals: St. Luke's-Roosevelt Hospital Center: The Roosevelt Hospital at 428 West 59th Street, NYC 10019, 523-4000; St. Clare's Hospital and Health Care Center, 415 West 51st Street, NYC 10019, 586-1500.

Libraries: Columbus Branch, 742 10th Avenue, NYC 10036, 586-5098.

Public School Education: Clinton falls within Community School District #2 (see **Chelsea**).

Adult Education: John Jay College of Criminal Justice, 445 West 59th Street, NYC 10019, 237-8000.

Cultural Resources: St. Clement's Episcopal Church, 423 West 46th Street, NYC 10036, 246-7277, has a special mission to the arts community, and its services are as likely to consist of theatrical performances as liturgy. The Intrepid Sea-Air-Space Museum, Pier 86 at West 46th Street and 12th Avenue, 245-0072, is housed in and around the aircraft carrier Intrepid and contains, among other permanent and changing exhibits, the USS Growler submarine and the USS Edson destroyer.

Transportation—Subway: #1, #2, #3 at 59th Street, 50th Street, 42nd Street (Exp), 34th Street (Exp); A, C, E at 59th Street (Exp), 50th Street, 42nd Street (Exp), 34th Street (Exp).

Transportation—Bus: Crosstown *57th Street* (#57, #58); Crosstown *49th/50th Streets* (#27, #50); Crosstown *42nd Street* (#42); Crosstown *34th Street* (#16, #34); Uptown *Tenth Avenue*—Downtown *Ninth Avenue* (#11); Uptown *Eighth Avenue*—Downtown *Seventh Avenue* (#10); Downtown Broadway (#104) to 42nd Street and then crossing to the East Side along 42nd Street.

Lincoln Center Area

Boundaries and Contiguous Areas: North: 72nd Street and the Upper West Side; **East:** Central Park West; **South:** 59th Street and Clinton; **West:** Hudson River.

This neighborhood, dubbed Lincoln Square, is a prime example of the change a major new facility can effect in a marginal New York location. Just as Cinderella's slipper transformed the hapless char girl, so the construction in 1960 of the glass and travertine Lincoln Center complex with theaters, opera and ballet houses, concert halls, library and the Juilliard School transformed a dreary stretch of rundown tenements and warehouses. Now it seems every other pedestrian carries a musical instrument or moves with the marked grace of a ballet dancer, and limousines queue up where once trucks double-parked.

Columnar apartment and office buildings rise above the cafes, restaurants and boutiques lining Broadway, Columbus and Amsterdam Avenues. Fordham University's West Side Campus and ABC/Capital Cities are also firmly planted in the neighborhood. The whole adds a boost to the renaissance of Columbus and Amsterdam Avenues, which cater to the food, drink and clothing needs of the West Side's relatively affluent young residents. Tall white brick luxury buildings compose most of Lincoln Square's housing: typical is the huge Lincoln Towers co-op— 3,897 apartments contained in eight high rises fronting West End Avenue between 66th and 70th Streets. Recently condo spires and columns have shot up south and west of the culture complex, even on barren Tenth Avenue, which may be the new frontier of Lincoln Square.

There are probably more rental apartments on the Upper West Side than around Lincoln Center. However, this will change if Trump City, the much-heralded river front project, ever gets off the drawing board. When Donald Trump purchased the site of the now-defunct railroad yards fronting the Hudson River between 59th and 72nd Streets, plans for the development of an enormous housing (condos, most likely), shopping and business complex to the west of Lincoln Center received a boost. Alexander Cooper, lauded for his humane master plan for Battery Park City, is designing what amounts to a new city from scratch. But resistance to the Trumping of Lincoln Square has solidified among residents and community planners, NBC has backed out, and future development, now at a crawl, is likely to be less dense, less grandiose than the original Trump model.

Area Code: 212

Post Office: Columbus Circle Station, 27 West 60th Street, NYC 10023, 265-7858.

Zip Codes: 10023, 10019

Police Precinct: Midtown North, 306 West 54th Street, NYC 10019, 767-8400.

Emergency Hospital (nearest): St. Luke's-Roosevelt Hospital Center: The Roosevelt Hospital at 428 West 59th Street, NYC 10019, 523-4000.

Library: Library of the Performing Arts at Lincoln Center, 111 Amsterdam Avenue, NYC 10023, 870-1630.

Public School Education: School District #3, 300 West 96th Street, NYC 10025, 678-2800; Committee on Special Education, 234 West 109th Street, NYC 10025, 865-2002.

Adult Education: Fordham University, 113 West 60th Street, NYC 10023, 636-6000; The Juilliard School, Lincoln Center Plaza, NYC

10023, 799-5000; Art Students League of New York, 215 West 57th Street, NYC 10019, 247-4510; The Elaine Kaufman Cultural Arts Center, 129 West 67th Street, 362-8060, offers courses in music, dance, art and the theater.

Cultural Resources: For the plethora of cultural events, theaters, library, shops, restaurants, exhibits and tours at Lincoln Center, consult the telephone directory; Merkin Hall, 129 West 67th Street, 362-8060, presents a variety of concerts, primarily ethnic and chamber music. Museum of American Folk Art, 2 Lincoln Square, NYC 10023, 595-9533.

Transportation—Subway: #1, #9 Broadway at 66th Street, 59th Street;#2, #3 Broadway at 72nd Street Exp); A, B, C, D at 59th Street (Exp).

Transportation—Bus: Crosstown *72nd Street* (#72); Crosstown *66th/67th Streets* (#66); Crosstown *57th Street* (#57, #58); Uptown *Tenth Avenue*—Downtown *Columbus Avenue* (#11); Uptown *Eighth Avenue*—Downtown *Central Park West/Seventh Avenue* (#10).

The Upper West Side

Boundaries and Contiguous Areas: North: 110th Street and Morningside Heights; **East:** Central Park West; **South:** 72nd Street and Lincoln Center; **West:** Hudson River.

Large sprawling apartments and an active community life have been luring writers, musicians, intellectuals, psychiatrists—in general, those seeking an alternative to the Upper East Side's more constrained life-style—to the West Side for decades. Indeed, the city's first large apartment buildings, with lofty ceilings, thick walls and space to waste, were built here around the turn of the century. Grand structures rose first along Central Park West (note the famed Dakota at 72nd Street), claimed by some aficionados to be the most architecturally elegant avenue in New York; next on Broadway (the neoclassical Ansonia between 73rd and 74th Streets and the block-square Apthorp between 78th and 79th are particularly grand), which was to be Park Avenue West but isn't; and then on West End Avenue and Riverside Drive.

Most buildings along the apartment-lined avenues—with the notable exception of Columbus and Amsterdam, which have only recently emerged from the Dickensian 19th to enter the trendiest century—managed to remain sufficiently attractive to hold the middle class. But the rows of brick, limestone, and brownstone townhouses built for the newly affluent on the cross streets during the early 1900s declined into squalid tenements and SRO (Single Room Occupancy) rooming houses. Not until the 1960s, when an ambitious urban renewal plan spurred building and renovation, did this veritable architectural museum again become an address for affluent achievers. Today, the typical brownstone houses the owner's family on the garden or parlor floors and tenants on the original bedroom floors above.

A golden ghetto has never been the goal of West Side planners. They have fought long and hard to keep the neighborhood diverse and representative of the city as a whole. However, the vogue-ish and often short-lived gourmet emporiums, bijou boutiques, clothing shops featuring somber Japanese designs, and fashionable hangouts decorating Columbus and Amsterdam Avenues attest to the fickle wants of the upwardly mobile.

Lately, ranks of condo towers have shot up along Columbus and, more recently, Amsterdam between 87th and 97th Streets—just outside the boundaries of the Central Park West historic district. These svelte and pricey (though cheaper than Lincoln Square) condominiums provide residents with plenty of play space: health clubs, pools, rooftop gardens, party rooms and in-house parking are standard. Meanwhile, Upper Broadway is being transformed as high rises are slotted, sleek cheek by shabby jowl, among the wearier old-timers between 97th Street and Columbia University. A short-term rental in one of these buildings offers the undecided newcomer an opportunity to try out the neighborhood before making a long-term commitment.

Most of the handsome stone buildings fronting Central Park—the San Remo, the Beresford, the Majestic, etc.—are cooperatives now, and as sought after and as pricey as those on Fifth Avenue across the park. The vast apartment co-ops lining West End Avenue and curving along Riverside Drive are more accessible. Pioneers are staking their claims in the area known as Manhattan Valley east of Broadway in the upper 90s and 100s. For the less adventurous and thicker of purse, existing rental apartments are well worth pursuing, if only to live between Manhattan's greenest playgrounds, Central and Riverside Parks, and near one of its cultural stalwarts, the massive Museum of Natural History, which devotes almost 25 acres of floor space to some of the finest scientific collections in the world.

Area Code: 212

Post Offices: Cathedral Station, 215 West 104th Street, NYC 10025, 6629191; Planetarium Station, 127 West 83rd Street, NYC 10024, 873-3701; Ansonia Station, 138 Columbus Avenue, NYC 10023, 362-7486.

Zip Codes: 10025, 10024, 10023

Police Precincts: Twenty-fourth, 151 West 100th Street, NYC 10025, 678-1811; Twentieth, 120 West 82nd Street, NYC 10024, 580-6411.

Emergency Hospital (nearest): Both branches of the St. Luke's-Roosevelt Hospital Center: The Roosevelt Hospital at 428 West 59th Street, NYC 10019, and St. Luke's Hospital, 114th Street and Amsterdam Avenue, NYC 10025, both 523-4000.

Libraries: Bloomingdale Branch, 150 West 100th Street, NYC 10025, 222-8030; St. Agnes Branch, 444 Amsterdam Avenue, NYC 10024, 877-4380; Riverside, 127 Amsterdam Avenue, NYC 10023, 870-1810.

Public School Education: School District #3 (see **Lincoln Center Area**).

Adult Education: Bank Street College of Education, 610 West 112th Street, NYC 10025, 875-4400.

Cultural Resources: Central Park, stretching from 59th Street over 840 acres up to 110th Street. For literary events, Gilbert and Sullivan, live jazz, Afro-Cuban rhythms and the new modern directions: Symphony Space, 2537 Broadway at 95th Street, 864-5400. For a multiplicity of musical styles, played live: the Beacon Theater, Broadway and 74th Street, 496-7070. American Museum of Natural History and the Hayden Planetarium, Central Park West from 79th Street to 81st Street, museum information: 796-5100, Planetarium information: 769-5920. The Bard Graduate Center for Studies in the Decorative Arts, 18 West 86th Street, NYC 10024. Nicholas Roerich Museum, 319, West 107th Street, NYC 10025, 864-7752. Children's Museum of Manhattan, 212 West 83rd Street, NYC 10024, 721-1234.

Transportation—Subway: #1/#9, #2, #3 Broadway at 110th Street, 103rd Street, 96th Street (Exp), 86th Street, 79th Street, 72nd Street (Exp); B, C at Central Park West and 110th Street, 103rd Street, 96th Street, 86th Street, 81st Street, 72nd Street.

Transportation—Bus: Crosstown *96th Street* (#19); Crosstown *86th Street* (#86); Crosstown *79th Street* (#79); Crosstown *72nd Street* (#72); Crosstown *66th/67th Streets* (#66) ending at Central Park West and 72nd Street; Uptown *Riverside Drive*—Downtown *Riverside Drive* (#4, #5); Uptown *Amsterdam Avenue*—Downtown *Columbus Avenue* (#7, #11); Uptown *Broadway*—Downtown *Broadway* (#104).

Morningside Heights

Boundaries and Contiguous Areas: North: 125th Street and Harlem; **East:** Morningside Drive; **South:** 110th Street and Upper West Side; **West:** Hudson River.

Academia amidst a gritty urban-scape, this lively community occupying the formerly rocky slopes of northern Manhattan is dominated—physically, economically and socially—by Columbia University, one of the nation's oldest, richest and largest educational institutions. In addition, Barnard College as well as two important religious seminaries, the Manhattan School of Music, a large teaching hospital, and two major churches share the Heights with a mixture of students, professors, professionals and urban poor. Up here next to the granite bulk of Ulysses S. Grant's pompous tomb, upper west side grey is relieved by Riverside Park, used extensively by residents as a front yard, and by Morningside Park, seldom used because it is safe only to contemplate from a distance.

When finally completed decades hence, the Episcopal Cathedral Church of St. John the Divine will literally tower over the community; now spireless, the world's largest Gothic cathedral just looms. (The tall Gothic church tower you do see rising northwest of Columbia belongs to Riverside Church, the Rockefellers' non-denominational gift to the city.) St. John's caters to cultural as well as spiritual needs, sponsoring a particularly rich and wide-ranging series of concerts from chamber music through liturgical works to jazz and other events including poetry readings, craft fairs and dance programs. The church dedicates a side altar to victims of AIDS.

Broadway, Morningside Heights' Main Street, showcases bookstores, coffee shops, all night fruit stands, student bars cum jazz joints, boutiques and restaurants ranging from fast food to ethnic and elegant. The lively street life that continues late makes the neighborhood relatively safe and certainly interesting.

As owners of one-third of the community's housing stock, over half of which is occupied by tenants affiliated with the university, Columbia is the Heights' biggest landlord. Rent control is pervasive here and tenants unrelated to the university often came with their buildings; when these original tenants leave, their apartments are usually taken by university people. However, an occasional rental does hit the open market, and sometimes space becomes available when Columbia-connected roommates separate (graduate, marry or move) leaving behind an empty room and half the monthly rent bill.

Area Code: 212

Post Office: Morningside Station, 232 West 116th Street, NYC 10026, 864-6968.

Zip Codes: 10027, 10026, 10025

Police Precinct: Twenty-sixth, 520 West 126th Street, NYC 10027, 678-1311.

Emergency Hospital: St. Luke's-Roosevelt Hospital Center: St. Luke's Hospital, 114th Street and Amsterdam Avenue, NYC 10025, 523-4000.

Library: 115th Street Branch, 203 West 115th Street, NYC 10026, 666-9393; Columbia Branch, 514 West 113th Street, NYC 10025, 864-2530.

Public School Education: School District #3 (see **Lincoln Center Area**).

Adult Education: Barnard College, 3009 Broadway, NYC 10027, 854-5262; Columbia University, Broadway and 114th Street to 120th

Street, NYC 10027, 854-1754; Union Theological Seminary, Broadway and 120th Street, NYC 10027, 662-7100; Bank Street College of Education, 610 West 112th Street, NYC 10025, 875-4400; Jewish Theological Seminary, 3080 Broadway, NYC 10027, 678-8000; Manhattan School of Music, 120 Claremont Avenue, NYC 10027, 749-2802.

Cultural Resources: Cathedral Church of St. John the Divine, West 112th Street and Amsterdam Avenue, NYC 10025, 316-7540, also has on its large grounds a Biblical Garden with plantings inspired by the Old Testament; north of St. John the Divine, Riverside Church, 400 Riverside Drive (at West 122nd Street), NYC 10027, 222-5900, offers educational and cultural programs in addition to religious services.

Transportation—Subway: A, B, C, D at 125th Street (Exp), 116th Street, 110th Street.

Transportation—Bus: Crosstown *116th Street* (#20); Uptown *Riverside Drive*—Downtown *Columbus Avenue* (#11); Uptown *Broadway*—Downtown *Broadway* (#104).

The Harlems

Boundaries and Contiguous Areas: East Harlem: North and East: Harlem River; **South:** 96th Street, Upper East Side and Yorkville; **West:** Central Park. **Harlem: North:** 155th Street and Washington Heights; **East:** Harlem River; **West:** Hudson River; **South:** 125th Street and Morningside Heights.

This neighborhood, rich in culture, remains the spiritual focus of black America. Although Harlem pockets some of the worst poverty and crime in New York City, many of its high-stooped, row-house-lined streets are perfectly safe.

Originally settled in 1636 by Dutch tobacco farmers, Harlem blossomed into a prosperous suburb in the 1800s. Around 1900, black New Yorkers began settling into an abundance of apartment buildings left empty when real estate developers' plans for a white middle class neighborhood never materialized. In addition to brand new housing stock, Harlem offered its first black residents a less racially hostile environment than in other parts of the city.

Harlem in the 1920s is synonymous with the Harlem Renaissance. Musicians, playwrights and novelists flocked to the neighborhood bursting with jazz clubs and casinos.

Since the 1930s prominent African-American Harlemites have lived on Striver's Row, on 138th and 139th Streets between Seventh and Eighth Avenues. Dominated by brownstones now part of the St. Nicholas Historic District, this block is where Spike Lee filmed some of *Jungle Fever*. Abyssinian Baptist Church, New York's oldest Black church, is located at 132 West 138th Street. Equally appealing to professionals, and to City College professors, is the Hamilton Heights area just north of the college, in particular Hamilton Terrace, with its handsome, land-marked brownstones. Vacancies are rare. A little more affordable per-haps are the brownstones in the Mount Morris Park Historic District, 119th to 124th Streets west of rocky Mount Morris/Marcus Garvey Park. Further north, Sugar Hill with its mixture of high rise and pleasing brown-stone apartments in the 140s and 150s between St. Nicholas and Edgecombe Avenues, has an enduring appeal.

In the heart of Harlem at Lenox Avenue and West 135th Street is the Schomburg Center for Research In Black Culture, housing the world's largest collection of Black history. On West 135th Street is the facility's outdoor sculpture garden; the outdoor amphitheater is on West 136th. Another neighborhood treasure at its western extreme is the splendid Riverbank State Park, 28 acres of landscaped greenery with spectacular sunset views over the Hudson at 145th Street. Completed in 1993 atop an award-winning waste treatment plant, the recreational complex com-prises indoor and outdoor swimming pools, a gym and fitness room, soft-ball fields, basketball, tennis and handball courts outdoors, an indoor the-ater and an amphitheater, an ice and roller skating rink. Admission is free daily from 6 a.m. to 11 p.m., with a fee for the use of tennis courts and a nominal fee for the pool (see **Sports and Recreation**).

Harlem's East side is known as Spanish Harlem or El Barrio. Here you'll find mostly tenements and housing projects. Above 100th Street, newcomers should take care and know where they're going. La Marqueta, a Latino produce, meat and houseware market keeps things bustling along El Barrio's busiest street, 116th to Park Avenue.

Harlem celebrates its past and present history each August by host-ing a one-week African-American and Hispanic festival. Call the Uptown Chamber of Commerce, 427-3315, for details.

Class and racial tensions have kept Harlem somewhat isolated from the rest of Manhattan, but many say it is bringing itself to a second Renaissance. Indeed, with new families restoring many of Harlem's brownstone buildings and a thriving cultural scene (see **Cultural Resources** below), this neighborhood is pumping with life. And if the good life is defined by the availability of lobster, French cheeses and filet mignon, Harlem has that too now and at competitive prices, 7 days a week at the vast Fairway market on Marginal Street right on the Hudson between 132nd and 133rd Streets. But it's not all brie; along with milk, juice, chittlins and collards, there's a Kosher butcher and fish depart-ment. With all this and free parking too, Manhattan is beating a path to Harlem. Moreover, Harlem and the South Bronx have been designated an "Empowerment Zone," which will mean that in the late 1990s, $300 million in federal money will start to flow into this neighborhood, begin-ning with the ambitious Harlem USA complex on West 125th Street and Eighth Avenue, where a 6,000-square foot Disney store and entertain-ment complex will anchor a glassy structure containing a Chase bank, a cineplex, restaurants, stores and a skating rink. Start your search for

Harlem housing in the *Amsterdam News* real estate section.

Area Code: 212

Post Office: Hamilton Grange Station, 521 West 146th Street, NYC 10031, 281-8401; Manhattanville Station, 365 West 125th Street, NYC 10027, 662-1901; Hell Gate Station, 153 East 110 Street, NYC 10029, 860-3557; Triborough Station, 167 East 124th Street, NYC 10035, 534-0865.

Zip Codes: 10026, 10027, 10029, 10030, 10031, 10032, 10035, 10039

Police Precinct: Twenty-third, 164 East 102nd Street, NYC 10029, 860-6411; Twenty-fourth, 151 West 100th Street, NYC 10025, 678-1811; Twenty-fifth, 120 East 119th Street, NYC 10035, 860-6511; Thirty-second, 250 West 135th Street, NYC 10030, 690-6311.

Emergency Hospital: Harlem Hospital, 506 Lenox Avenue at 135th Street, NYC 10037, 939-1000, includes a crisis intervention center for battered wives, children and rape victims; Mount Sinai Hospital, 101st Street and Madison Avenue, NYC 10029, 241-6500.

Library: A regional branch of the New York City Public Library, Countee Cullen, is located at 136th Street and Lenox Avenue, NYC 10037, 491-2070. The Schomberg Center for Research In Black Culture, 515 Malcolm X Boulevard (135th Street at Lenox Avenue), NYC 10037, 491-2200, houses the city's African-American archives and presents local artists' works.

Public School Education: East Harlem: District #4, 319 East 117th Street, NYC 10035, 860-5910; further West: District #5, 433 West 123rd Street, NYC 10027, 769-7600. High schools include the Manhattan Center for Science and Mathematics, FDR Drive and 116th Street, NYC 10029, 876-4639; and A. Phillip Randolph Campus, Convent Avenue and 135th Street, NYC 10031, 926-0113.

Adult Education: City College, City University of New York (CUNY) 138th Street and Convent Avenue, NYC 10031, 650-7000; Boricua College, a private Hispanic liberal arts college, 3755 Broadway at 155th Street, NYC 10032, 694-1000.

Cultural Resources: Apollo Theater, 253 West 125th Street, NYC 10027, 749-5838; Harlem Third World Trade Center on 163 West 125th; Studio Museum in Harlem, 144 West 125th Street, NYC 10027, 864-4500; Hamilton Grange, 287 Convent Avenue, NYC 10031, 283-5154; Black Fashion Museum, 157 West 126th Street, NYC 10027, 666-1320; The Museum of the City of New York, Fifth Avenue at 103rd Street, NYC 10029, 534-1672; El Museo del Barrio at Fifth Avenue and 104th Street, NYC 10029, 831-7272, (art, culture, heritage of Puerto Rico and Latin

America); Dance Theater of Harlem, 466 West 152nd Street, NYC 10031, 690-2800 (see Dance section); Harlem School of the Arts, 645 St. Nicholas Avenue between 141st and 145th Streets, NYC 10030, 926-4100.

Transportation—Subway: #4, #5, #6, Lexington Avenue at 125th (Exp), 116th, 110th, 103rd Street and 96th Streets; #1 at 157th, 145th, 137th (Exp), 116th, 110th, 103rd Street and 96th Street (Exp), all on Broadway; #2, #3, Lenox Avenue Terminal (Exp), Lenox Avenue at 145th Street (Exp), 135th (Exp), 125th (Exp), 116th, 110th (Exp), Central Park West at 103rd Street, Broadway at 96th Street (Exp); A, B, C, D, St. Nicholas/8th Avenues at 155th, 145th (Exp), 135th, 125th (Exp), and 116th, Central Park West at 110th, 103rd, 96th; #1/#9, Broadway at 157th, 145th, 137th (Exp), 125th.

Transportation—Bus: Crosstown *96th Street* (#19); Crosstown *116th Street* (#20); Uptown *Riverside Drive*—Downtown *Columbus Avenue* (#11); Uptown/Downtown *Broadway* (#7,#100,#104); Uptown/Downtown *St. Nicholas Avenue* (#3); Uptown/Downtown *Amsterdam Avenue* (#101).

Washington Heights-Inwood

Boundaries and Contiguous Areas: North: Harlem River and Riverdale; **East:** Harlem River; **South:** 155th Street and Harlem; **West:** Hudson River.

Up here, where outcroppings from the Hudson riverbed rise to form Manhattan's highest ground, the tawny stone arches rhythmically lining the central courtyard at The Cloisters are echoed by the exceptionally graceful curve of the steel suspension cables looping the twin towers of the silvery George Washington Bridge. Long before John D. Rockefeller gave the city the magnificent medieval Cloisters Museum as well as Fort Tryon Park, the land on which it stands, and long before the bridge was built in 1931, George Washington headquartered Revolutionary forces on the strategic terrain now called Washington Heights.

Six hundred acres of park land, much of it boulder-strewn and covered with healthy trees and brush, refresh and beautify one of the most densely populated, and narrowest, sections of New York. On the map, the neighborhood looks like a knobby finger pointing across the Harlem River at The Bronx from the elongated fist of Manhattan. Washington Heights and Inwood are *all* "West Side"; the Harlem River lops off the "East Side" at 138th Street.

Commercial Broadway cuts through the area on a north-south bias, dividing the almost solidly Hispanic, Harlem River (eastern) half from the middle-income, Hudson River (western) half of the neighborhood. The western section contains the most coveted housing—solidly constructed one-and two-bedroom apartments, many with pleasing river and park views—situated in square, five- and ten-story buildings. The clusters of yellow, buff and occasionally red brick Art Deco buildings clumped along the riverbank have special appeal: Chittenden Avenue between 187th and 189th Streets contains some beauties and there's a beguiling section bordering forested Inwood Hill Park. Hudson View Gardens between 183rd and 185th Streets and Castle Village nearby, two of the most desirable complexes, are cooperatives.

In recent years a violent drug trade has made parts of Washington Heights, the 150s and 160s in particular, a dicey neighborhood. However, in the healthier parts of Washington Heights and Inwood, community feeling is strong, largely as a result of a ten-year program that renovated an estimated 18% of the housing stock. Buildings have been going co-op on Riverside Drive and along the 181st Street corridor in Washington Heights. Another tangible sign of change in this working-class neighborhood are the several condos reconstructed from the shells of abandoned buildings in Inwood.

To get a sense of this other Manhattan—to feel fresh breezes blowing off the Hudson, to experience its slower pace and to realize that there are a few pubby hangouts or one-of-a-kind boutiques in these latitudes— amble the Heights' main thoroughfare, 181st Street, and pick up a copy of the *Uptown Dispatch*, which is filled with local lore, or the Spanish-English *Washington Heights & Inwood Report*, either of which can be found in a local bank. For another dimension, travel up to Inwood and stroll the grassy banks of Inwood Hill Park. If you find the friendly unassuming neighborhood attractive, plan to search, and search hard, on foot, questioning supers and building managers. Certainly, you can check with a reputable real estate agent. However, few apartments ever reach a broker's office here; word of mouth is still the best way to find a rental in Manhattan's northernmost neighborhood.

Area Code: 212

Post Offices: Audubon Station, 511 West 165th Street, NYC 10032, 568-3311; Washington Bridge Station, 555 West 180th Street, NYC 10033, 568-7601; Fort George Station, 4558 Broadway, NYC 10040, 942-0052; Inwood Station, 90 Vermilyea Avenue, NYC 10034, 567-3032.

Zip Codes: 10034, 10040, 10033, 10032

Police Precinct: Thirty-fourth, 4295 Broadway, NYC 10033, 927-9711; Thirty-third, 2120 Amsterdam Avenue, NYC 10032, 927-3272.

Emergency Hospital: Columbia-Presbyterian Medical Center, 622 West 168th Street, NYC 10032, 305-2500.

Libraries: Fort Washington Branch, 535 West 179th Street, NYC 10033, 927-3533; Washington Heights Branch, 1000 St. Nicholas Avenue, NYC 10040, 923-6054; Inwood Branch, 4790 Broadway, NYC 10034, 942-2445.

Public School Education: School District #6: Community School Board, 665 West 182nd Street, NYC 10033, 927-7777.

Adult Education: Yeshiva University, 500 West 185th Street, NYC 10033, 960-5400; Inwood Community Services, 651 Academy Street (just north of Dyckman Street), NYC 10034, 942-0043.

Cultural Resources: The Cloisters, division of the Metropolitan Museum of Art, Fort Tryon Park (193rd Street and Fort Washington Avenue), NYC 10034, 923-3700; Audubon Terrace Museum complex, Broadway between West 155th and 156th Streets, NYC 10032, including the National Museum of the American Indian Smithsonian Institution, 3753 Broadway, NYC 283-2420, the American Academy and National Institute of Arts and Letters, 1633 West 155th Street, NYC 368-5900, and American Numismatic Society (public display on the history of money), Broadway and 156th Street, NYC 234-3130; Yeshiva University Museum, 2520 Amsterdam Avenue at 185th Street, NYC 10033, 960-5390; Morris-Jumel Mansion and Museum, 1765 Jumel Terrace, NYC 10032, 923-8008, a colonial home in garden surroundings used by Washington during the Revolution and later redecorated by Eliza Jumel; Dyckman House, 4881 Broadway at 204th Street, NYC 10034, 304-9422, is a restored 18th century Dutch farmhouse-museum belonging to the city and well worth a visit.

Transportation—Subway: A, 207th, Dyckman, 190th, 181st, 175th, 168th (all Exp) 163rd Streets: stops along Fort Washington Avenue, Broadway; B, C 168th, 163rd, 155th Streets on Amsterdam Avenue; #1/#9 215th, 207th, Dyckman, 191st, 181st, 168th and 157th Streets: all stops along St. Nicholas Avenue.

Transportation—Bus: Crosstown *181st Street* (#3, #11, #13, #35, #36, #38); Uptown/Downtown *Fort Washington Avenue* to Broadway (#4); Uptown/Downtown *Broadway* (#7, #100); Uptown/Downtown *St. Nicholas Avenue* (#3); Uptown/Downtown *Amsterdam Avenue* (#101).

THE BRONX

Poor the Bronx, a borough that's seldom mentioned without its article. The northernmost and smallest, though not by much, of New York City's five parts is more often celebrated for a rude cheer and for Fort Apache, the south central section that has begun to struggle back from dilapidation and worse, than for large verdant parks, colleges and top-flight high schools or for some singularly attractive neighborhoods. To set the record straight, then, you should know that The Bronx boasts all of these.

Just south of Westchester County, New England-esque City Island floats rather quaintly in placid Long Island Sound. And over on the Hudson shore, Riverdale shelters estates and sylvan lanes worthy of suburban Scarsdale. In between these two neighborhoods, apartment buildings embellished with Art Deco motifs line the once-elegant Grand Concourse.

Four of the city's finest high schools are situated in The Bronx: the prestigious public Bronx High School of Science, from which so many Westinghouse Science Award winners graduate, as well as private Fieldston, Horace Mann and Riverdale Country Day School. Eight universities and colleges enhance the borough's scholastic character.

A wealth of public land is probably The Bronx's greatest asset; park land accounts for almost a quarter of the 43-square-mile borough. Partially forested Van Cortlandt Park, a mecca for cross-country skiers in the winter, is the spot for soccer, rugby and football in the summer. Even larger Pelham Bay Park, from which little City Island dangles, harbors Orchard Beach along its sandy shore. But the star is Bronx Park with 500 acres about equally divided between two of the city's most illustrious scientific institutions: the Bronx Zoo (now officially renamed the New York Zoological Society's International Wildlife Conservation Park) and the New York Botanical Garden. The Haupt Conservatory, a sparkling crystal greenhouse complex, displays thousands of plant varieties in natural micro-climates and must be seen. Kids of all ages, naturalists and explorers, too, frequent the Zoo, using the tram-like Skyfari for an overview of the African exhibit as well as to commute between pavilions that include the World of Darkness and World of Birds.

While chunks of The Bronx do flourish, the loft buildings and brownstones so dear to middle-income colonizers in search of inexpensive digs are in short supply. Cooperatives and condominiums continue to replace rental apartments, but The Bronx has few neighborhoods that attract the younger singles in the fashion of Brooklyn and Hoboken. Bronx realtors are listed under **Apartment Hunting.**

Riverdale

Boundaries and Contiguous Areas: North: 263rd Street and Yonkers; **East:** Broadway and Van Cortlandt Park; **South:** Harlem River and Washington Heights-Inwood; **West:** Hudson River.

Our boundaries outline a rather generous Riverdale, incorporating as

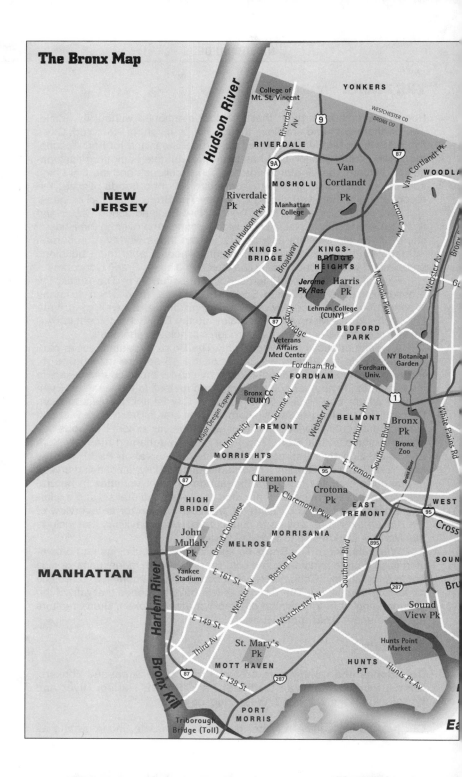

The Bronx Map

they do the communities of Kingsbridge, Fieldston, Spuyten Duyvil as well as Riverdale. Each enclave has its own personality, but the first-time renter will probably head to Spuyten Duyvil or Riverdale in search of a post-war apartment that has yet to go co-op.

Spuyten Duyvil, a colony of apartment buildings edged by the Harlem River and the Hudson, faces Manhattan. Tall red-brick apartment towers cluster in clumps along Riverdale's narrow potholed lanes. There are plenty of mini-mansions in Riverdale, too, although perhaps the single largest concentration of elegant single-family residences is located in adjoining Fieldston, a somewhat exclusive community with private streets. All three communities share the same rocky outcropping beside the Hudson. The urban grid and bustle so typical of New York is found on the flats below in Kingsbridge.

The Riverdale that for most of its well-to-do length ridges the river seems more Westchester than New York. Posh private schools attract kids who drive in from New Jersey and the suburbs as well as those who arrive by subway and bus from New York. Shops are discretely curtailed to a few zones of Mom and Pop businesses. Supermarket complexes are built elsewhere. Riverdale's low, tree-shaded profile appeals not only to affluent New York professionals but to resident foreigners. The Russians built their white high-rise complex here, and many of the local estates house UN personnel and foreign executives.

For a great day in this country visit Wave Hill (call 718-549-2055 for directions; express buses run by Liberty Lines, 718-652-8400, provide direct service to West 252nd Street). The Hudson-side complex at 249th Street and Independence Avenue consists of two stone manor houses offering occasional chamber music, a greenhouse and 28 acres of perfectly gorgeous gardens, where in summer outdoor sculpture exhibits compete for your attention with lovely river views.

Area Code: 718

Post Offices: Riverdale Station, 5951 Riverdale Avenue, Bronx 10471, 549-7519; Kingsbridge Station, 5517 Broadway, Bronx 10463, 549-5500.

Zip Codes: 10463, 10471

Police Precinct: Fiftieth, 3450 Kingsbridge Avenue, Bronx 10463, 543-5700.

Emergency Hospital (nearest): Montefiore, 210th Street and Bainbridge Avenue, Bronx 10467, 920-4321.

Library: Riverdale Public Library, 5540 Mosholu Avenue, Bronx 10471, 549-1212.

Public School Education: School District #10: Community School Board, 1 Fordham Plaza, Bronx 10458, 584-7070.

Adult Education: Manhattan College, Manhattan College Parkway and West 242nd Street, Bronx 10471, 920-0100; College of Mt. St. Vincent, Riverdale Avenue and West 263rd Street, Bronx 10471, 549-8000.

Cultural Resources: Wave Hill, West 249th Street and Independence Avenue, Bronx 10471, 549-2055; Riverdale YM-YWHA, 5625 Arlington Avenue, Bronx 10471, 548-8200.

Transportation—Subway: #1/#9 at 242nd, 238th, 231st and 225th Streets (all in Kingsbridge).

Transportation—Bus: Commuters in Spuyten Duyvil, Fieldston and Riverdale tend to use Liberty Line, 652-8400, express buses to mid-Manhattan. Get a Bronx bus map for local MTA routes.

BROOKLYN

"For safety and real rental value, Brooklyn beats Manhattan hands down." The chauvinistic local real estate broker quoted might have added a qualifying "certain neighborhoods" in Brooklyn. But it is true that by crossing the East River to Long Island's westernmost purchase you can pay less for housing than you might in Manhattan. Even rents in staid, lovely old Brooklyn Heights are a bit cheaper than equally prestigious Manhattan locations. It follows that relative bargains can be found in the four and five-story row houses, more often than not lovingly restored by a Brooklyn brownstoner, that line the streets in less securely established communities such as Boerum Hill or Fort Greene/Clinton Hill. Among the salient features of these neighborhoods are the brick, board and, yes, brownstone row houses representing a virtual catalog of architectural styles from 1820s Federal through 1910s late Victorian.

Other pluses? Brooklyn boosters boast about excellent subway transportation, the quality of the public schools in District 15, and the lively cultural climate engendered by the culture scene's Big Three: the Brooklyn Museum, Brooklyn Botanic Garden and Brooklyn Academy of Music (BAM).

The city's most populous borough is stirring. Immigration, most recently from the countries of the former Soviet Union and from Asia have added to the population, especially in Sunset Park and in some of the further reaches of the borough. This and other factors are feeding commercial growth in Brooklyn. 1987 marked the beginning of the long-overdue revitalization of downtown Brooklyn. First, 1 Pierrepont Plaza opened, with 800 computer and back-office workers from Morgan Stanley. Now several mixed-use developments are in various stages of progress in the area. Metrotech, the largest, with 11 buildings, is nearly finished and already headquarters Brooklyn Union Gas and some 6,000 Chase Manhattan workers, among others. Just across Jay Street, Renaissance Plaza will house corporate offices in a 32-story tower and the first new hotel in Brooklyn in 50 years, opening in 1998. The Atlantic Center, a mixed office, retail and residential complex on Flatbush Avenue, is rising, with a major part of its retail facilities up and running. These developments represent the most important change in Brooklyn since the completion of the Brooklyn Bridge. They are bringing more than 37,000 new workers to the area. Over time, the ripple effect should be immense.

Names of Brooklyn realtors can be found under **Apartment Hunting**.

Brooklyn Heights

Boundaries and Contiguous Areas: North: Fulton Ferry Landing and Cadman Plaza West; **East:** Cadman Plaza and Court Street; **South:** Atlantic Avenue and Cobble Hill; **West:** The Esplanade overlooking the East River and Brooklyn-Queens Expressway (BQE).

A New York Times article described two young lawyers walking home along Henry Street in the Heights one summer evening discussing cooperative apartments they had just bought. Not only did they estimate the purchase prices to be about 20% lower than comparable real estate in Manhattan, but they believed the location couldn't be topped professionally. And as generalizations go, that is a fair one. A large percentage of Heights residents have arrived, are established and will continue to lead the good life in carefully restored 19th and early 20th century townhouses built by earlier generations of successful Manhattan professionals.

Robert Fulton's steamboat ferry service, inaugurated in 1814, spurred the development of the rural Brooklyn settlement. Newly accessible to lower Manhattan, and cooled by East River breezes, the Heights attracted merchants and lawyers, who built the substantial homes and noteworthy churches which characterize the community today. Brooklyn Heights boasts 684 pre-Civil War houses alone, and more than a dozen mostly-Gothic Revival churches.

The opening of the Brooklyn Bridge in 1883 brought the Heights that much closer to Wall Street and provided its most spectacular landmark, the gossamer span flung from Gothic tower to Gothic tower over the busy East River. Wealth crossed the bridge to Brooklyn Heights and created one of the richest communities in the nation by the turn of the century. But the Depression wiped out many residents, the bankers and businessmen who worked on Wall Street, and blight came to the Heights.

In the 1950s and early 1960s, Brooklyn's first "brownstoners", attracted by the innate quality of the rundown housing stock, discovered Brooklyn Heights. These pioneers began a wave of renovation that, in the ensuing decades, has swept over row upon row of dilapidated Brooklyn townhouses. Today, the Heights' relatively cohesive population resides in stolid prewar apartment buildings and lovingly restored brownstones, as well as in striking warehouse conversions down at Fulton Ferry Landing. Besides the obvious, a five-minute subway zip to Manhattan, other commuting modes include the feet. Hearty residents stride briskly along the soaring raised center walkway of the Brooklyn Bridge to their jobs in Lower Manhattan.

From the start, accessibility to Wall Street attracted residents to the Heights, and the exceptional view of Manhattan and the harbor kept them there. The magnificent panorama brings a steady stream of day-trippers, who come to absorb the view while strolling the wide and gracious Esplanade and to enjoy the quiet, landmarked district with its informal restaurants and pleasant shops.

Area Code: 718

Post Offices: General Post Office, 271 Cadman Plaza East, Brooklyn 11201, 348-3000; Municipal Building Station, Municipal Building, 210 Joralemon Street, Brooklyn 11201, 875-1332.

Zip Code: 11201

Police Precinct: Eighty-fourth, 301 Gold Street between Tillary and Johnson Streets, Brooklyn 11201, 875-6811.

Emergency Hospital (nearest): Long Island College Hospital, 340 Henry Street at Amity Street, Brooklyn 11201, 780-1000.

Libraries: The Business Library, 722-3333, and Brooklyn Heights Branch, 780-7789 share the same address: 280 Cadman Plaza West, Brooklyn 11201. The Brooklyn Historical Society's private library, 128 Pierrepont Street, Brooklyn 11201, 624-0890, houses excellent historical and genealogical collections.

Public School Education: School District #13: Community School Board, 355 Park Place, Brooklyn 11238, 636-3204; and School District # 5: Community School Board, 360 Smith Street, Brooklyn 11231, 330-9300.

Adult Education: Long Island University, University Plaza, Brooklyn 11201, 488-1000; New York City Technical College, 300 Jay Street, Brooklyn 11201, 260-5000.

Cultural Resources: St. Ann's and the Holy Trinity Episcopal Church, 157 Montague Street, 834-8794. This church and day school complex sponsors numerous concerts and other cultural events as well. Bargemusic, Ltd., Fulton Ferry Landing, Brooklyn 11201, 624-4061: chamber music concerts accompanied by gentle lapping from the East River. St. Francis College, 180 Remsen Street, Brooklyn 11201, 522-2300. The Brooklyn Arts & Culture Association, Inc. (BACA), 195 Cadman Plaza West, Brooklyn, 11201, 625-0080, coordinates and supports the efforts of a wide range of cultural programs within the borough; call to receive BACA's monthly Calendar of Cultural Events.

Transportation—Subway: #2, #3, Clark Street, Borough Hall; #4, #5, Borough Hall; A, C High Street/Brooklyn Bridge; N, M, R at Court Street.

Transportation—Bus: Stop by Brooklyn Transit Headquarters Information Center, 370 Jay Street, for a bus map of Brooklyn.

Cobble Hill

Boundaries and Contiguous Areas: North: Atlantic Avenue and Brooklyn Heights; **East:** Court Street and Boerum Hill; **South:** DeGraw Street and Carroll Gardens; **West:** Hicks Street.

If it were possible to walk across the Mediterranean, a stroll starting at Atlantic Avenue down Court, Cobble Hill's main shopping street, to Carroll Gardens could be compared to a walk from Lebanon and the Middle East to Italy. Atlantic's famed Near and Middle Eastern spice and grocery stores and restaurants filter along Court south for a couple of blocks before meeting up with the pizzerias, Neapolitan bakeries and shops selling Italian housewares that take over the street as it approaches heavily Italian Carroll Gardens on Cobble Hill's southern boundary.

This intriguing ethnic mix results in topnotch food sources which attract shoppers from all over Brooklyn.

The row upon row of brownstones—cheaper and not quite as grand as those in Brooklyn Heights—shaded by large, leafy trees (note particularly the plane trees that completely cover Clinton Street as it crosses Baltic, Veranda and Congress Streets on the way to the Heights) attract a young professional crowd. Cobble Hill is probably the most homogeneous of all the Brooklyn brownstone neighborhoods. Apartment buildings and converted industrial properties are beginning to spring up in Cobble Hill, notably The Henry Street Mews condos and One Tiffany Place, just west of the Brooklyn Queens Expressway. Other recent conversions include Cobble Hill Towers, the city's first low income housing project when it was built in 1878, and the P.S. 78 condominiums, lodged in a late-19th century public school on Pacific Street.

Area Code: 718

Post Office (nearest): Municipal Building Station, Municipal Building, 210 Joralemon Street, Brooklyn 11201, 875-1332.

Zip Codes: 11201, 11231

Police Precinct: Seventy-sixth, 191 Union Street between Hicks and Henry Streets, Brooklyn 11231, 834-3211.

Emergency Hospital: Long Island College Hospital, 340 Henry Street at Amity Street, Brooklyn 11201, 780-1000.

Library (nearest): Carroll Gardens Branch, 396 Clinton Street at Union Street, Brooklyn 11231, 625-5838.

Public School Education: School District #15: Community School Board, 360 Smith Street, Brooklyn 11231, 330-9300.

Adult Education: See **Brooklyn Heights** and **Boerum Hill**.

Cultural Resources: See **Brooklyn Heights** and **Boerum Hill**.

Transportation—Subway: #2, #3, #4, #5, Borough Hall; F, G, Bergen Street.

Transportation—Bus: Stop by the Brooklyn Transit Headquarters Information Center, 370 Jay Street, for a bus map of Brooklyn.

Carroll Gardens

Boundaries and Contiguous Areas: North: DeGraw Street and Cobble Hill; **East:** Gowanus Canal; **South:** Hamilton Avenue; **West:** Brooklyn-Queens Expressway.

In Carroll Gardens, singularly deep and lushly planted gardens front the four- and five-story row houses so characteristic of Brooklyn's brownstone neighborhoods. These splendid yards, with trees as tall as the high-stooped townhouses, form part of an eleven-block tract laid out in the 1850s. Verdant block fronts are, however, only part of the reason urban homesteaders began moving to Carroll Gardens in the 1970s. This predominantly Italian community has a lower crime rate than many other areas in Brooklyn. And furthermore, just like Cobble Hill, another "tight" neighborhood to the north, Carroll Gardens boasts better-than-average public elementary and secondary schools.

Other pluses? Great food shopping. Shiny eggplants, firm-fleshed peppers, snowy mushrooms—a veritable caponata—heap the Italian vegetable stands lining Court Street, where bulbous *pecorino* cheeses intersperse salamis and whole prosciuttos hanging from grocery store ceilings. Subway transportation to Manhattan by F Train is fast and direct.

Less expensive, and less gentrified than the Heights and Cobble Hill, Carroll Gardens has limited housing stock, although conversions become available now and then. The largest and most appealing of these is The Mill on President Street. Fifty-five condos, some of which should be available as rentals from their owners, are contained in the converted rope factory with exposed brick walls and massive red oak beams.

To be sure, Carroll Gardens isn't paradise. Those garden blocks exist only north of Fourth Place. Shanties and derelict buildings still border Red Hook to the south. Use a real estate agent to find an apartment here, if after a stroll of the park-like streets between Fourth and President you find the area appealing.

Area Code: 718

Post Office: Red Hook, 615 Clinton Street, Brooklyn 11231, 624-5632.

Zip Code: 11231

Police Precinct: Seventy-sixth, 191 Union Street, Brooklyn 11231, 834-3211.

Emergency Hospital (nearest): Long Island College Hospital, 340 Henry Street at Amity Street, Brooklyn 11201, 780-1000.

Library: Carroll Gardens Branch, 396 Clinton Street at Union Street, Brooklyn 11231, 625-5838.

Public School Education: School District #15: Community School Board, 360 Smith Street, Brooklyn 11231, 330-9300.

Adult Education: See Brooklyn Heights and Boerum Hill.

Cultural Resources: See Brooklyn Heights and Boerum Hill.

Transportation—Subway: F, Carroll Street, Smith Street; G, Carroll Street, Smith Street.

Transportation—Bus: Stop by the Brooklyn Transit Headquarters Information Center, 370 Jay Street, for a bus map of Brooklyn.

Boerum Hill

Boundaries and Contiguous Areas: North: Schermerhorn Street; **East:** Third Avenue; **South:** Wyckoff Street; **West:** Court Street and Cobble Hill.

The Boerum Hill Historic District, bounded roughly by Hoyt and Nevins, Pacific and Wyckoff Streets, contains an outstanding assemblage of pre-Civil War Italianate and Greek Revival row houses: a monument to the efforts of new homeowners who in the early 1960s fought off a city effort to tear down the then-dispirited rooming houses to make way for urban renewal. Boerum Hill's turnaround—from near-slum to tight residential community—was achieved by a dedicated band of pioneers sophisticated enough to see the area's potential.

Often referred to as the Golden Oak Capital of America, the Boerum Hill section of Atlantic Avenue is the city's prime source for oak furniture and Victorian bric-a-brac. It seems only fitting that the devoted homesteaders living nearby should have appropriate furnishings close at hand. Antique stores lining both sides of the avenue have made way for a French bistro and a deli or two—a sure sign that the middle class has moved in.

Area Code: 718

Post Office: Times Plaza Station, 542 Atlantic Avenue, Brooklyn 11217,875-7882.

Zip Code: 11217

Police Precincts: Seventy-sixth, 191 Union Street between Hicks and Henry Streets, Brooklyn 11231, 834-3211; Seventy-eighth, 65 Sixth Avenue between 6th and Bergen Streets, Brooklyn 11217, 636-6411.

Emergency Hospital: Long Island College Hospital, 340 Henry Street at Amity Street, Brooklyn 11201, 780-1000.

Library: Pacific, 25 Fourth Avenue, Brooklyn 11217, 638-5180.

Public School Education: School District #15: Community School Board, 360 Smith Street, Brooklyn 11231, 330-9300.

Adult Education: Brooklyn YWCA, 30 Third Avenue, Brooklyn 11217, 875-1190, offers a health program plus a variety of adult classes.

Cultural Resources: New York Transit Museum (located in a former subway station), Boerum Place and Schermerhorn Street, Brooklyn 330-3060.

Transportation—Subway: #2, #3, Hoyt Street, Nevins Street; #4, #5 Nevins Street; F, Bergen Street; G, Bergen Street, Hoyt/Schermerhorn Streets; A, C, Hoyt/Schermerhorn Streets.

Transportation—Bus: Stop by Brooklyn Transit Headquarters Information Center, 370 Jay Street, for a bus map of Brooklyn.

Park Slope

Boundaries and Contiguous Areas: North: Flatbush Avenue; **East:** Prospect Park West; **South:** Windsor Place; **West:** Fifth Avenue.

If Cobble Hill is the most homogeneous of Brooklyn's brownstone neighborhoods, Park Slope is the most heterogeneous, and proud of it. (It is also by far the largest of these communities.) The fact that the population is still economically, ethnically and racially mixed appears for a majority of residents to be the neighborhood's most attractive attribute. Second place is probably a tie between 526-acre Prospect Park, designed by Frederick Law Olmsted and Calvert Vaux, Central Park's architects, and Park Slope's proximity to Brooklyn's three imposing cultural bastions: the Brooklyn Museum, the Central Library at Grand Army Plaza and the Brooklyn Botanic Garden. A recent addition to Prospect Park is the re-opened Wildlife Conservation Center, a state of the art children's zoo with a restored 1912 carousel (50¢ rides).

Park Slope's development paralleled that of Prospect Park in the 1880s. Sites with a park view were most highly prized, and small Victorian mansions line Prospect Park West. Closeness to the park and Grand Army Plaza determined the quality and appointments also of the vigorously Victorian bow-fronted townhouses which march row upon stolid row down the sloping streets. North Park Slope, nearest Prospect Park West and the Plaza, is considered the classiest part of the neighborhood. South Park Slope, east of 9th Street, is the less expensive, still-developing section. Old industrial properties, such as the Ansonia Clock factory complex on 12th Street, once the country's largest clock works and now deluxe condominiums, have been converted to apartments and co-ops. Seventh Avenue, the principal shopping street and scene of a hugely successful fair each spring, reflects neighborhood needs: the boutiques, card shops and unisex hair cutters once found exclusively at the North Slope end of Seventh have infiltrated blocks in South Park Slope as well. With the arrival of a Barnes & Noble the neighborhood is officially literate and upscale.

Without qualification Park Slope, together with Brooklyn Heights, has arrived as a suitable address for middle class professionals, especially those with—or about to be with—families. P.S. 321, district 15's progressive, well-regarded elementary school, has served as an additional attraction to young families. But don't go looking for bargain basements; in real estate parlance, the neighborhood is "hot" (and has been for a while), especially along the park. Prices are lower down the slope and in adjoining Windsor Terrace and Prospect Heights, two revitalizing communities nicely situated near Prospect Park.

Area Code: 718

Post Office: Van Brunt Station, 275 9th Street, Brooklyn 11215, 768-6284.

Zip Code: 11215, 11217

Police Precincts: Seventy-second, 830 Fourth Avenue between 29th and 30th Streets, Brooklyn 11230, 965-6311; Seventy-eighth, 65 Sixth Avenue between 6th and Bergen Streets, Brooklyn 11217, 636-6411.

Emergency Hospital: Methodist Hospital, 506 6th Street between Seventh and Eighth Avenues, Brooklyn 11215, 780-3000.

Library: Brooklyn Central Library, Grand Army Plaza at Flatbush Avenue, Brooklyn 11238, 780-7810.

Public School Education: School District #13: Community School Board, 355 Park Place, Brooklyn 11238, 636-3204; and School District #15: Community School Board, 360 Smith Street, Brooklyn 11231, 330-9300.

Adult Education: Brooklyn Museum Art School, 200 Eastern Parkway, Brooklyn 11238, 638-5000. Brooklyn Botanic Garden, 1000 Washington Avenue, Brooklyn 11225, 622-4433, holds classes for plant enthusiasts. Brooklyn Conservatory of Music, 58 Seventh Avenue, Brooklyn 11217, 622-3300. St. John-St. Matthew Emmanuel Lutheran Church Community Center, 415 Seventh Street between Sixth and Seventh Avenues, Brooklyn 11215, 768-0528, allocates space to community educational and cultural groups.

Cultural Resources: Brooklyn Museum, 200 Eastern Parkway at Washington Avenue, Brooklyn 11238, 638-5000. Behind the six Ionic columns of McKim, Mead and White's famed building are housed a number of exemplary collections as well as facilities for the cultural and educational programs sponsored daily by the museum.

Transportation—Subway: With the exception of the A and C trains, subways stop near one part of Park Slope or the other. #2, #3, #4, #5 trains stop at Grand Army Plaza; F stops at Fourth Avenue, Seventh Avenue and 15th Street; D stops at Seventh Avenue and Atlantic Avenue; B, M, N, R stop along Fourth Avenue at Pacific Street, Union Street, 9th Street and Prospect Avenue.

Transportation—Bus: The Information Center at Brooklyn Transit Headquarters, 370 Jay Street, is the place to get a bus map of Brooklyn.

Fort Greene/Clinton Hill

Boundaries and Contiguous Areas: North: Myrtle Avenue; **East:** Classon Avenue; **South:** Atlantic Avenue; **West:** Flatbush Avenue and Boerum Hill.

"To the rear of the boisterous city hall quarter was Brooklyn's other fine residential district, the Hill…. Its elegant residences were fewer in number [than Brooklyn's Heights'] and their owners slightly further removed from the traditions of genteel respectability. It abounded in churches and middle class houses, the majority of whose owners worked in New York." So wrote a Brooklyn historian of late 19th century Fort Greene and Clinton Hill. Despite a decline in the intervening years, that description is valid once again. Except for the fringe areas, especially to the north and west. Today they are even fringier. What occasioned the turnabout? Historic designation and the brownstone revival, mainly.

Revival came late, in the 1970s, to Fort Greene. Even the once-elegant brownstones on the choice streets nearest Fort Greene Park had become dilapidated wino rows. But beneath the grime and neglect the original detailing remained, awaiting the attention of determined urban pioneers. Now, perfectly restored Anglo-Italianate brownstones line Washington Park, South Oxford and South Portland Streets. And sweeping 33-acre Fort Greene Park, the community's centerpiece designed by Olmsted and Vaux, has been restored to its rather English graciousness.

Homeowners are as likely to be black or Hispanic as they are white, as likely to be filmmakers or musicians as investment bankers. Fort Greene is integrated, both racially and socio-economically, and determined to stay that way. The throbbing cultural presence of the Brooklyn Academy of Music (BAM) helped stimulate the growth of a substantial community of black artists in Fort Greene. Yet a perception of crime persists, a perception which is greater than the reality, many residents insist. Besides, they say, with what you save on rent here, you can afford to take a cab from the subway station at 1 a.m.

Clinton Hill, like Fort Greene, which it borders and from which it is barely distinguishable, contains an astonishing treasury of late 19th century urban architecture. The key word in this neighborhood is Pratt. Kerosene magnate Charles Pratt built several handsome mansions on Clinton Avenue, including the present residence of the Bishop of Brooklyn. Charles Pratt also founded, built and, until his death in 1891, ran Pratt Institute, the focal point and cultural center of the community. And now it is the students, grads and faculty of Pratt (art, design, architecture, engineering, computers and library sciences) who fill the streets and much of the local housing.

Clinton Hill has a few high rises and therefore a somewhat wider variety of housing than Fort Greene. But Clinton Hill has only one subway line. The G train, which stops at Clinton and Washington Streets and requires long waits as well as a transfer to reach Manhattan, is a definite minus. Fort Greene, on the other hand, is well tended by the subway system (see below) and offers easy on-street parking.

Both the nearly-finished Metrotech commercial development to the west on Flatbush Avenue and the Atlantic Center mixed-use development on the southeast edge of Fort Greene, should profoundly effect Fort Greene and Clinton Hill when completed at the end of the century. Expect the cost of housing to rise. Meanwhile, apartment hunting here is best done through a knowledgeable real estate agent.

Area Code: 718

Post Offices: Pratt Station, 524 Myrtle Avenue, Brooklyn 11205, 622-8581; General Post Office, 271 Cadman Plaza East, Brooklyn 11201, 834-3000; Times Plaza Station, 542 Atlantic Avenue, Brooklyn 11217, 875-7882.

Zip Codes: 11201, 11205, 11217, 11238

Police Precinct: Eighty-eighth, 298 Classon Avenue, Brooklyn 11205, 636-6511.

Emergency Hospital: Brooklyn Hospital, 121 DeKalb Avenue, Brooklyn 11201, 250-8000.

Libraries: Brooklyn Public Library, Clinton Hill Branch, 380 Washington Avenue, Brooklyn 11238, 857-8038; Walt Whitman Branch, 93 St. Edwards Street, Brooklyn 11205, 855-1508.

Public School Education: School District #13, Community School Board, 355 Park Place, Brooklyn 11238, 636-3204.

Adult Education: Pratt Institute, Continuing Education, 200 Willoughby Avenue, Brooklyn 11205, 636-3453; Medgar Evers Community College, 1150 Carroll Street, Brooklyn 11225, 270-4900; St. Joseph's College, 265 Clinton Avenue, Brooklyn 11205, 622-4690.

Cultural Resources: Brooklyn Academy of Music (BAM), 30 Lafayette Avenue, Brooklyn 11217, 636-4100. The borough's premier cultural resource, BAM contains four theaters of differing sizes presenting a spectrum of performances by artists from all disciplines and hosting the annual Next Wave Festival. Nearby: Long Island University, University Plaza, Flatbush at DeKalb Avenues, Brooklyn 11210, 650-8114; and the Brooklyn Children's Museum, splendidly renovated, at 245 Brooklyn Avenue (Crown Heights), Brooklyn 11213, 735-4400.

Transportation—Subway: A, C, Lafayette Avenue; B, D DeKalb Avenue; M, N, Q, R, DeKalb Avenue; #2, #3, Nevins Street; #4, #5, Nevins Street; G Fulton Street, Clinton/Washington Avenues.

Transportation—Bus: The Information Center at Brooklyn Transit Headquarters, 370 Jay Street, is the place to get a bus map of Brooklyn.

Greenpoint/Northside, Williamsburg

Boundaries and Contiguous Areas: North: Newtown Creek and Queens; **East:** Newtown Creek and the Brooklyn-Queens Expressway (BQE); **South:** Grand Street; **West:** the East River.

This northernmost portion of Brooklyn, protruding into the underbelly of Queens and just 20 minutes by subway from Manhattan, is one of Brooklyn's best-kept secrets, and that's just fine with Greenpoint. Or Greenpernt, as they pronounced it in the gangster movies of the 1930s. Just across the East River from 23rd Street in Manhattan, it might as well be another country. Modest two-, three-, and four-story houses, colorfully sided and impeccably tidy, line quiet streets. The feel is 1940-something small town. Housewives chat on front steps, and they are as likely to be speaking Polish as English.

Along Manhattan Avenue, Greenpoint's Main Street, kielbasi drape the butcher shops, restaurants offer *pierogi* and *golumpki*, and the travel agencies advertise Lot Airline flights to Poland. Italian restaurants, bodegas along Franklin street and the occasional shamrock define the ethnic composition of this largely blue-collar community. In the Historic District just west of Manhattan Avenue, Java and India Streets with their handsome brownstones and churches recall the coffee and spice trade that once flourished along the docks here. And in the rather British-feeling Monsignor McGolrick Park a monument to the Civil War battleship Monitor, which was built here, memorializes Greenpoint's shipbuilding past as well.

Just to the south beyond McCarren Park and the stunning, copper-domed Russian Orthodox Cathedral of the Transfiguration lies **Northside, Williamsburg**, with nothing to mark the boundary between it and Greenpoint, so similar are the two communities. Numbered streets—declining from North 15th to Grand—cross Bedford Avenue, Northside's tidy, quiet Main Street. To the east traffic roars along the elevated Brooklyn-Queens Expressway. From the undeveloped waterfront area to the west comes the occasional scent of molasses from the Domino sugar plant and now and then of garbage from the processing concerns there. No sign now of the fashionable resorts which florished here near the ferry landings until the Williamsburg Bridge and trolley service in 1905 brought immigrants streaming from the Lower East Side to make Williamsburg the most populous neighborhoood in Brooklyn in 1920. But signs of change here are evident in the cafes, the futon shop, the Thai restaurant and the pet shop.

Young artists discovered the peace, quiet and relatively low cost of living here, carving lofts out of former manufacturing space in Greenpoint in the 1980s and in Northside in the 1990s. Driven by rising rents in Manhattan, adventurous young professionals followed. There's talk of developing the waterfront, with its spectacular view of lower Manhattan. Meanwhile, you probably won't find a doorman in Greenpoint or Northside, nor an indoor pool or health club. But the 35 acres of McCarren Park includes ballfields, tennis courts, a running track and a fitness course. Available housing, though occasionally appearing among the rental listings in The Village Voice, is best found through local real estate agents. Expect few amenities and rents at least a third below the Manhattan rate for a small one- or two-bedroom. Allow six weeks to two months to find a suitable spot in this tight little community. Walk around to get a feel of the neighborhood, pick up a copy of the weekly Greenpoint Gazette for the apartment ads, and drop in on a real estate office.

Area Code: 718

Post Office: Greenpoint Station, 66 Meserole Avenue, Brooklyn 11222, 389-5929; Williamsburg Station, 256 South 4th Street, Brooklyn 11211, 387-2459.

Zip Code: 11222, 11211

Police Precinct: Ninety-fourth, 100 Meserole Avenue, Brooklyn 11222, 383-3879.

Emergency Hospital (nearest): Woodhull Medical Center, 760 Broadway, Brooklyn 11206, 963-8000.

Library: Greenpoint Branch, 107 Norman Avenue, Brooklyn 11222, 383-6692.

Public School Education: School District #14, 215 Heywood Street, Brooklyn 11206, 387-8698.

Transportation—Subway: L, Bedford Avenue; G, Greenpoint Avenue, Nassau Avenue.

Transportation—Bus: The Information Center at Brooklyn Transit Headquarters, 370 Jay Street, is the place to get a bus map of Brooklyn.

You might also want to consider...

- **Windsor Terrace**, a safe, old-fashioned community of small detached houses nicely sandwiched between Prospect Park and beautiful, park-like Greenwood Cemetery.

- **Flatbush**, fairly vast and varied, geographically and psychologically the heart of Brooklyn. Its most appealing neighborhoods are Prospect Park South and Ditmas Park, both of which feature lovely old Victorian homes along stately, tree-lined streets, and strong community spirit.

- **Bay Ridge**, way out by the Verazanno Bridge and overlooking the Narrows, studded with parks and restaurants. This conservative community with a Scandinavian and Italian heritage is peacefully 50 minutes by subway from Manhattan.

- **Fort Hamilton**, just beyond Bay Ridge around the base of the Verazanno Bridge, has more co-ops and condos among their one-family houses, with a similar perch on the Narrows and about an hour by subway to Manhattan.

QUEENS

"Queens is not New York!" exclaims a character in the film *Quiz Show*. Many Manhattanites would agree—but that is a Manhattan state of mind.

Among the five boroughs, Queens is the acknowledged bastion of New York's middle class. As skyscrapers identify Manhattan and brownstones Brooklyn, so solid brick buildings—free-standing, Tudor-inspired houses, semi-detached, two-, three-and four-family dwellings and six-story apartment blocks—define a good part of the largest borough in the city.

Until 1909 and the completion of the Queensborough Bridge, semi-rural Queens was a backwater connected only by ferry boat to Manhattan across the East River. But the bridge, followed almost immediately by train and then by subway service through new tunnels under the East River, opened the way for commuters and commerce. Great parcels of land were snapped up by developers, and 1908 saw the beginning of a building spree that continued, with few pauses, until World War II. While some communities are architecturally noteworthy—Forest Hills Gardens, a carefully designed 1909 enclave planned down to its English rustic street signs, and Malba, a charming melange of lawns, leafy lanes and handsome, mostly 1920s homes nestled under the Whitestone Bridge—most of the housing is sturdy, unremarkable pre-World War II stock often laid out, suburban-style, in tracts.

Although many Queens neighborhoods are identified with various ethnic groups—Greeks gravitate to Astoria, Latin Americans to Jackson Heights, Russians to Rego Park, Asians to Flushing—a multi-national mix of businessmen, engineers and other professionals continues to move into the area. Immediately across the river from Manhattan new life is being breathed into Long Island City, not only by artists attracted by P.S. 1, a highly successful alternative art, dance and theater space, but also by the re-establishment of the enormous old Astoria movie studios, the new Silver Cup Studios, the Eaves-Brooks costume company and the gargantuan International Design Center, which contains more than 100 acres of showroom space. The 42-story, glass Citicorp spire, towering over these industrial surrounds like a giant among midgets, now dominates Long Island City. Just to the south in the Hunters Point section, the 42-story Citylights, with 522 apartments, opens in late 1997, the beginning of a long-planned residential/commercial development which will rise along the East River there. When completed, Queens West will comprise 6,385 tower and low-rise apartments, a hotel and office complex spread over a 74-acre waterfront site across from the United Nations and connected with it by passenger ferry.

New York magazine was perhaps premature in proclaiming Long Island City "The New Hot Neighborhood" a few years ago, at least as far as newcomers are concerned; although a number of artists are residents of this factory town, there is a paucity of houses and residential lofts. Astoria just to the north and Sunnyside to the southeast, both equally accessible to Manhattan, are moderately priced alternatives.

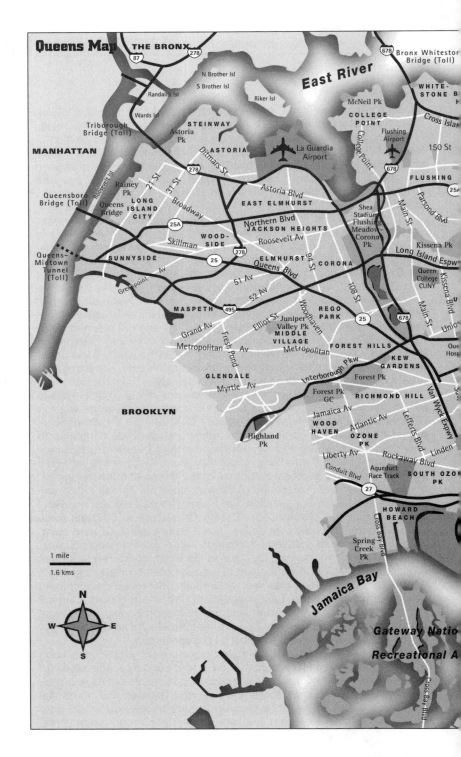

Queens Map

THE BRONX

87

278

East River

678 Bronx Whitestor
Bridge (Toll)

N Brother Isl

S Brother Isl

Randall's Isl

Riker Isl

McNeil Pk

WHITE-
STONE B
H

Wards Isl

COLLEGE
POINT

Cross Islar

STEINWAY
Astoria
Pk

Triborough
Bridge (Toll)

Flushing
Airport

150 St

Ditmars St

ASTORIA

La Guardia
Airport

College Point

678

MANHATTAN

278

Astoria Blvd

FLUSHING

25/

Rainey
Pk

21 St

31 St

Broadway

EAST ELMHURST

Parsond Blvd

Main St

Queensboro
Bridge (Toll)

**LONG
ISLAND
CITY**

Northern Blvd
JACKSON HEIGHTS

Shea
Stadium
Flushing
Meadow-
Corona
Pk

Queens
Bridge

25A

**WOOD-
SIDE**

Roosevelt Av

Kissena Pk

Skillman

278

Long Island Espw

Queens–
Midtown
Tunnel
(Toll)

SUNNYSIDE

25

ELMHURST
Queens Blvd

CORONA

Queen
College
CUNY

Kissena Blvd

51 Av

94 St

Main St

Greenpoint Av

108 St

Un

52 Av

MASPETH

495

**REGO
PARK**

25

678

Que
Hos

Grand Av

Elliot St

Juniper
Valley Pk
**MIDDLE
VILLAGE**

Woodhaven

FOREST HILLS

Metropolitan Av

Fresh Pond

Metropolitan

**KEW
GARDENS**

Van Wyck Expwy

GLENDALE

Interborough Pkw

Forest Pk

Myrtle Av

Forest Pk
GC

RICHMOND HILL

BROOKLYN

Jamaica Av

Lefferts Blvd

**WOOD
HAVEN**

Atlantic Av

Highland
Pk

**OZONE
PK**

Liberty Av

Rockaway Blvd

Linden

Conduit Blvd

Aqueduct
Race Track

**SOUTH OZON
PK**

27

**HOWARD
BEACH**

Spring
Creek
Pk

Cross Bay Blvd

Jamaica Bay

**Gateway Natio

Recreational A

Cross Bay Blvd

1 mile

1.6 kms

N

W   E

S

Within subway reach, Rego Park, Forest Hills and Kew Gardens are popular established communities where one, and even two, bedroom apartments rent for the same amount as a Manhattan studio. Further east, the new condominium units renting in big Bayside high rises seem to have appeal for those who don't find the trip by express bus or Long Island Railroad too daunting.

Names of Queens real estate brokers will be found in the chapter on **Apartment Hunting.**

Astoria

Boundaries and Contiguous Areas: North: East River; **East:** Grand Central Parkway, Brooklyn-Queens Expressway and LaGuardia Airport; **South:** 35th Avenue and Sunnyside; **West:** East River.

You don't have to be Greek (or Italian, Yugoslavian, German or Bohemian either) to live in Astoria, but it can't hurt. With a population that is nearly 60% Greek or Hispanic, this community has a distinct Old World feel. With and without belly dancers, the tavernas on Ditmars Boulevard and Broadway vibrate long and late to the keening of Greek dance music. The most recent wave of immigrants has brought an infusion of Irish, South Americans, Slavs and Asians.

Urban professionals have discovered the apartments in the decently maintained but unprepossessing two-story houses and small apartment buildings bordering Astoria's relatively safe streets, in particular the area between Crescent and 35th Streets, which is within distance of the N line and a 20-minute commute from Midtown. (A caveat: presumably Astorians have no problem with the improbably numbered streets, drives and avenues here; outsiders find them incomprehensible.)

The Olympic-sized city pool in spacious Astoria Park, just beneath the Triborough Bridge on the East River, is free, as is the uncrowded running space around the park. Condo living, with a free health club and unobstructed view of the Manhattan skyline, came to Astoria with the opening of the 405-unit Shore Towers in 1990 at the southern end of the park.

Astoria was the home of Paramount Studios from 1919 until the 1930s, when the business moved—lock, stock and W.C. Fields—to Hollywood. The movies are back, however, sharing with television the enormous, refurbished Kaufman Astoria Studios on 35th Avenue between 34th and 37th Streets. The complex also houses the Museum of the Moving Image, the only museum in the country dedicated to movies, TV and the interactive media. Several production facilities have sprouted up nearby including Silvercup Studios, a maker of commercials and feature films. The revitalization of southern Astoria's movie and television industry has suggested a new moniker for the area: Hollywood East.

Still, with the noteworthy exception of two extraordinary sculpture collections and the recent addition of a 750-seat public theater, Athens

Square, cultural institutions and parks are in short supply in mainly blue-collar Astoria. Unlikely as it may seem, the prime showcase of Isamu Noguchi's sculpture—some 350 pieces by the famous artist—is located in the Noguchi Garden Museum on Vernon Boulevard at 33rd Road. And sculptor Mark Di Suvero organized the Socrates Sculpture Park, with a changing display of monumental works in a vacant East River lot just across Vernon Boulevard. Could a branch of Washington's Hirschhorn Gallery be next?

Area Code: 718

Post Offices: Astoria Station, 27-40 21st Street, Astoria 11102, 726-1005; Steinway Station, 43-04 Broadway, Astoria 11103, 726-1107; Woolsey Station, 22-68 31st Street, Astoria 11105, 274-5563; Broadway Station, 21-17 Broadway, Astoria 11106, 726-1007.

Zip Codes; 11102, 11103, 11105, 11106

Police Precinct: One Hundred Fourteenth, 34-16 Astoria Boulevard at 35th Street, Astoria 11102, 626-9311.

Emergency Hospital: Elmhurst Hospital Center, 79-01 Broadway, Elmhurst 11373, 334-4000.

Library: Astoria Branch, Queens Public Library, 14-01 Astor Boulevard, Astoria 11102, 278-0601; Steinway Branch, 21-45 31st Street, Long Island City 11105, 728-1965.

Public School Education: District #30, Community School Board, 49-05 20th Avenue, Jackson Heights, 11106, 777-4600.

Cultural Resources: The Noguchi Garden Museum, 32-37 Vernon Boulevard, 204-7088, is open Wednesday and Saturday afternoons, April-November; Socrates Sculpture Park, Broadway at Vernon Boulevard, 956-1819, open 10 a.m. to dusk daily; Museum of the Moving Image, 36-01 35th Avenue, 784-4520, open Tuesday to Friday, Noon to 4, Saturday and Sunday to 6 p.m.

Transportation—Subway: N, Queensboro Plaza, 39th Avenue, 36th Avenue, Broadway, 30th Avenue, Astoria Boulevard-Hoyt Avenue, Ditmars Boulevard; E, F, 23rd Street, Queens Plaza; G, R, Queens Plaza, 36th Street, Steinway Street and 46th Street; B, Q, 21st Street/Queens Bridge.

Transportation—Bus: Stop by the Queens Transit Headquarters Information Center, 124-15 28th Avenue, Flushing, for a bus map of Queens.

Sunnyside

Boundaries and Contiguous Areas: North: Barnett Avenue and the Sunnyside Amtrak Yards; **East:** 52nd Street and New Calvary Cemetery; **South:** Long Island Expressway; **West:** 36th Street and Long Island City.

This traditionally blue-collar community bounded by railroad yards, industrial tracts, cemeteries and the legendary LIE (the Long Island Expressway, known, among other sobriquets, as the world's longest parking lot) won't be the next "in" New York neighborhood. But the sensible, mostly-brick homes and apartments lining Sunnyside's residential streets ten minutes by train from Manhattan do attract young professionals, as well as immigrants from overseas, with more space for lower-than-Manhattan rents.

Newcomers are especially drawn to Sunnyside Gardens. "The Gardens," the first U.S. development to be modeled on the English garden community, occupies 55 leafy acres north of bustling Queens Boulevard. Towering London plane trees shade the 650 one-, two-and three-family brick townhouses which enclose long, communal gardens. The effect is English village, with shrub-lined walks penetrating the landmarked blocks. "Like Greenwich Village and far more than Brooklyn Heights, it was a mixed community, in which one might mingle without undue intimacy with one's neighbors," recalls urban critic/historian Lewis Mumford, who lived in The Gardens from their inception in 1924 until 1936. They seem little changed.

There are private homes and rentals in greater Sunnyside as well, but most of the brick apartment blocks are non-rentable co-ops. The three main shopping thoroughfares are small-town Skillman Avenue at The Gardens' southern edge, Queens Boulevard in the shadow of the elevated IRT Flushing Line, and running diagonally southwest from the Boulevard, Greenpoint Avenue. There and on the side streets you can rent Korean movies, buy Irish imports, eat Italian, Middle European or Oriental, or lift a pint at Moriarty's Pub Restaurant. The city's only Spanish language theater, The Thalia on Greenpoint, plays to sellout crowds on weekends.

Thanks in large part to the efforts of the Sunnyside Foundation whose staff works on planning and preservation issues, Sunnyside is an appealingly cohesive community, for all its ethnic diversity. Stop by the Foundation's office at 41-13 47th Street (392-9139) for information, advice and a free copy of *The Sunnyside Herald* if you're thinking of moving here.

Area Code: 718

Post Office: Sunnyside Station, 45-15 44th Street, Sunnyside 11104, 729-1438.

Zip Code: 11104

Police Precinct: One Hundred Eighth, 5-47 50th Avenue, Long Island City 11104, 784-5411.

Emergency Hospital (nearest): Elmhurst Hospital Center, 79-01 Broadway, Elmhurst 11373, 334-4000..

Library: Sunnyside Branch, 43-02 Greenpoint Avenue, Sunnyside 11104, 784-3033.

Public School Education: School District #24, Community School Board, 43-31 39th Street, Sunnyside 11104, 361-0750.

Transportation—Subway: #7, 40th Street, 46th Street, 52nd Street.

Transportation—Bus: Stop by the Queens Transit Headquarters Information Center, 124-15 28th Avenue, Flushing, for a bus map of Queens.

Rego Park

Boundaries and Contiguous Areas: North: Queens Boulevard; **East:** Yellowstone Boulevard and Forest Hills; **Southwest:** Woodhaven Boulevard.

What distinguishes Rego Park from neighboring Forest Hills and Kew Gardens, which it very much resembles, is the appreciably higher ratio of apartment buildings to private dwellings, slightly lower rents, somewhat older population and proportionately more recent immigrants. While the number of Indians, Pakistanis and Asians has been increasing throughout the three communities, Rego Park has also attracted a sizable Russian population, a large Israeli group and a nucleus of Iranians.

One of the borough's largest malls, the Queens Center housing Macy's, among others, with Stern's and Sears nearby, is quartered on the Rego Park stretch of Queens Boulevard. Smaller, more intimate shops line 63rd Drive.

It should be noted that the imposition of a rigid grid pattern was foiled in this part of Queens by circuitous streets laid out in "crescents" by the original developers. Wherever possible, each numbered thoroughfare has an Avenue, Road and Drive to its credit. For example, 63rd Avenue, 63rd Road, 63rd Drive in that order. The streets tend to be named, not numbered. Rego Park was first developed in 1923 and named for the company that built it: the Rego (for Real Good) Construction Company.

Area Code: 718

Post Office: Rego Park, 92-24 Queens Boulevard, Rego Park, NY 11374, 429-2696.

Zip Code: 11374

Police Precinct: One Hundred and Twelfth, 68-40 Austin Street, Forest Hills, NY 11375, 520-9311.

Emergency Hospital: St. John's Hospital, 90-02 Queens Boulevard, Elmhurst, NY 11373, 558-1000.

Library: Rego Park, 91-41 63rd Drive, Rego Park, NY 11374, 459-5140.

Public School Education: Public School District #28 (see Forest Hills).

Adult Education: Queens College (see **Flushing**); St. John's University (see **Forest Hills**).

Transportation—Subway: R, Rego Park Station, 67th Avenue; G, Rego Park Station, 67th Avenue.

Transportation—Bus: Stop by the Queens Transit Headquarters Information Center, 124-15 28th Avenue, Flushing, for a bus map of Queens.

Forest Hills

Boundaries and Contiguous Areas: The neighborhood is shaped roughly like a lower case "d". **North:** Long Island Expressway; **East:** Grand Central Parkway and Corona Park; **South:** Union Turnpike and Kew Gardens; **West:** Yellowstone Boulevard and Rego Park.

Practical Queens Boulevard, a major shopping thoroughfare which sensibly separates curbside businesses from through traffic with narrow cement dividers, belies the charm of Forest Hills as it cuts through the heart of the neighborhood. Bordering Corona Park northwest of the boulevard, the "Cord Meyer" district consists of gracious, white-trimmed brick homes begun in 1904 and large apartment buildings constructed later by the Cord Meyer Development Co., which is still the largest landlord in the area. South a block just off Austin, considered one of the most enticing shopping streets in Queens, lies "The Gardens." Forest Hills Gardens, designed in the eclectic tradition by an architect of the Beaux Arts school and sponsored by the Russell Sage Foundation, has few peers in the half-timbered world of Victorian Tudor. Brick-fronted Cotswoldian houses face curving drives and landscaped plots originally planned by Frederick Law Olmsted, Jr. Instantly successful, the development spawned housing decorated with Tudor clichés throughout central Queens.

Until 1977, when the US Open Tennis Championships moved to Flushing, Forest Hills was the self-described "lawn tennis capital of the Western Hemisphere." But the West Side Tennis Club, still occupying ten acres next to the Gardens, continues to add luster to the community by hosting the men's World Champion matches each spring, among other tournaments. Shopping and noshing opportunities also add allure. In addition to the attractive Austin Street spots, appealing cafes, craft and antique stores are cropping up on Metropolitan Avenue.

Old, established, and mostly—about 90% according to the last census—white, Forest Hills is becoming increasingly cosmopolitan. (A local real estate agent reports a Japanese language map of Forest Hills on sale in Tokyo bookstores.) And increasingly, its brick apartment buildings have gone co-op. The few six-to ten-story rental buildings congregating on either side of Queens Boulevard and the IND/BMT subway lines, as well as major arteries like Ascan, Metropolitan and 108th Street, are worth pursuing for their quality pre-war construction as well as convenience to public transportation. Semi-detached apartments and units in private homes may require a slightly longer walk but offer landscaped lots and winding streets as dividends.

Area Code: 718

Post Office: Forest Hills, 106-28 Queens Boulevard, Forest Hills, NY 11375, 268-1696.

Zip Code: 11375

Police Precinct: One Hundred and Twelfth, 68-40 Austin Street, Forest Hills, NY 11375, 520-9311.

Emergency Hospitals: LaGuardia Hospital, 102-01 66th Road, Forest Hills, NY 11375, 830-4000; Parkway Hospital, 70-35 113th Street, Forest Hills, NY 11375, 990-4100.

Library: Forest Hills, 108-19 71st Avenue, Forest Hills, NY 11375, 268-7934.

Public School Education: School District; #28, 108-55 69th Avenue, Forest Hills, NY 11375, 830-8800.

Adult Education (nearest): St. John's University, Grand Central and Utopia Parkways, Jamaica, NY 11439, 990-6161.

Community Resources: West Side Tennis Club, 1 Tennis Place (bounded by Burns and Dartmouth Streets and 69th and 70th Avenues), 268-2300.

Transportation—Subway: E, F, G, R, all to 71st and Continental Avenues, Forest Hills.

Transportation—Bus: Stop by the Queens Transit Headquarters Information Center, 124-15 28th Avenue, Flushing, for a bus map of Queens.

Kew Gardens

Boundaries and Contiguous Areas: Northeast: Queens Boulevard; **South:** Metropolitan Avenue and Forest Park; **West:** Union Turnpike and Forest Hills.

Bracketed by LaGuardia Airport and John F. Kennedy International, Queens is home to thousands of airline employees. Kew Gardens in particular is popular with flight crews, who can spy their very own red-tiled roofs as the jets they man pass over the community en route to the airports. Real estate agents report more rentals available and more singles residing in Kew Gardens than in Forest Hills and Rego Park.

The neighborhood's oldest section dates to 1912, when the Kew Gardens Corporation was formed. The substantial Colonial and Tudor-accented private homes built on high, comparatively hilly ground between Maple Grove Cemetery and Forest Park have cachet even today. After some years heavy with co-op conversions, the blocks of red brick apartment buildings that ring Kew's center are becoming more affordable and turning co-op at a slower rate. Austin Street and Metropolitan Avenue together with Lefferts and Queens Boulevards make up Kew's main shopping area.

At its southeastern most tip, Kew Gardens hosts not only the borough's newest commercial skyscraper, a tall, rectangular gray block with cutout circles at the corners, but also Queens Borough Hall just across the Van Wyck Expressway, a long bureaucratic brick and limestone structure usually filled with politicians and, occasionally, useful publications about the borough.

Area Code: 718

Post Office: Kew Gardens, 83-30 Austin Street, Kew Gardens, NY 11415, 847-1978.

Zip Codes: 11415, 11375, 11365

Police Precinct: One Hundred and Second, 87-34 118th Street, Richmond Hill, NY 11418, 805-3200.

Emergency Hospital (nearest): LaGuardia Hospital, 102-01 66th Road, Forest Hills, NY 11375, 830-4000.

Libraries: Lefferts Branch, 103-34 Lefferts Boulevard, Richmond Hill, 843-5950; Glen Oaks, 25604 Union Turnpike, Forest Park, NY 11426, 347-8200.

Public School Education: Public School District #28 (see **Forest Hills**).

Adult Education (nearest): Queens College, 65-30 Kissena Boulevard, Flushing, NY 11367, 997-5411.

Community Resources: Queens Borough Hall, 120-55 Queens Boulevard, Kew Gardens, NY 11424, 520-3220.

Transportation—Subway: E, Kew Gardens/Union Turnpike; F, Kew Gardens/Union Turnpike; R, Kew Gardens/Union Turnpike.

Transportation—Bus: Stop by the Queens Transit Headquarters Information Center, 124-15 28th Avenue, Flushing, for bus map of Queens.

Flushing

Boundaries and Contiguous Areas: North: Cross Island Parkway and Whitestone; **East:** Utopia Parkway and Francis Lewis Boulevard and Bayside; **South:** Union Turnpike; **West:** Grand Central Parkway and Forest Hills.

Middle class Flushing sprawls on either side of the Long Island Expressway, embraced by two great parks, at the center of thriving northern Queens. The nexus of multiple bus routes, rail lines and traffic arteries, downtown Flushing looks like the crossroads of the world as well. In recent years a strong influx of Asians—Chinese, from Taiwan primarily, Koreans, Indians and Pakistanis—have revitalized commercial Flushing, enriched it culturally and changed its face. On weekends the colorful Chinese fish-fruit-and-vegetable venders, Muslim butchers, and sari shops along Main Street draw shoppers from outside the area. Religious observances are as likely to be in Korean, Hindi or Mandarin as in English or Hebrew.

Away from commercial Main Street, Union Turnpike and Northern Boulevard, the grid of shady residential streets has changed little, except perhaps to have become more presentable. The profusion of well-established trees, 2,000 varieties throughout Flushing, constitute a treasure and a living remnant of the nursery industry which flourished here from pre-Revolutionary times until recently. Among these is the venerable Weeping Beech in a small, landscaped park behind historic Kingsland House. Another survivor, its back turned to Northern Boulevard, the austere Friends' Meeting House has been a place of worship since 1694, except during the Revolutionary War, when it was a British hospital, prison and stable. Bowne House, built nearby in 1661, was an earlier site of Quaker worship and of the struggle for religious freedom in what was then a Dutch settlement. Down Bowne Street from this museum of colonial life, in a modest residential neighborhood, is an extraordinary Hindu temple covered with stone statues. That's Flushing.

Equally characteristic are the great tracts of green breathing space which surround and bisect Flushing. Along the town's western flank Flushing Meadow Corona Park contains within 1,200 acres the site of two world fairs (1939 and 1964), two lakes, a marina, the Queens Zoo, a botanical garden, the Queens Museum, Theatre in the Park, the New

York Hall of Science, an indoor ice-skating rink, Shea Stadium, home of the New York Mets, and the USTA National Tennis Center, site of the annual U.S. Open Tennis Championships. A green band connects this vast park with the more intimate and landscaped Kissena Park, which contains an appealing Nature Center. Along the eastern flank of Fresh Meadows the grassy stretches of Cunningham Park provide an outlet for all manner of amateur sports teams.

As might be expected, the presence of Queens College and the rich ethnic mix here support an unusually vibrant cultural life: music, art, literary pursuits and theater flourish here. The Flushing Branch of the Queens Borough Public Library on Main Street is bursting its seams with readers in 30 languages; hence its temporary relocation while it is demolished and rebuilt. Simultaneous renovation of the subway station nearby will be a temporary nuisance in downtown Flushing, but a long-term boon to the 100,000 commuters who use it, many of them transferring from the web of bus routes which cross here.

Besides the convenience of transportation and the physical amenities, what Flushing has to offer is more space at less-than-Manhattan rents. For luxury condos look elsewhere, **Bayside** perhaps. High-rise apartments cluster near downtown Flushing. The rest is two-story brick apartment enclaves, one and two-family houses, detached and semi-attached, all with on-street parking. Ads to sell or rent these properties are often placed in *Newsday* and *The New York Times* by their owners; consult these same pages and the list of realtors in **Looking for a Place to Live** to find brokers who handle other properties.

Area code: 718

Post offices: Flushing Main Station, 41-65 Main Street, Flushing 11355, 670-4700; Fresh Meadow Station, 192-20 Horace Harding Expressway, Flushing 11365, 454-6647; Station "B", 136-50 Roosevelt Avenue, Flushing 11368, 424-273l; Pomonok Station, 158-05 71st Avenue, Flushing 11366, 591-6611; Utopia Station, 182-04 Union Turnpike, Flushing 11366, 380-0902; Station "A", 40-03 164th Street, Flushing 11358, 353-28l9; Station "C", 75-23 Main Street, Flushing 11367, 544-0989; Linden Hill Station 29-50 Union Street, Flushing 11354, 461-1512.

Zip Codes: 11354, 11355, 11358, 11365, 11366, 11367, 11368

Police Precincts: One Hundred and Ninth, 37-05 Union Street, Flushing 11354, 321-2250; One Hundred and Seventh, 71-01 Parsons Boulevard, Flushing 11365, 969-5100.

Emergency Hospitals: New York Hospital Medical Center of Queens, Main Street at Booth Memorial Avenue, Flushing 11355, 670-1231; Flushing Hospital Medical Center, 4500 Parsons Boulevard, Flushing 11355, 670-5000.

Libraries: Flushing Main Branch, 36-41 Main Street (temporarily), Flushing 11355, 445-0800; Hillcrest Branch, 187-05 Union Turnpike, Flushing 11366, 454-2786; McGoldrick Branch, 155-06 Roosevelt Avenue, Flushing 11354, 353-0839; Mitchell-Linden Branch, 29-42 Union Street, Flushing 11354, 539-2330; Pomonok Branch, 158-21 Jewel Avenue, Flushing 11365, 591-4343; Queensboro Hill Branch, 60-05 Main Street, Flushing 11355, 359-8332; Vleigh Branch, 72-33 Vleigh Place, Flushing 11367, 261-6654.

Public School Education: District #25, 70-30 164th Street, Flushing 11365, 480-4100; District #26, 61-15 Oceania Avenue, Bayside 11364, 639-6900.

Adult Education: Queens College, 65-30 Kissena Boulevard, Flushing 11367, 997-5000.

Cultural Resources: Queens Historical Society, Kingsland House, 143-35 37th Avenue, Flushing 11354, 939-0647; The Bowne House, 37-01 Bowne Street, Flushing 11354, 359-0528; Godwin-Ternbach Museum, Queens College, 65-30 Kissena Boulevard, Flushing 11367, 520-7129; Art Center, Benjamin S. Rosenthal Library, Queens College, 65-30 Kissena Boulevard, Flushing 11367, 997-5000; New York Hall of Science, 47-01 111th Street, Flushing Meadows-Corona Park, Flushing 11368, 699-0005; Queens Museum of Art, New York City Building, Flushing Meadows-Corona Park, Flushing 11368, 592-2405; Colden Center for the Performing Arts, Queens College, Long Island Expressway and Kissena Boulevard, Flushing 11367, 793-8080; Flushing Council on Culture and the Arts at Town Hall, 136-73 41st Avenue, Flushing 11355, 463-7700;Tung Ching Chinese Center for the Arts, 147-17 45th Avenue, Flushing 11355, 539-4682;Kissena Park Nature Center, Rose Avenue and Parsons Boulevard, 699-4202; Queens Botanical Garden 43-50 Main Street, Flushing 11355, 886-3800; Queens Theatre in the Park, Flushing Meadow Corona Park, Flushing 11368, 760-0064.

Transportation—Subway: #7, Willets Point-Shea Stadium, Main Street; E, F, Union Turnpike-Kew Gardens.

Transportation—Bus: Stop by the Queens Transit Headquarters Information, 124-15 28th Avenue, Flushing, for a bus map of Queens; Queens Surface Corp., at the same address, 445-3100, offers express service on several routes to midtown Manhattan.

Transportation—Train: Regular Long Island Railroad service from Main Street Station.

Bayside

Boundaries and Contiguous Areas: North and East: Cross Island Parkway; **South:** Long Island Expressway; **West:** Francis Lewis Boulevard and Utopia Parkway.

The bright barn-red Long Island Railroad station, white-trimmed and snappy, differentiates Bayside from other Queens stops. So does the concentration of pubs and restaurants—some dim and glitzy, others homey-comfortable with fireplaces—that surround the station. These places attract singles and have a bubbling atmosphere after work and on weekend nights. North of this Bell Boulevard and 41st Avenue junction, one-and two-family homes re-establish that urban/suburban quiet which typifies residential Queens until you reach Bay Terrace. Here, newly con-structed condominiums and co-oped garden apartment buildings again break the mold.

While the older, free-standing homes contain rental apartments, con-dominium rentals in the Bay Club, though expensive, are probably the biggest draw. The enormous development consists of 1,036 condomini-ums in two three-pronged towers, a glass-domed swim club, a health club and five tennis courts. The Bay Bridge condo development nearby, with some 2,000 luxury townhouses, is a shorefront village in itself. From the Bay Club windows, and from those in the older co-ops, you can see how the community got its name—Bayside is bounded on two sides by Little Bay and Little Neck Bay—and the Whitestone, Triborough and Throgs Neck Bridges connecting Queens to The Bronx as well.

Bayside has water views but no direct subway connection to Manhattan. Commuters have three public transportation choices: the Long Island Railroad, express buses, or Queens buses to Flushing's Main Street Station and the # 7 Flushing Line subway.

Area Code: 718

Post Office: Bayside, 212-35 42nd Avenue, Bayside, NY 11361, 229-0699.

Zip Codes: 11360, 11361, 11359

Police Precinct: One Hundred and Eleventh, 45-06 215th Street, Bayside, NY 11359, 279-5200.

Emergency Hospital: St. Mary's Hospital for Children, 29-01 216th Street, Bayside, NY 11360, 281-8800.

Library: Bayside Branch, 214-20 Northern Boulevard, Bayside, NY 11361, 229-1834.

Public School Education: Public School District; #26, 61-15 Oceania Street, Bayside, NY 11364, 631-6900.

Adult Education: Queensborough Community College, 222-05 56th

Avenue, Bayside, NY 11364, 631-6262.

Community Resources: Crocheron Park, 33rd Avenue and Little Neck Parkway, 7225-2620, 45 acre park; Queensborough Community College Gallery, 222-05 56th Avenue, Bayside, call 631-6396 for information.

Transportation—Train: Regular LIRR service.

Transportation—Bus: Stop by the Queens Transit Headquarters Information Center, 124-15 28th Avenue, Flushing, for a bus map of Queens.

You might also want to consider...

• **Richmond Hill**, with Victorian houses, golf and tennis in Forest Park, and a variety of ethnic stores, but less expensive than neighboring Kew Gardens and Forest Hills, for the most part. An easy commute by train or subway.

• **Douglaston**, an upper middle-class community on Little Neck Bay at the northeastern end of Queens, having mostly one- and two-family houses and co-ops, relatively low real estate taxes and lower prices than upscale Great Neck to the east. A 25-minute commute to Manhattan on the Long Island Railroad (LIRR).

• **Whitestone**, on the East River between the Whitestone and Throgs Neck Bridges in northern Queens and 30 minutes on the #7 from Times Square (45 minutes by express bus). Mostly houses, co-ops and condos, few rentals. Includes exclusive Malba and Francis Lewis Park along the riverfront.

• **Jamaica Estates,** with its winding roads, shady streets, Tudor houses and English street names, 45 minutes by the E or F train to Manhattan. Expensive.

Staten Island Map

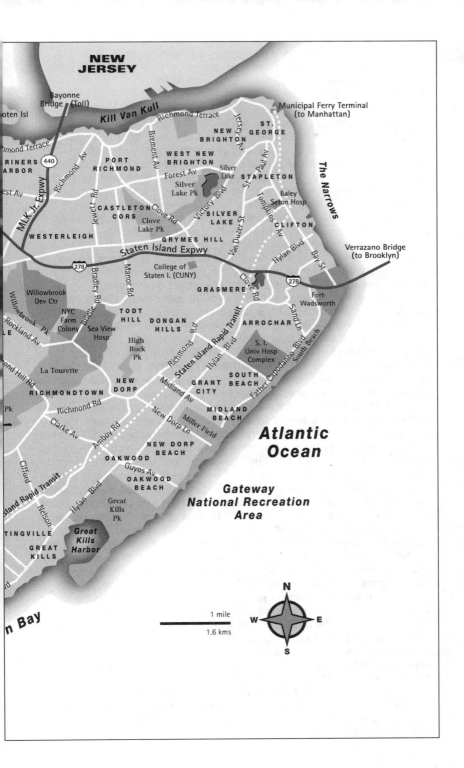

STATEN ISLAND

New York's least-populated borough is, for many, simply the turn-around point for New York's most beloved, and cheapest, boat ride. Not that Staten Islanders mind. The 400,000 residents would just as soon keep their 61-square-mile island off the coast of New Jersey to themselves. In fact, November 2, 1993, marked a red-letter day when islanders voted overwhelmingly to secede from New York City. Final word rests with Albany and this question is not likely to be settled soon.

Dreams of remaining far from the madding New York crowd were, in fact, conclusively shattered when the austerely beautiful Verrazano-Narrows Bridge connecting Staten Island with Brooklyn was opened in 1964. The island's semi-rural isolation ended once and for all as Brooklynites flocked across the longest single-span bridge in the world to take up residence in dozens of new tract developments.

Giovanni da Verrazano discovered hillocky Staten Island in 1524 but, until the dedication of his namesake bridge 440 years later, the island remained something of a backwater. Henry Hudson claimed *Staaten Eylandt* for the Dutch East India Company in 1609; however, Britain acquired Staten Island when the British took over New Amsterdam in 1644. Farming, and then oystering, flourished. By the mid-1800s, a railroad, trolley cars and ferry service made the island's seashore and salubrious air accessible to the gentry.

The fickle fashionables had moved on though by the time Staten Island became part of New York City in 1898. Too bad, because the city improved the new borough's ferry service immeasurably: by 1904 there were a number of sturdy seaworthy boats running on schedule for the first time since young Cornelius Vanderbilt instituted ferry service to Manhattan around 1810. Today, three sunset-yellow ferries ply the choppy waters of the Upper Bay between St. George and the Battery during the rush hours. Off-peak, two just-modernized 1,200-passenger boats handle the immensely scenic 25-minute crossing. Now, not only do tracts and shopping malls flourish south of the Staten Island Expressway, straining the island's over-taxed infrastructure, but a modest renaissance is underway in communities within walking distance of the ferry landing. Wall Streeters cherish the office-to-ferry walk, as well as the uphill stroll home, almost as much as they cherish the 50¢ round-trip fare.

Hills—precipitous slopes reminiscent of San Francisco—and stunning views from the craggy ridge that rises between St. George and Richmondtown characterize that quarter of Staten Island nearest Manhattan. On leafy Todt, Emerson and Grymes Hills, million-dollar homes look over the tree tops to Brooklyn and Manhattan. Wood-frame Victorian houses, salted among the stucco mini-mansions and angular contemporary homes, are the darlings of homesteaders. You're more likely to find a rental apartment in a converted one-or two-family house than in an apartment building on Staten Island—although red brick apartment towers do exist.

The Staten Island Chamber of Commerce, 130 Bay Street, Staten Island, NY 10301, 727-1900, sells an excellent street map for $2; the

MTA's Staten Island Bus Map (free at the Chamber) is equally useful. Rental classifieds in the *Staten Island Advance* are more numerous on Saturday and Sunday but this afternoon paper publishes real estate ads every day. In Manhattan, pick up a copy of the *Advance* at the news-stand located inside the ferry terminal. *The Village Voice* is also a good source for listings. Some Staten Island realtors are listed in the section on **Apartment Hunting.**

St. George

Boundaries and Contiguous Areas: North: Richmond Terrace; **East:** Bay Street; **South:** Victory Boulevard and Stapleton; **West:** Jersey Street.

Flags aflap, the beguiling limestone and brick Borough Hall caps a rise to the right of St. George's ferry terminal. To the left as you exit the terminal a stunning structure, at once public sculpture, bridge and lighthouse-like tower, crowns a plaza, inviting visitors to climb to its glassy top for a smashing view of the harbor and lower Manhattan beyond. The two are symbolic of St. George's struggle against blight. The ragtag downtown sector defies gentrification, but uphill, within sight of the neo-Gothic spires of Curtis High School (between St. Mark's Place and Hamilton Avenue), you'll find restored Victorian, Tudor and 1920s-stucco houses as well as a few apartment buildings.

In contrast to the maple-shaded period homes, the three converted grain and coffee warehouses that comprise Bay Street Landing are very 1980s. Arguably the borough's trendiest housing, these waterside condo-miniums a five-minute walk east of the ferry terminal are the first stage in a projected harbor front revival. Here, black pines and juniper separate the public marina, esplanade and the glass-enclosed Landing Cafe from the access road. Shades of Sausalito. New rentals, rare in Staten Island, are to be found in moderately-priced waterfront mid rises at Harbor View. What's next? Development of the abandoned, park-like U.S. Coast Guard base which lies between the ferry terminal and The Landing.

Come spring, fishing enthusiasts flock to the charter boats tied up at The Landing's pristine new docks. The Joseph L. Lyons Pool, one of Staten Island's four municipal swimming pools, and the George Cromell Center, an indoor recreation center with tennis courts and a track situat-ed on a pier, are both located near The Landing's complex.

Check the classifieds and our list of Staten Island real estate brokers in the **Looking for a Place to Live** chapter for rentals, and after filing off the ferry, walk through the gradually reviving community of St. George. Sustenance for your search? La Fosse aux Loups, a Belgian bistro wedged between City Hall and the court buildings at 11 Schuyler Street, serves imaginative (and inexpensive) lunches on weekdays. Moules, waterzooi, carbonnades flamandes and other Belgian specialties are fea-tured at dinner six nights a week.

Area Code: 718

Post Office: St. George Station, 45 Bay Street, Staten Island, NY 10301, 981-1313.

Zip Code: 10301

Police Precinct: One Hundred Twentieth, 78 Richmond Terrace, Staten Island, NY 10301, 876-8500.

Emergency Hospitals (nearest): Bayley Seton Hospital, 75 Vanderbilt Avenue (at Bay Street), Staten Island, NY 10304, 390-6000; St. Vincent's Medical Center of Richmond, 355 Bard Avenue, Staten Island, NY 10301, 876-1234.

Library: St. George Library Center, 5 Central Avenue, Staten Island, NY 10301, 442-8560.

Public School Education: School District; # 31: Community School Board, 211 Daniel Low Terrace, Staten Island, NY 10301, 273-9559.

Adult Education: College of Staten Island, St. George campus (part of the City University of New York), 130 Stuyvesant Place, Staten Island, NY 10301, 390-7733

Cultural Resources: Snug Harbor Cultural Center, 1000 Richmond Terrace, Staten Island, NY 10301, 448-2500, is located in a clutch of handsome Greek Revival buildings on 80 arboreous acres. Once a haven for indigent sailors, the colonnaded buildings are now the locus of Staten Island's cultural rebirth. Concerts, art exhibits and plays fill the high-ceilinged halls. Also on the grounds you'll find: The Staten Island Botanical Garden, 273-8200, and the Staten Island Children's Museum, 273-2060; the Staten Island Institute of Arts and Sciences, 75 Stuyvesant Place, Staten Island, NY 727-11135, this museum offers tours and cultural events.

Transportation—Train: The Staten Island Rapid Transit train costs $1.25 one way and provides service between the St. George Ferry Terminal and Tottenville at the southern tip of the 13.9-mile-long island. The second stop, Tompkinsville Station, is used for Bay Street Landing. Call 718-447-8601 for information.

Transportation—Bus: Local buses cost $1.25 one way. The #101, #42 bus leaves from and returns to the ferry terminal after circling northwestern St. George. Express buses to Manhattan via the Verrazano Bridge and Brooklyn Battery Tunnel cost $3.50 one way. Call 718-330-1234 for bus information.

Transportation—Ferry: Passenger ferries run every 15 or 20 minutes during rush hours, every half hour at other times, every hour from 11 p.m. to 6 a.m. Service is less frequent on holidays and weekends. The fare is 50¢ round trip. Car ferry service, suspended in 1991 after fire damaged the Whitehall terminal, is available between 4:30 and 11 p.m. and costs $3.50 per car plus 50¢ per passenger. Call 718-390-5253 for information.

Stapleton

Boundaries and Contiguous Areas: North: Victory Boulevard and St. George; **East:** Bay Street and Upper New York Bay; **South:** Canal and Broad Streets; **West:** Louis Street, Van Duzer Street and Grymes Hill.

Bordering Bay Street, Stapleton boasts a batch of more-collectibles-than-antiques stores and Staten Island's only glade of fern bars. These cafes, tarted up with Tiffany style lamps, polished brass and old-fashioned bottle vases, point to the presence of newcomers in Stapleton's craggy hills.

Located only two stops from the ferry terminal on the SIRT train, Stapleton for some time has attracted artists and young families looking for a third bedroom. Now, here come bankers and stockbrokers from Lower Manhattan. Sturdy 19th century homes characterize housing in Stapleton Heights and adjacent Ward Hill. Asphalt shingles sheath houses down on the flats near the gourmet takeout shops, the library and handsome Tappan Park. The Mud Lane Society, a group of community boosters, promotes Stapleton with an annual house tour.

Area Code: 718

Post Office: Stapleton, 514 Bay Street, Staten Island, NY 10304, 727-2207.

Zip Code: 10304

Police Precinct: One Hundred Twentieth, 78 Richmond Terrace, Staten Island, NY 10301, 876-8500.

Emergency Hospital (nearest): Bayley Seton Hospital, Bay Street and Vanderbilt Avenue, Staten Island, NY 10304, 390-6000.

Library: Stapleton Branch, 132 Canal Street, Staten Island, NY 10304, 727-0427.

Public School Education: School District #31 (see **St. George**).

Adult Education (nearby): St. John's University, 300 Howard Avenue, Staten Island, NY 10301, 390-4545.

Cultural Resources (nearby): The Jacques Marchais Center of Tibetan Art houses Tibetan monastery artifacts at 338 Lighthouse Avenue in Richmondtown, call for an appointment, 987-3478; the Richmondtown Restoration, a historic village comprised of 14 buildings operated by the Staten Island Historical Society at 441 Clarke Avenue, Staten Island 10306, 351-1617; The Conference House, a pre-Revolutionary manor house, at 7455 Hylan Boulevard, Staten Island 10307, 984-2086; Alice Austen House Museum and Garden, 2 Hylan Boulevard, Staten Island 10305, 816-4506.

Transportation—Train: The Stapleton Station is the third stop on the SIRT train. (Details under **St. George**.)

Transportation—Bus: The #74, #76, and #51 travel Bay Street as far as Canal; the #78 runs along Van Duzer Street and St. Paul's Avenue in Stapleton Heights. (Details under **St. George**.)

Grymes Hill and Silver Lake

Boundaries and Contiguous Areas: North: Louis Avenue; **East:** Stapleton, Van Duzer Street, and Vanderbilt Avenue; **South:** Clove Road and the Staten Island Expressway; **West:** Victory Boulevard.

One blustery afternoon, a salty sea breeze rattled maple and birch branches, garnishing Grymes Hill with russet fall leaves. Save for the outline of Wall Street's mist-shrouded skyline, you could have been in Westchester. Interspersed with narrow blacktop lanes and imposing houses, the hills of Staten Island radiate a rustic sub-urbanity.

The higher you climb any one of the island's myriad hills, the more imposing the homes become. Four-hundred-foot high Todt Hill, the tallest of Staten Island's peaks, is the toniest. Grymes Hill, nearer the ferry terminal, is the most intellectual: St. John's University and Wagner College cluster its slopes, the College of Staten Island lies in an adjacent valley. Though 12-story Sunrise Tower is co-op, there are 475 two-and three-bedroom rental apartments in the Grymes Hill Apartments Complex, built by Donald Trump's father in the 1940s. In addition, rental apartments can be found in remodeled one-family homes.

Silver Lake combines with Clove Lakes Park to form a sylvan greenbelt. There are tennis courts, bridle paths, ice skating rink and a municipal golf course laid out around the reservoir, and between Clove Road and Broadway a small, accessible zoo with a first-rate reptile collection.

Area Code: 718

Post Offices: St. George Station, 45 Bay Street, Staten Island, NY 10301, 981-1313; Stapleton Station, 514 Bay Street, Staten Island, NY 10304, 727-2207.

Zip Codes: 10301, 10304

Police Precinct: 120th, 78 Richmond Terrace, Staten Island, NY 10304, 876-8500.

Emergency Hospitals (nearest): Bayley Seton Hospital, Bay Street and Vanderbilt Avenue, Staten Island, NY 10304, 390-6000; St. Vincent's Medical Center of Richmond, 355 Bard Avenue, Staten Island, NY 10301, 876-1234.

Library (nearest): Stapleton Branch, 132 Canal Street, Staten Island, NY 10304, 727-0427.

Adult Education: College of Staten Island, Sunnyside campus (nearby), 715 Ocean Terrace, Staten Island, NY 10301, 390-7733;

St. John's University, 300 Howard Avenue, Staten Island, NY 10301, 390-4545; Wagner College (and Wagner College Planetarium), 631 Howard Avenue, Staten Island, NY 10301, 390-3100.

Cultural Resources: Staten Island Zoo, 614 Broadway, Staten Island, NY 10310, 442-3100. (See also **Stapleton.**)

Transportation—Train: A steep climb is required to reach Grymes Hill from Stapleton, the nearest stop on the SIRT line. (Details under **St. George**.)

Transportation—Bus: The #74 bus traverses Van Duzer Street along the base of Grymes Hill; the #61, #62, #66, and #67 traveling Victory Boulevard connect with the #60 shuttle bus at Clove Road. The shuttle follows Howard Avenue as far as the St. John campus. (Details under **St. George**.)

You might also want to consider...

- **West New Brighton,** a stable community across the Kill van Kull from New Jersey and southwest of the ferry, where Victorian houses and apartments offer golf, tennis and extensive parkland in Silver Lake Park and Clove Lakes Park, which includes the Staten Island Zoo. The Snug Harbor Cultural Center is nearby. Bus to the ferry to the subway to work, about 50 minutes.

- **Port Richmond**, just south of West New Brighton on the Kill van Kull, offers reasonably priced housing, much of it pre-War one- and two-family homes a 50-minute commute by express bus or bus/ferry from Manhattan.

NEW JERSEY

Fort Lee and Edgewater

Boundaries and Contiguous Areas: North: Englewood and Englewood Cliffs; **East:** Hudson River; **South:** Cliffside Park and West New York; **West:** Leonia and Palisades Park.

Apartment towers in Fort Lee ride the Palisades above the Hudson like so many schooner masts, their rigging blown loose, flung across the river and fixed there as the lacy George Washington Bridge. Beneath these rocky cliffs, its back to the wall in fact, little Edgewater was virtually invisible until the mid-1980s, when low structures began to take shape, seemingly afloat on the river, and Manhattanites wondered "What's that over there?" For the most part, they're still wondering.

It was in what is now Edgewater that George Washington and his Continental Army landed in November, 1776, after the battle of Washington Heights. General Charles Lee had supervised the fortifications above on the site which bears his name, and their remnants are still to be found there. Fort Lee remained a sleepy little town with a ferry landing throughout most of the 19th Century. Civil War gunboats used the volcanically formed Palisades for target practice, and these same cliffs provided the Belgian paving stones for the streets of Manhattan. In the late 1800s an amusement center and resorts flourished on The Bluffs, as they were known, but as business waned and ferry service finally ceased, Fort Lee declined.

The location of a nascent movie industry here from about 1910 into the 1920s offered a reprieve, but Hollywood won the climate competition, and the village languished. Completion of the George Washington Bridge in 1931 gave Fort Lee a suburban future. The tallest high-rise in Bergen County rose in Fort Lee in 1972. As rapidly and as large as they rose along Palisade Avenue, they filled up in this fastest growing town in Jersey's most affluent county. Fort Lee straddles the approach to the bridge, but the most sought-after housing lies south of the bridge. An estimated 80% of the approximately 35,000 inhabitants commute to jobs in the city, largely by Jersey Transit to the Port Authority Bus Terminal in Manhattan. In recent years this population has included a strong infusion of affluent Japanese and Korean residents, as is evident in the store and office signs along Main Street. An appealing diversity of restaurants is the result.

No longer sleepy, Fort Lee has maintained a small town feel, despite its having grown faster—and taller— than it could plan for. Along the quiet streets off Palisade Avenue tidy homes nearly fill their lovingly manicured postage-stamp lots (they're expensive, nonetheless). It's The View—Manhattan afloat on the Hudson—which determines the price of real estate and rentals. Apartments with a view fetch near-Manhattan prices, whether they are co-ops, condos or rentals; but you use the same pool and health club at a lower rent without the view. Away from the edge, garden apartments and two-family houses are less expensive

At the eastern, river end of Main Street in 33-acre Fort Lee Historic Park visitors trace the Revolutionary history of the area in the museum and discover the remnants of Continental Army dugouts. The park lies within the greater Palisades Interstate Park, a narrow strip of wooded land stretching for miles between the Hudson and the Palisades Parkway above, with marinas, picnic areas and a scenic drive known to few outside the immediate area. This constitutes an extraordinary recreation asset for residents of Fort Lee and Edgewater.

Main Street winds down the steep hill into River Road in **Edgewater**, surely one of the more unusual small towns in New Jersey. A blue-collar pocket with an industrial history, Edgewater hunches under the Palisades along steep, narrow streets, some of whose modest houses have recently been replaced by clutches of tidy condos. There's a somewhat funky feel to the town, especially in the artists' colony called Shadyside

Construction of four or five up-scale but low-rise condo and co-op developments along the river side of River Road has brought a wave of affluent young professionals, and change, to Edgewater. Sprawling handsomely at water's edge, or suspended over it on piles, these complexes with aquatic names such as Admiral's Walk, Grand Cove and Independence Harbor offer all the amenities—tennis, pool, health club— and The View, at a price. Cinemas, supermarket, restaurants, a restaurant/club in a restored old Hoboken Ferry boat and a Comfort Inn comprise a small mall; and to the south Yaohan, a Japanese mall complete with Japanese supermarket, restaurant and specialty shops, attracts shoppers from throughout the tri-state area. Interspersed helter-skelter between these waterside centers, are the occasional industrial site, a golf driving range, and marinas.

Edgewater is again abuilding, with three rental and condo projects underway and plans for additional retail space and a cineplex. Office complexes are being carved out of abandoned industrial sites. And with this critical mass, the megastores—Bed, Bath and Beyond, Barnes and Noble, Staples etc.—have ventured in. Starbucks, too.

Although there is commuter bus service to the Imperial Ferry in Weehawken and to the Port Authority, a car is a necessity here in the relative isolation of Edgewater's narrow, winding River Road. Realtors handling Fort Lee and Edgewater properties are listed in the next chapter, **Looking for a Place to Live.**

Area Code: 201

Post Office: Main Branch, 229 Main Street, 944-1853, and Palisade Station, 1213 Anderson Avenue, Fort Lee, 224-8787; Edgewater Station, 33 Hilliard Avenue, Edgewater, 945-0310.

Zip Codes: Fort Lee, 07024; Edgewater, 07020

Police Station: 1325 Inwood Terrace, Fort Lee, 592-3500; 916 River Road, Edgewater, 943-2200.

Emergency Hospital: Englewood Hospital and Medical Center, 350 Engle Street, Englewood 07631, 894-3000; Palisades Medical Center, 7600 River Road, North Bergen, 07047, 854-4000.

Libraries: Fort Lee Free Public Library, 320 Main Street, 592-3614; Edgewater Free Public Library, 49 Hudson Avenue, 224-6144.

Public School Education: Board of Education, 255 Whitman Street, Fort Lee, 585-4600; Board of Education, 257 Undercliff Avenue, Edgewater, 945-4106.

Transportation—Bus: Call New Jersey Transit, (201) 762-5100 or 212-564-8484, for routes and schedules, or pick up same at the Port Authority Bus Terminal at Eighth Avenue and 41st Street in Manhattan.

Transportation—Ferry: See **Weehawken.**

Weehawken

Boundaries and Contiguous Areas: North: West New York; **East:** Hudson River; **South:** Union City and Hoboken; **West:** Union City.

Compact little Weehawken (.85 square miles) crests the Jersey Palisades three watery miles across the Hudson from midtown Manhattan. Longtime residents of Irish, German and Italian heritage, the more recent Latino families, and commuter expatriates of the Big Apple prize that distance and the peace and quiet which it guarantees. The Lincoln Tunnel at the foot of the rocky heights provides Weehawken an enviable half-hour access to Manhattan by car or mini-bus. Little wonder, then, that the modest mansions shoulder to shoulder along cliffside Boulevard East fetch prices in the neighborhood of $1 million for the magnificent skyline view which they command.

The Dutch bought this site in the 17th Century from the Leni Lenape Indians and modified its Indian name to suit Dutch tongues. Little had changed in 1804, when Aaron Burr killed Alexander Hamilton in a duel on a grassy plot near the shore here. Shipyards and industry along the shoreline came later, and with them, the mansions on the Heights. Frame, brick and brownstone row houses were built along the side streets heading west from the cliffs and remain the chief source of prime housing in Weehawken. Most prized are houses in the tiny Bluffs section just south of Hamilton Park.

The housing stock in Weehawken was increased a few years ago by the conversion of a factory complex to 177 condos with Manhattan views, now Gregory Commons. Further expansion will have to be along the waterfront. Hartz Mountain's 95-acre, mixed-use Lincoln Harbor development has transformed Weehawken's southern shore with two 10-story blue glass office buildings, restaurants, a hotel and marina. The residential component, pricey beige-and-pastel Riva Pointe wrapped around a courtyard on a 1,000-foot pier has attracted an affluent young clientele with its amenities and adjacent commuter ferry, not to mention the view. Just to the north at Port Imperial, developer Arthur Imperatore operates NY Waterway, continuous five-minute ferry service to Manhattan with connecting van service to midtown and the Wall Street area. His grander plan for a "Venice-on-the-Hudson" comprised of a convention center, commercial and residential complex has been limited by the economy so far to a marina, golf driving range and waterfront restaurant. Stay tuned. Meanwhile Port Imperial and Lincoln Harbor have given nine acres to New York University for playing fields, clubhouse and bleachers to be used jointly by the University's teams, Weehawken schools and residents. In time, a planned 18.5-mile walkway from the George Washington Bridge to Bayonne will pass along Weehawken's shore.

Many Weehawken properties are handled by Hoboken real estate brokers, or by their owners. Check the ads in *The Jersey Journal* (see **Jersey City**) and in *The Weehawken Reporter*, available locally in stores and apartment building lobbies, as well as the list of real estate brokers in **Apartment Hunting** in this book.

Area Code: 201

Post Office: Weehawken Substation, 3504 Park Avenue, 867-0081; Park Avenue Branch, 4708 Park Avenue, 867-0081.

Zip Code: 07087

Police Station: 400 Park Avenue, Weehawken 07087, 863-7800.

Emergency Hospital (nearest): Palisades Medical Center 7600 River Road, North Bergen 07047, 854-5000.

Library: Weehawken Free Public Library, 49 Hauxhurst Avenue, Weehawken 07087, 863-7823.

Public School Education: Board of Education, 53 Liberty Place, Weehawken -07047, 867-2243.

Transportation—Bus: Mini-buses troll Boulevard East for passengers to the Port Authority Bus Terminal in Manhattan continuously weekdays, less frequently on weekends. Jersey Transit service is also l0 minutes to the terminal; call (201)762-5100 or (2l2) 564-8484 for routes and schedules, or pick up same at the Port Authority Bus Terminal, Eighth Avenue and 41st Street in Manhattan.

Transportation—Ferry: Service by NY Waterway between Port Imperial and midtown Manhattan and Whitehall is every 15 minutes daily 6:45 a.m. to midnight, to 1 a.m. Fridays, Saturday 8 a.m. to 1 a.m. and Sunday 9 a.m. to midnight. The five-minute ride costs $4.50 each way to midtown, with monthly commuter tickets costing $l40, and $5 each way to Whitehall. Parking at the vast lot in Weehawken is $4.50 for the day. Call 800-533-3779 for information.

Hoboken

Boundaries and Contiguous Areas: North: Weehawken; **East:** Hudson River; **South:** Jersey City; **West:** Jersey City and Union City.

Physically, Hoboken hasn't changed much since the early 1900s. Until recently. Most of this tidy, small (population 45,000) "Mile Square City" sandwiched between the Hudson River and Jersey bluffs was built between 1860 and 1910. By 1900 Hoboken was famous as the first American port of call for tens of thousands of immigrants, many of whom stayed close by finding jobs in the city's numerous light manufacturing plants. Industrious working and middle-class citizens built the simple, unadorned brownstone and brick row houses that comprise most of Hoboken's real estate, although the patrician Stevens family, who bought what was to become Hoboken soon after the Revolution, lived in relative isolation and splendor in the Castle Point section of town. This tract is now occupied by the Stevens Institute of Technology, the engineering school founded by the family. (And it is here beside the Hudson that a state-of-the-art scientific research center will rise when a partner can be found for the joint venture.)

Laid out in a grid that encompasses several pleasant, leafy squares, Hoboken, with its workingman's bars and sizable Hispanic population, still retains a blue collar tinge.

But with the closing of Maxwell House Coffee, the last employer of any size within Hoboken's boundaries, the housing here has increasingly been occupied by refugees from across the Hudson, who now gaze back at a Manhattan skyline visually afloat on the river, gleaming in the morning sun and ablaze with lights at night.

In the early 1970s a tide of disaffected New Yorkers, many of them singles, was attracted to this community just ten minutes from Manhattan by subway (PATH). Artists and rock musicians as well as young professionals discovered Hoboken, and the row house renovations, the cafes, interesting shops and galleries dotting the original downtown and Washington Street neighborhoods show it. Where homesteaders pioneer, serious developers almost always follow. Certainly, the conversion to condos of tenement blocks along Monroe, Adams and the other "presidential" streets west of Washington, as well as a new rental complex rising on once heavily industrial land in the northwest quadrant, bear decided witness to *that* fact.

Development of Hoboken's mile-long river front is now being planned. Phase I, at the southern end, is slated to begin sometime in 1996. The huge Erie-Lackawanna Terminal building has been spruced up to house commercial tenants and a handsome Art Deco waiting room. Once again the Hoboken Ferry, abandoned for 30 years, plies the Hudson between Hoboken and Battery Park. The very *idea* of waterfront transformation jolted Hoboken's housing market, which is expanding. *The Hoboken Reporter*, available free at 1311 Washington Street, is an excellent source of rentals, which tend to run about 10% below comparable Manhattan dwellings. For names of local brokers and a shares agency, refer to the chapter on **Apartment Hunting**.

Area Code: 201 (North and Central New Jersey).

Post Offices: Main Office, 89 River Street, Hoboken 07030, 659-3220. All branches have the same telephone number and zip: Castle Point Station, Stevens Institute of Technology; Uptown Station, 57 W. 14th Street; Washington Street Station, 734 Washington Street; and West Side Station, 502 Grand Street.

Zip Code: 07030

Police Station: #1 Police Plaza, 108 Newark Street, Hoboken, 07030, 420-2100.

Emergency Hospital: St. Mary's Hospital, 308 Willow Avenue, Hoboken, 07030 792-8100.

Library: Hoboken Public Library, 500 Park Avenue, Hoboken, 07030, 420-2346.

Public School Education: Hoboken Board of Education, 1115 Clinton Street, 420-2162.

Cultural Resources: The Hoboken Civic Theater troupe uses the Union Club for performances; the Hoboken Chamber Orchestra gives concerts at the Demarest Grammar School. Membership in the Hoboken-North Hudson YMCA, with its tiled pool, workout rooms and movement classes, is an inexpensive alternative to the health and fitness centers proliferating here. New rock reigns at a number of clubs on Washington Street like The Elysian Cafe, #1001, 659-9344, and Maxwell's, #1039, 656-9632.

Transportation—Subway: PATH trains, 800-234-7284 shuttle between the Hoboken Station next to the Conrail (old Erie and Lackawanna Railroad) Terminal and Manhattan every 10 minutes from about 6:30 a.m. to 8:30 p.m., every 15 minutes between 8:30 and 11:45 and from then on every 30 minutes until 6:30 a.m. A direct line runs between Hoboken and the World Trade Center, and another between Hoboken and West 33rd Street and Sixth Avenue, making stops at Christopher near Hudson Street, then at 9th, 14th and 23rd Streets, all on Sixth Avenue.

Transportation—Bus: Frequent commuter bus service on the #126 line operated by New Jersey Transit, 212-564-8484 (and be prepared to wait) for schedules, and on buses operated by Red Apple Transit, 201-420-9697 and 212-564-8484, connect Hoboken Terminal and Manhattan's Port Authority Bus Terminal at Eighth Avenue and 40th Street (the South Wing).

Transportation—Ferry: Service between Hoboken and Battery Park. Ferries run every six to eight minutes, 6:50 a.m to 9 a.m. and 4 p.m. to 8 p.m., every 15 minutes in between and till 11 p.m., every half hour weekends 10 to 10. Tickets are $2 each way, $18 for 10 trips, $62 for a monthly pass. Call 800-533-3779 for information.

Jersey City

Boundaries and Contiguous Areas: North: Hoboken; **East:** Hudson River; **South:** Bayonne; **West:** Brunswick Street.

Jersey City, directly across the Hudson River from the World Trade Center, is not yet New York's "sixth borough." If, however, comparatively inexpensive commercial office space, river front development and a large stock of 19th century brick and brownstone townhouses are requisites for boroughhood, then Jersey City may yet make its point.

New Jersey's first city—"settled in 1630" says the historical marker erected in Paulus Hook, the oldest section of town—has survived three and a half centuries largely as a working-class community. Today it has a population of 280,000 and an enviable position five minutes by PATH train under the Hudson from Lower Manhattan.

The arrival of brownstoners presaged the current Jersey City revival. Twenty-five years ago expatriate New Yorkers began buying and reclaiming townhouses in the historic districts bordering Hamilton and Van Vorst Parks. Co-ops and condominium conversions sprung up in these neighborhoods and in the adjoining Paulus Hook historic district. And once Banker's Trust leased space at the vast Harborside Financial Center (as the rehabilitated Pennsylvania Railroad warehouse is now called), it became clear that back-office operations of large Manhattan corporations would prove a boon to the local economy. Now, gleaming skyscrapers soar along wide boulevards that connect Harborside with Newport, the enormous, $10-billion apartment, mall and townhouse-marina complex across the Hudson River from Manhattan's Battery Park City. Riverside Towers is on the rise there, due to open in 1997, adding some 340 rentals to the original 1500 which opened in 1986.

The opening of Avalon Cove, twin five-story, brick buildings with unobstructed views of lower Manhattan, in 1996 marked the end of a six-year lull in residential building along Jersey City's Hudson River front. Amenities accompanying the one- to three-bedroom rentals at prices well below their Manhattan counterparts include tennis and racquetball courts, swimming pool and a river-front walkway. In the historic district at the foot of Washington Street, Portside's luxury rentals feature mostly balconied studios to three-bedroom spreads with shuttle service to the Exchange Place PATH tubes and the ferry. Completion of the luxury condos at Port Liberte to the south will increase the range of waterfront choices.

West of the harbor developments and 35 minutes from Manhattan by PATH, a 1,176-unit condominium community, Society Hill, offers middle-priced town houses and apartments with marina, tennis courts, and two pools. With other projects already in the works, this K. Hovnanian project has spurred the revitalization of this up-and-coming area.

The Jersey Journal published every day but Sunday is the best source for Hoboken or Jersey City classified rental ads. In Manhattan, buy *The Journal* at newsstands in the World Trade Center, the 14th Street Downtown PATH station and outside the 33rd Street PATH station. See **Looking for a Place to Live** chapter for names of brokers.

Area Code: 201

Post Office: The main Post Office, 69 Montgomery Street, 915-7000, is located in Downtown.

Zip Code: 07302 covers the Downtown area; Port Libert≥, 07305; Newport, 07310

Police Station: East District, 207 Seventh Street, 547-5408.

Emergency Hospital: St. Francis Hospital, 25 McWilliams Place, 714-8900.

Library: The main branch of the Jersey City Public Library, 472 Jersey Avenue, 547-4500, is located in Downtown.

Public School Education: Jersey City Board of Education, 241 Erie Street, 915-6000.

Adult Education: St. Peter's College, 2641 Kennedy Boulevard, 333-4400, Jersey City State, 2039 Kennedy Boulevard, 200-2000, and the Jersey City branches of Hudson County Community Colleges, headquartered at 168 Sip Avenue, 656-2020, all offer evening classes but most are held in campuses up in Jersey City Heights, not in the Downtown area.

Cultural Resources: The Jersey City Museum, fourth floor, Jersey City Public Library, 472 Jersey Avenue, 547-4514. Liberty Science Center, 25 Phillip Street, Jersey City, 07305.

Transportation—Subway: On PATH, 800-234-7284, the trip between the four stops in Jersey City (Journal Square, Grove Street, Exchange Place and Pavonia-Newport) and the World Trade Center takes 10 minutes at most and trains run at four to six minute intervals during rush hours, every 10 to 15 and 30 minutes at other times. It takes 20 minutes at most from Journal Square or Grove Street to 33rd Street in Manhattan (with stops at Sixth Avenue and Christopher, 9th, 14th and 23rd Streets in between). Service is almost as frequent on the 33rd Street line as on the World Trade Center line. PATH trains also run to Hoboken and Newark from all four Jersey City stations.

Transportation—Bus: The Hudson Bus Co., 212-564-8484 or 201-653-2220, operates frequent service between Jersey City and Wall Street or the Port Authority Bus Terminal in Manhattan.

New Jersey Suburbs

- **Cliffside Park**, on the Palisades just south of Fort Lee, an affordable family neighborhood with an ethnically mixed population.

- **Leonia**, west of Fort Lee but less glitzy and not as high rise, middle-class with a village-like feel. Proximity to the George Washington Bridge makes it a quick commute, by bus, to the city.

- **Englewood**, cosmopolitan with its multi-racial population and housing ranging from low-income to turn-of-the-century estates. Traditionally home to affluent business executives, it boasts good shopping and restaurants and a 30-minute bus commute to Manhattan.

- **Teaneck**, just west of Englewood and without the estates, is similarly hilly and tree-shaded, more middle-class and proud of its ethnic diversity. A 30-40-minute commute.

- **Tenefly**, north of Englewood and more homogeneous a suburb, boasts a nice village center clustered around the railroad station and an excellent high school. Also an easy commute.

- **Montclair**, cosmopolitan and affluent, enjoys a hilly perch from which Manhattan is visible at a distance to the east. Single family housing is shaded by towering oaks. The bus commute takes about 30 minutes.

- **South Orange,** with its downtown railroad station, is convenient, small towny. Housing is varied, from modest to upscale up the hill, and 60 acres of park land with three town pools add to the comfort level.

- **Ridgewood**, a 60-minute commute northwest of the city, houses a homogeneous white-collar population along manicured, tree-shaded streets. Schools are excellent, taxes high, and the downtown shopping district seems not to have changed in 50 years. The Paramus malls nearby make up for that.

- **Westfield** nestles among the rolling Watchung hills of Union County, about an hour by bus or 35 minutes by train and PATH tubes from mid-town. A strong sense of community, excellent schools, extensive sports and recreation activities in three county-run parks make this culturally rich old town attractive to commuters.

Long Island Suburbs

Rockville Centre, 30 minutes from Manhattan by the Long Island Railroad (which is not the island's finest feature), Rockville Centre has easy access to Long Island beaches, an arts guild, eight parks, a thriving shopping center and a variety of housing. But it is best known for its municipal power plant, which gives its residents the cheapest electricity on the island.

- **Garden City** was once a summer resort for Morgans and Vanderbilts, and it's still expensive, tidy and manicured. Squarely in the middle of the island, it's an easy 30-40 minutes to Penn Station.

- **Manhasset** lives in single family homes and condos, the former most attractively and expensively set around Manhasset Bay in Plandome to the north. Because of the department stores along Miracle Mile, real estate taxes are low here, just about 35 minutes from Manhattan on the LIRR.

- **Port Washington**, formerly a glamorous summer resort on a peninsula in the Long Island Sound, is still attractive to boaters. The 40-minute train commute is a relatively easy one.

- **Old Westbury** once housed the North Shore estates of high society and still has 25 miles of horse trails and a polo club. Besides its rolling hills, the high cost of living here gets you good schools, three colleges and Old Westbury Gardens.

- **Cold Spring Harbor**, with its cedar shake colonials on a natural inlet on the Sound one hour from the city by train, has the feel of old Long Island. It also has good schools. This is Talbot's country.

Westchester County (NY) Suburbs

- **Pelham,** just over the line and a 20 minute train ride north from the city, is cosmopolitan and relatively unknown. Fine old trees line its winding roads, and you can walk to everything, which includes beaches, a golf course and woodland hiking and fishing. Taxes are high.

- **Bronxville**, also on the city's northern border and hilly, feels rather English and looks rather Tudor. There are also co-ops and condos, rather elegant ones near the railroad station. Known for its good schools.

- **Mamaroneck**, which includes Larchmont, houses a heterogeneous population just west of toney Rye on a neck of land in Long Island Sound. Co-ops, condos, single-family homes, few rentals. Waterfront is what it's about, with good recreational facilities including boating and beaches on Harbor Island Park. A 35-minute commute.

- **Edgemont** is adjacent to Scarsdale, less known and more affordable. Its good schools have attracted a growing foreign-born population, especially Japanese. Houses are traditional in style, co-ops and condos relatively plentiful and reasonable.

- **White Plains**, 35 minutes from *the* city, is a city, offering a quick commute by train or express bus, good shopping, ethnic restaurants, a variety of housing choices, and relatively low taxes. Recreational facilities include a golf course, outdoor pools, tennis and an ice skating rink.

- **Hastings-on-Hudson** is diverse, in its housing, its population and its terrain, albeit hilly and with river views. Besides one-family houses behind stone walls, apartments are available. The arts are strong here, shopping very small-town. Nature trails and bike paths are an added feature.

- **Dobbs Ferry** on the Hudson just to the north, and about 40 minutes by Metro North's Hudson line from the city, also offers a variety of housing possibilities and a heterogeneous population, which makes it appealing to academics and people in the arts.

- **Scarsdale**, rocky, wooded and upscale, has few rentals or coops, but it does have beautiful homes along winding, wooded roads and about a quarter of the town's area in open land. Its highly competitive public schools have attracted a diverse population, many of them Asian, altering the town's once-waspy image. The commute to Manhattan is about 45 minutes.

Connecticut Suburbs

- **Greenwich** (pronounced Gren itch), a 45-minute train commute from the city, offers genteel seclusion for the wealthy, the bustle of corporate headquarters as well as upscale shopping and eateries, excellent schools, beaches and recreational facilities. Less expensive than Greenwich "backcountry" is the livelier downtown area. Cos Cob, Byram and Old Greenwich are also somewhat more affordable.

- **Norwalk** is diverse and less expensive than the surrounding towns, on the whole. Partially rehabilitated, south Norwalk, with its condos, galleries and restaurants, appeals to a young crowd, many of whom work in nearby corporate offices. Boating, fishing, beaches, tennis and paddle tennis are also a draw. Silvermine to the west and Rowaton on the southwestern tip are more upscale.

- **Westport** on Long Island Sound became a colony of artists and writers in the 1930s and 1940s, and it is still more sophisticated, more like New York City than the rest of Connecticut. There is a summer theater, and the arts are still a presence, as are pricey boutiques and good shopping in nearby Stamford. Water and woods, a variety of single family homes, a few rentals and condos characterize the town. The train to New York takes about an hour.

RENTING an apartment in New York City is once again a daunting task. The market has tightened considerably, even at the high end, with rents rising about 10% a year in recent years. Less expensive apartments (the affordable one-or two-bedroom, hold the Jacuzzi) are even harder to find. Non-subsidized middle income housing starts in Manhattan are nil.

In Manhattan's established neighborhoods, location doesn't much influence price. One rental expert estimates that in Greenwich Village and the neighborhoods between 23rd Street and 96th Street (Chelsea, the Upper East and West Sides, Murray Hill, Gramercy Park), the price difference between comparable apartments is negligible. If cost is a serious concern, it is best to search in the developing Manhattan neighborhoods and in the boroughs.

Another option, especially attractive now at the studio and one-bedroom level, is to purchase a condo or a co-op. Until recently, these apartments languished on the market; with the income tax deduction for mortgage interest factored in, these apartments are now often less expensive than renting an equivalent space. To see what's involved in buying an apartment or a house, turn to **Buying** at the end of this chapter.

But first, renting. With pluck, imagination and fortitude you *can* find an adequate place in an appropriate neighborhood. Various strategies for doing so are listed below in order of conventionality and practicality, but to start, some golden generalities:

- **Don't panic.** Don't be immobilized by what you may have heard. Negativism will get you nowhere—to live. Start your search a month or more before you expect to move, if possible.

- **Be prepared for high rents**. Newcomers, especially, are subject to shock at New York rents. In the long run it may just be possible to find that charming, sun-drenched apartment in the neighborhood of your dreams for a reasonable sum, but such gems take time and contacts, so brace yourself.

- **Be adventuresome but prudent**. The housing squeeze has intensified gentrification of neighborhoods throughout the city.

Yesterday's marginal areas are meccas for today's trend-setters. Behind dusty facades from the Bowery to upper Broadway lurk attractive apartments, but before getting too carried away, realize that not all areas are suitable, especially not for single women.

• **Inquire about a neighborhood.** Local police precincts (see listings under **Neighborhoods**) can supply valuable safety information about a particular neighborhood, street or block within their boundaries. Stop by the precinct for candid and well-founded opinions about the characteristics and police problems of a particular area.

• **Consider subletting or sharing to start.** If you are in desperate need of a roof and have not discovered a feasible rental, seriously consider these alternatives. Subletting or sharing buys time to find the optimum situation in the most suitable neighborhood.

Generalities out of the way, on to ways of finding space.

Newspaper Classified Advertisements

Because individual landlords as well as brokers place ads, classifieds sometimes are a means of avoiding brokerage commissions. Chances are, however, you will end up using a broker. The classifieds provide a good way of finding one and of discovering which brokers are active in a particular neighborhood.

The Sunday *New York Times* Real Estate section, printed Friday night and delivered to dealers sometime on Saturday, contains the best rental listings in the city. *The Times* actively discourages sale of the Sunday edition before the multi-sectioned paper is completed Saturday evening. However, many outlets sell the sections they have on hand (for full newspaper price) Saturday morning. While far fewer in number, daily ads in *The Times* are also worth checking. Since the race is to the swift, the cyber-connected will do well to check the *Times'* web site (http://www.nytimes.com), where the Sunday ads appear before 5 a.m. Saturday morning, with daily updatings.

The *Village Voice* is a good source of rental listings for Manhattan as well as other boroughs. Newsstand deliveries are made around 5 a.m. Wednesday morning; the newsstand on the island behind the Seventh Avenue IRT Uptown Christopher Street subway entrance at Sheridan Square is one of the first places to receive delivery. You can also get early copies Tuesday night at the Village newsstand on Astor/Lafayette; get there between 5 and 6 to beat the line. Easier yet, the *Voice* listings are on-line (http://www.villagevoice.com/re) at 1 p.m. Tuesday.

The *Wall Street Journal's* Friday edition lists apartments for rent in "The Mart" classified section.

The *New York Post's* rental classifieds are best consulted on Friday. The Friday edition is printed Thursday night and delivered to all-night newsstands in the mid-Manhattan area (try stands at Grand Central or Pennsylvania Stations Thursday night around midnight). *The*

Post (once again, Rupert Murdoch's toy) is a particularly good source for apartments in Queens, Brooklyn and The Bronx.

The Daily News' Brooklyn and Queens editions carry numerous rental classifieds for those boroughs. Listings in the Manhattan edition are negligible.

New York Press is a free weekly distributed each Wednesday. Look for it in restaurants, stores and street boxes all over town. A good source for sublets and shares. *Press* listings are on-line (http://www.adone.com/nypress) at 10 a.m. Tuesday.

The Jersey Journal, published in Jersey City Monday through Saturday, is the paper to consult for rentals in Hoboken and Jersey City. *The Journal* can be purchased at the World Trade Center and at newsstands adjoining the 14th Street and 33rd Street PATH stations in Manhattan.

New York City neighborhood newspapers—*The Villager*, *Chelsea-Clinton News*, *The West Side Spirit* (Upper West Side), *Our Town* (East Side) and others—occasionally carry a rental ad or two but are not prime sources. In Brooklyn, however, two weeklies, the **Brooklyn Heights Press**, 129 Montague Street, second floor, and **The Phoenix**, 33 Flatbush Avenue, carry sublet and rental advertisements. First copies of the *Press* are delivered to the office around 2 p.m. Thursday afternoon, and *The Phoenix* reaches Brooklyn newsstands early Friday morning.

On-Line Classifieds. Prospective newcomers with a connection to the Internet can start their housing quest at home in, say, North Dakota now through Real Estate On-Line's Metro New York Real Estate Guide (http://www.nyrealty.com). The service provides detailed listings, photos and floor plans of nearly 5,000 houses and apartments for rent or sale in the city and Westchester County. They're updated hourly, and they're free; owners pay a monthly advertising charge. You can search by location, price-range and size, with E-mail notification as properties in your categories come on-line. For information call 212-734-9191. See also **No Fee Apartment Listings**, below.

Real Estate Brokers

New York City's real estate brokers focus on sales rather than rentals. However, some agencies specialize in rentals, and many have brokers who handle nothing else. Below, we've listed the names of real estate brokers as a service. Their presence in this book indicates no endorsement. Rather, firms and the neighborhoods they cover are given as possible starting points for your search.

Real estate agencies tend to concentrate their efforts on one or a series of contiguous neighborhoods, for example: the Upper East Side; Chelsea, the Village and SoHo; Gramercy Park and Murray Hill. If your heart is set on one location, it is important to discover the most savvy brokers in that area. If almost any neighborhood will do, make sure you list with several knowledgeable firms in order to get the coverage you need.

Count on spending some time and effort discovering a broker sympathetic to your needs and capable of showing you suitable places. In the long run, a broker may well be the best lead to a decent apartment, and she (the majority seem to be women) can save you hours of calling and traipsing on your own. Broker commissions for unfurnished apartments currently run 15% of one year's rent, paid up front by the tenant, and in New Jersey, where rentals are more generally available, one month's rent or, in rare cases, no commission at all.

Recommendations for finding a real estate broker:

- Ask friends, colleagues, your firm and family for recommendations of brokers who are particularly helpful. As previously mentioned, not all capable agents with good lists advertise widely.

- Gather names from appealing classified listings.

- If your heart is set on one locale try some of the smaller firms whose storefronts you'll notice when pounding the pavements. These firms seldom advertise but are often good sources for listings in the immediate vicinity.

- As a start, we've compiled a list of brokers who handle rentals in Manhattan, parts of The Bronx, Brooklyn, Queens, Staten Island and New Jersey.

Manhattan Real Estate Brokers (Area Code 212)

- **Ambrose-Mar Elia Co.**, 770 Lexington Avenue, NYC 10021, 752-7789: Upper East and West Sides. 137 Waverly Place, NYC 10004, 675-6980: Gramercy Park to the Battery.

- **Brocor Realty**, 654 Madison Avenue, NYC 10028, 223-7554. East Side from 96th Street to Gramercy Park.

- **Douglas Elliman**, 575 Madison Avenue, NYC 10021, 891-7000. Upper East and West Sides.

- **Dwelling Quest Corp.**, 360 Lexington Avenue, Suite 1601, NYC 10022, 681-9200. Upper East and West Sides.

- **Edwards Sisters Realty Associates**, 740 St. Nicholas Avenue, NYC 10031, 281-8830. Harlem.

- **Eychner Associates Inc.**, 90 Hudson Street, NYC 10012, 274-1414. Greenwich Village and downtown.

- **The Feathered Nest**, 310 Madison Avenue, Suite 630, NYC 10017, 867-8500. All Manhattan.

- **Selena Godeau**, 88 University Place, NYC 10013, 645-1800. SoHo, Chelsea, East and West Village.

- **Joseph H. Green Realty**, 4310 Broadway, NYC 10033, 795-0144. Washington Heights and Inwood.

- **Sandra Greer Real Estate**, 201 East 77th Street, NYC 10021, 472-1878. Mostly East Side, Upper and Lower.

- **Gumley-Haft Inc.**, 110 East 59th Street, NYC 10022, 371-2525. Luxury rentals, Upper East Side.

- **Kain Realty**, 37 West 84th Street, NYC 10024, 877-5100. Upper East and West Side and Midtown.

- **Macklowe**, 142 West 57th Street, NYC 10019, 265-5900. All Manhattan.

- **Alice F. Mason**, Ltd., 635 Madison Avenue, NYC 10022, 832-8870. Luxury rentals on the Upper East Side primarily.

- **Moss Realty**, 2508 Broadway, Suite 1-A, NYC 10025, 222-4040. All Manhattan.

- **Prolific Realty**, 202 Waverly Place, NYC 10014, 989-3012. Greenwich Village.

- **Frederick M. Reed and Co.**, 405 Park Avenue, NYC 10022, 826-2150. Upper East Side.

- **Eugene Rooney**, 191 Avenue of the Americas, NYC 10013, 691-8380. Chelsea and West Village.

- **Salon Realty Co.**, 316 East 89th Street, NYC 10128, 534-3131. Upper East Side.

- **Schein Realty Co.**, 1425 Second Avenue, NYC 10021, 861-2400. Upper East Side, Upper West Side and Clinton   primarily.

- **Stafford International Realty**, 7 West 122nd Street, NYC 10027, 996-0939. Harlem, Mt. Morris Park area especially.

- **Stein, Perry**, 764 West 181st Street, NYC 10033, 928-3805. Washington Heights.

- **Willie Kathryn Suggs**, 412 West 145th Street, NYC 10031, 690-7636, 690-3461. Harlem and Washington Heights.

- **Stevens Real Estate Co.**, 2350 Broadway, NYC 10024, 580-3737. Upper West Side.

- **Wendy Walters & Associates**, 201 West 77th Street, NYC 10024, 874-4396. Upper West Side.

- **Webb & Brooker Realty Inc.**, 2534 Adam Clayton Powell Jr. Boulevard, NYC 10039, 926-7100. Harlem.

- **Mary Woods**, 645-7158, by appointment only. Brownstones primarily, Chelsea, Greenwich Village and downtown.

The Bronx (Area Code 718)

- **E.R.A. Susan Goldy & Co.**, 6114 Riverdale Avenue, Bronx 10471, 549-4116. Riverdale.

- **Robert Hill, Inc.**, 279 West 231st Street, Bronx, 10463. Riverdale and Kingsbridge, 884-2200.

- **Spero Real Estate**, 33 South Broadway, Yonkers, 10701, 914-968-7862, (800) 897-7862. Riverdale and lower Westchester County.

- **Trebach Realty**, 3801 Greystone, Bronx 10463, 543-7174. Riverdale.

Brooklyn Real Estate Brokers (Area Code 718)

- **Flood Company**, 7403 Fifth Avenue, Brooklyn 11209, 238-9800. Bay Ridge and Fort Hamilton.

- **Heights Cranford Agency**, 144 Montague Street, Brooklyn 11201, 624-7000. Brooklyn Heights, Cobble Hill, Boerum Hill, Park Slope.

- **Kenn Firpo Realty Corp.**, 158 Bedford Avenue, Brooklyn, 11211, 384-4949. Greenpoint and Williamsburg.

- **Kazeroid and Aberman Realty**, 196 Seventh Avenue, Brooklyn 11215, 499-8200. Park Slope.

- **William B. May Co.**, 150 Montague Street, Brooklyn 11201, 875-1289, Brooklyn Heights, Cobble Hill, Carroll Gardens; 397 Flatbush Avenue, Brooklyn 11238, 230-5500, Park Slope, Prospect Park.

- **Naida McSherry**, 275 Clinton Avenue, Brooklyn 11205, 230-0030. Fort Greene and Clinton Hill.

- **Brooklyn Landmark Realty**, 174 Court Street, Brooklyn 11201, 935-9800. Brooklyn Heights, Cobble Hill and vicinity.

- **David Perlman**, 32 Court Street, Brooklyn 11201, 855-8708. Brooklyn Heights, Park Slope, Cobble Hill, Boerum Hill, Carroll Gardens.

- **Renaissance Properties**, 102 Hoyt Street, Brooklyn 11217, 875-5650. Fort Greene and Clinton Hill.

Queens Real Estate Brokers (Area Code 718)

- **Bay Benjamen**, 212-89 26th Avenue, Bay Terrace Shopping Center, Bayside 11360, 225-0800. Bayside.

- **Century 21 Alexiou Realty**, 31-23 23rd Avenue, Astoria 11105, 204-0101. Astoria.

- **Crest Haven Realty**, Inc., 28-17 Astoria Boulevard, Astoria 11102, 545-7669. Astoria.

- **Roslyn Deller**, 39-68 45th Street, Sunnyside 11104, 786-0995. Sunnyside.

- **First Choice Real Estate**, 61-43 186th Street, Fresh Meadows 11365, 800-875-4111. Flushing, Forest Hills, Kew Gardens, Rego Park, Bayside.

- **Golden Choice Realty**, 37-11A Prince Street, Flushing 11354, 359-1700. Queens, especially Flushing.

- **Green-Ways Realty**, 2 Tennis Place, Forest Hills 11375, 544-1952. Forest Hills, Kew Gardens, Rego Park.

- **Lane Realty**, 107-40 Queens Boulevard, Forest Hills 11375, 268-3500. Forest Hills, Kew Gardens, Rego Park.

- **Nu Place Realty**, 120-10 Queens Boulevard, Kew Gardens 11415, 793-9500. Forest Hills, Kew Gardens, Rego Park, Briarwood.

- **Owner's Club Realty**, 31-15 Ditmars Boulevard, LIC 11105, 956-5757. Astoria, Long Island City, Sunnyside.

- **Re/Max Today**, 32-75 Steinway Street, LIC 11103, 274-2400. Astoria, Long Island City, Sunnyside.

- **Lois Schenck Real Estate**, 46-15 Skillman Avenue, Sunnyside 11104, 706-0957. Sunnyside, Woodside.

- **Terrace Realty**, 16 Station Square, Forest Hills Gardens, Forest Hills 11375, 268-1045. Forest Hills, Rego Park, Kew Gardens.

Staten Island Real Estate Brokers (Area Code 718)

- **Appleseed Agency-Century 21,** 2043 Richmond Avenue, New Springville 10314, 698-9797. North Shore.

- **Rachel Gannon Realty, Inc.**, 963 Post Avenue, SI 10302, 273-9200. All Staten Island, specializing in Port Richmond.

- **Gateway Real Estate**, 285 St. Marks Place, St. George 10301, 273-3800. St. George, Snug Harbor. No fee.

- **Rainbow Realty**, 364 Decker Avenue, Port Richmond 10302, 720-2002. Victorian properties in St. George, Stapleton, Snug Harbor and Port Richmond.

- **Vitale-Sunshine Realty**, 1444 Richmond Road, SI 10304, 979-3333. All Staten Island.

New Jersey Real Estate Brokers (Area Code 201)

- **Action Agency**, 4301 Bergenline Avenue, Union City 07087, 348-8741. Fort Lee, Edgewater, Weehawken.

- **Apartments & Homes of NJ.**, Fort Lee Inc., 214 Main Street, Fort Lee 07024, 947-6464. Fort Lee, Edgewater, Weehawken.

- **Boyne Real Estate**, 303 Grove Street, Jersey City 07302, 451-0950. Jersey City.

- **Eileen Cappock**, 115 Washington Street, Hoboken 07030, 792-5200. Hoboken.

- **Severino Realty**, 920 Washington Street, Hoboken 07030, 653-1800. Hoboken.

- **Singleton and Galman**, 1106 Washington Street, Hoboken 07030, 656-5400.

- **West Bank Realty, Inc.**, 313 First Street, Hoboken 07030, 792-0100. Hoboken.

- **Weichert Realtors**, 310 Main Street, Fort Lee 07024, 592-6888. Fort Lee, Edgewater, Weehawken.

New Buildings

Renovated factories, warehouses and other commercial buildings occasionally add new rental units to the city's supply. Apartments in reconstructed or totally new buildings command top dollar. However, it is often possible to avoid brokers' commissions in these buildings when landlords and managers pay on-site rental agents to fill the buildings as quickly as possible. The agents, as employees of the landlord, charge no commission.

Direct Action

In a town where single-minded apartment hunters have been known to read the obituary columns with as much intensity as the real estate classifieds, no one need feel self-conscious about tackling landlords, managing agents, superintendents or local merchants in order to locate a place in a particular neighborhood or building.

Consider trying some of these alternatives:

- **Call the managing agent of a likely building.** The firm's or agent's name is usually posted near a building's entrance. If no telephone number is given, check the phone book.

- **Speak with the superintendent directly.** To find him, check the building directory, buzzer listings or, in the case of the smaller brownstones with shared part-time supers, your man could be the person sweeping the steps or putting garbage cans out on the sidewalk.

If an apartment is available, the super or manager will sometimes send you to a broker to gain access. If a vacant apartment is found through independent efforts, you are not liable for the broker's fee. However, since reasonable apartments are in short supply, need usually overrides the fine points of the legal situation; most people prefer to pay the commission rather than go without the apartment. Once secure in your nest, if you want redress, file a complaint with the Division of Licenses, New York Department of State, 270 Broadway, NYC 10007, 212-417-5747. This may eventually result in a settlement.

- **Pavement pounding** accompanied by incessant querying of merchants, stoop sitters, dog walkers, postmen—indeed anyone who looks like a resident of the neighborhood—can yield results as well as blisters.

- For those intrepid souls determined to find an apartment in a specific building or block there is always **Cole's Metropolitan Householders Directory**, known familiarly as "Cole's Directory" or the "criss cross directory." This reverse telephone book lists addresses first and residents second. The names and telephone numbers of those living at any given address are listed by building, block by block.

Cole's does not note building owners per se, but it does carry the building's phone number if there is one. If the place is small, you can gamble on finding the owner by dialing the residents listed at the given address. Reference copies of Cole's Directories for all five boroughs are available at the New York Public Library's Science, Industry and Business Library at 188 Madison Avenue at the corner of 34th Street.

- For the record, some but not all apartment buildings are listed in each borough's **Yellow Pages** by street and number under the alphabetical heading "Apartments and Apartment Houses." Others are listed alphabetically by name.

No-Fee Apartment Listings

You may have noticed among the newspaper listings ads for no-fee services, and if you're determined to avoid a stiff broker's fee one of these may help, at a fraction of the cost of a broker. Here's how they work: pay a flat fee, up to $175, phone or fax your specifications and receive a list of no-fee apartments being offered by management companies and private owners, as well as the occasional broker's listing and co-op and condo for sale. Updates are daily or weekly, and you do the rest of the work. However, listings can be off-base or out-of-date, and the reliability of some of these services is questionable. We mention two which may be useful.

• **HOMEline**, 212-271-HOME (http://www.mlx.com), the first of the listing services (1993), considers itself a city-wide data base rather than a service. The subscriber pays $175 and receives an account number and a personal ID number (PIN) which covers specifics such as desired location, apartment size, whether pets are allowed, maximum rent, etc. By fax or on-line he/she receives a list of all the apartments in the data base fitting these specifications, with updates on request for as long as necessary. You can change specifications to receive listings in other categories: different neighborhoods or rent limits, for example. Included among the listings, which are updated daily, are properties handled by some 70 brokerage companies; these would involve fees. Also included as of 1997, co-ops, condos and houses for sale by owners as well as brokers, photos and layouts included.

• **Apartment Fone**, 212-278-3663 (http://www.aptfone.com). The first thing you hear when you call this number is a commercial for a mini-storage company, who happen to sponsor this service, along with the management companies, brokers and private owners who pay a fee to list here. So it's *free* to the caller. Choose from a menu of specifications and hear the appropriate listings on the phone, receive them by fax or by E-mail. Most of the listings are in Manhattan and mid-range. Co-op and condo sales are listed as well. For free, it's worth a try.

A final word about no-fee apartment guides sold in book form at bookstores and some newstands. They tend to be unreliable and not up-to-date.

Word of Mouth

The grapevine approach—broadcasting your need through a network of local friends—is often an effective means to a desired apartment. However, when you're new to town the chances of having such a network are probably slim. But do use any contacts available. Parents can call old college chums. Who knows, their children may be leaving a desirable place. Your college friends may have a lead; their in-laws may, too. Nine phone calls may an apartment produce—but may not either. In any case, personal contacts are often a shot at the type of place that never makes it as far as *The Times* or a broker's office.

Bulletin Boards

Certain neighborhoods, particularly the newer, more homogeneous communities such as SoHo and Tribeca, as well as some large buildings, have bulletin boards (or blank wall space—cork isn't a prerequisite) where an occasional apartment turns up among the sheets offering children's skis, a ride to California and opportunities for self-improvement. Inquire locally to find out which bar, supermarket or grocery store serves this neighborhood function. Bulletin boards in university areas also include valuable information, notably New York University, Columbia, and Hunter College.

House Organs

Many corporations and organizations publish newsletters or magazines for their personnel that print employee advertisements (Time-Warner's *F.Y.I.* comes to mind).

Sublets and the occasional rental turn up in these columns, and it is worth asking friends working for likely concerns to check their in-house publication for leads.

College-Related Associations

Various New York alumni associations are trying to address the difficulty graduates have settling or relocating in the city. Contact your alumni office or local group to see if they can help. Some university clubs also offer advice and an occasional lead. Alumni magazines and newsletters may also offer sublet opportunities.

Employers and Relocation Firms

Frequently large companies pay for the services of relocation firms to find suitable long- and short-term apartment rentals for their mid and upper level hires and to help solve the various problems associated with moving and settling in. The fortunate employee is saved money and headaches in the bargain. Presumably you'll be informed by the company for which you are working if it is prepared to offer help with your search for living quarters.

A variety of relocation services are also available to individuals through real estate firms which are part of nationwide franchise networks such as Re/Max, Century 21, Prudential and Coldwell Banker or networks of independent brokers such as Genesis and Relo. Also, there are independent services such as Relocation Consulting Services, located in Bedford, NY. While they exist primarily to service relocating homeowners, or potential homeowners, these services are also sometimes available to renters. Contact a broker near you affiliated with one of these networks before you move. They will help you sell your home, if you own one, and put you in touch with a realtor here who will take you in hand, provide you with information and show you communities which interest you, find you a place, get you pre-qualified for a mortgage, help you with insurance, get you a mover at a discount, help your spouse find a job, find a veterinarian for your cat, a painter for your bathroom, a school for your children. And it's free.

Sublets

Most brokers offer long-term sublets and advertise them, together with regular rentals, in local newspapers. Leaseholders of rent stabilized or exceptionally reasonable apartments have been known to ask for fixture fees or key money in a sublet situation. While some people do pour money and energy into rehabilitating an inexpensive rental apartment and may deserve compensation for their efforts when they move, fixture fees that reflect no real value are tantamount to key money, which is illegal.

Consider the furnished sublet as a useful interim measure. Available long or short term, sublets often provide the time needed to discover the optimum rental apartment. Then, too, there is always the possibility that the original tenant will decide not to return, *et voila*, no need to move until the original lease runs out.

Prime sources for sublets include:

- *The Village Voice* with its special "Sublets" classified section.

- *The New York Times*, which lists sublets under "Apartments—Furnished" and "Apartments—Unfurnished," # 1501 to # 1516.

- *New York Press* is a free weekly distributed each Wednesday. Look for it in restaurants, stores and street boxes all over town. Good source for sublets.

- **Brokers** A number of sublet specialists advertise in the *Voice* and *New York Times*. Typically, commissions on furnished rentals run between one-half and one month's rent for periods of less than nine months. Most agencies charge 15% for longer sublets.

Four brokers and one service currently specializing in sublets:

- **Apartment Placement Services,** 160 East 56th Street, NYC 10022, 212-750-6125. Specializes in short-term sublets uptown for an $850 fee; also places college graduates and young professionals in shared apartments throughout the city for $550. Call for appointment.

- **The Feathered Nest,** 310 Madison Avenue, NYC 10017, 212-867-8500. Call for appointment.

- **J. Senter,** 211 East 51st Street, Suite 4E, NYC 10022, 212-935-8730. Call for appointment.

- **Short Term Housing**, 862 Lexington Avenue, NYC 10021, 212-570-2288. Call for appointment.

- **Urban Ventures,** 38 West 32nd Street, NYC 10001, 212-594-5650. Call for appointment.

- **Bulletin boards** in large buildings, bars or other neighborhood locations. Large apartment complexes have lists for rental apartments the proverbial block long. However, leaseholders arrange sublets directly and occasionally post notices on community bulletin boards. Check with the management of these big units to see if they have a central sublet source.

• **In-house publications** tend to be a better source of sublets than of rentals.

Sharing

One of the best solutions to cutting high housing costs, particularly for young, single people, is an apartment share. But if you are just arriving in the city and don't know anyone, you may not have anyone to share with. If networking with old college buddies fails to turn up anything, your best bet is probably the newspapers or a roommate-finding service.

To find a room or bed in someone else's apartment check the *Times* ads under "Apartments to Share," #1696, and the *Voice*'s "Shares." Some leaseholders prefer to have roommates pre-screened and list with agencies that arrange apartment shares for a flat fee up front. Reputations ebb and flow; we can't guarantee satisfaction. But if you want to investigate this option, two of the firms in Manhattan are:

• **Roommate Finders,** 250 West 57th Street, Suite 1629, NYC 10019, 212-489-6862, open Monday-Friday noon to 8, Saturday and Sunday noon to 6. For the $200 fee the client, after filling out a registration sheet covering personal habits and preferences and discussing specifications in a half-hour interview, is given information sheets on prospective apartments and/or roommates. You can call daily for new listings for up to one year, and if you find your own roommate or apartment, you are entitled to a 50% refund. Listing is free.

• **The Roommate Solution, Inc.,** 488 Madison Avenue, Suite 1700, NYC 10022, 212-313-1004. By appointment Monday through Thursday noon to 7, Friday to 6, Saturday to 5. After an hour's screening and listing of preferences the client has nine-months' access to a computerized data base covering the five boroughs and New Jersey, with new leads available daily. The fee is $195 in advance, with a 50% money back guarantee. Apartment holders list free, with a $35 placement fee if they find a roommate through the service.

• *A Tenant's Guide to Subletting and Apartment Sharing*, published by The New York State Tenant and Neighborhood Coalition, 198 Broadway, Room 1000, New York, NY 10038, 212-695-8922, has recently gone out of print. The Coalition still sells photocopies of last edition, which is still relevant, for $9 (join the Coalition for $20 and get a tenants' rights newsletter as well as the pamphlet free), this invaluable 22-page guide details the practical and legal ramifications of apartment sharing and the ins and outs of subletting to, as well as from, another individual.

Buying

In a city of renters, why buy? Real estate values have risen in the 1990s and so have rents. Factoring in the income tax exemption for mortgage interest, which is highest in the early years of the mortgage, the cost of renting now can approach, or even exceed the cost of buying, especially in the studio and one-bedroom apartment category. For some, the idea of building equity, which is portable, as opposed to paying rent to some-one else, has a strong appeal. For others, it's the satisfaction and securi-ty of home ownership.

That said, nevertheless, the newcomer to New York City would be well advised to rent or sublet for a year at least before buying: become comfortable in the city, familiar with some of its neighborhoods, and develop a sense of how you use the city. Furthermore, the case can be made that, given the expenses incidental to buying (described below) and the fact that real estate values tend to rise and fall in roughly ten-year cycles, it makes sense to buy only if you expect to spend at least ten years in the city.

As with renting, the search for a condo, a co-op or a house generally begins in the classified ads in *The New York Times, The Wall Street Journal* or *The New York Observer,* a weekly newspaper distinctively pink in color and available at most newstands. Web sites on the Internet offering national real estate listings proliferate, and some fade. Below, a few which may be useful:

- **Real Estate On-Line's Metro New York Real Estate Guide**, (http://www.nyrealty.com)

- **Homes&Land Magazine**, (http://www.homes.com)

- **Home WEB**, (http://www.us-digital.com:8080/homeweb), incorporat-ing Better Homes & Gardens Real Estate Service listings.

- **Homenet,** (http://www.netprop.com), especially strong in the New York-New Jersey area.

- **Realty Guide**, (http://www.xmission.com/-realtor1), with links to bro-ker Web sites, lenders, for-sale-by-owner directories and home-for-sale magazines.

For those who are contemplating buying, a few considerations now, which apply whether you are looking for a house, a co-op or a condo. First, what can you afford to pay? The rule of thumb, and one which lenders use, is it is safe to pay three or four times the buyer's yearly income, depending on a variety of factors. The required down payment will generally be 20% of the purchase price; it may go as low as 10%, in which case origination fees (points) to the bank will probably be higher. Be prepared for a thorough examination of your finances, your credit record and your employment status. This, of course, assumes the buyer is not paying cash but obtains a mortgage from a bank.

Know that the transaction you are about to make is going to cost more than the agreed upon price. How much more? Generally, closing costs run 5% to 8% of the purchase price. This includes points, attorney's fees, title insurance, a title search, inspection and survey, recording tax, various fees, and the deposit of some real estate tax payments and homeowners insurance premiums in escrow. The lender (bank) is required to give a good-faith estimate of closing costs. In New York, the seller pays the broker's fee.

Whatever and wherever you are looking to buy, you'll need a good broker who listens to you, knows what is out there and takes you to it, knows the neighborhood, potential lenders and perhaps mortgage brokers, and who can work equitably for you as well as for the seller. (See **Looking for a Place to Live, Recommendations for finding a real estate broker**). You must also have a good real estate lawyer, who you can find through the recommendations of friends, your own lawyer or your broker. If you have no idea where to find an attorney who handles real estate transactions, call legal referral (212-626-7373) at the Association of the Bar of the City of New York, 42 West 44th Street. If you are buying a **house,** you will do well to hire a building engineer to check the structure of the house, the heating and plumbing systems, fireplaces etc.; a thorough inspection may save you thousands of dollars or prevent your making a disastrous purchase.

When you buy a **co-op** (cooperative apartment) you are buying shares in the ownership of a building, the other shareholders of which must approve your purchase through their board. And, should you choose to sell or rent your apartment later, the same approval process must be repeated, which can be a problem. In the most desirable buildings approval may prove more difficult than getting a mortgage, as shareholders seek to guarantee the financial reliability *and* the social acceptability of their new partners. Your finances will be scrutinized, and your life-style may be considered. A good broker will help by running interference for you. Get a prospectus, minutes of the last meeting of the board and a financial statement from the cooperative, and go over them with your broker and your lawyer. If your purchase is rejected, expect no explanation. Be aware that co-op size may affect your ability to get a mortgage; in co-ops with less than 12 units, lenders may be more likely to reject a mortgage application because the relatively small number of shareholders in such buildings raises the collective risk of a default. Also, keep in mind that co-op maintenance fees (the cost of upkeep for everything outside the walls of your apartment) can be more than your mortgage, depending on the building, and only some of the maintenance fee (the portion of the fee that is allocated for property tax payments) is tax deductible. Forty-fifty percent is a ballpark figure.

The purchase of a **condo** involves fewer hurdles, though some condo management organizations are requesting letters of recommendation from prospective buyers. Here you are buying an apartment, a piece of a building, outright, with the right to rent or re-sell when and as you choose. Of course, this means neither you nor the other residents has any control over who your neighbors are. In making this purchase you will also want your lawyer to examine a prospectus and financial statement on the building to avoid buying into a financially unstable property.

Finally, a word about **mortgage brokers**. Banks are once again competing to lend mortgage money, and in an effort to win new business they offer a somewhat confusing array of loans. Mortgage broker to the rescue! Think of a mortgage broker as a financial advisor who helps her client get a suitable mortgage. At no charge to you, she will examine your financial situation (age, income, assets, debt load etc.) and the property you want to buy and recommend the most likely lender and the best type of mortgage for your needs. Given her relationship with various banks, she can ease your way through the process, especially on co-op loans. If you're the ruggedly independent sort, keep in mind that in New York City your chances of getting a good mortgage are much higher with a qualified mortgage broker than without.

AFTER apartment-hunting, the newcomer's first order of business will probably be opening a bank account and establishing credit. The following information about personal savings and checking accounts, on-line banking, credit and debit cards should make the task less daunting. And, finally, for your edification come April 15, federal, state and city income tax procedures.

Bank Accounts and Services

While most people tend to choose their bank for its location, services, interest rates and minimum balance requirements can be important determinants in where you decide to put your money. If the range and quality of services a bank offers is more important to you than convenience, particularly now that ATM's provide access to cash and account information outside the branch, shop around. The city's three largest retail banks—**Citibank, Chase Manhattan** and **Chemical**— became two in 1996, when Chemical swallowed Chase but got rid of the less prestigious Chemical name. The remaining giants still operate more than 100 branches in Manhattan alone. Some of the smaller banks may be more user-friendly for the small-wallet customer; Republic National, for example, at this writing, requires a smaller minimum balance for personal checking than Citi and Chase and charges less if you go below your minimum balance. If you're determined to do your banking by phone, be prepared to deal with annoying recorded menus, waits and disembodied voices.

Beyond the telephone, technology has transformed banking and continues to do so daily. What's more, traditional distinctions between commercial banks, savings banks and brokerage houses have become blurred. And financial software has crossed all these lines. In this fluid situation, "It's a consumer's market," says one bank officer. "Our bank's strategy is to establish a relationship with each customer." That's why special windows for affluent customers and business clients are commonplace.

- **Checking accounts** Take a completed application—two references are required, usually the name of your current bank and that of your employer—to the branch where you intend to bank, together with two signed pieces of identification: driver's license, credit card, student ID with photo. Some banks require a minimum start-up deposit. Your account can be opened immediately, but checks and deposit slips won't be issued until your signature is verified. "Regular" non-interest-bearing personal checking accounts carry no charges as long a minimum daily balance is maintained. A certificate of deposit, money market or savings account linked to your regular checking account also gets you free checking. Similarly, interest-earning NOW checking accounts charge a fee if they fall below required minimum balances.

- **Savings accounts** Follow the procedures detailed above for checking accounts to apply for a "statement" savings account, which provides monthly statements of all transactions and can be linked to your checking account. Most banks require an average minimum balance of $1,500 to avoid maintenance charges.

- **Debit cards** Bank cards for use in cash machines are issued automatically to new customers. Most can be used to make withdrawals through the nationwide network of CIRRUS and NYCE ATMs. Increasingly, however, these cards can also be used at retail outlets to pay for groceries or gasoline, debiting your account directly rather than billing you monthly as credit card companies do. Chase has introduced a debit card which looks like a VISA card and for which you must be credit-approved; use it wherever you would use a VISA card, to buy clothes, a meal, whatever, paying directly from your account.

- **Banking on line** With a PC, a modem and an account in one of the major banks (increasingly the smaller banks, also) you can do most, if not all, of your banking at home electronically. Using software provided by Citibank or Intuit or Microsoft you can review your accounts, transfer funds from one account to another, check the latest stock market figures, assess the current worth of your portfolio, buy and sell stock, and pay your bills without leaving the apartment or touching paper, and it's free. At other banks the services vary, there are charges depending on the number and range of services used, and in some cases on the level of combined balance. But change in this area is at a dizzying pace, leaving the customer to investigate and shop around for the banking services which fit her needs.

- **Banking by phone** A touchtone telephone gives access to all the banking services performed by an ATM, except making deposits and cash withdrawals: you can check account balances and make transfers between accounts. For a small monthly charge (or free with a minimum combined balance of, say, $10,000) the bank will make scheduled bill payments such as rent, mortgage or car payments, as well as payments on request to designated payees such as stores, credit card companies and utilities. A year-end annual statement may be provided on request. Again, inquire about the latest refinements and the fees involved.

Credit Cards

On the off chance that your mailbox hasn't been filled with credit card applications, you can call to request one. An important twist to consider: frequent-flyer miles earned as you use your card. Shop around for the one best suited to your travel needs.

- **American Express**, 800-528-4800. All cards except the free Optima Card for students have a minimum income requirement. A Green Card costs $55 per year. The Optima True Grace card, $25 per year with no fee if used three times a year, gives the user 25 interest-free days for all purchases. The Gold Card costs $75 annually. For $300 per year you can possess a Platinum Card; but don't call American Express, they'll call you.

- **Diner's Club**, 800-234-6377. The Diner's card costs $80 per year, $25,000 minimum annual income.

- **Discover Cards**, 800-347-2683, are issued by Dean Witter with no annual fee for the basic card; minimum income is judged on a case-by-case basis. The Private Issue Card carries a $40 annual fee and requires higher income. With both cards you may get cash back at the end of each anniversary year.

- **VISA and MasterCard** can be obtained from a variety of financial service organizations, usually banks. Interest rates vary, annual fees may even be waived, and many cards offer frequent flyer miles. It pays to shop around, especially if you don't pay off your balance every month.

- **Department stores** Most accept personal checks for the amount of purchase, given the required identification. Store charge accounts can offer advantages over other forms of payment: advance notice of sales, mail or phone orders, no annual fee. Accounts are approved within three to eight weeks after application. Macy's and Brooks Brothers offer instant store charge account privileges to credit card holders who apply in person with two pieces of identification.

If you don't like wasting hours dialing 800 numbers after a credit card loss, register your cards with an agency that will cancel them for you. Hotline Credit Card Bureau of America, for example, 800-327-1284, charges a yearly fee to guarantee card replacement. Major banks offer a similar service to their VISA customers for an annual fee.

Income Taxes

Heralded by freshly painted H&R Block signs and black-bordered boxes in the newspapers warning "Only 10 more days to file your income tax returns," April 15 arrives every 365 days. In New York City, the Internal Revenue Service and New York Department of Taxation and Finance provide literature and telephone taxpayer information services designed to answer your tax questions year round.

- **Federal** income tax forms can be obtained by calling 800-829-3676, or call 212-732-0100 (for residents of Manhattan). Call 800-829-1040 to obtain explanatory literature as well as answers to specific questions, such as which of the three tax forms—1040EZ, 1040A or 1040—you should use. If you're comfortable on the world wide web, visit the IRS's well-regarded URL (http://www.irs.ustreas.gov) where you can find answers to tax questions as well as downloadable tax forms. The staff at the Internal Revenue Service office, open weekdays 7:30 a.m. to 5 p.m. downtown at 120 Church Street, provides instruction in the fine art of calculating your Federal income tax but won't do it for you.

- **New York State and New York City** use a combined income tax form. Call 800-462-8100 to receive forms: if you use either IRS 1040EZ or 1040A, choose the IT 100, which you fill in and let the State tax people calculate for you, or the IT 200, which you calculate yourself; if you file the Federal 1040 long form, you'll need the IT 201. The number for taxpayer assistance is 800-C-A-L-L-T-A-X.

Your Federal Adjusted Gross Income is the tax base for state and city taxes. New York State Taxable Income is calculated by adding and subtracting various New York State "modifications." The New York City Resident's Income Tax is based on New York State taxable income. Residents pay a percentage of the State category into which their income falls.

PC devotees have been filing their **income tax returns electronically** for several years now, with mixed results. Using tax-preparation software to complete the return, the taxpayer transmits the return via modem, through Compuserve or America Online, or on diskette by mail to the service bureau used by the software's publisher. The service bureau checks the return, puts it in an I.R.S.-acceptable format and transmits it to the agency, for a fee. Ideally, the returns are correct and the acknowledgment rapid, but a typing error can cause frustrating delays. However, there are hundreds of practitioners—CPA's and tax preparation firms, generally— registered to file electronically, and they will file your federal returns, long or short form, for a fee, approximately $50 per return. If they prepare the return as well, the fee is greater. You will need two forms of identification, including a driver's license or a passport. Your refund, if you have one, should come in two to three weeks instead of six, and by direct deposit if you wish. Within 24 hours your filer will receive acknowledgment of receipt and acceptance of the returns. See the Yellow Pages under Tax Returns if you do not have a recommendation from an acquaintance.

Taxpayers with incomes below a specified amount (about $30,000) can file electronically at no cost at the I.R.S. office at 120 Church Street in Manhattan, at 625 Fulton Street in Brooklyn or at 59-17 Junction Boulevard in Corona, Queens. Call the agency's help line, (800) 829-1040, for information on electronic filing or its Tele-Tax number (800) 829-4477 for recorded tax information 24 hours a day.

At this writing New York State and City are not yet ready to process electronic returns. Note: advertisements offering instant or rapid refunds are actually offering Refund Anticipation Loans (RALs), for which you pay an extra fee, approximately $50. As there has been some fraud associated with this practice, the quick refund may not be worth the fee.

ONCE theory has been put into practice and an apartment found, be prepared to sign the lease and a check or two. But before you do, we suggest you read Rent Smart, a 37-page booklet that untangles lease legalese and describes tenants' rights in New York State. Call 518-474-1471 or write to the State Consumer Protection Board, 99 Washington Avenue, Albany, NY 12210, for a free copy.

Deposits

Your first check will undoubtedly be a deposit held by the broker or landlord while credit references are being researched. Don't go apartment hunting without money in the bank and checkbook in hand; in fact, some landlords require certified check or traveler's check rather than personal check, so it pays to inquire in advance. The first person to put down a deposit (customarily one month's rent) stands the best chance of signing the lease. The credit investigation should take no more than a couple of days if you are already employed or can substantiate a reasonable income or net worth through bank accounts or financial statements. Some landlords ask to see your tax return or two or three years of bank statements as well as letters of reference. If your income, substantiated by a letter from your employer or pay stubs, is not at least four times the prospective rent, the landlord may require parents who own property in the tri-state area to co-sign the lease. And the landlord may want to se the past year's rent checks to verify that the prospective tenant tends to pay on time (generally the first or fifteenth of the month). You may be charged $50 for the credit check in a coop sublet.

Once you are pronounced credit-worthy, the deposit check should be accepted as your first month's rent, two months in advance for some short-term rentals. The interest-earning security deposit, payable now, will be refunded at the end of your lease, providing the apartment is left in the same condition in which it was found. If a real estate broker is involved, your third payment will be the broker's fee, which currently averages about 15% of the first year's rent. In some cases, the owner will pay all or part of the fee.

Leases

Read the lease carefully before signing it and all those checks. Married couples should have both names on the lease; unmarried couples should try to get both names on the lease, though the landlord is not legally obliged to do so. A standard form is customary. Be familiar with the content of the entire lease, but pay special attention to the end of the form where the qualifying clauses are printed. The document should specify any special arrangements made with the landlord about alterations, repairs, painting and new appliances. If you have a dog, be sure the lease states that dogs are allowed to inhabit the apartment.

Determine how the building is heated and who pays the bills. If the landlord is responsible, there must be a clause in the lease to this effect. Traditionally, landlords pay for steam heat and gas heat. Tenants customarily pay for exceedingly costly electrical heat. In some buildings gas and electricity charges for stoves and ovens are included in the rent, but, in general, count on being billed directly by Con Edison for all utilities in the apartment proper.

Since 1982 smoke detectors, essentially one per sleeping area, have been mandatory in New York apartments. Tenants are responsible for the repair and maintenance of these alarms.

The landlord is legally responsible for ridding apartments of cockroaches. Some provide routine exterminator services; others simply take care of the matter as it crops up. Obviously, the ounce of prevention method is preferable and you should know in advance if regular service is included in your lease.

Check for a sublet clause. Subletting is allowed "with the landlord's permission." This means he can say no. To avoid permission being withheld capriciously, the clause should mention that the apartment can be sublet with written permission from the landlord "which permission shall not be unreasonably withheld."

Conversely, if you are subletting an apartment from the original leasee, determine whether or not you have a legal right to be there. To address this and other questions the New York State Tenant and Neighborhood Coalition (NYSTNC) has a useful booklet, A Tenant's Guide to Subletting and Apartment Sharing, costing $9; write the NYST-NC, 505 Eighth Avenue, 24th floor, NYC 10018. Or, if you have questions about the propriety of a subtenancy and the apartment falls under city or state-enforced guidelines, try calling one of the organizations listed below (the Rent Stabilization Association, DHCR office or the New York Loft Tenants) with your concerns.

Subletting a cooperative apartment can be daunting. Not only is it necessary to prove yourself to the landlord but you must pass the scrutiny of the building's board of directors, too. However, the traditionally restrictive subletting practices of many cooperative buildings are slowly being liberalized. Though unlikely, if you sublet a co-op without the board's approval, beware that you could be evicted. Free from boards of directors, individuallyowned condominium apartments can be sublet at the owner's discretion.

Rent Stabilization and Rent Control

Although municipal rent controls have been eliminated in most of the country, they survive in New York City because of the sheer number of affected units: close to one million. Many—900,000 is a ballpark figure—apartments on the market today are rent stabilized. Few if any of the estimated 80,000 rent controlled apartments ever reach the market. They either are passed among qualifying members of one family like heirlooms or, once vacant, automatically become rent stabilized (apartments in large buildings) or decontrolled (apartments in buildings with five units or less). Buildings constructed before February 1, 1947, come under rent control. Instituted in 1969, rent stabilization covers apartments in buildings constructed between February 1, 1947, and December 31, 1973.

Rents for apartments built after January 1, 1974, are not bound by any laws except for those special few where real estate tax abatements or rehabilitation laws apply. Buildings with less than six apartments are free from any rent restrictions unless they contain rent controlled units. Rents in condominiums and cooperative apartments are left to the owner's discretion.

Stabilized rents negotiated each June under the aegis of the New York Rent Guidelines Board go into effect the following October 1. A rent stabilized landlord in New York City is not obligated to sign a lease for more than one year the first time around. However, when it comes time to renew, he or she must offer tenants the right to sign a one-or two-year lease. A three-year lease may be requested but the landlord is not required to provide one. The Board's Housing NYC web site (http://www.nycrgb.com) provides a trove of information concerning rent control and stabilization, subleasing, lease renewal, lead paint rules, small claims court, housing court, and more.

The Rent Stabilization Association (the landlord group), 1500 Broadway, NYC 10036, will answer questions about tenants' rights under rent stabilization. Call 212-214-9200. The Office of Rent Administration, State Division of Housing and Community Renewal (DHCR), 92-31 Union Hall Street, Jamaica 11433, 718-739-6400, answers questions and handles complaints from both rent stabilized and rent controlled tenants. Complaints as well as inquiries about co-op conversions can be addressed in writing only to the New York State Attorney General, 120 Broadway, NYC 10271.

If your apartment is rent controlled or rent stabilized, call the State DHCR office in your borough with any questions or problems: Upper Manhattan, above 110th Street, 163 West 125th Street, 212-961-8930; Lower Manhattan, below 110th Street, 156 William Street, 212-240-6010; The Bronx, 1 Fordham Plaza, The Bronx, 718-563-5680; Brooklyn, 91 Lawrence Street, Brooklyn, 718-722-4778; Queens, 164-19 Hillside Avenue, Jamaica, 718-739-6400; Staten Island, 350 St. Mark's Place, 718-816-0277.

Tenants of any stripe can call 212-960-4800, the Central Complaint Bureau of the New York City Department of Housing and Preservation, 215 West 125th Street, NYC 10027, 24 hours a day, seven days a week. Bureau operators answer questions and pass along housing complaints to the appropriate New York City agency.

Lofts

During the 1960s the trickle of hardy artists working and living illegally in industrial lofts located in zoned-for-manufacturing districts became a stream. Living in a vast, often high-ceilinged space with few if any partitions, a la boheme, became a desirable alternative life style. Add a few partitions, a restaurant gas stove, some antiques—instant chic. Illegal loft tenancies proliferated.

An amendment to the state's Multiple Dwelling Law legalized loft living in manufacturing buildings (buildings with no residential Certificates of Occupancy) containing three or more rental units. Some areas of the city were exempted, but in Chelsea and lower Manhattan, in the Fulton Ferry area of Brooklyn and Long Island City in Queens, loft dwellers breathed a legal sigh.

The loft law did not, however, create complete order out of chaos, and the legality of some loft-living situations is still in doubt. Anyone considering renting or subletting a loft is well advised to check with one of the three loft groups currently active in Manhattan before signing the lease:

- **The Housing Clinic**, 280 Broadway (at Chambers), Room 412, no telephone. An educational and informational, not-for-profit organization concerned with all aspects of residential lofts. They hold free weekly clinics Tuesdays 5:00—6:00 p.m. and will answer questions regarding updates to the loft law.

- **The New York City Loft Board**, 1 Center Street, 212-788-7610, is the city agency charged with overseeing the legalization of residential lofts.

- **The New York State Tenant and Neighborhood Coalition, Inc.** is, in their own words, "a statewide membership organization dedicated to passage of stronger tenant protection laws, stronger enforcement of existing laws, and creation of decent, affordable housing". They publish a concise and exceedingly useful pamphlet entitled A Tenant's Guide to Subletting and Apartment Sharing ($9 and available from the Coalition at 198 Broadway, Room 1000, New York, NY 10038).

L ET'S see. You've opened a bank account and have finally found an apartment. So now, keys and lease in hand, it's time to have utilities connected and the telephone installed. You can really make yourself at home once you can cook and call; really settle in once you possess a library card and can vote. The how-to's follow.

Consolidated Edison

Call Customer Service to have utilities turned on: in Manhattan, 212-338-3100; the Bronx, 718-409-7100; Brooklyn, 718-802-6000; Queens, 718-830-7400; Staten Island, 718-390-6400. A personal visit from Con Ed is not necessary unless the prior tenant's service was cut off for non-payment. Expect to wait at least one business day before service commences. Deposits are no longer required for residential accounts.

Telephone Service

So rapidly are communications technologies advancing, barriers crashing and regulations churning to keep up, that however you describe telephone service today, it will be out of date next year. Today local telephone service is provided by NYNEX/Bell Atlantic as well as that brash upstart MCI with its new local service (for now at least using NYNEX lines) available in 212, 718, 914 and 516 area codes. Cable television giants are poised to offer telephone service over their fiber optic cables, first to businesses then to homes. For their part, regional Bell telephone companies are aiming at the cable markets with video services. Today cellular phone service is offered by four operators (see below) offering a dizzying array of plans, now including digital personal communications services, or P.C.S., which may be superior to cellular, and may be cheaper. Confusing? Stay tuned. Meanwhile, you want a telephone in your apartment now.

To institute new **local service** in any borough, call NYNEX at 890-1550; for MCI's new local service call 888-624-5622. For NYNEX service, if you can answer three out of six credit questions positively, no deposit is required. If you flunk the test, the company requests a deposit, which accumulates interest and is refunded in a year's time. With MCI, no deposit is needed but a credit check is required.

Telephones can still be rented from AT&T, call 800-555-8111, but most people prefer to buy their telephones outright. For a wide variety, consider specialty shops such as the Fone Booth, 829 Third Avenue, NYC 10022, 212-564-0900

As a NYNEX customer you will be offered a bouquet of extra services, each carrying an extra monthly fee, among them: **Call Waiting** (the most popular), **Voice Dialing**, **Call Return**, **3-Way Calling**, and **Call ID**. **Call Forwarding** automatically forwards an incoming call to you at another number or to an answering service without the caller's knowing it (you pay for the forwarding). As a voice mail alternative to an answering machine or service **Call Answering**, once it is activated on your touch-tone phone ($20.15 installation charge for a residence, waived occasionally during advertised promotions), cuts in after, say, the third ring 24 hours a day and records up to 30 messages of up to two minutes. Messages are retrievable from any touch-tone phone. The service costs $6.23 per month, plus 10.6 cents for each incoming call and 10.6 cents for each retrieval call, regardless of the number of messages, billed on your monthly statement. For any of these services, call the number above.

As a NYNEX customer you can receive, at no cost, a calling card for use locally or long distance. When using the card on a pay phone, however, you will pay a surcharge for this non-regulated service, 40 cents local and 80 cents long distance if the phone is served by NYNEX, a stunner on your next bill if another carrier is involved. To avoid this shock dial 1-800-54-NYNEX first.

MCI local service promises all the same extra services as NYNEX (call waiting, voice dialing, 3-way calling, etc) *except* voice mail, which is not offered. MCI's basic rates are comparable to those of NYNEX but, borrowing a successful strategy from the long distance market, for regional toll calls such as from Manhattan to Rockland County, MCI charges a flat rate rather than the sliding scale offered by NYNEX.

Long distance service is provided by AT&T, 800-222-0300, and other carriers, which may quote cheaper residential rates. These companies include Sprint, 800-877-4646; and MCI, 1-800-950-5555. Variables, other than rates, include volume discounts, monthly minimums and the fact that AT&T may offer slightly more comprehensive overseas service. Check around.

Newcomers or not, most New Yorkers aren't aware of how much good information can be found in the city's telephone books. The **White Pages** includes an extensive listing of community service numbers as well as government listings and an emergency care guide. The **Yellow Pages** is almost in itself a guide to New York City. Seek it as a reference for historical sites and landmarks, public transportation maps, a yearly calendar of events, and sports stadiums and concert hall seating charts!

The **Business to Business Yellow Pages**, which lists all wholesalers and manufacturers, is free of charge and can be obtained by calling your local telephone office. Call 800-426-8686 to purchase consumer and business-to-business 800 directories.

For those whose business requires their constant telephone accessibility, as well as those who suffer separation anxiety away from the telephone, the **cellular phone** provides an umbilical cord, albeit an expensive one. Here, too, technology is rapidly changing, and cost will probably diminish. Currently, cellular service is provided in the area by four companies: Bell Atlantic Nynex, Omnipoint, AT&T Wireless and MCI. The equipment, ranging in price from about $10 to $1000, is available from a host of manufacturers through local vendors and service providers, whose ads and occasional promotions are to be found in the *Times* and in the Yellow Pages. The cost of operation, varying according to carrier and plan, includes a monthly access charge, air time charges, landline charges and roaming area charges for use beyond the home area. Users are billed for receiving as well as making calls. New users would do well to try out a plan that does not require a long-term contract and has no early termination penalty. Service will probably cost more than you expect. Whether you want cellular or **PCS** (personal communications service, which is clearer and can receive electronic mail), analog or digital, depends on how you will use your phone, how often and what you are willing to spend for the convenience; at this point analog equipment cannot receive digital calls, and vice versa. Members of AAA may want to purchase their cellular phone through that organization. Cellular phones can also be rented for short-term use such as a trip. **Caveat**: cellular fraud, the electronic theft and use of the identification numbers of legitimate phones, has been high in the metropolitan area.

Television Stations

So that you may tune in your favorite show immediately upon arrival, we list national television networks (and local independents) and their New York channels: **Channel 2**—WCBS; **Channel 4**—WNBC; **Channel 5**—WNYW (Fox); **Channel 7**—WABC; **Channel 9**—WOR (an independent New Jersey-based station); **Channel 11**—WPIX (independent community station serving the tri-state area); **Channel 13**—WNET (Public Broadcasting System). Note that an Ultra High Frequency station, **Channel 21**—WLIW (Long Island's public network channel), broadcasts many of the public network TV series ("Masterpiece Theater" and the like) carried on Channel 13 but at different times. When you miss an episode on Channel 13, you can usually catch it a night or two later on Channel 21.

You'll find weekly programs for the broadcast channels as well as cable channels (including HBO, Showtime and the like) printed in *TV Guide* and the Sunday *New York Times*' "Television". This supplement also carries a complete "Station Guide" detailing the ownership and/or focus of broadcast and cable stations.

Cable Television and The Dish

Expanded programming and famous skyscrapers make cable an attractive and often necessary option in New York City. Like the telecommunications industry, the cable industry is in the throes of change. Currently, service in Manhattan is quasi-monopolistic: Paragon has cable rights to the northern half of the borough, Time-Warner to the southern half. The situation is more fluid in outlying areas, where several firms vie for customers. With a few exceptions, both Manhattan distributors offer the same services: Home Box Office (HBO) for movies, MTV (music videos and rock/pop concerts), Nickelodeon for children, sports on Sportschannel (for events blacked out in the metropolitan area), Madison Square Garden Cable Network and ESPN, as well as channels broadcasting news, weather, health and stock market reports and entertainment. Time-Warner Cable offers Cinemax for still more movies, while Paragon has Showtime (also movies) and Uptown (R-rated movies from 9 p.m. to 1 a.m.) for its upper Manhattan subscribers.

If your building isn't already wired, the owner or manager must request hookup, which has been known to take anywhere from several months to a year. If you're living below 79th Street on the West Side or below 86th Street on the East Side, contact Time Warner Cable of New York City, 120 East 23rd Street, NYC 10010, 212-674-9100. Brooklyn and Queens residents should call Time Warner at 718-358-0900. In Manhattan above 79th Street on the West Side or 86th Street on the East Side, contact Paragon Cable, 5120 Broadway, NYC 10034, 212-304-3000.

"44 W. 62nd Street has been liberated from the cable monopoly...." You may have puzzled over tiny ads such as this at the bottom of the *Times* front page. You may even wind up in an apartment serviced by Liberty Cable, which provides cable service via satellite dish to more than 10,000 units in large apartment buildings, mostly on the East Side. In that case, you'll be billed about $12 to $17, either by Liberty or by the building management, for some 50 major cable channels, but not including New York One or public access cable.

The latest alternative to lousy reception via the rabbit ears and the tyranny of the cable companies is **direct broadcast satellite** (DBS), more commonly known as The Dish, which provides the clearest reception available and up to 200 channels, *not* including the local channels and only *if* you are in position suitable for mounting an 18- to 36-inch dish outside your home, a difficult proposition for most Manhattanites. Basically, you'll need to own your building so you can use the roof or have a southwest-facing balcony on which to mount the thing, and there can be no taller building to block the signal from the southwest. Clearly, TV junkies in the outer boroughs and the suburbs, where buildings are lower and spread out, have the advantage here. Currently three DBS signal providers compete in the metropolitan area: Digital Satellite System (DSS), with programming from DirecTV (800-347-3288) and US

Satellite Broadcasting (800-238-8378); Primestar (800-966-9615); and DISH (800-333-3474). Depending on the provider, you buy or lease the receiver and dish, pay a one-time installation fee and a monthly pro- gramming fee. AT&T long distance subscribers may get a price break by buying the hardware from AT&T and the service from DSS.

Radio Stations

Music lovers are best served by their FM dials; news and talk shows dominate the AM band. However, on either broadcast frequency most stations specialize further still, emphasizing one format or one sound. Check below to find your station. For program particulars, consult *The New York Times* daily radio listings and *New York* magazine's "Cue" entertainment guide, which publishes classical music "Highlights" weekly.

- **AM News:** CBS 880—"Newsradio"; WINS 1010—"Give Us 22 Minutes and We'll Give You the World."

- **AM Talk:** WABC 770; WMCA 570—"The Voice of New York"; WNYC 830—the city's own station features cultural and consumer- oriented broadcasts and National Public Radio's "All Things Considered"; WOR 710—insomniac radio (talk around the clock).

- **AM Nostalgia:** WEVD 1050—11 p.m. to 5:30 a.m.; WQEW 1560.

- **AM Sports:** WFAN 660.

- **FM Classical:** WKCR 89.9—classical when it isn't jazz, country or talk; WNYC 93.9—classical, swing and jazz interspersed with PBS programs including "All Things Considered" and "Prairie Home Companion"; WQXR 96.3—*The New York Times'* mostly-music but some-news-too station.

- **FM Jazz:** WBGO 88.3—contemporary jazz from Newark; WKCR 89.9—about half the time Columbia University's station plays jazz; WFUV 90.7—-Fordham University's station, playing classic rock to contemporary jazz.

- **FM Listener Sponsored Radio:** WBAI 99.5—just like the populace that supports it, this talk and music station is invigorating, madden- ing and appealing all at the same time.

- **FM Country:** WYNY 103.5. and WFMU 91.1—Saturday 1 to 3 p.m.

- **FM World Music:** WNYE 91.5, 1 to 6:30 a.m., musical map-hop- ping for insomniacs.

In hot pursuit of the all-important 20- to 35-year-old market, most New York FM stations feature "Top 40 Radio" and are fiercely competi- tive. According to a knowledgeable radio staffer, New York's contempo- rary FM music stations currently fall into the following trade categories:

- **Urban Contemporary** (dance music with a driving beat): WBLS 107.5 and WRKS (KISS) 98.7.

- **Album Oriented Rock**: WNEW 102.7 and WXRK 92.3.

- **Current Hit Radio**: WPLJ (Power 95) 95.5.

- **Hot Hits** (slightly wilder than Current Hit Radio; more novelties): WHTZ (Z100)100.3.

- **Adult Contemporary** (soft sounds aimed at 24-to 54-year-olds): WLTW 106.7.

- **Golden Oldies** (rock and roll from the 1950s and 1960s): WCBS 101.1.

- **Middle of the Road** ("easy listening" for over-35-year-olds; Sinatra triumphant): WPAT 93.

Driver's Licenses and Automobile Registration

New residents with valid foreign or out-of-state licenses have 30 days to apply for a New York State Driver's License and to register their cars and motorcycles. Licenses and vehicle registrations are issued by the District Office of the New York State Department of Motor Vehicles, 141-155 Worth Street, corner Centre Street, NYC 10013, open Monday through Friday 9 to 4:30,. Pick up a license application (which will have a convenient voter registration form attached), Driver's Manual and, if necessary, an Automobile Registration form at the District Office or have them sent by calling 212-645-5550. A valid out-of-state license exempts you from the road test, but you must pass the vision, road sign and written tests.

Unless you get lucky, happening by when the examiner has a time slot open, you must make an appointment in advance to take the written test. Write to the Preliminary Test Office of the Department of Motor Vehicles in whichever borough you live, or stop by in person. No appointment can be made by phone. The written tests, based on the Driver's Manual, are given from 9 to 3.

Because tests are scored there and then, you are issued a temporary license which allows you to drive immediately if you pass. Your official license, the one with the photograph, is mailed to you. You must have the completed application form, current license and $32.25, which includes the written test fee, license validation fee and picture, taken at the time your license is issued. New York State licenses are valid for four years.

If your license has lapsed or this is your first, pick up the materials and take the vision, road sign and written tests noted above. You'll then be eligible for a learner's permit. With this in hand, after a three-hour course at a licensed driving school, it is possible to take the road test, the ultimate qualification for the New York Driver's License. Examiners can be finicky, but the most frustrating aspect of the road test is getting an appointment to take it. If you can arrange to take the test out of town, or at least out of Manhattan, do so.

You need the following documents to register your car or motorcycle: Registration Application or Title completely filled out, proof of ownership, proof of insurance, proof of vehicle inspection, sales tax clearance, and proof of your identity and birth. Read the back of the Application for Registration to determine what "proofs" are acceptable. The registration fee depends on vehicle weight.

Long lines are a Department of Motor Vehicles tradition. Best time to go is early in the week. Fridays are particularly busy. The last workday of any month can find the line spilling out onto Worth Street's sidewalk and is to be avoided, period. **Note**: for a quickie (10-minute) **renewal** of your NY State driver's license, go to the DMV office at 300 West 34th Street between Eighth and Ninth Avenues, Monday-Wednesday, 8 to 5:30, Thursday to 7 p.m. The fee is $27.25.

Parking Your Car

You may have a very helpful helpmate, willing to spend long hours switching a car from one side of the street to another in order to conform with New York's alternate side of the street parking laws, or you may derive pleasure from driving through lonely streets at night looking for a legal spot. Either way, you had better be informed about alternate side of the street parking regulations. Call 212-442-7080 to find out if regulations are in effect on any given day or, better yet, get a free copy of the Department of Transportation's calendar showing the days your car doesn't have to be moved. Send a stamped, self-addressed envelope to Calendar, NYC Department of Transportation, 40 Worth Street, NYC 10013.

Most people working full time must find private parking for their cars. Monthly garage rates keep rising. In any of Manhattan's prime areas, count on paying between $200 and $400 a month. There are alternatives, however, to be found in garages around the fringe of town, on the Lower East Side, south of Greenwich Village along the West Side Highway and north of Morningside Heights. A favorite for the budget-conscious below 14th Street is Pier 40, West and Houston Streets. The problem here is that Pier 40 is not close to a subway line, and the buses that pass nearby (the #13 and #10) do so only seldom. Open lots are cheaper and some are better guarded than others. Again, however, the more reasonably priced lots tend to be on the periphery of town.

If you use a car only occasionally, consider a private garage in a nearby community that is easily accessible by public transportation. See **Transportation** section for information about car rentals.

Auto Services and Repair

Keeping a car in New York City is a luxury and a headache. You've stood on line (New Yorkers don't stand *in* line) for registration and license, what you're paying the garage would rent a studio apartment somewhere else, now who can you trust to repair your car without ripping you off? There are hundreds of auto repair shops throughout the city, and many of them are competent and honest. Which ones?

Alas, there is no consumer rating system for auto repair shops. Talk to friends and colleagues for their recommendations before you have a problem; you may find a gem of a repairman. Membership in AAA (American Automobile Association) for $55 the first year, $45 thereafter, is probably the best investment you can make in your car in the city. The emergency road service alone, with free battery charge and free towing within a three mile radius to an AAA-affiliated service station is worth the price of admission. Their list of affiliated stations is a valuable starting point. Members also receive free maps and trip planning services, trip interruption insurance, the services of AAA travel agents, travel discounts and a host of products and services highlighted in their monthly magazine, *Car and Travel*. Drop in to their Manhattan branch at 1881 Broadway at 62nd Street or call 212-757-2000 or 718-224-222.

Traffic Tickets and Towing

What's the price if you get caught? To help you decide whether to take that parking chance or not, here is what tickets currently cost below 96th Street in Manhattan (tickets in the boroughs are sometimes cheaper): $40 if the meter has expired; $55 if you're parked on the wrong side of the street in an alternate-side-parking zone; $55 for double parking or parking within 15 feet of a fire hydrant, in a No Parking or No Standing zone. No ticket costs more than $55, though fines increase by $10 per day after 30 days and by $20 per day after 45 days. If you are going to pay your fines, do it immediately.

But tickets are only a part of the penalty. The real deterrent to joining the ranks of New York's scofflaws is the threat of having your automobile towed. It costs $150 to retrieve your car from the pound on Pier 76 (Twelfth Avenue and 38th Street) in Manhattan, plus $15 a day (not including the day your car was towed) for storage. You must produce the car's registration and your driver's license to get the automobile back. If your name is on the registration papers, you can pay by check—that is, if your name is printed on the check. Otherwise, or if you have accumulated unpaid traffic tickets, you must produce cash, certified check or traveler's check for payment. The pound is open 7 a.m. to 6 a.m., seven days a week. Call 212-TOW-AWAY to determine whether your car has been towed; if it isn't in the pound (and you haven't misplaced it), your car has been stolen or the Marshall has towed it away for nonpayment of tickets.

To find out if you have an accumulation of tickets (they often blow off the windshield; then, too, other drivers swipe them to put under their windshield wipers in order to fool the cops) call the Parking Violations Bureau's Help Hot Line, 212-477-4430. All five boroughs have Help Centers where you can get a free computer printout of your tickets: One Centre Street, Manhattan; 1400 Williamsbridge Road, 1st floor, The Bronx; 89-61 162nd Street, Jamaica, Queens; 210 Joralemon Street, 9th floor Brooklyn; 350 St. Mark's Place, 3rd floor, Staten Island.

Don't Even Think of Parking Here! by Paul Trapido and Barbara Ensor covers just about every topic a car owner in New York needs to know (published by Simon & Schuster).

Keeping Pets

Can you bring your Portuguese Water Dog and your Burmese cat to New York? Will that pose a problem? Yes and maybe. The biggest hurdle to clear will be the first: finding a place to live that will accept pets (fish don't count). Increasingly, landlords are prohibiting pets in their buildings, which means you may have to choose between the perfect apartment and the perfect pet. Be sure to inquire as you search for a pet-friendly home; don't plan to sneak one in where they are prohibited. Dogs and cats being the most common city pets, we'll address their needs here. If yours is an exotic pet, a miniature pig, say, you're on your own.

You will want to have a vet lined up before you need one. Start by calling the Veterinary Medical Association of New York City, 212-246-0056, for a list of accredited vets in your neighborhood. Visit the dog run, park or vacant lot in your neighborhood where dog owners hang out with their dogs to glean information on local vets and the whole range of dog-owner concerns. Choosing a vet, like choosing a doctor, is largely a subjective thing. Beyond the cleanliness and user-friendliness of the establishment, you and your pet will want to be comfortable with this vet. You may want to inquire to be sure your vet is available or covered after hours by answering service. In case of a serious emergency after hours, the Manhattan Veterinary Group, a private animal hospital at 240 East 80th Street between Second and Third Avenues, 212-988-1000, is open till 1 a.m. daily; the Animal Medical Center at 510 East 62nd Street at York Avenue, 838-8100, is open 24 hours a day.

Dogs must be licensed by the city 's Department of Health, 212-566-2456, for which you will need proof of rabies vaccination. **Note:** Besides keeping your dog leashed outside of fenced dog runs, you must clean up after your dog. This last ordinance has made it possible to look up when walking in the city.

Dogs need to be walked at least three times a day, not a problem if you work at home. Being social animals, they suffer more than cats from being left alone for long periods. Consider the proposition that two dogs is not much more bother than one, and both are happier together than one alone. In any case, if you are away for more than eight hours a day, you will probably need a dog walker, a person who has your keys and who will come in and take your dog out for 15 to 60 minutes. Costly? Yes. To find a reliable walker check with other dog owners and your vet for recommendations. Some of the better pet care establishments keep a list of walkers whose credentials they can vouch for. Some dog walkers will also pet-sit when your are away, either staying in your home to care for your pets and plants or visiting three times a day to feed, water, play with, and walk your pet. The cost? Currently a minimum of $22 a day for cats, $25-$30 a day for dogs, more in some neighborhoods. There *are* kennels in the city, at least one without pens; those out of town, most of which pick up and deliver, tend to be roomier and less expensive.

If you're looking to acquire a dog or cat you might consult the classified ads in the Sunday Sports Section of the *New York Times*. There are purebred rescue groups in the city for most breeds; they find homes for animals of a particular breed which need to be placed, usually at less cost than from a breeder. And finally, if you adopt a pet from the ASPCA Shelter and Adoption Center, 424 East 92nd Street at First Avenue, 876-7700 ext. 4120, you are saving it from almost certain euthanasia. The Bide-A-Wee Manhattan Shelter at 410 East 38th Street east of First Avenue, 532-4455, does not destroy animals but offers dogs and cats for adoption at minimal cost.

A recent, probably inevitable, entry into the field of animal medicine here is the pet HMO, Pet Assure, which offers members 25% off all medical care and supplies for pets using participating veterinarians and 10% to 50% off of cost of pet foods, supplies, training, grooming and boarding at participating establishments in the five boroughs, Manhattan especially. Call 1-888-789-PETS (http://www.petassure.com).

Two books widely available in book and pet stores are useful compendiums of information for dog owners:

- *The Dog's Guide to New York City, With Jack, the City Dog*, by Jan Rohman, Richmond Press; and

- *The Great New York Dog Book*, by Deborah Loven, HarperCollins.

Finding a Physician

"What about how to find a doctor?" a plaintive reader inquires, adding, "it's been tough." Indeed. They're out there, about 13,000 of them in Manhattan alone, but choosing a personal physician is more like choosing a mate than buying a car. You're looking for a doctor who has graduated from an excellent medical school, done residency in a good teaching hospital, is board-certified, has practiced long enough to know what he/she is doing but not so long as to be out of touch with the latest research and technology, *and* has just the right professional manner—concerned, straightforward, a listener with, perhaps, a good sense of humor. If you put it off until you need one, you're apt to wind up sitting miserably in the nearest Emergency Room, followed by a big bill. Maybe worse.

If you are enrolled in an HMO (Health Maintenance Organization) by your employer or independently, you are probably limited in your choice of physicians to those listed by that HMO. This makes choosing somewhat easier, but the criteria for choosing remain the same as they are at-large. More about HMO's below.

You may choose a physician as many do, on the basis of the recommendation of friends, and there is something to be said for that. Do, at least, question your friend closely as to what exactly he/she does and does not like about this physician. If you had a physician you liked before moving here, he may be able to recommend a colleague here who will suit you.

Conventional wisdom says that one should have a doctor who is on staff or is an attending physician at one of the **teaching hospitals**. These physicians have been carefully screened and their credentials certified, the reasoning goes, and the teaching hospitals tend to offer a wider range of services and sophisticated procedures than do the smaller community hospitals. Bear in mind also, that as a patient in a teaching hospital, you may expect to be poked and probed by students and residents, and some care may be provided by residents without the proper supervision. Insist on seeing your own doctor. In any case, these hospitals have referral services, which is one place to start your search. Referrals are based on medical specialty and location and often come up by computer rotation. The major academic hospitals in Manhattan, with their physician referral lines, are:

- **Beth Israel Medical Center**, First Avenue at 16th Street, NYC 10003, 800-420-4004

- **Columbia Presbyterian Medical Center**, 622 West 168th Street, NYC 10032, 800-227-CPMC

- **Mount Sinai Medical Center**, Fifth Avenue at 101st Street, NYC 10029, 800-MD-SINAI

- **N.Y. Hospital-Cornell Medical Center**, 525 East 68th Street, NYC 10021, 800-822-2NYH

- **N.Y.U. Medical Center**, 550 First Avenue, NYC 10016, 212-263-5000

- **St. Luke's-Roosevelt Hospital Center**, 1000 Tenth Avenue, NYC 10019, 212-876-5432

- **St. Vincent's Hospital**, 153 West 11th Street, NYC 10011, 800-999-6266

Some of these hospitals also have treatment centers elsewhere, and their doctors practice throughout the metropolitan area. See the Yellow Pages for more hospitals in Manhattan and in the other boroughs.

Another source of referrals is the **county medical society**, which in Manhattan (N.Y. County Medical Society, 15 East 26th Street, NYC 10010, 684-4670) has some 6,000 members. The caller can specify the area of choice, hospital of choice, specialty, sex, and be given three names. **Note:** You can also check on the credentials, training, and board specialties of a physician recommended to you elsewhere.

Referral(s) in hand, call the specific doctor's office to ask about an introductory visit. Inquire about office hours and their procedure for an introductory interview, which may be by phone or in person, and what the charge will be. Is the office staff helpful? Before talking with the physician have your questions written down: what hospitals does he/she practice in, who covers for him/her when he/she is unavailable, can he/she be reached by phone after hours if need be, what are his/her billing procedures, etc. You may also want to discuss such sensitive issues as his/her views on abortion and life support. If you are satisfied so far, you will probably make an appointment for a physical exam and some tests to establish a baseline profile. Ask about that and what it will cost. If you are not satisfied, go elsewhere.

A word abut **HMO**s. If you are not covered by some form of health insurance and are not in an HMO connected with your place of employment, you can join one directly yourself on a "direct pay" basis. That means you pay, and it isn't cheap, at least until you consider the alternative, should you or a family member become ill or injured. Competition among HMO's is intense, and the field is rapidly changing. It's a good idea to request information from a number of organizations in order to determine what is available and what best suits your situation and your pocketbook.

To assist in this and/or in the choice of a physician or hospital, one book, known as "Best Doctors," is especially useful. Based on extensive surveys of health care professionals, statistics and other data, *How to Find the Best Doctors, New York Metropolitan Area* by John Castle and John Connolly is available in area library reference rooms.

Voter Registration

Registering to vote is as simple as calling the Manhattan Board of Elections, 212-886-3800, and requesting an Application for Registration and Enrollment by Mail, completing the form and returning it to the board. If you live in another borough, the Manhattan Board will pass the completed application along to the appropriate borough board: Bronx, 718-299-9017; Brooklyn, 718-522-3116; Manhattan, 212-868-3788; Queens, 718-392-8989; and Staten Island, 718-727-4300. Under the 1995 "Motor Voter" law, the pre-stamped applications are also available now in post offices, libraries and some public agencies. If you enroll in a political party, the form must be received by the Board of Elections 25 days before the primary or general election. You can also register in person during specific central registration periods at Election Board headquarters, 131 Varick Street, 9th Floor, NYC 10013.

Further questions about voting procedures? The candidates? Issues? The **League of Women Voters** will help you answer these questions by telephone, 212-677-5050, or through the materials they publish. Also, they will send you a voter registration application on request. You can stop by their offices at 817 Broadway corner of East 12th Street, 6th floor, for a copy of their useful guide, *What Makes New York City Run*, $4, or have it sent by mail for an extra dollar. Their pamphlet *They Represent You* lists the addresses and phone and fax numbers of community boards, city, state and federal boards and officers for $3.25, or $4.33 by mail. Also good to have is *The Green Book* ($12.99, Citybooks Store, 61 Chambers Street) which lists numerous elected officials as well as all city departments and offices. If you have a government-related problem, the telephone listings in this guide can be a powerful tool.

Library Cards

The New York Public Library, with four research libraries, numerous special divisions for various disciplines, famous reference collections and over 80 branches in Manhattan, The Bronx and Staten Island, is one of the city's great treasures. Residents of Brooklyn and Queens, however, aren't bookless: the Brooklyn Public Library has 59 branches, the Queens Borough Public Library, 60.

Library cards are free and entitle you to borrow or request circulating books from any branch in the system. To obtain a card, give your name, address and proof of residence to the staffer at the return desk of the nearest branch library. Call 930-0800 for library hours—which vary widely from branch to branch.

A wonderful resource is the library's Telephone Reference Service, 212-340-0849. Library researchers try to answer all viable questions and, if they cannot, will refer you to the department most likely to have the required data. If the Manhattan number is too busy, try the Brooklyn, 718-780-7700, or Queens, 718-990-0714, Telephone Reference Service numbers.

Passports

Whether you are applying for a passport for the first time or renewing, do not wait until just before your summer or Christmas vacation to do so. Apply early and relax. First, call 212-399-5290 to obtain recorded factual information. With luck, the recording will answer all your questions. For more detailed information and to download the proper mail-in forms, you can visit the Bureau of Consular Affairs' home page at http://travel.state.gov. Or call the National Passport Information Center (NPIC) at 900-225-5674 for detailed recorded information (35 cents a minute) 24 hours a day or to speak with a live operator ($1.05 a minute) from 8 a.m. to 8 p.m.

If you are applying for a passport for the first time, you must have 1) proof of citizenship: an original, or copy, of your birth certificate with a raised seal, or naturalization papers, and 2) proof of your identity: a driver's license or other ID with a photograph and signature. (If you don't have these papers, call the number above for alternatives.) You will need two passport photos (which can be made while you wait in most neighborhood photo shops) and $65 if you are over age 18, $40 for minors. You will find the necessary forms (DSP-II) at all of the addresses listed below, and you must appear in person to get your first passport. But don't go to the Passport Agency unless you have an appointment for a priority passport, covered below. These centers can process your application:

- **Clerks of the State Supreme Court:** (Manhattan) Court House, 60 Centre Street, 10007; (Brooklyn) New Supreme Court, 60 Adams Street, 11201; (Bronx) County Building, 851 Grand Concourse, 10451; (Queens) County Court House, 88-11 Sutpin Boulevard, 11435.

- **Post Offices:** (Manhattan) General Post Office, 8th Avenue and 33rd Street; Ansonia Station, 1960 Broadway; Church Street Station, 90 Church Street; Cooper Station, 93 Fourth Avenue; Franklin D. Roosevelt Station, 909 Third Avenue; and Manhattanville Station, 365 West 125th Street. (Call the General Post Office for stations with passport windows in the other boroughs.)

To renew a passport, pick up form DSP-82 (or, if you were under 18 when you obtained your previous passport, form DSP-11) at any of the addresses listed above and mail it as directed with two passport pictures, $55 and your expired passport. Allow four to six weeks, more if you're applying in high summer season, or mention the date of your departure on the form; passports are processed on the basis of departure date. A passport is good for ten years and can be renewed within two years after expiration.

If you must leave the country in a hurry, it is possible to obtain or renew a passport in three days by calling 212-399-5290 from a touch-tone phone to make an appointment at the Passport Agency, 630 Fifth Avenue, NYC 10111, open 7:30 to 3. You will punch in your Social Security number, the date of your travel ticket and other information and be given a choice of three appointments. Bring your ticket and other necessary papers and cash or check for the fee, plus an extra $30 for priority handling to your appointment, and be prepared to wait and to return for your passport. In high season (April through June, just before Christmas, Easter and other school holidays) an applicant with an appointment made by phone is likely to need two hours to get to the head of the line.

Suppose you've got to go to Botswana on short notice, you don't even know what documents and shots you need, and you're too busy to get it together. What to do? For a fee (up to $150 for a same-day passport renewal) a knowledgeable staff at Passport Plus, 677 Fifth Avenue at 53rd Street, 212-759-5540, will handle it for you.

Social Security

It is the rare American citizen who does not have a Social Security number, a virtual necessity for most. Non-citizens who are working or studying here will also need a number. This can be done by mail by first calling 1-800-772-1213 and answering five automated questions, then mailing a completed application form with the necessary documents. However, given the not-altogether-reliable mail service, it is preferable to visit the nearest Social Security office (see the telephone book or get the address from the 800 number above), no appointment necessary.

Bring with you a birth certificate, an original with raised stamp, not a copy, and two other pieces of identification: passport, driver's license, school or government ID, health insurance card, military records, an insurance policy. A Social Security employee will complete the application, and you should receive a card with your number within several weeks.

Non-citizens need a birth certificate and/or a passport and a green card or student documentation, as well as whatever immigration documents you have. It may take a month or more to receive a card.

If you already have a number but have lost your card, call the number above to apply for a new card.

Recycling

Like it or not, recycling has become a part of life in New York City and everywhere else. In most areas, residents are used to placing newspapers, magazines and corrugated cardboard neatly tied with string on the curb on appointed days. (To find out the pickup days for your neighborhood call the New York City Department of Sanitation at 212-219-8090.) If you're in an area where official recycling is in effect, you leave your separated garbage (i.e. washed cans, plastic and glass bottles, and aluminum foil) curbside in the blue drums provided by the Sanitation Department or in blue plastic bags. Newspapers, magazines and cardboard should be secured with twine in stacks of 18 inches or less. Returnable bottles and cans should be redeemed. For those without an ecological conscience, fines start at $25 for the first offense and go up with each succeeding violation.

If your neighborhood hasn't jumped on the bandwagon and you want to do a little conservation of your own, there are two recycling centers in Manhattan. Several mobile drop-off centers are operated by the Department of Sanitation; call the Sanitation Action Center, 212-219-8090, for their locations and hours.

- **The Village Green Recycling Team**, Avenue of the Americas at West 4th Street, 777-1422, open 5 to 7 Monday, 11 to 2 Wednesday, 8 to 11 Friday, 10 to 3 Saturday. Accepts newspapers, office papers, aluminum and tin cans, plastics, bottles and glass.

- **Upper West Side Recycling Center**, 1047 Amsterdam Avenue at the Cathedral of St. John the Divine, 316-7540. Accepts office paper, aluminum cans and foil, tin cans, plastic bottles and glass.

Building Staff

New Yorkers rely on the staff of their buildings in ways that are unique to the city—and they reward their staff in an equally unique manner.

Most multi-unit residences have a superintendent (the "super") who is responsible for the maintenance and day-to-day operation of the building. Many superintendents may be assisted by porters and hallmen. There are also doormen (and today, doorwomen) in many buildings. In luxury buildings, perhaps a concierge.

Because many New Yorkers do not rely on their cars to accomplish their daily tasks, goods and services are delivered by businesses to the consumer's home even when they are not there, hence the importance of the building staff. Other staff duties may include hailing cabs, supplying important building information, directing repair people, door holding and—in some buildings—even mail delivery. Most of all, your staff (particularly the doorman) is the first line of security in your building, making certain that anyone who desires entrance truly belongs there.

In addition to the generally higher rents found in staffed buildings, there is an unspoken cost associated with the extra service. It is widely expected that a building's residents tip the staff at Christmas-time for general services rendered throughout the year. (Anything beyond a general service, such as pet-walking or heavy lifting, is best attended to at the time the service is performed.) The tip is by no means mandatory but individual service has been known to decline precipitously for those more Scrooge-like residents. The custom varies widely from building to building both in terms of cost and how the money is dispersed. It is a good idea to find out what is customary in your building and budget for the holiday season accordingly.

Rip-off Recourse

It goes without saying that the best defense against fraud and consumer victimization is to avoid it. You read all contracts down to the smallest print, save all receipts and canceled checks, get the name of telephone sales and service people with whom you deal, check a contractor's license number with the Department of Consumer Affairs for complaints. But you've been stung. A dry cleaner returns your blue suit, but now it's purple and he shrugs. A shop refuses to refund as promised on the expensive gift which didn't suit your mother. Your landlord fails to return your security deposit when you move. After $458 in repairs to your automobile's engine, the car now vibrates wildly, and the mechanic claims innocence. Negotiations, documents in hand, fail. You're angry, and embarrassed because you've been had. There *is* something you can do.

- Call the **NYC Department of Consumer Affairs, Complaints Department**, 212-487-4444, for information on filing a complaint; have all your information organized before calling, and be prepared to spend some time on the phone.

- File a complaint with the **NY State Consumer Frauds and Protection Bureau**, office of the Attorney General, 120 Broadway, NYC 10271. You may want to call the bureau's complaint line, 416-8345, first for advice or a complaint form. Or go in to the office in person, third floor, open Monday-Friday 9:30 to 4:30. Again, have all your documentation organized and in hand.

• File suit for relief, up to $3,000, in **Small Claims Court**. You do not need a lawyer, and some 60,000 New Yorkers use this resource annually. There are six Small Claims locations in the city, two of them in Manhattan, all open one evening until 10. For details call 212-791-6000; ask for two excellent booklets, "A Guide to Small Claims Court" and "Preparing for the Collection of a Small Claims Judgment." Be advised that winning in court is easier than collecting on a judgment.

Before doing any of the above, inform your adversary of your intentions, politely but firmly. You may force a settlement, thereby saving yourself the trouble of following through.

Safety in New York City

For the past several years the incidence of violent crime in New York City has actually been decreasing and although many American urban areas have higher crime rates, an important part of getting settled in New York *is* learning to live safely. What follows are some basic guidelines:

• *Always* remain alert to what is around you (in front and in back); if you don't pay attention to your surroundings—for example, by walking and listening to a Walkman—-you make yourself a target for crime.

• Trust your instincts; they are usually right.

• Stay clear of deserted areas such as empty streets, uninhabited subway cars or platforms and lonely automatic teller machines.

• If you must take the subway late at night, always get in the car that houses the brakeman (generally one of the middle cars).Typically, there is a black and white "zebra" sign marking the spot where the brakeman's car stops—ask the token seller where it is. Alone in the station, wait near the token booth.

• Look for children playing outside or women walking on their own as signs that an area is safe.

• If you do find yourself on an ominous-looking block, avoid the sidewalk and walk directly in the street to be in view of traffic.

• If you feel you are being followed, walk into the nearest restaurant or store.

• Conceal your valuables, and if you wear a diamond ring turn it around so only the band is showing. Cover watches and necklaces.

• Hold your handbag close to you, wearing the strap across your chest. Don't hang a purse on a restaurant chair or restroom hook.

• Do not count your money in public or use big bills.

- Be discreet when using your phone card at a public phone; onlookers may read your calling card number by watching how you hit the phone pad.

- Resist the temptation to play three-card monte on the street; *you won't win!*

- Beware of operators working as a team: someone who tells you she just dropped her contact lens might well have a friend who is reaching in your handbag.

- *Remember:* you do not owe a response to anyone who asks for one. This may seem callous but it is better to err on the side of bad manners rather than bad judgment.

The New York City Police Department publishes free brochures on safety. These booklets include safety precautions addressed to men, women, children, the elderly—even to runners. Brochure topics also include how to safeguard your apartment, car and small business. See the final section of this book for emergency phone numbers.

Smart Business Travel: How to Stay Safe When You're on the Road by Stacey Ravel Abarbanel is a handy pocket guide to safe travel. If your security desires can only be satisfied by hi-tech gadgetry, you may want to pay a visit to the Counter Spy Shop at 444 Madison Avenue or in the lobby of the Waldorf-Astoria.

Finally, become involved in your neighborhood. Community is New York City's new buzzword. All over town, people are organizing block associations to monitor crime. To find out if a block association exists in your neighborhood, or to set one up, call Citizen's Committee for New York City at 212-989-0909.

I T should come as no surprise that the international service capital is as energetic in supplying the needs of New Yorkers as it is of those the world over. Multitudinous talents and supremely innovative minds combine to provide a mind-boggling array of services, for individuals as well as for industry. Shelter magazines and newspapers seldom let a month or week go by without feature articles about umbrella repair specialists, third-generation tapestry reweavers, or the pair of clever Upper East Side women now available to reorganize your closets. We'll leave these summaries of the city's more recherché services to the press and provide instead the names of a few representative firms and organizations which supply basics such as cleaning men and women, furniture rentals and computer repairs, or which address the concerns of the lesbian and gay communities and the needs of people with disabilities.

Furniture and Air Conditioner Rentals

Anyone arriving in New York unburdened by furniture can remain that way by renting. This option is great if you're in a state of flux or want to postpone paying for an apartment's worth of furnishings all at once. Monthly charges for the mainly contemporary styles stocked by our representative sampling of rental companies are usually pro-rated on the basis of a one-year lease. Most firms will credit rental charges already paid if you decide to purchase your furniture outright.

Prices quoted below for a one-bedroom apartment would include: bed, night stand, dresser, lamp, mirror, sofa, occasional chair, end table, cocktail table, lamp, dining table and four chairs. Be sure to take your floor plan; most showrooms provide decorator service. Delivery takes two to five days. Add 8.25% sales tax and 5% fire insurance to the monthly rates.

Furniture

- **AFR The Furniture Rental People**, 711 Third Avenue at 44th Street, 212-867-2800, open 9 to 6, closed Sunday. While AFR prices each piece individually, the items listed above would cost a minimum of $300 a month for three months, and $150 a month for six months to a year. Delivery is $150 round-trip, and a deposit of one month's rent plus a two-month security fee is required.

- **I.S. Furniture Rentals**, 49 West 23rd Street, 212-924-4800 or 800-255-6651, 9 to 5, closed Saturday and Sunday. Rentals here are by the piece. Our selection would cost between $100 and $200 a month, depending on the items chosen and the length of the contract. First month's rental in advance plus two months' security. There is a one-time fee of $95 for delivery and pickup.

- **International Furniture Rentals**, 345 Park Avenue, entrance on Lexington Avenue between 51st and 52nd Streets, 212-421-0340, open 9 to 6, 10 to 2 Saturday, closed Sunday. The price spread quoted for our one-bedroom apartment reflects quality differences: from $119 to $500 a month. Delivery is $80 each way. One-and-a-half month's rent required as a deposit.

Air Conditioners

- **A A B C O Amber Corp.**, 1594 York Avenue, 212-535-9578 or 212-734-5777. Average cost per unit for the hot season (May through mid-October) is $200, service included. Specifics depend on room size and BTU requirements. AE, MC, V.

- **Ace Air Conditioning Service Corp.**, 24-81 47th Street, Astoria, Queens, 212-406-2256 from Manhattan. Room size determines the cost of the unit: approximately $175 for a bedroom, $245 for a living room. Price includes delivery, removal and service, if required. MC, V.

- **Columbus Air Conditioning Center**, 529 Columbus Avenue, 212-496-2626. Rentals run $145 to $300 depending on the BTUs required, May through mid-October. Service and delivery are included. AE, MC, V.

House Cleaning

Word of mouth is your best bet for finding a cleaning person (women have no monopoly on the profession here). Ask friends and neighbors if they know of someone with a few hours available. If this doesn't work, you might try one of the services. The hourly rates quoted include dusting, changing linens, mopping, vacuuming, laundry, cleaning bathrooms and washing dishes. The same firms provide specialists to handle floor waxing, washing walls and other heavy duty jobs at higher fees. As noted above under Baby Sitters, the Irish Echo in its classified ads is also a place to look for house-cleaning personnel.

- **Lend-A-Hand, Inc.**, 200 West 72nd Street, 212-362-8200. Housecleaning is one of the many services provided by this agency's actors, musicians and dancers. The rate is $14 per hour, plus a $15 finder's fee, for one person, whose references are checked before going out on a job.

- **Maid in NY**, 200 Park Avenue South, 212-777-6000. Homes as well as industrial sites and business offices are serviced by some 100 employees, who currently work for $12 an hour (four-hour minimum) plus $2.50 for transportation. Times and schedules are arranged to suit the client: weekly, bi-weekly or just once for a thorough spring cleaning.

- **Maids Unlimited**, Flatiron Services, 230 East 93rd Street, 212-369-9100. $54 for four-hour minimum, $13.50 each additional hour in Manhattan. For regular service, the same person would be sent if possible. One or two days' notice required. Help is bonded. Maid uses your supplies.

Mail, Telephone and Beepers

You haven't found an apartment yet, or are out of town frequently and want to keep in touch. Telephone answering services either answer your own phone or assign you a number. Mail receiving agencies or "mail centers" hold or forward mail, receive and ship packages. Beepers keep you in touch with the telephone away from a telephone; they are also more affordable than cellular service.

NYNEX Call Forwarding allows you to use your own phone number with an answering service. You connect your phone to the answering service by dialing 72 plus the service number; to disconnect when you return, dial 73. The one-shot installation charge is $16; the carrying charge is $4.15 a month for residential use. Using an answering service-provided number you avoid installation and carrying charges and can begin receiving messages the day you sign up. In either case, the phone is answered and the message conveyed to you by a human being.

Elect service 24 hours a day, seven days a week or during business hours only (9 to 5 or 8 to 6, Monday through Friday). Monthly fees include a specified number of messages; additional messages cost about 50¢ each. Expect to pay the answering company about $70 a month for 24-hour service or $50 for service during business hours only, in addition to which there may be a one-time set-up charge of about $10. Voice mail service (recorded messages, no human bodies) after a set-up fee of about $20 runs at least $15 per month for 100 calls, with perhaps 15 cents charged for each extra call.

Some telephone answering services also offer mail service but you may prefer to use a mail service close to your home. Mail boxes rent from about $82 (including tax and $10 key deposit) for a standard size box for four months to $288 total for a large box for 12 months. Mail services will also forward and ship mail and typically offer fax and copy service.

Check the Yellow Pages under "Mail Receiving Services" and "Telephone Answering Services" for more comprehensive lists.

Beeper service, indispensable to doctors, photographers, drug dealers, and those on the go who need to be in touch, can be arranged in several ways. First, you buy a beeper/pager at an electronics store (see the Tuesday Times, the Yellow Pages or walk down the street); it will cost from $20 to $200, depending on its range and whether it is numeric, giving you simply the number of your caller, or alpha/numeric, giving you a message. At some stores the beeper will be activated on the spot for a one-time fee, generally about $20; you will be assigned a beeper number to give expected callers and you will pay for the first four months to two years. Numeric service costs from $6.50 to $12 a month, depending on length of payment in advance; an 800 number, giving access to long-distance callers, if available, will cost extra. Alpha/numeric service allows for an 800 number at no extra cost, and runs from $20 to $25 a month. Other stores, such as The Wiz chain, sell you the beeper, and you call the service which handles their equipment for activation and billing. Some telephone answering services also offer beeper service, but it is likely to cost more. Most beeper services cover the better part of the tri-state area.

Computer Repairs

Of course, you always back up your files. So when the crash comes...well, you know. But that won't save you from unscrupulous computer repair shops. Stories abound, but in fact there are reliable repair shops out there. We list a few which New York Magazine rated highly. First, a few guidelines. If you have a problem with your computer, call the repair shop first and describe the problem; a good shop may be able to talk you through a diagnosis and a self repair. Before taking the computer in, ask if there is a diagnostic fee, and if that fee will be deducted from the work done. Some shops do not charge a diagnostic fee. Ask if the shop stocks spare parts, what the cost of repairs is likely to be and get an assurance they will do no work until it is authorized. If the technician seems vague or intimidating, call someone else.

- **ABC Computer Services**, 14 East 40thStreet, 212-725-3511
- **Ampex Service Center**, 229 East 53rd Street, 212-593-2425
- **CompUSA, 420 Fifth Avenue**, 212-782-7775
- **Machattan**, 381 Park Avenue South, 212-545-7171, Macintosh only
- **Macvision**, 239 East 5th Street, 212-586-8445, Macintosh only
- **Tekserve**, 163 West 23rd Street, 212-929-3645, Macintosh only

Moving and Storage

Disagreeable moving experiences aren't obligatory but they do happen, and it's difficult to know where to begin listing moving companies. So, with the exception of a couple of storage companies and a few mini-warehouses that might be helpful to know about, we've dispensed with listing names in this section. The State Department of Transportation (DOT) says most people use the Yellow Pages to find a mover; you can consult the Village Voice classified for short hauls. Whoever you use, make sure they are certified.

Instead of a list of moving companies, we'll begin by describing what two government regulatory agencies, the New York State Department of Transportation and the Federal Interstate Commerce Commission (ICC), can do for you.

Interstate movers are licensed by the ICC, intrastate companies by the DOT. Neither agency gives out names, but if you call the ICC, 212-264-1072, or the DOT Motor Carrier Investigations Bureau, 718-732-4810, they'll tell you if the mover is licensed.

Before a move takes place, the ICC requires interstate movers to furnish clients with a copy of When You Move, Your Rights and Responsibilities prepared by the Commission. To receive these guidelines before hiring a mover, call the New York Office of the ICC, 212-264-1072, and they'll send you one.

After the move, if there has been a problem, call the appropriate agency to find out how to proceed. The ICC and the DOT can provide assistance only when you use a certified mover. Hire an unlicensed firm and you're on your own in case of damage or loss.

Storage facilities may be required when you have to ship your furniture without an apartment to receive it or if your apartment is too small for all your belongings. The New York City Department of Consumer Affairs licenses storage—but not self-storage—warehouses. Dissatisfied? Call the city's all-purpose complaint number, 212-487-4398.

Storage Warehouses

- **Approved Moving and Storage**, 718-622-2660, has a fireproof warehouse in Brooklyn. Charges are 20¢ a cubic foot per month, plus a one-shot warehouse handling charge that amounts to one month's storage. Estimates are based on the number of rooms of furniture and household goods you'll be storing.

- **The Seven Santini Bros.**, 201-340-8210, has a warehouse for the storage of household goods at 141 Lanza Avenue, Garfield, NJ 07026. The Manhattan warehouse is for fine arts storage only.

Self-Storage Companies

The ability to rent anything from 3 foot by 3 foot lockers to small storage rooms is a great boon to urban dwellers. Collectors, people with old clothes they can't bear to give to thrift shops and those with possessions that won't fit in a sublet or shared apartment all find mini-warehouses a solution to too-small living spaces.

Rates for space in Manhattan self-storage (you or your mover get the goods there) facilities are competitive: expect to pay about $55 a month for a locker 4' by 4' by 7', $90 a month for an 8' by 8' by 8' space, and so on. If you're looking for lower rates, check the prices for storage units located in the suburbs and boroughs other than Manhattan.

- **Keepers III**, 212-924-8484, has locations at 43 Clarkson Street near Houston Street, 444 East 10th Street between Avenues C and D, and at 2577 Forest Avenue on Staten Island. Prices at the East Side location are slightly less than those on the West Side and Staten Island.

- **Manhattan Mini Storage**, 212-786-7243 and 212-255-0482, with locations at 520 West 17th Street corner of Tenth Avenue, 600 West 58th Street corner of Eleventh Avenue and 570 Riverside Drive corner of 134th Street, offer private storage rooms from 5' by 5' to 10' by 25' (the size of some NYC studio apartments).

- **U-Haul Moving and Storage** has a mini-warehouse located at 562 West 23rd Street, 212-620-4177, with rooms 4' by 8' for $40 and 8' by 12' for $120, as well as facilities in Brooklyn, The Bronx and Queens.

For other names and addresses in the burgeoning self-storage field, check the Yellow Pages under "Moving & Storage —Self Service."

Lesbian and Gay Concerns

In a city with large and established lesbian and gay communities, there are many organizations, businesses and publications which address their various needs and interests—too many to detail here. We mention one important umbrella organization and one publication as starting points.

- **The Lesbian & Gay Community Services Center**, 208 West 13th Street, NYC 10011, 212-620-7310, is just that, and the services it offers in a 150-year-old former schoolhouse in Greenwich Village seven days a week are myriad. Besides cultural and recreational offerings and events galore there is alcohol and substance abuse counseling; adoption and parenting support for lesbians and gay men; a gender identity project; a variety of HIV/AIDS-related services, support groups, counseling and bereavement support; couples mediation; and public policy programs, among others. Social events, of course. And Center Orientation provides newcomers to the city "a map of New York's organized lesbian and gay community."

- *Gay USA,* by George Hobica, in its New York chapter provides gay men with a concise and entertaining introduction to the city.

Resources and Services for People With Disabilities

Living in New York City with a disability has never been easy, but after passage of the federal Americans with Disabilities Act (ADA) in 1990, it began to get easier as the city began to address the needs of the disabled more seriously. Increasingly, street curbs were restructured to become wheel-chair accessible, as did public buildings. Following are some of the services, organizations and resources which make life safer, easier and more pleasant for people with disabilities.

Getting Around

- **Buses** All buses operated by the Metropolitan Transit Authority (MTA) are wheelchair-accessible, with lifts at the rear door. Reduced fare for seniors and customers with disabilities means a bus ride costs 75 cents one way, using tokens or the pre-paid plastic MetroCard. To get the reduced fare card and for more information, call 212-878-9274, or for the deaf or hearing impaired, 878-7622 (TTY).

- **Subway** Accessible Transfer Points within the New YorkCity Subway, a pamphlet of the MTA, lists all the subway stations and transfer points in the system which are wheelchair-accessible by elevator, with a map of the system. Reduced fare by token or MetroCard as described above applies to the city's subway system as well, and to the Staten Island Ferry, the Long Island and Metro-North Railroads, except at morning peak hours. The pamphlet, also in large type and on audiotape, is available from Customer Assistance, MTA NYC Transit, 370 Jay Street, 8th Floor, Brooklyn, NY 11201, or by calling 718-330-3322.

- **ACCESS-A-RIDE**, administered by the MTA through contracts with private carriers, provides rides for customers who are unable to use city bus or subway service for some or all of their trips. Customers call in advance, or subscribe for transportation on a regular basis, to ride Monday through Friday 6 a.m. to 6 p.m., Saturdays and Sundays 10 to 6. The one-way fare is the same as is charged for buses and subways, and accompanying Personal Care Attendants ride free. For more information or to obtain an application contact ACCESS-A-RIDE, Paratransit Division, New York City Transit, 10 Columbus Circle, 17th Floor, NYC 10019, 718-694-358l or TTY 718-722-4403.

- **Parking Permits for People with Disabilities (PPPD)** The city Department of Transportation issues two types of permits for citizens with disabilities: the New York State permit, which allows the driver to park in spaces marked by the International Symbol of Access, which in the city are all off-street in parking lots; and the NYC permit, which allows the driver to park on city streets in all No Parking and restricted parking zones. For more information and to request an application for either or both permits write: Parking Permits for People with Disabilities (PPPD), NYC Department of Transportation, 28-11 Queens Plaza North, 7th Floor, Long Island City, NY 11101-4008, or call 718-433-3100 and on pickup push the # key, then 11, or for the deaf or hearing impaired, call TTY 718-433-3111.

Communication

The NYNEX Communications Center for People with Disabilities, 204 Second Avenue at 13th Street, NYC 10009, offers information, services and a variety of adaptive communications equipment necessary or useful to people with various disabilities. Some of these devices, such as enlarged number rings, are free; others, such as Weak Speech Handsets, may be rented, leased or purchased. The Teletypewriter Device for the Deaf, alternately referred to as TTY or TDD and available at cost through NYNEX, sends typewriten words over the phone lines to the New York Relay Center, from which special operators relay conversations verbally 24 hours a day. The service is confidential and free of charge, except for the cost of the call, and users get a 50% discount on the cost of NYNEX regional calls. Hearing callers to TTY users reverse the process, calling a number (below) from which a special relay operator types the message to the TTY recipient, etc. To qualify for this and other services you must be certified at the Center after providing an approved application and a letter from a doctor or an authorized social service agency.

- **NYNEX Communication Center for People with Disabilities**, 800-482-9020; TTY users call 800-342-4181.

- **New York Relay Center**, TTY 800-662-1220; others 800-421-1220

Other Resources

- **Andrew Heiskell Library for the Blind and Physically Handicapped**, 40 West 20th Street, 212-206-5400, TTY 212-206-5458. Wheel-chair accessible, it offers books in Braille and recorded books, an extensive collection of large-print books, print and non-print materials on disabilities, a Community Information Service collection on resources for people with disabilities, as well as recreational, cultural and service-oriented programming for and about people with disabilities. Materials are for use on site or by postage-free mail to those who are home-bound, 212-621-0564, TTY 212-621-0553.

- **Associated Blind**, 135 West 23rd Street, NYC 10011, 212-255-1122, operate 205 apartments for the blind and wheelchair bound at this address, but there is a long waiting list. Non-resident blind also have access to social workers, recreation and the fitness center there.

- **Cinema Village**, 22 East 12th Street, call Maria Flores 718-899-8800 for information; and the Walter Reade Theater, 70 Lincoln Center Plaza at 67th Street, 875-5601, show first-run features with open captions for the deaf once a month. Call after 3 p.m. for details.

- **Con Edison Concern Program** for the hearing-impaired and sight-impaired, 800-872-8846, TTY 800-642-2308; Con Ed's Life Sustaining Equipment Program, 212-338-4806,

- **Hospital Audiences** Inc. (HAI), 220 West 42nd Street, 13th floor, NYC 10036, 212-424-4685, publishes the indispensable Access for All: A Guide to New York City Cultural Institutions for People with Disabilities, which lists 300 cultural venues accessible to the handicapped, including major galleries and historical monuments ($5). Their hotline, 888- HAI-HOTLINE, provides similar information, with hotels and restaurants as well.

- **International Center for the Disabled** (ICD), 340 East 24th Street, NYC 10010, 212-585-6250, TTY 212-585-6060, provides primary medical care, vocational evaluation, job training and placement for learning and physically disabled.

- **League for the Hard of Hearing**, 71 West 23rd Street, NYC 10010, 212-741-6067, services and provides hearing aids. Call for their resource manual, $5.

- **Learning Disabled HelpLine**, 212-645-6703.

- **The Lighthouse, Inc.**, 111 East 59th Street, NYC 10022, 212-821-9200, ext. 251, or 800-334-5497, provides vision rehabilitation and other services to the visually impaired. Services include readers, mobility training, computer training, career services, a child development center and adaptive skills classes.

- **Mayor's Office for People with Disabilities**, 52 Chambers Street, Room 206, NYC 10007,212-788-2830 or TTY 212-788-2838. For information and referrals.

- **Metropolitan Museum of Art**, 1000 Fifth Avenue at 81st Street, NYC 10028-0198, 212-879-5500 or TTY 212-570-3828. The museum is wheel-chair accessible and has programs with sign-language interpretation for the hearing impaired, guides by appointment only for the visually impaired, tours and programs for the developmentally disabled.

- **New York Able**, a monthly newspaper "Positively For, By & About the Disabled", with news, commentary, a calendar of events and ads of interest to people with disabilities. Write P.O. Box 395, Old Bethpage, NY 11804, or call 516-939-2253 or 718-792-3533.

- **New York Public Library Branches** (see also Andrew Heiskell Library, above) which are wheel-chair accessible include the Donnell Library Center, 20 West 53rd Street, 212-621-0618; the Library for the Performing Arts, 40 Lincoln Center Plaza at 65th Street, 212-870-1630; Mid-Manhattan Library, 455 Fifth Avenue at 40th Street, 212-340-0833; Science, Industry, and Business Library, 188 Madison Avenue at 34th Street, 212-592-7000; the Fordham

LibraryCenter, 2556 Bainbridge Avenue, The Bronx, 718-594-4244; and St. George Library Center, 5 Central Avenue, St. George, S.I., 718-442-8561, among others. Project ACCESS, by appointment at the Mid Manhattan, St. George and Fordham branches, uses Kurzweil Personal Readers to give sight-impaired readers access to the full range of the library services and materials. Other assistive technology, such as Braille writers, is available here and at some other branches. For information about these and other services call 212-340-0843, TTY 212-340-0931.

- **New York Society for the Deaf**, 817 Broadway at 11th Street, 7th Floor, NYC 10003, 212-777-3900, providing multiple services for the deaf.

- **Resources for Children With Special Needs**, 200 Park Avenue, NYC 10003, 212-677-4650. Comprehensive resources, and excellent.

- **Rusk Institute of Rehabilitation Medicine**'s driver training program, 400 East 34th Street, Room RR312, 212-263-6070. Their technicians evaluate the particular needs of prospective drivers with physical handicaps, adapting each car with special devices, and train the driver to operate the adapted car.

- **Technology Resource Center**, operated by United Cerebral Palsy of New York City, at 120 East 23rd Street, NYC 10010, 212-979-9700. You can come in to the demonstration center here to view, learn about and try a range of adaptive products and get information about others through a resource specialist and catalogues. Products range from adapted toys to augmentative communication devices, computers, home products and accessibility modifications.

- **Visions Services for the Blind and Visually Impaired**, 120 Wall Street, 16th Floor, NYC 10005, 212-425-2255, offers free and low-cost rehabilitation and social services to the blind and multi-handicapped, including those who are non-English speaking. Self-help audio guides at cost teach life skills, and there are peer support groups and recreation year-round at Vacation Camp for the Blind in Rockland County, transportation provided.

BIG city living encourages idiosyncratic life styles. The idea of proximity breeding privacy seems contradictory, but in New York City that's the way it works. Freed from small-community pressures to pay token respect to values not necessarily shared, New Yorkers pursue their interests and goals singularly unencumbered by considerations as to "what the neighbors might think." Home decoration is a striking case in point. Anything (within the terms of the lease) goes, and while stingy with space, when it comes to providing all the goods and services necessary for us to feather our wildly divergent, albeit mainly minuscule, nests, the city really comes through for its residents. Generally speaking, there are at least three approaches to shopping in Manhattan: 1) largish, fairly priced, standard sources; 2) famous signature shops and upscale boutiques; and 3) discounters and/or alternative resources such as wholesale districts and sample sales.

Note from the shopping strategies department: unless you are literally sitting and sleeping on the floor of your new apartment, it pays to wait until the annual winter furniture and housewares sales city-wide to make those major purchases. In both the department stores and the specialty shops the savings in January and February are considerable, 20% to 50% off. Watch for the ads in the Times. One final caveat. If the idea of shopping is appalling, there's always furniture rental. See the chapter on Helpful Services for a list of firms. Unless otherwise noted, all stores mentioned accept American Express, MasterCard and VISA.

Full Service Department Stores

As designer boutiques fragment row upon heretofore sensibly labeled row of merchandise into seemingly hundreds of glass-sheathed cubicles, one-stop shopping the full service store has lost cohesiveness but still beats 15 stops in a 20-block neighborhood. Although more difficult than it once was, it's comforting to take a 15-item list, silk pins through box springs, and pass the afternoon under one roof. So, we lead off with the royalty of New York's merchandise scene, listed alphabetically, before splintering into our own smaller sections.

- **Bloomingdale's**, Third Avenue at 59th Street, 355-5900, open 10 to 6:30, to 9 Thursday, 11 to 6 Sunday. AE, DC, MC, V, Bloomingdale's charge. Along with other mink-wrapped legends, Bloomingdale's has worked hard to achieve entertainer status and like all top stars, not content to rest on laurels, sets trends and discards old routines as it tears along. But for all the zap and glitter, Bloomie's has a sturdy core; you can leave your watch for repair, order Christmas cards, shop the best white sales in town January and August, buy a TV, a mattress and sweat socks as well as try out glittery red Dorothy of Oz shoes to a funky beat, arrange an assignation over Izod shirts or nosh the food of the moment at one of five chic cafes. Services include Beatrice Dale personal shoppers (705-2380) and translators, a bridal registry, decorators, and 24-hour telephone order service.

- **Lord & Taylor**, Fifth Avenue at 39th Street, 391-3344, open 10 to 7:00 Monday through Thursday, to 6:30 Friday and Saturday, noon to 6 Sunday. AE, Lord & Taylor's charge. The trim, self-confident customers here, dressed in "updated contemporary classics" and often found around the Soup Bar on Ten sipping vichyssoise in summer, Scotch broth in winter, tend to mirror the American look championed by the store. "Young American" designers on Six and the model rooms on Eight displaying a substantial collection of contemporary American furnishings are among the current darlings. Multilingual, the "Red Rose" personal shopping staff on Three handles international mail orders and, for an extra fee, a fashion adviser is available for counseling.

- **Macy's**, Broadway at 34th Street, 695-4400, open 10 to 8:30 Monday, Thursday and Friday, to 7 Tuesday, Wednesday and Saturday, 11 to 6 Sunday. AE, MC, V, Macy's charge. Enormous! Complete! And can it be overwhelming! First-timers take advantage of the multilingual information booths and descriptive giveaway location maps at first floor information booths. Others use Macy's Buy Appointment, the personal shopping service, and the 24-hour telephone ordering service, 800-528-6602. A total revamp of the beloved behemoth began at the basement level with the creation of the superb Cellar, a bazaar-like warren of individual food and homewares shops, and moved skyward as each floor was completely redone with pizzazz and flair. A merchandising tour de force and, equally miraculous, the sales help's attitude and quality of service has improved beyond belief.

- **Macy's** (formerly A & S), 420 Fulton Street, Brooklyn, 718-875-7200, open 9:45 to 6, to 7 Monday, to 9 Thursday, noon to 5 Sunday. AE, MC, V, A & S charge. Talk about full service! Lucky Brooklyn residents need travel no further than the Hoyt Street stop on the #2 or #3 train for practically any nicety or necessity. Macy's has both an optometrist and a podiatrist on duty and a fur storage and restyling service. From

TVs, furniture and electronics on the Lower Level to fabric on Six, this rather reserved no-nonsense institution also heeds the latest fashions with up-to-the-minute styles from leading designers on Three.

- **Saks Fifth Avenue**, 611 Fifth Avenue at Rockefeller Center, 753-4000, open 10 to 6:30, to 8 Thursday, noon to 6 Sunday. AE, DC, MC, V, Saks charge. Carefully coifed customers, self-assured and tan, and elaborate bouquets spraying nonchalantly into the glowing, wood-paneled aisles characterize Saks Fifth Avenue. So do the most refined escalators in New York. They float you silently past eight well-lit shopping floors against a backdrop of perfectly placed plants, mirrors and pinky-beige marble Luxurious Saks exudes well-being from every tasteful counter. Faced with the largest selection of Vuitton luggage in town, a Revillon fur boutique and the stylish men's department on Six, you may forget that Saks harbors a useful set of shops along 49th and 50th Streets. Housewares, luggage, bathing suits and sportswear, the bath and linen shop and the art gallery all have private entrances. Recently, the store has made a fetish of personalized service. The Fifth Avenue Club, 753-4000, ext. 4200, on Three shelters five personal shopping services, among them the Executive Service for women executives.

- **Stern's**, Avenue of the Americas at 32nd Street, 212-244-6060, open 10 to 8 Monday, Thursday and Friday, to 7 Tuesday, Wednesday and Saturday, 11 to 6 Sunday. AE, MC, V and Stern's card. Like a smaller, more restrained Macy's, Stern's opens onto and backs up Manhattan Plaza, a gleaming chrome-and-glass vertical mall in midtown. Float up to Six in a theatrically-lit glass bubble elevator at the edge of the soaring mall atrium, choose from a gaggle of fast-food eateries for lunch, walk back into electronics, home furnishings, and housewares (no major appliances, however), and drift down the escalator through wearing apparel and jewelry to toys and children's clothes below ground level. It's not chic, but the clothes are au courant and reasonably priced. Adjoining boutiques stacked around the mall offer books to records to toys to ski equipment as the bubbles rise and fall. It's Trump Tower downtown (and downscale).

Discount Stores

- **Century 21**, 22 Cortlandt Street (across from the World Trade Center), 227-9092 and 472 86th Street, Bay Ridge, Brooklyn, 718-748-3266, open 7:45 to 7:30 Monday through Friday, 10 to 7:30 Saturday. Not the nationwide real estate broker but something that is unique to New York City—a full service department store where everything is discounted. There are many real bargains here and the service is pleasant and no-nonsense. Beware: the Manhattan store can be a zoo especially around Christmas-time.

Appliances, Electronics, Cameras

These three categories have been lumped together because many of the stores listed below cross merchandise lines.

- **Macy's** is the only full service department stores which sells washing machines, stoves and other major appliances.

- **Willoughby's Camera Store**, 110 West 32nd Street, 564-1600, open 9 to 7, to 8 Thursday, 10 to 6 Sunday. Phone quotes. Complete rental and service departments complement the most extensive new and used photographic stock in the city. Willoughby's also has a computer department.

Specialty Shops

- **Alkit Camera Shop**, 866 Third Avenue between 52nd and 53rd Streets, 832-2101, open 7:30 to 6:30, 9 to 5 Saturday. "Generally" gives phone quotes. Full video and stereo line but fame rests on the quality and quantity of the professional and amateur cameras and other photographic equipment offered, as well as Alkit's custom order department and rental and repair services.

- **Innovative Audio**, 150 East 58th Street between Lexington and Third Avenues, 619-6400; and 77 Clinton Street, Brooklyn Heights, 718-596-0888, open 10:30 to 7, Thursday to 9, Saturday to 6, Sunday noon to 5. Opening in 1997, the Manhattan store is perhaps a bit higher end, though both stores offer the full range of quality equipment. The home theater demo setup for projectors and surround sound at the new site is especially advanced. Noted for their user friendliness.

- **Lyric High Fidelity**, 1221 Lexington Avenue at 83rd Street, 535-5710, open 10 to 6, noon to 5 Sunday. "Only the finest stereo components." A strong selection of speakers.

- **Sound by Singer**, 18 East 16th Street, 924-8600, open 10 to 6, to 8 Tuesday and Thursday, noon to 5 Sunday. High-end audio equipment and an extremely knowledgeable sales staff. Specializes in American brands.

Discount Stores

The Lower East Side doesn't have a monopoly on good buys. Appliances and electronics are sold all over the city at less than retail. A few of the many discounters in Manhattan:

- **ABC Trading Co.**, 31 Canal Street near Essex, 228-5080, open 10 to 6, to 1 p.m. Friday, closed Saturday. No credit cards. No phone quotes. Photographic equipment, small as well as major appliances, audio equipment and supplies, TVs and VCRs. ABC's special department for merchandise adapted to cycles and broadcast standards found throughout the world is a favorite of UN personnel and others living overseas.

- **Cambridge Camera Exchange**, Seventh Avenue and West 13th Street, 675-8600, open 9 to 6, 10 to 3 Sunday, closed Saturday. MC, V, Discover. No phone quotes. Complete photographic line, mostly mail order (free catalog) but good buys available to the walk-in trade.

- **Goodman Electronics**, 37 Essex Street near Grand, 673-3220, open 9:30 to 5:30, closed Saturday. AE, MC, V. No phone quotes. Name-brand luggage, dishes, calculators, hair dryers, TVs, radios and lots, lots more.

- **J&R Music World**, 31 Park Row across from City Hall for audio-video hardware and 27 Park Row for kitchen and small personal appliances and fitness equipment, 238-9000, open 9 to 6:30 Monday through Saturday, Sunday 11 to 6. It's definitely not all music, though their stereo selection is perhaps the best among the discounters. This string of outlets along Park Row also draws shoppers from all over for CDs, cameras, camcorders, cellular phones, television and video equipment, home office equipment, computer hardware and software (see Computers).

- **Uncle**, 343 Canal Street near Church, 226-4010, open 10 to 7 every day. Stereos, TVs, camcorders, radios, car sound systems.

- **Vendome**, 345 Seventh Avenue at 29th Street, 279-3333, open 8:30 to 5:30, 11 to 3 Saturday, closed Sunday. All major credit cards. Phone quotes. A member of a cooperative buying group that has its own warehouse, Vendome sells air conditioners, washing machines and other major, as well as small, appliances, computers, TVs and stereos. Major credit cards on small appliances but not on electronic equipment.

- **Nobody Beats The Wiz**, 12 West 45th Street, 302-2000, 404 Sixth Avenue, 677-2100, 726 Broadway, 475-1700, are three of the many city locations. Open 10 to 10, to 8 Saturday, 11 to 5 Sunday. No phone quotes. Their claim: "no one goes lower" on stereo, small electronics and TV prices.

Alternative Sources

Head to **lower First Avenue** for discounts on brand name appliances. Try both **Gringer & Sons** at 29 First Avenue at Second Street, 475-0600, and **Bloom & Krup**, 504 East 14th Street between Avenues A and B (for years at First and 12th Street), 673-2760, for bargain prices on dishwashers, freezers, refrigerators and stoves. Garland, SubZero, Traulsen, GE, KitchenAid and European manufacturers such as Gaggenau and Miele, among others, are in stock or can be ordered.

Beds and Bedding

Department stores can take care of all your bedding needs under one roof. Lay in supplies during January and August, traditional White Sale months. **Bloomingdale's** becomes particularly generous at these times, stocking irregular Martex towels and name brand sheets at great savings.

Specialty Shops

- **Ad Hoc Softwares**, 410 West Broadway at Spring Street, 925-2652, open 11:30 to 7, to 6 Sunday. The high tech bed and bathroom furnishings displayed in this lightstruck corner store are softened by the inclusion of a few more traditional, even old fashioned, lines. Pale blue and rose French Jacquard hand towels, napkins and placemats and Carpe Diem lace curtains and lampshades add a little romance to Ad Hoc's own somber, rather austere collection of all-cotton sheets and to bed linens by international manufacturers including Wamsutta, Palais Royale and Castelini

- **Arise Futon**, 265 West 72nd Street, 212-496-8410, open 11-7 Monday to Saturday, until 8 on Thursday, 12-5 on Sunday. You'll find a large and reasonably priced selection of futons, frames, pillows and covers.

- **Bed & Bath & Beyond**, 620 Sixth Avenue, 255-3550, as the name declares, this popular (and affordable) newcomer to the Manhattan bedding scene, has almost everything for your household needs.

- **Carlyle Custom Convertibles**, main store 1056 Third Avenue near 62nd Street, 838-1525; studio collection at 1375 Third Avenue near 79th Street, 570-2236, and Chelsea collection at 122 West 18th Street between Sixth and Seventh Avenues, 675-3212; open 10 to 7 Monday through Friday, Saturday to 6, Sunday 12 to 5. Quality custom-made sofas in a variety of fairly conservative styles and fabrics. Allow four to six weeks for delivery.

- **Castro Convertibles**, main store, 43 West 23rd Street, 255-7000, open 10 to 7, to 9 Monday and Thursday, to 7 Saturday, 11 to 6 Sunday; branch, 51 East 34th Street, 679-6099, open 10 to 6 seven days a week. First major distributor of the time-honored (since WW II anyhow) sofa bed solution for a one-room apartment.

- **Dixie Foam**, 104 West 17th Street, 645-8999, open 10 to 6, closed Sunday. In this factory/showroom, 4" and 5 1/2" thick foam mattresses are the forte. Choose standard sizes or have irregular sizes cut and covered to order.

- **Gracious Home**, 1217 Third Avenue between 69th and 70th Streets, 988-8990, open 8 to 7, Saturday 9 to 7, Sunday 10 to 6. Imported linens for the Upper East Side, bathware, fabrics, stationary and giftware. Free gift wrapping and delivery in Manhattan, not to mention phone orders.

- **Jennifer Convertibles**, largest store, 1530 Second Avenue at 79th Street, 535-1242; other stores: 1014 Second Avenue at 54th Street, 751-1720; 404 Park Avenue South at 28th Street, 532-4697; 750 Broadway at 8th Street, 677-1539; 1770 Broadway at 57th Street, 581-1559; 2424 Broadway at 89th Street, 787-8507; and 206 Eighth Avenue at 20th Street, 924-8828; also in Brooklyn at 142 Montague Street, 718-852-3400, 280 Livingston Street at Bond Street, 718-643-8581, and 498 Fifth Avenue at 12th Street, 718-788-8119; and in Jersey City, Hudson Mall at Route 440, 201-451-2211; open 10 to 9, to 6 Saturday, noon to 5 Sunday. AE, MC, V. No question, stores in this chain, which bills itself "America's largest sofa bed specialist", have the city's biggest selection of relatively inexpensive convertible sofas, including Sealy and Simmons models.

Alternative Sources

Household linens on the **Lower East Side** are squooshed into two blocks on Grand Street between Allen and Forsyth. An uptown look has intruded on the cramjammed bargain basement fustiness always considered de riguer in the city's most raffish bazaar area. The uninitiated will find comparatively sleek Harris Levy, 278 Grand, 226-3102, and Homeworks Design (this trendy name would have been unthinkable a few years ago), 281 Grand, 226-4644, easier to take, but the same Laura Ashley, Marimekko, Martex, Wamsutta, Cannon and Stevens lines are handled by Ezra Cohen, 307 Grand, 925-7800, and other unreconstructed firms along Grand. All closed Saturday, open Sunday. Department store White Sale prices match those you're likely to find on the Lower East Side but, if you avoid the Sunday crush, you'll discover sales personnel often more knowledgeable and helpful than their uptown counterparts.

- **ABC Carpet & Home**, 888 Broadway at East 19th Street, 473-3000, open 10 to 7, to 8 Monday and Thursday, to 6 Saturday, 11 to 6 Sunday. It's certainly not just carpets anymore, but "the ultimate in home furnishings adventure": uptown imported and domestic designer lines, spreads and towelings at downtown prices, along with a fetching array of country furniture, folk art objects, decorative pieces and scatter pillows. Now there's crystal, earthenware, Limoges, bone china and flatware as well and The Parlour Cafe to sink into for refueling when energy flags.

- **Dial-A-Mattress**, showroom at 31-10 48th Avenue, Long Island City, 11101, 800-628-8737. Checks and all major credit cards. But you don't go there, unless you want to try out a mattress, or look at their bedding, sofa beds, frames or accessories. Simply dial, 24 hours a day, and a bedding consultant will help you choose among discounted Sealy, Simmons, Certa or Spring Air mattresses according to size, firmness and price range. Delivery ($19 to $39) is within 24 hours, on approval, with a 36-day comfort exchange (softer or firmer). It's hard to beat for the busy.

- **Kleinsleep**, 962 Third Avenue at 58th Street, 755-8201, open 10 to 7, 11 to 6 Sunday. Remainders from the six-store chain's extensive line of innerspring and foam mattresses and beds of all shapes and sizes are sold in the clearance center downstairs.

- **J. Schacter Corp.**, 5 Cook Street, Williamsburg, Brooklyn, 718-384-2100, open 10-5 Monday to Thursday, 10-1 Friday, Sunday by appointment only, closed Saturday. MC, V. New York's leading feather merchants, famous for standard and custom-made pillows and comforters in various mixes of feathers and down and for reprocessing and cleaning already fabricated down bedding and garments.

- **Soho Mill Outlet**, 490 Broadway at Broome, 226-0656, open 10 to 6 Monday through Wednesday, to 7 Thursday and Friday, 11 to 7 Saturday, to 6 Sunday. No effort is made to disguise the manufacturing past of this second-floor loft space, where manufacturers' closeouts in bedding and towelings are the main attraction. Down and feather pillows, duvets and cotton duvet covers way off-price are worth the trip, as are an assortment of cotton sheets, towels, scatter pillows and terry cloth items.

Carpets and Rugs

For an overview, check the department stores, in particular **Macy's** for broadlooms and **Bloomingdale's** for imports.

- **Einstein Moomjy Inc.**, 150 East 58th Street, 758-0900, open 9:30 to 6:30, to 8 Monday and Thursday, noon to 5 Sunday. At this self-described "Rug Department Store" located in the Architects and Designers Building, the very best broadlooms share floor space with luminous Orientals as well as domestic and imported carpets of all kinds. Don't worry about missing an Einstein Moomjy sale: newspapers and TV are flooded with ads.

Specialty Shops

Oriental rug dealers are concentrated on, but by no means limited to, **Madison Avenue** from 57th Street up past the Carlyle Hotel as far as

86th Street. **A. Beshar & Co. Inc.**, 611 Broadway, Room 405, 288-1998, not only sells Orientals but is a cleaning specialist of top repute. In **Brooklyn, D. Kalfaian & Son**, 475 Atlantic Avenue between Third Avenue and Nevins Street, cleans and repairs Orientals as well as selling them; watch for their annual unclaimed Orientals sale.

Discount Stores

- **ABC Carpet & Home**, carpets at 881 Broadway at East 19th Street, rugs across the street at 888 Broadway, 473-3000, open 10 to 7, to 8 Monday and Thursday, to 6 Saturday, 11 to 6 Sunday. An overwhelming selection of broadlooms from all the mills. The rug store carries new imports and, down in the basement, an in-depth stock of carpet remnants at bargain prices. As noted above under Beds and Bedding, you can furnish your home at ABC after you carpet it.

- **Central Carpet**, 426 Columbus Avenue between 80th and 81st Streets, 787-8813, and 81 Eighth Avenue at 14th Street, 741-3700, open 10 to 7, Thursday to 8, 10 to 6 Saturday, 11 to 6 Sunday. For over 50 years, Central has been supplying New Yorkers with antique and semi-antique Oriental rugs—from earthy Kilims to elegant Kashans. Go upstairs for more mundane mill ends and discounted broadlooms. The downtown store, resplendent in a landmarked former bank building, has a larger selection of machine-made rugs and wall-to wall carpeting, and all but the smallest rugs are hanging, not stacked.

- **The Rug Warehouse, Inc.**, 220 West 80th Street at Broadway, 787-6665, open 10 to 6, Thursday, 11 to 5 Sunday. Discounted semi-antique and antique rugs fill a barn-like space above a vitamin store on the Upper West Side.

Alternative Sources

Carpets and rugs also turn up at thrift shops, auctions and flea markets. See Home Furnishings for details.

Computers and Software

Personal computers can be bought in a variety of places comparatively cozy neighborhood centers to barn-like discount warehouses. Many outlets offer courses as well as literature on the subject. For an overview of current prices and trends, check the Science section of the Tuesday edition of *The New York Times,* where the weekly computer columns are flanked by ads for hardware, software and allied services.

- **CompUSA**, 450 Fifth Avenue at 37th Street, 764-6224, and 1775 Broadway at 57th Street, 262-9711, open 9 to 8 Monday through Friday, 10 to 7 Saturday, and noon to 6 Sunday. Astonishing, this hardware/software supermarket, 26,000 square feet of PCs, laser printers, modems, "scuzzys" and "gooeys," joysticks and trackballs, and, yes, the latest games. The enthusiastic help can talk techie, but the computer-challenged may feel more comfortable at a smaller, more personal computer shop. CompUSA also offers many courses, from PC fundamentals to advanced graphics.

• **J&R Computer World**, 15 Park Row across from City Hall, 349-4727, open 9 to 6:30 Monday through Saturday, 11 to 6 Sunday. A knowledgeable sales staff and a showroom with all the major computer hardware lines, including the latest Apple clones, available to try out, in stock and discounted have made this the largest single (non-chain, that is) computer store in the country. With some 40 different digital notebooks to try out among the PCs, accessories, peripherals, CD-ROM equipment and titles, software and digital cameras, it's a techie playground. They'll install your upgrades for you or repair your old PC. Call for a catalogue, and if you know what you want, phone order, 800-221-8180.

• **Personal Computer Power Center**, 1650 Broadway at 51st Street, 315-0809 by appointment. Writers and other professional computer users who need occasional hand-holding, or at least guidance, with their systems swear by this former SoHo outfit, which went from retail to selling and consulting. For $75 to $100 a consultation they'll advise you on what you need, help you build a system and, if you like, sell you what you need. They also offer a consumers' guide course and a bookkeeping conversion course.

• **User Friendly**, 128 West 72nd Street, 580-4433; 200 East 83rd Street, 535-4100; and 401 Sixth Avenue at 8th Street, 675-2255, open 9 to 10 Monday through Thursday, 9 to 6 Friday, 11 to 7 Saturday, noon to 8 Sunday. Is your computer on the blink? Computer illiterates and literati can rent personal computers equipped with laser printers, scanners, modems, and graphic capabilities. Rates are calculated by the hour and functions used. A knowledgeable sales staff is on hand to lead you through any unfamiliar terrain with audio tutorials and advice, or, for a per-page rate, do the work for you.

Fabric—Decorating

Ringed around the **Decoration & Design Building**, 979 Third Avenue between 59th and 60th Streets, wholesale fabric showrooms marked "To The Trade Only" usually require shoppers to be accompanied by a decorator or to possess a decorator's card. No entree? Try the department stores or the retail fabric importers or discount merchants listed below, all of whom stock dress goods as well as slipcover, curtain and upholstery fabrics.

Specialty Shops

Retail Imports Fabrics identified with a specific nation form the basis for some of Manhattan's most enchanting retail outlets. You can buy yardage as well as decorative accents, clothes and accessories made from the goods featured at the following shops: **China Seas**, 979 Third Avenue, 752-5555, has few direct imports but a wide array of Orient-inspired patterns; **Handblock**, 487 Columbus Avenue between 83rd and 84th Streets, 799-4342, with hand-stamped and hand-woven Indian cottons and an outstanding Dhurrie rug selection; **Laura Ashley**, 714 Madison Avenue at 63rd Street, 735-5000, and at 79th Street and Columbus Avenue, 496-5110, displays three floors of furnishings, accessories and yardage in sprigged Victorian-style cottons.

Discount Stores

- **K Trimming & Zippers**, 519 Broadway at Spring, 212-431-8929, open 9:30 to 6. Dig through boxes stuffed with grommets, braids and hundreds of buttons for low, low prices on all the trimmings.

- **Samuel Beckenstein**, 125 Orchard Street, 212-475-4525, open 9 to 5:30, closed Saturday. Big selection, low prices for decorating fabrics, men's suiting, and dress fabrics.

- **Long Island Fabric**, 406 Broadway at Canal Street, 431-9510, open 9 to 6, to 7:30 Thursday, 10 to 5 Saturday and Sunday. MC, V. Right in the heart of the fabric jobbing district between SoHo and City Hall, this ramshackle three-story outlet houses notable bargains.

- **Paterson Silks**, 36 East 14th Street, 929-7861; 151 West 72nd Street, 874-9510; 152-154 East 86th Street, 722-4098, open Mondays and Thursdays 9 to 8, Tuesday, Wednesday, Friday and Saturday to 7, Sundays 10 to 5. Besides a wide selection of fabrics, this old standby specializes in custom draperies, slipcovers and re-upholstery. Shops in Flushing and Astoria as well. Call 800-522-5671 for shop-at-home decorating.

- **Silk Surplus, Inc.**, 223 East 58th Street, 753-6511, open 10 to 5:30, 11 to 4 Saturday, closed Sunday. MC, V. While noted for Scalamandre seconds, crewel-work, heavy embroideries and other elegant coverings, including silks, are stocked here at their new boutique in ABC Carpet and Home.

Alternative Sources

Mecca to home decorators and seamstresses are the Lower East Side fabric shops clustered on **Grand Street at the Eldridge Street intersection** (between Forsyth and Allen). These discount stores, like the household linen outlets adjacent, are open Sunday through Friday, closed on Saturday. Prices for the curtain, upholstery and slipcover fabrics in stock are almost always a better bargain than materials you select from the sample books. But these too are discounted. About half the stores have workshop facilities on premises. You'll find stellar names printed on the selvages of velvets, embroideries, cottons and tapestries: Brunschwig & Fils, Givenchy, Schumacher, and Stroheim & Roman were sighted. **Interiors by Royale**, 289 Grand Street, 753-4600; **Martin Albert Interiors**, 288 Grand Street, 226-4047; and **Harry Zarin Company**, 292 Grand Street, 925-6112, are among the shops to investigate.

Furniture

Antique furniture dealers (at least in their shops) tend to cluster. Rare pieces from the 17th, 18th and 19th centuries, the quality found at the Winter Antiques Show held late each January at the Seventh Regiment Armory, are most likely to be found in elegant shops along Madison Avenue north of 63rd Street. Increasingly, retail outlets for less prestigious pieces are infiltrating the wholesale "To The Trade Only" antique district located in the quadrant formed by University Place, Broadway, East 9th and East 12th Streets in the Village. Art Deco dealers and those specializing in the Depression era, in retro furniture and the now-fashionable Fifties clump together in SoHo. A handful of good sources can also be found in Greenwich Village. The more upscale antique stores, dealing mostly in Early American and French country furniture, line Bleecker west of Seventh Avenue.

Look for furniture sales post-Christmas. Those held by New York department stores at their warehouses in the boroughs and suburbs offer especially large savings for anyone with a car and enough stamina to brave the stampede.

- **Crate & Barrel**, 350 Madison Avenue, 308-0004, open 10 to 8, Saturday to 7, Sunday 12 to 6. Somewhat incongruously located at the base of a sleek office tower, this emporium of handsome, countryish furniture, dish and cookware, decorative items and linens is theme-decorated in natural pine which you can smell. The earthtones are muted, and reasonably priced glassware is extensive. It's affordable and stylish one-stop home furnishing.

- **The Door Store**, 1 Park Avenue at 33rd Street, 679-9700; other stores: 1201 Third Avenue at 70th Street, 772-1110; 123 West 17th Street west of Sixth Avenue, 627-1515; 130 Cedar Street off West Street, 267-1250; all open 9:30 or 10 to 5:45 or 6, later Monday and Thursday, noon to 4:45 or 5 Sunday; 1 Carlton Avenue, Brooklyn, 718-596-1938, open 9 to 4:30, noon to 4 Sunday. AE, MC, V. An excellent source of reasonably priced contemporary furniture, especially desks, wall units, chairs and tables in oak, teak and pine—but no doors. Their sales are well worth watching for.

• **IKEA**, 1000 Center Street, Elizabeth, NJ, 908-289-4488, open 10 to 9 Monday through Saturday, 10 to 6 Sunday; Broadway Mall, Hicksville, Long Island, 516-681-4532, same hours as NJ, except on Sundays when it is open 11 to 7. Those without wheels can take the LIRR from Penn Station to the Hicksville station; or call 800-287-4532 for details about the bus service from Mid-town to the Elizabeth location. Borrow a car, if you can, to stock up on inexpensive pine dressers, kitchen tables, beds, all designed Swedish-style with clean lines and natural materials. Pick up sheets, glasses, wallpaper, lamps and more—for less. At the Jersey store have a Swedish meatball lunch for less than $5 in IKEA's spacious, clean (if slightly antiseptic) cafeteria, also open for breakfast and dinner. IKEA does not accept American Express but they do accept Visa, MasterCard, Discover as well as personal checks. Delivery is available.

• **Jensen-Lewis**, 89 Seventh Avenue at 15th Street, 929-4880, open 10 to 7, to 8 Thursday, noon to 5:30 Sunday. Famous for deck chairs, satchels, backpacks and other canvas products in lots of zippy colors. In big, bright quarters puffy sofas and easy chairs, beds and an expanding housewares department fill the showroom as canvas seems to recede as Jensen-Lewis' bag.

• **Maurice Villency**, 200 Madison Avenue at 35th Street, 725-4840, open 10 to 6, to 9 Monday and Thursday, noon to 5 Sunday. If sleek and modern, embellished with glass and brass, is the look you favor, then head for this sparkling showroom where furniture lines exclusive to Maurice Villency are displayed.

• **Workbench**, main store, 470 Park Avenue South at 32nd Street, 481-5454; other stores: 161 Avenue of the Americas at Spring Street, 675-7775; 336 East 86th Street between First and Second Avenues, 794-4418; 2091 Broadway off 72nd Street, 724-3670; 130 Clinton Street, Brooklyn Heights, 718-625-1616; all open 10 to 6:30, to 8 Thursday, to 6 Saturday, noon to 5 Sunday. Excellent resource for clean-lined wood and tubular steel furniture, platform beds, lamps and all sorts of desks.

• **Zona**, 97 Greene Street between Spring and Prince Streets, 925-6750, open 11:30 to 6, to 7 Thursday, noon to 5 Sunday. Oh-so-tasteful, hand-crafted Southwestern furniture, antique and contemporary, plus Navajo rugs, wood and clay artifacts. It's Santa Fe in SoHo.

Alternative Sources

• **Salvation Army**, main store, 536 West 46th Street between Tenth and Eleventh Avenues, 757-2311, and seven other outlets, open 9 to

4:45, closed Sunday. MC, V for purchases over $50. With great pride, the Army explains that the two huge warehouse floors on 46th Street contain everything a homemaker needs to set up housekeeping.

• **Thrift Shops** Charities and hospital research programs benefit from the proceeds of these stores, just as donors benefit from the tax deductions and buyers benefit from the bargains in designer clothes to silver pitchers to down sofas. Head to Third Avenue between 80th and 86th Streets and east to Second Avenue for new and gently used goods. **Spence-Chapin Corner Shop**, 1430 Third Avenue, 737-8448; **Irvington House Thrift Shop**, 1534 Second Avenue, 879-4555; and **Memorial Sloan-Kettering Cancer Center Thrift Shop**, 1440 Third Avenue, 535-1250 are just three among many thrift stores concentrated in this neighborhood.

• **Housing Works Thrift Shops**, 143 West 17th Street at 7th Avenue, 366-0820, and 202 East 77th Street between Second and Third Avenues, 772-8461, open 10 to 6 Monday through Saturday. Selling clothes, books, records, bicycles and whatever, but furniture is the best buy here, where proceeds go to house and service homeless people living with AIDS/HIV. Come at 10 a.m. for best buys.

• **Atlantic Avenue**, Brooklyn *The Village Voice* describes this as the best strip in the five boroughs for vintage furniture above the junk category. Beware of pricey delivery costs, the *Voice* warns, and think about renting a van. Atlantic Avenue between Nevins and Bond Streets.

• **Auction Houses** Diverting, and occasionally rewarding, auctions are another way of obtaining basic necessities such as mattresses, as well as moth-eaten moose heads, which, in fact, make poor hatracks. Check the auction pages at the back of the Arts and Leisure section of the Sunday Times for sale descriptions and viewing hours. The big three, **Christie's**, 502 Park Avenue, 546-1000; **Phillips**, 406 East 79th Street, 570-4830; and **Sotheby's**, 1334 York Avenue, 606-7000, hold specialty auctions of interest to collectors and connoisseurs (and voyeurs) once or twice a week in season. The second tier, including **Christie's East**, 219 East 67th Street, 570-4141 (weekly); **William Doyle Galleries**, 175 East 87th Street, 427-2730 (every other Wednesday); and **Sotheby's Arcade Auctions**, 1334 York Avenue, 606-7000, usually auction off a varied selection of household goods in a single session. Note: Interior designers prowl the tag sale operation where Doyle's disposes of high-class flotsam from the adjacent gallery 8:30 to 4:30 Monday through Friday, 10 to 5 Saturday; you can too. For erratic quality, more fun and lower prices try: **Lubin Galleries**, 30 West 26th Street, 924-3777 (alternate Saturdays); and **Tepper Galleries**, 110 East 25th Street, 677-5300 (alternate Saturdays).

- **Flea Markets** This raffish country custom adapts well to New York's jostling sidewalks. Check the "Antiques" classified column near the back of the Weekend section in the Friday Times for flea market listings. All but the hardiest markets (and those held indoors) shut down from late fall until spring. **The Annex Antiques Fair**, Avenue of the Americas at 26th Street, 243-5343, 9 to 5 Saturday and Sunday, levies a $1 admission charge, but 80 to 100 dealers make it the largest and best of the lot. On Sundays, also, the same management runs the **Annex Flea Market** two blocks south at 24th Street, where new and used clothing and housewares are sold. These two markets have now been joined by **The Garage** on 112 West 25th Street, Manhattan's largest indoor flea market. All three markets are run by Alan Boss, and they are the closest thing in New York to a European flea market a la London's Portobello Road or Paris' Marche aux Puces.

- **Public school PTAs** sometimes sponsor flea markets on school grounds in order to raise funds. These are rain-or-shine affairs; sometimes they take place on Saturdays and Sundays and sometimes they don't. The most consistent markets include the one held in the Greenwich Avenue school yard of PS 41 between Seventh Avenue and 10th Street and in the Columbus Avenue yard of IS 44 between 76th and 77th Streets. Other markets include the SoHo-Canal Street Flea Market, at Broadway and Grand and the Indoor Antiques Fair, 122 West 26th Street.

- **The Street** A *New York Times* Home section featured the apartment of a dedicated young middle-class scrounger who furnished his two rooms with street finds. The comfortable living room looked just like home in the heartlands, traditional with overstuffed chairs, a coffee table and standing lamp. Resourcefulness, a strong back and willing cabbies are all that's required for street shopping—well, that and a knowledge of the Sanitation Department's bulk collection day for whatever area you're combing. It's legal to put large items on the sidewalk after dark the evening before the appropriate Sanitation Section's assigned day for bulk pickups. Days vary by neighborhood. Because bulk is collected Wednesday on much of the Upper East Side, Tuesday night is the best time to scout this fertile territory. Try Wednesday nights in the West Village, where pickups are scheduled for Thursdays. If found furniture is your style, call Manhattan West Bulk Collection, 265-7550, for pickup days in sections near your apartment.

Hardware, Paints and Wallpaper

On Saturdays, slow-moving lines as long as the lists new residents clutch make local hardware stores as good a way of meeting people as local bars later that night. But once you've made new friends along with those seemingly endless purchases, you may require more than the good old all-purpose neighborhood reliable to fill decorating needs. Some specialty resources, then.

- **Gracious Home**, 1220 Third Avenue at 70th Street, 517-6300, and 1217 Third Avenue, 988-8990, open 8 to 7, Saturday 9 to 7, Sunday 10 to 6. Sprawling along one full block of Third Avenue, this hardware-houseware-and-home-furnishings center for the Upper East Side is exceedingly well organized and staffed. From screws to decorative bathroom fixtures, paints to electrical fixtures to power tools to glassware to hard to find vacuum cleaners.

- **Janovic Plaza**, main store, 1150 Third Avenue at 67th Street, 772-1400, open 9:30 to 6, 9:30 to 5:30 Saturday, 11 to 4:30 Sunday; other stores: 245 Broadway at 92nd Street, 769-1440, open 7:30 to 6:30, Saturdays 9 to 6, and Sunday 11 to 5; 159 West 72nd Street between Broadway and Columbus Avenue, 595-2500, open 7:30 to 6, to 8 Thursday, 9 to 6 Saturday, 11 to 5 Sunday; 771 9th Avenue at 52nd Street, 245-3241; 215 Seventh Avenue between 22nd and 23rd Streets, 645-5454; 161 Avenue of the Americas at Spring Street, 627-1100;125 4th Avenue at 13th Street, 477-6930; 350 Third Avenue at 26th Street, 689-2222; and 1555 Third Avenue at 87th Street, 289-6300, open 7:30 to 6:30, 9 to 6 Saturday, 11 to 5 Sunday. MC, V. The Bloomingdale's of the paint-and-wallpaper scene, Janovic's image is as glossy as its enamels and printed foil papers. At the Third Avenue store, they can computer-match any color you bring in. For the latest colors and trends, as well as an overall view of what's available, Janovic can't be beat.

- **Simon Hardware**, 421 Third Avenue near 30th Street, 532-9220, open 8 to 5:30, 10 to 5 Saturday. AE, MC, V. Take a number and join the inevitable throng of contractors and decorators shopping Simon's first-rate stock of brass, bronze, pewter, plastic, wood, steel—whatever!—decorative hardware.

Discount Store

- **Pintchik**, 22nd Street and Third Avenue, 777-3030; and 2475 Broadway at 92nd Street, 769-1440; open 8:30 to 6:50, 9 to 6 Saturday, 11 to 6 Sunday. Whether you select from books or open stock, all wallpapers are discounted here and so is the rest of the color-coordinated merchandise, which includes name-brand floor tiles, linoleum, paint, window shades and blinds.

Alternative Sources

Hardware and plastics—nuts and bolts made dingy by neighboring bright, bouncing baubles—overflow rows of cut down cardboard boxes that alternate with the racks of surplus and flea market clothing lining Canal Street between West Broadway and Broadway. Most of this sidewalk hardware and pretty plastic bric-a-brac is useful only to the professional, handyman or collagist, but inside, generalists revel in complete selections of quality merchandise at exceptionally fair prices. Try any of the stores sitting side by gray dilapidated side on Canal west of Broadway.

- **Pearl Paint Co.**, 308 Canal Street, 431-7932, open 9 to 5:30, Thursday to 7, 10 to 5:30 Sunday. Listed here because of the discounted house paints, including Benjamin Moore, sold on One, Pearl Paint is in fact renowned for art-related materials and accessories and its four upper floors are usually swamped with an international array of fine artists.

Housewares

- **Bazaar Stores** are a six-store chain easily identified by bright yellow plastic signs with bold blue letters: Broadway Bazaar, 2025 Broadway at 69th Street, 873-9153; First Avenue Bazaar, 1453 First at 75th, 737-2003; Second Avenue Bazaar, 501 Second at 28th, 683-2293; Third Avenue Bazaar at 1145 Third at 67th, 988-7600, and 1362 Third at 77th, 861-5999; and the Third Street Bazaar, 125 West Third off Sixth Avenue, 673-4138, open 10 to 6:30, 11 to 5:30 Sunday. All-purpose emporiums with adequately tasteful, moderately priced rattan chairs, painted glasses, curly plastic cords, greeting cards, black pressboard stacking tables, aluminum and enamel pots, etc. etc. etc.

- **Lechter's Housewares**, 15 locations, home store at 60 East 42nd Street, 682-8476, open 8 to 8, Saturday 9 to 5:30, Sunday 11 to 5. With outlets from 112th Street and Broadway south to the World Trade Center in Manhattan, you're never far from a Lechter's, and a good thing too. They've filled the void left by disappearing Woolworth's, nicely organized and well stocked with all the basic kitchen cookware and gadgetry, bathroom and closet essentials, plus frames, gift items, gizmos and much more. Hours vary from store to store.

- **Macy's Cellar**, Broadway at 34th Street, 494-2283 (see Macy's, above, for hours). A vast emporium in its own right, The Cellar stocks everything from traditional Pyrex bakeware to imported kitchen cutlery, dinnerware and the like, all at highly competitive prices.

- **Pottery Barn**, 117 East 59th Street between Lexington and Park, 753-5424; 250 West 57th Street at Eighth Avenue, 315-1855; 51 Greenwich Avenue between Sixth and Seventh Avenues, 807-6321; 700 Broadway at 4th Street, 505-6377; Pier 17 Pavilion, 89 South Street, 233-2141; 1451 Second Avenue at 76th Street, 988-4228; 2109 Broadway between 73rd and 74th Streets, 595-5573; 1292 Lexington Avenue between 87th and 88th Streets, 289-2477, open 11 to 9, noon to 7 Sunday. Pottery Barn keeps growing, so look for a new outlet in your neighborhood. It's not all pottery, for sure. There's a selection of inexpensive to moderately-priced imported glassware, china and table settings, augmented by quality cookware, sometimes below list price, and occasional gourmet items. But increasingly it's home furnishings in a country mode, well-priced chairs, cotton rugs, decorative items—whatever meets their sharp-eyed buyers' high standards for good design—- that fill the chain's catalogs, if not the stores. Their periodic sales of specific merchandise are worth catching, and see Williams-Sonoma for savings on remainders at the store on Tenth Avenue.

- **Zabar's**, 2245 Broadway at 80th Street, 787-2000. Housewares department on the mezzanine open 8 to 6 daily. Food shops downstairs open 8 to 7:30, to midnight on Saturday and 6 on Sunday. Expansive Zabar's, mecca to millions for unequaled edibles, houses an equally esteemed and often bargain-priced selection of supplies for the home and kitchen in four rooms on the mezzanine.

Specialty Shops

- **Bridge Kitchenware**, 214 East 52nd Street off Third Avenue, 688-4220, 9 to 5:30, 10 to 4:30 Saturday, closed Sunday. MC, V. Purveyors of durable, professional, high quality kitchen equipment—for example, chrome-topped glass shakers found on every lunchonette counter worth its salt, an enviable selection of French tin-lined copper pots, huge Hobart dough mixers—to the city's food establishment and serious cooks the world over.

- **Broadway Panhandler**, 477 Broome at Wooster Street, 966-3434, open 10:30 to 6, 11 to 6 Saturday, noon to 5 Sunday. AE, MC, V, $20 minimum. Discounted cookware (Calphalon, All Clad, Le Creuset) and quality kitchen tools for the serious cook. Hit the Gourmet Garage at 453 Broome for your ingredients.

- **Fishs Eddy**, 889 Broadway at 19th Street, 420-9020, and 2176 Broadway at 77th Street, 873-8819, open 10 to 8 Monday through Saturday and 11 to 7 on Sunday. Surplus restaurant china where you can buy just one piece. Everything guaranteed chip and crack-free. Their outlet store, 551 Hudson Street at Perry, is worth a look.

- **Hammacher Schlemmer**, 147 East 57th Street, 421-9000, open 10 to 6, closed Sunday. Accordion-like, the size of this establishment stalwart seems to expand and contract. Like its growing catalog business, Hammacher's features a collection of premier quality kitchen and barware, electronic products and gadgets galore.

- **Tiffany and Co.**, 727 Fifth Avenue at 57th Street, 755-8000, open 10 to 5:30, closed Sunday. Something a bit more upscale than rainbow plastic dinnerware from the Third Avenue Bazaar? Head past the world famous array of jewels and jewelry on Tiffany's high-ceilinged hallowed first floor and up to Three where, against shimmering ivory walls, plates by Picasso nudge Royal Crown Derby place settings. Tired of jelly glasses? Crystal's to your right.

- **Williams-Sonoma**, 20 East 60th Street, 980-5155; 110 Seventh Avenue, 633-2203; 1309 Second Avenue, 288-8408; 1175 Madison Avenue, 289-6832; 580 Broadway at Houston Street, 343-7330, open 10 to 7, Sunday 11 to 6. Known through their appealing catalogue to serious cooks nationwide, this California-based firm specializes in quality cookware, handsome glassware, and mostly imported, country-style tableware. The familiar pieces, and then some, are available here, along with gourmet food items and cookbooks. For lovers of blue and color-coordinated kitchens it's a treasure trove. Where else would you find a blue Kitchen Aid mixer? Their 15,000-square foot outlet location, 231 Tenth Avenue at 23rd Street, offers great discounts on remainder items from Williams-Sonoma and their other three stores: Chambers Gardener's Eden, Hold Everything, and Pottery Barn, 206-8118.

Alternative Sources

- **The Restaurant Supply District** As the use of professional kitchenware in the home increases, the wholesale restaurant strip along the seedy Bowery between West Houston and Broome Streets has become an accepted destination for retail shoppers in spite of its derelict state. Pots, pans, butcher block, Robot Coupes, Garland ranges, barware and thick, nigh on to unbreakable, dishes are available from most stores at less than uptown retail. Outlets include Bari Restaurant Equipment Corp., 240 Bowery, 925-3786 for a grand assortment of pots, pans, strainers, stirrers and such must-haves as pizza ovens and gigantic wooden pizza spatulas; and Chef Restaurant Supply, 294 Bowery, 254-6644, "unbelievably cheap" and favored by uptown chefs.

- **Secaucus Outlet Center**, Secaucus, NJ and Flemington, NJ. Don't go around Christmas without armor plate. At other times, values obtained in these two discount meccas may well be worth the shlep.

To get to Secaucus, about 15 minutes from the Lincoln Tunnel, follow signs to Route 3 West continuing about 6 miles to the "Meadowlands Parking" exit, take the down ramp to the light, then a left and continue past two more sets of lights to American Way, take another left and you will be confronted by a number of warehouses. Bring boxes for your gleanings and a companion to watch them as you gather. Get a booklet containing a map and brand names by merchandise category from the first warehouse. Mikasa and Copco both have large outlets here. While you're at it, if you've the stamina, load up on discount Gucci shoes, Liz Claiborne goodies, Oleg Cassini and the like. It takes an hour or so to reach Flemington and Dansk, Mikasa and an interminable number of other housewares outlets, but if quality doesn't give you the vapors, the quaint Victorian houses (filled with discount operations) lining the main street make shopping here less onerous. Fastest route is via NJ Turnpike South to Exit 10 "Methuen," picking up I 287 North to Exit 10 (again), marked "22 West," and "202/206" continuing 2 1/2 miles to a circle exiting on Route 202, to "Flemington/Princeton."

Lamps and Light Fixtures

You can't beat the department stores for variety and choice. But if you want better prices, or the newest imports, shop some of the sources below.

Specialty Shops

• **Cho Lite & Shade**, 1264 Second Avenue at 66th Street, 737-8512, open 10 to 7, Saturday to 6. Repair a lamp, buy one or get a new shade in this tiny shop among the apartment megaliths. There's a surprising selection of contemporary and traditional light fixtures and lamps, some of them fashioned from antique objects.

• **Just Bulbs Ltd.**, 936 Broadway between 21st and 22nd Streets, 228-7820. An eclectic and funky mix of bulbs (and more bulbs!). The sister store next door at 934, Superior Lamp, specializes in residential lighting, including track lights and low-vision lights.

• **The Lighting Center**, 1097 Second Avenue between 57th and 58th Streets, 888-8383, open 10 to 6, 11 to 5:30 Saturday, closed Sunday. Although a large selection of mainly American contemporary lighting fixtures crams the center's small, gray-walled retail shop, the specialty is track lighting. Have a system custom designed or choose from the Halo, Lightolier, Lighting Services or Altalite lines already on hand.

• **Lightforms**, 168 Eighth Avenue, 255-4664; 509 Amsterdam Avenue, 875-0407. Interesting, moderate to expensive contemporary light fixtures; unfortunately, at the downtown location customer service may seem a forgotten art.

• **Rosetta Electric**, 21 West 46th Street, 719-4381, open 9 to 6, Thursday to 7:30, Saturday to 5. A wide variety of lighting fixtures, more traditional than chic or high tech, at reasonable prices makes this a source worth investigating, especially if you live or work in midtown.

Alternative Sources

The Lamp and Light Fixture District concentrated on **The Bowery between Broome and Canal Streets** abuts wholesale restaurant supply stores that begin at Broome and end a few blocks north at Houston. If you know what you want, don't be daunted by lurid window displays of fantasy fixtures. Push on past high kitsch, find a salesman and describe your product. Chances are the fixture can be ordered or will be in stock at less than retail. But don't count on tender loving care. That's reserved for large wholesale buyers. **Try Bowery Lighting Corp.**, 132 Bowery, 941-8244, one of the largest stores in the district. **Just Shades**, 21 Spring Street, 966-2757, covers the gamut from burlaps to fine pleated ivory silks in all sizes; and **Grand Brass Lamp Parts**, 221 Grand Street, 226-2567, just around the corner from the lamp stores, is the place to go for fittings.

Greenmarkets/Farmer's Markets

One of the surprises and joys of New York shopping has the been the great success of the many greenmarkets that now take place throughout the city. The Council of the Environment of New York City sponsors these affairs by arranging for farmers and bakers from the tri-state area to sell their produce and goods at various outdoor locations within Manhattan, Brooklyn, the Bronx and Staten Island In addition to fruit and vegetable growers, the Council invites suppliers of beef, pork, lamb, poultry, eggs, honey, dairy, wine, flowers, maple syrup and other delectable items. Prices are competitive and the offerings are fresher than anything else except homegrown. All this and a general air of festivity is the reason why so many urbane New Yorkers have made greenmarkets a regular part of their shopping routine. Keep in mind that because the produce does come from the tri-state area, the warmer months are the most bountiful time to shop the markets. Unless otherwise noted, market hours are from 8 to 6.

Manhattan

Bowling Green . . . . .Thursday . . . . .Year round

City Hall . . . . .Tuesday, Friday . . . . . .Year round

World Trade Center . . . . .Tuesday, Thursday . . . .June-December

Church & Fulton Street ......Thursday ....Year round

Federal Plaza ....Friday ....Year round

Washington Market Park .....Saturday ....Year round
(Greenwich and Reade Sts.)

St. Mark's Church ....Tuesday ....June-December
(10th St. & 2nd Ave.)

West Village ....Saturday 8 to 3 ......May-December
(Abington Square & Hudson)   •

Union Square ....Mon., Wed., Fri., Sat. ..Year round
(17th & B'way)

Sheffield Plaza ....Wed., Sat. ....Year round
(57th St. & 9th Ave.)

West 70th Street ....Saturday ....June-November
(Amsterdam-West End)

I.S. 44 ....Sunday 10 to 5 ......Year round
(77th & Columbus)

West 97th Street ....Friday ....June-December
(at Amsterdam Ave.)

Minisink Townhouse ....Tuesday ....July-October
(Lenox Ave. and W. 143rd St.)

West 175th Street ....Thursday ....June-December
(at Broadway)

The Bronx

Lincoln Hospital ....Tuesday, Friday .....July-October
(149th St. & Park Ave.)

Poe Park ....Tuesday ....June-November
(Grand Concourse & E. 192nd)

Brooklyn

Borough Hall ....Tuesday & Saturday ...Year round
(Court and Remsen)

Grand Army Plaza . . . . .Saturday . . . . .Year round
(Prospect Park entrance)

Albee Square . . . . .Wednesday . . . . .July-November
(Fulton St. & DeKalb Ave.)

Windsor Terrace . . . . .Wednesday . . . . .May-November
(15th Street & Prospect Pk.)

Williamsburg . . . . .Thursday . . . . .May-November
(Havemeyer & B'way)

Staten Island

Municipal Lot . . . . .Saturday 8 to 2 . . . . . . .July-November
(Hyatt and St. Marks)

Personal tours may be arranged of the **Union Square** greenmarket, the acknowledged granddaddy of them all. These tours take place on Wednesdays, Fridays and Saturdays and take about 1 and 1/2 hours. Call the Council on the Environment of New York City at 212-477-3220 for more information.

Sample Sales

Being new to New York, you're probably not familiar with a great New York amenity: sample sales. These are special sales of a designer's left-over inventory (from jewelry to furniture to whirlpools). Typically, designers do not advertise their sample sales, but predominant sale months are November, December, April and May. Scan New York magazine's "Sales & Bargains" section for some sale times and locations. Better yet, subscribe to the **S&B Report**, 212-683-7612, a monthly publication stating every major designer showroom sale in the city. A one-year subscription is $50. The "preferred" subscription, at $104, includes weekly updates throughout the year listing 5-15 additional sales (by fax or mail).

I F YOU'RE planning to raise children in New York City, friends and relatives (from out of town) will look at you with concern, pity, disbelief perhaps. And it *is* a challenge to raise children here. But it is also richly rewarding, for child and parent alike. In fact, it isn't so much difficult as it is just a little different here. This chapter attempts to make it a little easier by describing the available options in child care, daycare, nursery schools, primary and high schools—public, private and parochial—with information to help parents choose between them. We begin with baby sitters and infant care and wind up with high schools.

Quality day care is hard to find and more expensive in New York than anywhere else in the country, thanks to the tremendous cost of real estate and the need for stringent standards governing the operation of day care centers. Asked what is required to open a day care center here, Frances Alston, program director of the not-for-profit Day Care Council, says, "First thing is, rob a bank. You can't start a day care center in New York for less than a quarter million dollars."

Non-profit agencies which act as go-betweens for parents and day care providers are proliferating. Some corporations have begun to distribute day care information to their employees, while others have gone so far as to add on-premises facilities. Nursery schools which used to start with three-year-olds now have toddlers' groups for twos.

Listed below you'll find thumbnail descriptions of the kinds of preschool care (and education) available in New York City. Arranged chronologically by ages covered—from birth through six years—these categories are followed by the names of organizations which provide specific day care recommendations.

It should be noted that New York State establishes the eligibility requirements for publicly funded day care, be it Family Day Care in a private home or Group Care at a center. To be eligible, a family of two must have a combined income of less than $27,432, a family of three less than $29,880, a family of four less than $31,728, and so on. Almost all those entitled to assistance still pay something; currently fees range from a low of $2 per week per child up to $85 per week.

Baby Sitters and Nannies

When it comes to sitters, New York's no different than the suburbs. Neighborhoods are stocked with reliable teenagers looking for jobs. But it takes time to meet them and, occasionally, local kids aren't available on short notice or for New Year's Eve. As with many services, the best source for good baby sitters or nannies is often friends, relatives or colleagues who can recommend one. That failing, we've listed a number of alternatives. Some of the agencies also provide full-time, sleep-in or live-out help.

Note: An invaluable source of full- and part-time nannies, both live-in and out, as well as house-cleaning personnel is the classified ad section in the *Irish Echo,* published in the city and available at newsstands throughout the city. Those seeking positions are not necessarily Irish, and some of the ads under "situations wanted" are placed by the satisfied employers of nannies whose services they no longer need.

Agencies

- **Avalon Nurses Registry**, 162 West 56th Street, 212-245-0250. Rate is $9 per hour for babies to six weeks; $8 per hour for tikes over six weeks; four-hour minimum. Travel is $3 during the day, $6 after 8 p.m. Each additional child over seven months is $1 per hour. You can call them 24 hours a day, seven days a week. Fees include the agency commission.

- **Baby Sitter's Guild**, 60 East 42nd Street, 212-682-0227. The hourly fee for one or two children is $10, $1 per hour extra for each additional sibling and $3/hour extra for a visiting friend. With enough advance notice a sitter with a nursing background is provided for children under one year. and will cost $12.50 per hour. There is a four-hour minimum plus $4.50 to $7.00 for travel, depending on time of day. For an extra $2 per hour the Guild can provide a baby-sitter fluent in one of 16 languages. Fee includes the agency's commission. Call between 9 a.m. and 9 p.m. seven days a week. While requests made during the day for that evening can usually be filled, it is better to call a day ahead.

- **Fox Agency**, 30 East 60th Street, NYC 10022, 212-2686, providing baby nurses and nannies since 1936. Rates are hourly, daily or weekly. Nannies, screened by the agency, run $350 to $550 living out weekly, $350 to $650 living in (the rate may or may not include the legally mandated Social Security taxes and unemployment insurance).

- **Pavillion Agency, Inc.**, 15 East 40th Street. NYC 10016, 212-889-6609, specializes in nannies (as well as butlers, domestics and chauffeurs), who negotiate their rates depending on the needs of their clients. Currently nannies, living in or out, cost $350 to $500, plus Social Security taxes and unemployment insurance.

- **Pinch Sitters**, 799 Broadway, NYC 10003, 212-260-6005. Baby sitters, on short notice if necessary, at $10 per hour, plus transportation at night, four-hour minimum. Call Monday through Friday, 7 a.m. to 5 p.m.

- **Town & Country's Gilbert Child Care**, 157 West 57th Street, #303, 212-245-8400. The hourly rate is $7.25 for children over nine months ($8 to $9 under nine months) with a four-hour minimum; add $1/hour per sibling; $2/hour per visiting child. Daytime carfare is $4, nighttime carfare is $8. Call Monday through Friday 9 to 5. Same-day service is possible but plan a few days ahead for weekends.

- **Hand-in-Hand Agency**, 116-55 Queens Boulevard, Forest Hills, Queens, 718-268-6666. They provide sitters city-wide on a permanent and temporary basis: $7 per hour for one or two children, $1 per hour each extra child, on a regular basis; $10 per hour on a temporary basis, four hour minimum in either case. Live in or out for permanent sitters. Call Monday through Friday, 9 to 5, and allow one to two day's notice.

Non-profit

- **Parents League**, 115 East 82nd Street, 212-737-7385. The League's baby-sitting service is just one of several benefits included in the $35 annual membership fee. Sitters are students, ages 13 to 18, who attend League member schools or who are the children of members. Riffle through the sitter files, arranged by neighborhood, in the League's office between 9 and 4 Monday through Wednesday, 9 to 7 on Thursday or until noon on Friday.

Schools

- **Barnard College Baby-sitting Service**, 606 West 120th Street, 212-854-2035. To pre-register, call in your name, address, phone number and name of your pediatrician. Once you are in their file, call Monday through Friday between 10 and 5, two days in advance of your needs. The student will call you back. Rates are $6 per hour. There is also a $15 annual fee.

- **St. Francis College**, 180 Remsen Street, Brooklyn, 718-522-2300, ext. 260. If you live in the Brooklyn Heights area, phone in your needs; minimal information is posted and the student who wants the job goes to the Student Placement Office for details. Rates are up to the individual.

- **St. Vincent's Hospital School of Nursing**, 27 Christopher Street, don't call. Mail or bring a notice to Re: Tina to be posted on the school's bulletin board. Negotiate a rate with the student who calls you.

Infant Care

Formal programs for the two-month-old to two-year-old set are almost all publicly funded and appended to day care centers. Call the New York City Health Department's Division of Day Care, 212-334-7803, for the names of city-licensed facilities. Infants can also be placed in Family Day Care homes.

Family Day Care

More and more, middle-class parents are electing family care for their toddlers. Said to be the most widely used form of day care in the country, here in New York City the Health Department and/or other agencies involved in the field certify and supervise individuals caring for infants and toddlers in their apartments. These "providers," often mothers of young children drawn to child care as a means of remaining at home with their own youngsters, are allowed to oversee up to six children—no more than two of whom can be infants—in their dwelling at one time. Typically, parents who do not qualify for assistance pay between $30 and $40 per child for a six-to eight-hour day.

Group Day Care Centers

These city-licensed facilities, be they in the private or public sector, offer educational as well as caretaking programs for groups of children primarily, but not exclusively, between the ages of two and six years for an extended (beyond normal nursery school hours) or a full eight-hour day.

- **Publicly funded day care centers** are usually found in, or contiguous to, neighborhoods with the greatest economic need. Even with an income above the maximum allowed by the state (see introduction for specifics) parents proving "social" need—those working full time qualify—can apply to publicly funded day care centers if they are prepared to pay the full cost for their child's care, currently between $80 and $217 a week, depending on the facility.

- **Private centers** tend to be either nursery schools which have added all-day care to the regular school curriculum or centers established to supply day care which also offer education.

Playgroups

Neighborhood parents often band together informally, usually in cooperative fashion, to care for a small group of pre-schoolers for a half-day or so, one, two or three times a week.

Toddlers' Groups

Formal groups with a paid trained professional in command cater to the 18-to 36-month-old set. Groups with more than five children must be licensed by the Department of Health. Toddlers' groups are also appended to nursery schools and even a few private elementary and secondary schools.

Information Sources

New York Parents' Book by Lois Gilman (Penguin) covers everything from having the baby to care to entertainment. Several non-profit organizations as well as the Agency for Child Development, jointly sponsored by the city, state and Federal governments, provide accurate information about local facilities. To determine the most suitable day care solution for your family's needs, consult these sources while pursuing the other leads suggested below.

- **Agency for Child Development,** 30 Main Street, Brooklyn 11201, call 718-260-6000 for pre-school information and referrals from the ACD's Vacancy Information Service. Their staff provides names and addresses of private as well as publicly funded and Head Start child care facilities located in the five boroughs. This information is supplied ACD by the Department of Health's Bureau of Day Care, 212-334-7803, the group charged with licensing pre-school facilities. Their Directory of Day Care Services in New York City is available by mail free of charge.

- **Child Care Inc./The Pre-School Association**, 275 Seventh Avenue, NYC 10001, 212-929-4999, a knowledgeable, non-profit group, has a corporate program. Member firms receive counseling on child care in New York City as well as detailed publications on the subject for distribution to employees. The organization, funded also to assist individual parents, offers telephone counseling to all callers. They also provide three packets ($5 each), one each on in-home care, family day care and early childhood programs— which contain an informative booklet, checklist, licensing information sheet and, most helpful of all, names of day care providers appropriate to your needs in your specific neighborhood.

- **The Lower East Side Family Resource Center**, 137 East Second Street, NYC 10009, 212-677-6602, houses among a variety of other services the Community Child Care Exchange, an information, referral and counseling group. Targeted at Lower Manhattan residents, the exchange helps parents to locate child care centers, family day care providers and sitters and to establish informal cooperative play groups.

- **The New York Public Library's Early Childhood Resource Center** at the Hudson Park Branch on Leroy Street off Seventh Avenue in Greenwich Village, 212-929-0815, devotes one whole floor to resource materials for parents and a playroom for kids.

- **Solving the Childcare Puzzle**, a booklet covering the range of child care options in the city, is available on request from the Office of the Manhattan Borough President, 1 Centre Street, 19th Floor South, NYC 10007, 212-669-395l.

Other Leads

Check out some of the following resources for referrals in your particular neighborhood:

- **Churches**, large and small; **bulletin boards**, most often, but not exclusively, found in the larger supermarkets; **private schools**, ask the admissions director for the names of feeder schools, day care centers or playgroups; **pediatricians**; **hospitals**, talk with the administrative officer in charge of residents and interns; and, last but perhaps most accessible and knowledgeable of all, **playground and park bench parents.**

Nursery Schools

It is at this point, typically, that parental anxiety sets in. And it needn't. In Manhattan alone there are more than 175 privately run pre-school programs, generally geared to three-, four- and five-year-olds, often including toddlers' groups and sometimes all-day care as well. They vary widely in educational philosophy and style, and admission to none of them is essential to a child's later success at Harvard. The *Manhattan Directory of Private Nursery Schools* by Linda Faulhaber (SoHo Press) is a detailed listing of more than 150 nursery and all-day programs plus other useful information. It's a good place to start. Meanwhile, talk with mothers in the parks you frequent and with parents of children in neighborhood nursery schools. The search process typically begins just after Labor Day preceding application, and many schools will have open houses; this is also the time to request information from the schools you might wish to consider. And finally, in helping you decide what might be the best school for your child (and for you), the two sources below should be helpful:

- **The Independent Schools Admissions Association of Greater New York** (ISAAGNY) publishes the *New York Independent Schools Directory* containing page-long descriptions of more than 120 private member schools enrolling pre-schoolers through high schoolers. Nursery schools and toddlers groups, as well as numerous elementary and secondary schools with pre-school groups, are listed, and a useful geographical index is included in the appendix. This directory provides an excellent overview of New York's varied private schools. Copies cost $10 and can be picked up at the office of the Parents League of New York (212-737-7385) or ordered from them by mail ($11.50).

- **Parents League of New York, Inc.**, 115 East 82nd Street, NYC 10028, 212-737-7385, with 106 member schools, mainly in Manhattan, is an excellent source of private school information. One counseling session with a specialist from their School Advisory Service—for example, their expert on toddlers' groups and nursery schools—is well worth the League's annual $30 membership fee. A panoply of other child-related services, not the least of which is their reliable Baby Sitter-Young Helper listing, a great boon to any newcomer with kids, also come with League membership, as does their 80-page Toddler Activities directory.

Grade Schools

Here, decision-making becomes more difficult because there are so many options. To begin with, the choice between public, private and parochial school. For some it is a choice easily made; they know they want one or the other, or they can't afford private school. A word to the undecided: know that there are some excellent public schools in the city, just as there are some dreadful ones.

If your child is in a nursery school in the city, you can expect some guidance in choosing a primary school, both in general and specific to your child's temperament and style of learning. Beyond that, you want a school which reflects your values. Those opting for **private school** will find the resources above under **Nursery Schools** helpful. The *Manhattan Family Guide to Private Schools* by Catherine Hausman and Victoria Goldman (Soho Press, 1992), offers an independent evaluation of the specific schools; however the focus is distinctly uptown, giving scant attention to some excellent downtown schools. They do provide useful information and advice on navigating the admissions process.

Catholic **parochial schools**, which cost considerably less than the city's private schools, have found favor in recent years with non-Catholics as well as Catholics as an attractive alternative to public schools. The Archdiocese of New York operates 144 elementary and 39 high schools in Manhattan, The Bronx and Staten Island. For information about schools in your neighborhood or about which you may have heard, call (800) SCHOOL4. The Diocese of Brooklyn and Queens operates 156 elementary schools and 22 high schools. Call the Superintendent's office, 718-492-1800, for more information. There is no source of comparative evaluation of the parochial schools, which are independently run, so interested parents are left to make their own evaluation on a school by school basis.

Visit the schools which seem to suit your child's needs, and yours.

Read the school literature carefully. Examine the physical plant. Observe the relationships between children, staff and administration. Consider the program, in theory and in practice. Finally, what is your gut reaction? Remember, you and your child may spend the next eight to twelve years here, and no decision is irrevocable. Just hard.

Parents considering **public school** should begin by contacting the community school board in their district (see **Neighborhoods**) for a list of schools in the district and to find out what school they are zoned for. Many of the boards have brochures describing the various schools in the district, from which it is possible to get a sense both of the character of this school district and of the particular schools. In most districts there is a variance procedure allowing a child to go out of his zone within the district, space permitting. Plan to start such a procedure in January for the following year. Register at your school and arrange to visit for a good look at the physical plant, teacher-student interaction, student engagement and interestedness, the feel of the school. Ask questions.

It is often possible to send a child to a school out of district, space permitting, if the process is begun early enough. A child may be enrolled in a school in another district if a parent's workplace is in that district; inquire in that district about the required variance procedure.

In recent years several grade groupings have evolved among the city's schools, making choice more complicated. And within these groupings are schools with varying focus. The most common configurations below the high school level are:

- **Early childhood schools**, pre-kindergarten to second or third grade, popular for their focus on the needs of young children.

- **Elementary schools**, K-fifth or sixth grade, and the most common configuration. Many districts are now shifting sixth grade to middle schools to avoid crowding.

- **Grammar schools**, K-8, making a comeback and popular with parents as an alternative to middle school.

- **Middle schools**, or intermediate schools, containing sixth through eighth grades or seventh and eighth. Many of these are theme schools, focusing on a particular subject area, such as the performing arts or technology. Junior high schools, seventh through ninth grades, once common, are in decline.

For further guidance and encouragement in choosing a public school for your child, turn to *The Parents' Guide to the Best Public Elementary Schools In New York City* by Clara Hemphill, researcher at the Public Education Association, published in 1997 by Soho Press. She profiles 100 (out of 676) of the top elementary schools in the city.

High Schools

Decisions at this level, however fraught, are made somewhat easier by the guidance procedures at whatever school the child is already enrolled in and (or more difficult) by the fact that the child will participate in the decision. Again, public or private? Information sources for the private schools are as noted above.

Admission to many of the high schools is city-wide, a trend which is increasing as theme schools proliferate at this level. The various categories of high school include the following major groupings:

- **Competitive** schools to which admission is by competitive exam. Bronx High School of Science, Brooklyn Tech, Hunter High School and Stuyvesant are the most well-known and desirable schools in this group.

- **Audition** schools, such as Fiorello LaGuardia High School of Music and Art and the Performing Arts and High School of Art and Design, to which the student must be recommended and must audition or present a portfolio for admission.

- **Special Interest** schools such as the School of Fashion Industries and the New York School of Printing.

- **District** schools, which range from abysmal to excellent.

Information Sources

The annual public school options fair, with workshops and guides to schools in several Manhattan districts, at the 92nd Street YMHA, 212-996-1100, is worth a visit. The Parenting Center there has a variety of seminars on public and private schools, and one need not be a member to attend. Call the Center for particulars.

- **The Board of Education**, in conjunction with the Fund for New York City Public Education publishes *The Directory of Public High Schools* annually. Call or write Office of Access and Compliance, Division of High Schools, Board of Education, 110 Livingston Street, Brooklyn 11201, 718-935-3415.

- **The Division of Assessment and Accountability of the Board of Education**, 110 Livingston Street, Brooklyn 11201, 718-935-3767, publishes an *Annual Report,* commonly known as the Report Card, which describes each of the public schools statistically for the previous year. It's a source of information on enrollment, ethnic composition, reading scores etc.

- **The Manhattan Borough President's Office**, 1 Centre Street, 19th Floor South, NYC 10007, 212-669-3951, will send *Parent's*

Guide to Choosing a Public Elementary School in New York City, on request, free.

• **The Public Education Association**, 39 West 32nd Street, NYC 10001, 212-868-1640, offers seminars for parents and publishes a free *Consumers Guide to High Schools,* a *Consumer's Guide to Middle Schools* for the cost of the postage, and *Lend a Hand to N.Y. City Public Schools,* which is a guide to the system and to organizations that help the schools. Judith Baum at PEA is an understanding source of particular information and advice.

• **The Toussaint Institute**, 212-422-5338, offers an annual springtime seminar on New York City public schools for African-American and Hispanic parents. Call for details.

F YOU came from a small town, you may have gone to the Methodist church, *the* Catholic church, or *the* synagogue. No problem. But there are an estimated 2,300 churches (not counting storefront pentecostals) and some 650 synagogues in New York City. You'll find some, but by no means all, of them listed by denomination in the Yellow Pages. Connecting with a church or synagogue may be as simple as that or the suggestion of an acquaintance. Or it may be as intensely personal and complex as choosing a spouse. The churches and synagogues listed below by denomination were chosen specifically for their possible appeal to newcomers. It's a place to start.

Roman Catholic Churches

Most Catholics attend Mass near their home or office. But there are a few churches which, for one reason or another, attract worshipers from beyond the parish confines. One of these may suit you.

- **Cathedral-Basilica of St. James**, 230 Cathedral Place (at Jay Street near Tillary Street), Brooklyn Heights 11201, 718-852-4005. Built in 1822 and restored in recent years to a Georgian brick elegance befitting its prominence, St. James is Brooklyn's cathedral, a bishop's church, but it is also a non-territorial parish, especially popular among young professionals in the area, for whom the daily business communion at 12:10 is a special convenience. Mass here is traditional, and the music quite wonderful.

- **Church of the Epiphany**, Second Avenue and 22nd Street, NYC 10010, 475-1966, is at once striking and modest, an unusually successful modern structure of rounded verticals in brown brick. It's a family church, with a traditional Mass at 11:15 and a popular family Mass to guitar accompaniment at 10. But there's a difference. For one thing, altar girls. Nuns are involved in work traditionally done by priests, and women's issues are addressed. The church is popular with young professionals in the community, and there is a social action group.

- **Church of St. Agnes**, 141 East 43rd Street at Lexington Avenue, NYC 10017, 682-5722, hard by Grand Central Station was once a family parish, then a bustling commuter church until it burned in 1992. But it remains a busy church with multiple daily masses in the chapel of a former boys' high school at 158 East 44th Street at Lexington Avenue. St. Agnes will rise again, and it continues to be one of two churches in Manhattan offering a Latin Mass, Sundays at 10:30. (The other, less conveniently located, is St. Ann's Armenian Catholic Cathedral at 110 East 12th Street, 477-2030, where the Latin Mass is at 2 p.m. Saturdays.)

- **Church of St. Thomas More**, 65 East 89th Street between Park and Lexington Avenues, NYC 10028, 876-7718, stone Victorian Gothic, was built as an Episcopal Church and still feels a bit like one, with its intimately peaceful, fragrant interior beneath a timbered ceiling. Ever so decorous. You can linger for coffee in the Rochester Room after 10 o'clock Mass.

- **Holy Trinity Chapel**, 58 Washington Square South, NYC 10012, 674-7236, is the Catholic chapel at New York University, but its congregants are by no means all students. A moderately liberal intellectual approach and active social life attract a committed band of Catholics from the surrounding Village and beyond to this modest but appealing modern brick structure. Communicants run the Monday soup kitchen, deliver food to homebound AIDs victims, tutor and provide legal advice to the homeless. A women's group meets regularly, and there are sessions of silent Christian meditation.

- **St. Francis Xavier**, 46 West 16th Street, NYC 10011, 627-2100. This hulking, grey stone Jesuit presence dominates the block between Fifth and Sixth Avenues. The style here is rather less formal than you might expect, perhaps because the congregation covers such a broad social spectrum: Hispanics, knowledgeable Catholic activists and young professionals. Actively involved in the community, the church shelters the homeless and serves 1,000 meals a week. It's equally busy on the spiritual front, with lay spirituality group retreats, healing Masses and discussion groups for a fiercely devoted following.

- **St. Ignatius Loyola**, Park Avenue at 84th Street, NYC 10028, 288-3588, solidly limestone Italian Baroque, is definitely high church and upscale: incense, ornate vestments, and a fine professional choir at the traditionally sung morning High Mass. But the rigorous Jesuit approach is apparent in a strongly social and economic outlook from the pulpit. At 11 a.m. you can attend a folk Mass in the undercroft (Wallace Hall) and linger over coffee. Young adults meet monthly in the Rectory. The church is also known for its series of formal musical programs featuring the fine choir and organist as well as visiting musicians.

• **St. John's**, 210 West 31st Street, NYC 10001, 564-9070, as a distinct sideline to its normal parish activities, is host to the Catholic charismatic movement in Manhattan. There are seminars, prayer meetings and a monthly charismatic Mass.

• **St. Joseph's**, 371 Avenue of the Americas at Washington Place, NYC 10014, 741-1274, in the heart of Greenwich Village, appeals to a variety of Catholics in the neighborhood and even outside the city. At once a bustling family church and an esthetic experience, with professional musicians performing at formal, traditional Masses and at evening concerts. Distinctly high church. The lovely stone and stucco Greek Revival structure, resplendent inside with creamy plaster, crystal chandeliers and wide, carved balconies, is the oldest Catholic church in the city (1833), and the first to open a shelter for homeless men.

• **St. Paul's Chapel at Columbia University**, 116th Street and Broadway, NYC 10027, 854-6242(Catholic Campus Ministry Office), is an architecturally stunning Episcopal chapel but other denominations hold services here, and the 5 p.m. Sunday Catholic Mass, with its modern liturgy, lay participation and challenging intellectual content, attracts communicants from beyond campus. In addition to the Sunday Mass while school is in session, there is a daily Mass at 12:15.

Protestant Churches

Baptist

• **Calvary**, 123 West 57th Street between Sixth and Seventh Avenues, NYC 10019, 975-0170, across from Carnegie Hall, is probably the largest Baptist Church in Manhattan. You might begin a typical Sunday at the 9:30 Young Professionals' topical Bible study and fellowship, followed by traditional worship service at 11 along with some 1,400 other fellow Baptists, mostly young educated singles, and then coffee in Fellowship Hall downstairs. The Worship Team (singers) might perform at the 6 p.m. service. Young Adult Ministries offers occasional weekend retreats, and there are outreach programs to the prison population, the poor and welfare hotel children.

Episcopal

• **Cathedral of St. John the Divine**, 1045 Amsterdam Avenue at 112th Street, NYC 10025, 316-7540, dwarfs its rather shabby surroundings even as it awaits completion of its stone towers. The largest cathedral in the world, at once Byzantine, Romanesque and Gothic, it is truly awesome, especially inside, where spectacular stained glass windows light the vast dark vaults and music echoes ethereally. It is also a bustling and exciting community church, a leader in the movement to feed and house the poor. And the performing arts flourish here almost around the clock.

- **Church of the Ascension**, 36 Fifth Avenue at 10th Street, NYC 10011, 254-8620. Its communicants find this church especially challenging intellectually and pleasing esthetically. A LaFarge altar fresco and a St. Gaudens altar relief enliven the quietly tasteful interior, and liturgical music of the highest quality is performed by an exceptional choir Sundays and at special evening concerts.

- **Church of the Heavenly Rest**, 2 East 90th Street at Fifth Avenue, NYC 10128, 289-3400, sits confidently but un-ostentatiously, stripped contemporary Gothic in pale grey stone, facing Central Park. It's an upscale, neighborhood family church, where the congregants linger casually for coffee after the morning service while the children play decorously about the door.

- **Grace Church**, 802 Broadway at East 10th Street, NYC 10003, 254-2000, despite its rather patrician, lacy English Gothic elegance, is relatively low church. Worship is traditional, however, with wonderful music, especially on holy days. The congregation runs to young families and a variety of artists. Pastoral counseling is available as well as adult classes on a variety of topics, and there are outreach groups to college students and AIDS victims, programs for children and families and a thrice-yearly Alpha Course, a 10-week introduction to Christianity.

- **St. Bartholomew's**, Park Avenue at 51st Street, NYC 10022, 751-1616. This landmarked Romanesque-Byzantine church houses a friendly, welcoming community numbering about 1,000 worshipers each Sunday. Lay participation in all aspects of church life is encouraged. Sundays feature a stimulating Rector's Forum and Sunday School, in addition to several services, and Bible studies are offered during the week. Several adult social clubs offer a wide variety of social, athletic and theatrical activities, among them St. Bart's Players, "the longest running off-Broadway theater group in the city. Communicants and non-members alike volunteer at the homeless shelter and the feeding program operated by the church.

- **St. James'**, 865 Madison Avenue at 71st Street, NYC 10021, 288-4100. Distinctly Upper East Side, this trim brownstone is a warm, neighborhood family church which is also decidedly activist in the community and beyond: feeding, mentoring, supporting, and sometimes even demonstrating. Despite its rather liberal bent, St. James' is moderately high church. Its education programs for adults and children are worthy of note.

Latter-Day Saints/Mormons

- **The Church of Jesus Christ of Latter-Day Saints** (the Mormon church) in Manhattan, is located at 125 Columbus at W. 65th Street (across from Lincoln Center), 724-0539 or 799-6090. Several different congregations (called "wards" and "branches") conduct worship services every Sunday in three-hour blocks, beginning at 9 a.m. These include two English-speaking "family" wards, one English-speaking ward for single adults, two Spanish-speaking wards, and one deaf branch. Also, each congregation offers social and musical activities during the week.

Lutheran

- **Holy Trinity**, Central Park West at 65th Street, NYC 10023, 877-6815, offers challenging preaching at traditional, rigorously Lutheran services. But it is music, at the regular services and at the Sunday vespers featuring Bach cantatas with professional musicians, for which Holy Trinity is widely known. The sturdy Gothic revival church is the setting for frequent evening concerts as well.

- **St. Peter's**, 619 Lexington Avenue at 54th Street, NYC 10022, 935-2200, nestles, sleek and angular like a modern stone tent, beneath the towering Citicorp Center. A large Louise Nevelson sculpture punctuates the stark, light interior, scene of a sung Mass with traditional liturgy in the morning and Jazz Vespers with jazz as the sermon Sunday afternoons. Classical and jazz concerts, often free, theater and provocative adult Forum lectures attract an ecumenical following, to say the least.

Methodist

- **Christ Church**, 520 Park Avenue at 60th Street, NYC 10021, 838-3036, is sedately Byzantine outside, dazzlingly so inside, every inch covered with mosaics in blazing blues, greens and gold. It's a wonderful setting for the religious music-dramas occasionally performed here. The congregation, though relatively small, supports a weekly soup kitchen and excellent pastoral counseling.

- **John Street**, 44 John Street between Broadway and William Street, NYC 10038, 269-0014. To step into this landmarked little Italianate brownstone church (1841) among the towering monoliths of the financial district is to step out of place and time into a peaceful haven of creamy modest proportions and brass sconces. It's the oldest Methodist society in the US, and few know about it. Inquire about the occasional Wednesday noon hymn-sings.

- **Park Avenue**, 106 East 86th Street, NYC 10028, 427-5421. A mixed and growing congregation, mostly young families and singles, is attracted by the moderately liberal approach and active social scene at this smallish, restfully intimate, Moorish-looking church. Adult Bible study precedes and a coffee hour follows the traditional Sunday service with volunteer choir. Weekday activities include a Tuesday evening gathering for informal sharing and a Wednesday evening service of prayer and meditation. An adult fellowship group organizes social activities.

Presbyterian

- **Brick Church**, Park Avenue at 91st Street, NYC 10128, 289-4400, staid neo-Georgian with a rather ornate interior, is distinctly Park Avenue. But the welcome is friendly, including a popular Coffee Hour after the Sunday service. Adult Bible study Tuesday mornings and "Mid-Week at Brick" religious studies Wednesday evenings are intellectually meaty. The church's day school is prestigious.

- **Fifth Avenue**, Fifth Avenue at 55th Street, NYC 10019, 247-0490. The city's largest Presbyterian church has a warm, woody interior behind its otherwise undistinguished brownstone facade. A variety of social adult fellowship groups attract large numbers of youngish adults to the traditional services. Activities of these groups include Sunday night church suppers, after-church brunch, movies and ski retreats, as well as monthly dinner meetings with outside speakers at the Women's Roundtable for business women and the Men's Fellowship. The church's Center for Christian Studies offers challenging five-week courses with outside lecturers on several levels of Christian thought. Fees are minimal, and non-members are welcome.

- **Madison Avenue**, 921 Madison Avenue at 73rd Street, NYC 10021, 288-8920, has a cozy, Scottish feel, with its Gothic-timbered white walls, carved pews and galleries. The music program is strong, including a volunteer choir and frequent Sunday afternoon concerts. The adult education program at 10 a.m. is sandwiched between the two Sunday services. A young adult fellowship group meets regularly for Bible study, discussion and socializing.

- **Redeemer**, church office at 271 Madison Avenue, Suite 1600, NYC 10016, 808-4460. This recently organized and rapidly growing congregation of the PCA holds two Sunday services in the Hunter College Auditorium, 69th Street between Park and Lexington Avenues. The scripturally-based emphasis is on preaching which is intellectually engaging and an array of spiritual, social and outreach activities.

Unitarian

- **All Souls**, 1157 Lexington Avenue at 80th Street, NYC 10021, 639-9385. New England simple and elegant, this Federal-style brick church looks Unitarian. As might be expected here, the busy church calendar tends to activism on a variety of fronts and a fairly intellectual approach to adult education, which features book groups, films and lectures. Music is stressed. Social activities are many and varied, including a Career Networking Group.

Interdenominational

- **Judson Memorial** (Baptist-United Church of Christ), 55 Washington Square South, NYC 10012, 477-0351. Worldly young adults and seminarians are attracted to this ornate Romanesque church and its fairly traditional Protestant liturgy with progressive elements, including a monthly Agape Meal. There is a consumer health library and support for AIDS victims.

- **Riverside**, 490 Riverside Drive at 122nd Street, NYC 10027, 870-6700 This towering Gothic gift of John D. Rockefeller, Jr. dominates the heights overlooking the Hudson River. Inspired by Chartres, it boasts spectacular stained glass and beautifully carved stone in the large but simple nave and chancel and about the entrance. Activist concerns under the leadership of the Rev. Dr. James Forbes, Jr. are dizzying, as are the opportunities for involvement in activities musical, intellectual and social, not to mention spiritual.

Synagogues

Reform

- **Brooklyn Heights Synagogue**, 131 Remsen Street, Brooklyn 11201, 718-522-2070, has moved up the street from its brownstone home of 20 years to the larger brownstone formerly housing the Brooklyn Club in order to accommodate its after-school religious school for children and extensive adult education classes. Services here are characterized by a greater use of Hebrew and more congregational singing than is generally found in reform synagogues. The warmth and friendliness of this relatively small (some 260 families) congregation and their purposeful inclusiveness makes this a particularly appealing synagogue for newcomers. Congregants come from all the boroughs, and their numbers swell sufficiently on the high holy days that these services are held in the (Protestant) Plymouth Church nearby.

- **Central**, 123 East 55th Street, NYC 10022, 838-5122, is the oldest Jewish house of worship (1872) in continuous use in New York. The Moorish brownstone structure has an interior richly stenciled in red, blue and gold. Traditional in orientation and ritual, the temple tends to the manifold interests, worldly as well as spiritual, of its 1,400-member congregation in groups and classes ranging from Hebrew and Yiddish to Bible to bridge, teens' and singles' groups, and 8 a.m. Women's Focus speakers for working women.

- **Temple Emanu-El**, 1 East 65th Street, corner of Fifth Avenue, NYC 10021, 744-1400, is perhaps a little less traditional, nevertheless classical Reform in approach, and it is the largest Reform temple in the US, with over 3,000 members. The landmarked limestone Moorish-Romanesque temple facing Central Park seats 2,500 beneath a high, colorfully painted wood ceiling and stunning stained glass windows. The temple has a large staff to run its many facilities, classes and community outreach programs, as well as a large religious school. Services are broadcast every Friday evening at 5:30 over WQXR (1560 AM, 96.3 FM).

Conservative

- **Ansche Chesed**, 251 West 100th Street at West End Avenue, NYC 10025, 865-0600, houses four separate congregations, each with a different approach to Conservative Judaism, in one medium-sized, squat, brick building. Alternatives within a framework of Jewish tradition are stressed at this much-talked-about West Side synagogue, which offers an adult beginners' service, courses on a wide range of Jewish topics, and social action projects aiding elderly Jews.

- **Baith Israel Anschei Emes/Kane Street**, 236 Kane Street at Tompkins Place in Cobble Hill, Brooklyn 11231, 718-875-1550, has grown considerably in recent years, partly, perhaps, because of the emphasis on egalitarianism in its observances. Vibrant and involved, with challenging study groups, it is regularly packed with congregants, mainly young, from Cobble Hill and nearby Brooklyn Heights.

- **B'Nai Jeshurun**, 257 West 88th Street between Broadway and West End Avenue, NYC 10024, 787-7600. Under the charismatic leadership of the late Rabbi Marshall Meyer, "BJ", as it is affectionately known, burst its ornately Byzantine/Romanesque seams. Successor rabbis, his former students, continue to hold traditionally musical services in the larger Methodist Church of St. Paul and St. Andrew, 86th Street and West End Avenue, as well as in the more intimate, richly colorful home temple. Emphasis is on study, with a wide variety of adult courses and lectures as well as a Hebrew school for children. And the diverse congregation thinks of itself as a community, with a strong commitment to social action, Tikkun Olam, in the wider Jewish and non-Jewish community beyond. Plan to come early for services, which tend to fill up fast; non-members will want to call about high holy days.

- **Brotherhood**, 28 Gramercy Park South, NYC 10003, 674-5750, occupies a landmarked (1859) Friends' Meeting House, starkly beautiful in Italianate brownstone and overlooking lovely Gramercy Park. About its courtyards are housed a shelter for the homeless, a religious school, adult education, an educational program for the developmentally disabled, and facilities to aid Jewish immigrants.

- **Park Avenue**, 50 East 87th Street at Madison Avenue, NYC 10128, 369-2600, is the city's largest Conservative temple and an East Side Moorish landmark in carved golden stone. The rich interior boasts fine stained glass, sculpture and paintings, and the traditional services are distinctly formal, with organ and choir. There are many programs for children, singles, young marrieds and seniors, and a Food Pantry for the neighborhood's hungry.

- **Shaare Zedek**, 212 West 93rd Street between Broadway and Amsterdam Avenue, NYC 10025, 874-7005. This congregation, founded 160 years ago on the Lower East Side and housed now in a grey stone Greek revival temple, has experienced a revival in the mid-1990s with an infusion of college students and young professionals. Friday evening services, usually downstairs in the social halls, can be especially busy, and once a month there is a post-worship dinner. Bridge Club, occasional seders and special events fill out the social calendar.

- **Tifereth Israel/Town and Village**, 334 East 14th Street between First and Second Avenues, NYC 10003, 677-8090, stresses sexual egalitarianism in its informally innovative, traditional services and attracts an involved family congregation, largely from the adjacent community, including Stuyvesant Town and Peter Cooper Village. Adult education and a young marrieds group are popular. The Sol Goldman YW-YMHA of the Educational Alliance next door, with whom it shares a Hebrew school, offers members the advantages of a social center with pool, gym, and classes.

- **United Synagogue of Hoboken**, 830 Hudson Street at Ninth, Hoboken 07030, 201-659-2614, is one congregation with two temples, the other being at 115 Park Avenue, a tan brick structure with copper onion domes. Friday evening and Sabbath services are in the converted Victorian brownstone Hudson Street temple, the last of many serving the predominantly German Jewish community here at the turn of the century. The small but growing egalitarian congregation is youngish and welcoming. Extensive adult education courses include Hebrew reading and Jewish history, a Hebrew discussion group, a book club, Jewish women's and men's discussion groups, karate, adult bar and bat mitzvah instruction. There is also a Hebrew school for children.

Orthodox

- **Civic Center**, 49 White Street west of Broadway, NYC 10013, 966-7141, occupies a small, award-winning, modern structure scrunched among the cast iron manufacturing lofts and loading docks. Its flame-shaped interior houses a membership of about 100 families with about 1,000 supporters, including elderly members of long standing as well as artists and young professionals from surrounding

Tribeca, Independence Plaza and Battery Park. There are both Hebrew and adult education, as well as parenting sessions conducted by Educational Alliance West.

• **Kehilath Jeshurun**, 125 East 85th Street between Lexington and Park Avenues, NYC 10028, 427-1000. Though old and rich and housed in classical Romanesque grey stone, this is probably the most progressive of the Orthodox congregations. Its size makes possible a host of activities for singles, couples and children, recreational facilities, and an educational program including the Ramaz School and "Lunch and Learn" classes. Emphasis is placed on outreach to beginners and singles, with classes, special services and Friday night dinners for them.

• **Shearith Israel**, 8 West 70th Street at Central Park West, NYC 10023, 873-0300, known as the Spanish and Portuguese synagogue, is the oldest Jewish congregation in the US, dating from 1655, when a group of Sephardic Jews arrived from Brazil. In the formal sanctuary scholarly rabbis conduct very formal services, which offer the best opportunity to observe Sephardic tradition and music. Excellent adult education explores Sephardic and Ashkenazic culture and tradition, with visiting scholars leading seminars. There are special educational and social events for young adults.

• **Lincoln Square**, 200 Amsterdam Avenue at 69th Street, NYC 10023, 874-6100, sometimes referred to as "the hip synagogue", might be described physically as synagogue-modern. Its nickname and popularity among the young professionals who pack four Saturday services is due in large part to the charm and zealous outreach efforts of Rabbi Ephraim Buchwald, who hosts the 9:15 "Learners' Minyan", which is followed by wine and cookies and, if you like, lunch with an experienced family. There are courses at all levels on Jewish law and thought as well as singles and youth groups.

Other

• **Society for the Advancement of Judaism**, 15 West 86th Street off Central Park West, NYC 10024, 724-7000. Known as the SAJ, this is the original Reconstructionist synagogue. Reconstructionism, which attempts to reconcile traditional Conservatism with modern life, views Judaism as evolving rather than divinely inspired. The Torah is observed, and services are largely traditional but egalitarian. The approach here is distinctly intellectual, not social.

• **West End**, 190 Amsterdam Avenue at 69th Street, NYC 10023, 579-0777, is a popular Reconstructionist congregation flourishing with a slightly more emotional, interpersonal emphasis and monthly Shabbat dinners as well as concerts, debates and social action programs.

• **Young Israel of Fifth Avenue**, 3 West 16th Street at Fifth Avenue, NYC 10011, 255-4826, is one of three such temples in Manhattan. Young Israel can be defined as modern Orthodoxy, observing all the Orthodox forms, including separate seating of the sexes, but emphasizing programs serving the entire family. This includes communal singing and participation, youth and singles programs, outreach, adult education, and attention to community needs.

Mosques

• **The Mosque of New York**, in the Islamic Cultural Center, 1711 Third Avenue, NYC 10029, 722-5234. This imposing structure, the gift of a group of Islamic countries, houses a large Mosque. The design is modern, with numerous references to traditional elements of Muslim architecture. The effect is at once peaceful and spiritual. In addition to the weekly congregational prayer service, the Mosque is open for daily prayer at the five prescribed times. Sunday classes for children and adults, held in the main hall until the school building is completed in late 1997, cover a range of Islamic topics. There are Saturday classes for women only.

• **The Muslim Center of New York**, 137-58 Geranium Avenue off Kissena Boulevard, Flushing, NY 11355, 718-460-3000, serves the growing Muslim community in Queens and Long Island. In a modest neighborhood an octagonal minaret rises from the polished rose quartz structure. Congregational prayers Friday at 1:15 are followed by Koranic studies. There is a Sunday school and afternoon religious school for children weekdays. Call for hours.

THE diversity and incredible depth of the city's cultural, intellectual and artistic life is a magnet for many. Nowhere else can such an enormous range of interests and avocations be accommodated on so many levels. While it is impossible to cover all the opportunities New York offers, we *can* help the newcomer assimilate culturally by providing a compilation of ticket, subscription and membership information for leading opera companies, symphony orchestras, dance companies, theatrical repertory groups and museums. And we've added at the end a list of the major colleges and universities in the city, with the emphasis on Manhattan. In addition to graduate degrees and an inviting array of evening courses, these schools also offer lectures and workshops of interest, not to mention musical and theatrical performances.

First, a list of publications which cover what is showing where and when.

- **"Weekend," *New York Times* Friday Edition**, features reviews, articles and tips on the endless entertainment possibilities for Friday, Saturday and Sunday. This special section also contains an up-to-the-minute Movie Clock, useful in a town where movie schedules are notoriously unreliable.

- **"Arts and Leisure," *New York Times* Sunday Edition**, besides reviews and critical articles on current trends and upcoming events in the arts, includes listings for the arts with thumbnail reviews.

- ***The New Yorker,*** on the stands Wednesday, includes not just plays, opera and museums in its comprehensive "Goings on About Town," but also poetry readings, sporting events and night life. Most listings include abbreviated reviews.

- ***New York*** magazine, on the stands Monday, incorporates Cue, "A Complete Guide to Entertainment, the Arts, and Dining for the Week." Included are brief movie and theater reviews. Comprehensive.

- *Time Out New York,* on the stands Wednesday, offers comprehensive listings in all aspects of entertainment and the arts, as well as gay and lesbian features and listings, reviews and articles on who's doing it this week, all for a somewhat younger audience than the above.

- *The Village Voice,* free on the street Wednesday, is filled with entertainment ads and carries a "Listings" column of weekly free events. Particularly good for alternative events.

- *New York Press* is distributed free in restaurants, stores and in street boxes below 28th Street, sparsely uptown. A favorite with downtowners as a reference for what's going on in arts and music, the weekly also includes restaurant reviews and feature stories.

The latest wrinkle in performance information is New York City/On Stage. Dial 212-768-1818 for up-to-the-minute information and ticket availability. Once connected with this 24-hour recorded service, you are asked to choose a category: Press 1 for Theater and Performance, 2 for Dance and Music, 4 for family entertainment, 5 for events accepting TDF vouchers, 8 for information on TKTS booths, and so on. Recorded information is also available in Spanish.

Suppose you don't know what you want to see, or your bowling league wants to buy a block of seats to a musical. Call the Broadway Show Line, operated by the League of American Theatres and Producers, 212-563-BWAY, for descriptions of Broadway and off-Broadway shows, performance schedules, seat locations and group sales information. You can also order tickets here, with service charges the same as from Tele-charge.

Tickets

How can you buy tickets to New York's plays, concerts, ballets, operas and special mega-events? Let us describe the ways.

Box Office

To get the best seats for the day you want, go to the appropriate box office in person well in advance of the performance desired, cash or charge card in hand. Not only can you check the theater's seating diagram (usually posted near the ticket window) but you won't pay a fee for using a credit card. When ordering by telephone or mail, you have no control over the exact row or seat issued because orders are filled automatically on a "best available" basis. Box offices are usually open from 10 or 11 a.m. until the evening performance. Note: Sometimes producers, directors or actors release their personal tickets and these go back to the box office for sale at the last minute, making it possible for the persistent to see a hot show which has officially sold out. Line up.

Telephone Orders

Most theaters list a special number to call for reservations. Billed to credit cards, tickets are mailed if time allows; otherwise pick them up at the theater the day of the performance. Tele-charge, 212-239-6200, represents some 20 Schubert Theaters in New York City and adds $4 per ticket to your bill. Ticketmaster, 212-307-7171, originally an outlet for children's and sports events and rock concerts, now handles theater productions as well, collecting $3 to $5 per ticket plus a one-shot handling fee of $2.

Ticketmaster

Promoters determine how tickets to their events will be sold: at Ticketmaster outlets, by calling Ticketmaster, or both. First call 212-307-7171 to find out what performances they are offering and whether tickets can be ordered by phone and charged to a credit card (fees range from $2.50 to $3.75 per seat) or whether they must be picked up in person and paid for in cash ($2.50 extra for Broadway shows; $1.25 for all other events) at one of Ticketmaster's 2200 outlets in the US and Canada. There are 160 outlets in the tri-state area; prime locations in Manhattan include Tower Records, 692 Broadway corner of East 4th Street and Broadway at 66th Street; Tower Video, 215 East 86th Street, and 42nd Street east of Avenue of the Americas. Call 212-307-7171 for the location nearest you.

Brokers

Unless you have a friend with a personal broker or an "in" with a hotel concierge or unless your corporation runs a ticket service, don't expect to walk into a ticket agency and get front row center for the town's hottest musical the day of performance. These seats are held for valued clients. However, for most events brokers, who usually handle only orchestra, mezzanine and box seats, are still probably the easiest way to get into a show or sporting event in a hurry. Expect to pay 10%-50% over the total price for their service. **Note:** Deal only with licensed brokers in the city; out-of-town brokers operating with 800 numbers are not regulated, and you can get burned. See "Ticket Sales—Entertainment and Sports" in the Yellow Pages for names, among whom American Tickets and Continental Guests Services, operating out of major hotels, are large and well-established.

Discounts

TKTS is one of the city's great bargains. The Theater Development Fund operates two outlets for half-price, day-of-performance tickets to Broadway and off-Broadway shows as well as to music programs and dance events. Availability information is posted on large boards near ticket sales booths, and a small fee—currently $2.50—is charged for each ticket. Cash or travelers' check only.

- **TKTS Times Square**, West 47th Street and Broadway, sells Broadway and off-Broadway tickets for evening performances from 3 to 8 p.m. daily. Matinee tickets go on sale on Wednesdays, Saturdays 10 to 2, Sundays noon to 7.

- **TKTS Lower Manhattan**, 2 World Trade Center, mezzanine, open Monday through Friday from 11 to 5, Saturday 11 to 3:30. Seats for Broadway evening performances go on sale here earlier—at 11 a.m.—than those at Times Square, and the lines are a lot shorter at the World Trade Center TKTS, where half-price off-Broadway evening tickets are also sold from 11 a.m. to 1 p.m. on the day of performance. Matinee tickets are sold from 11 to 5 on the day prior to performance.

- **Bryant Park Tickets Booth**, 42nd Street and Sixth Avenue, 212-382-2323 open noon to 2 p.m. and again 3 p.m. to 7 p.m., Tuesday–Sunday, operated by the Bryant Park Restoration Corporation, sells half-price, day-of-performance tickets for dance and music concerts throughout town. You can call for a recording listing tickets available that day. Tickets for Monday may be purchased on Sunday. Sharing this booth is a Ticketmaster outlet for full-price tickets to all events.

- **Twofers** resemble theater tickets but are, in fact, passes. When exchanged at Broadway (and some off-Broadway) box offices, twofers entitle the bearer to two tickets for little more than the price of one. A convenient way to keep a show open after bad reviews or at the end of a long run, twofers can be found all over town, for example at restaurant cash registers, the New York Convention and Visitors Bureau at 2 Columbus Circle, in college dorms and on hotel desks.

- **The Theater Development Fund**, 1501 Broadway, Attention: Applications, NYC 10036, 212-221-0013, offers tickets to a variety of plays, musicals, dance and jazz performances at about $10 each to its members. If you are retired, a student or teacher, a clergyman, performing professional, union member or in the armed forces, you can get a membership application by mailing a self-addressed, stamped envelope with your request. Upon acceptance and payment of $14 or more, you'll be on the mailing list to receive their offerings. You will also be eligible to purchase their TDF Vouchers for off-off-Broadway shows, music and dance events. For $15 you get vouchers good for five performances over a six-month period, plus a calendar of events to which they apply.

- **ArtsPassNY**, 250 West 57th Street, Suite 1222, NYC 10107, 212-307 6655, offers its members discounted tickets to the best seats at selected performances of Young Concert Artists, the American Ballet Theatre, the Roundabout Theatre and the New York City Opera. Membership, costing $115 and open to adults under 40, entitles you to choose one of the selected performances from each of the participating companies. The same seats without the discount would run $205. Call 307-6655 to inquire or subscribe.

• **Audience Extras**, 109 West 26th Street, NYC 10001, 212-989-9550, provides free tickets to plays in preview and post opening (whose producers wish to "paper" the house, i.e., fill it with freebies to stimulate word-of-mouth) to its members in the theater industry. For $130 you get a one-year membership card with a reserve fund against which a $3 service charge per ticket is charged as well as access to their 24-hour hotline, which lists available shows. There is no limit on free shows, and you can bring up to three guests.

• **Quicktix**, a small allotment of seats for each of the various performances at the New York Shakespeare Festival's Public Theatre on Lafayette Street (see Theater section) go on sale at 5:30 p.m. the day of performance for about half the price of regular tickets. Call 212-598-7150 for information on general availability.

Student tickets at half price or less are often available to those holding bona fide student IDs as follows:

• **New York Philharmonic** at Avery Fisher Hall, Lincoln Center, has two arrangements. They sell $10 tickets for the Thursday morning rehearsals about a month before the actual date. In the Student Rush Program you should line up with ID and $10 at Window 6 about an hour and a half in advance of a Tuesday or Thursday concert. At 7:30 p.m. available tickets go on sale. Call 212-875-5656 to check ticket availability first.

• **New York City Opera**, also at Lincoln Center, sometimes has student tickets for those who line up at the theater by 10 a.m. on the morning of a performance, 11:30 on Sunday. Tickets, if available, are $10. Call 212-870-5570 for more information.

• **Carnegie Hall** sells $5 tickets, when available, on a first-come, first-served basis. You can call 212-247-7800 between noon and 1 p.m. on the day of performance to see if tickets will be available.

• **Grace Rainey Rogers Auditorium** at the Metropolitan Museum of Art sells standing room tickets for half price on the day of a concert. Call the box office at 212-570-3949 to check on availability.

High school students have access to the best deal of all on tickets to music, theater, museums, dance and more through **High 5 Tickets to the Arts**. Students 13 to 18 years old can get $5 tickets to weekend (Friday through Sunday) performances, two for $5 for weekday performances by presenting school ID at any Ticketmaster outlet, including Rite Aid pharmacies, at least a day before the performance. Museum admission is two for $5 any day, with ID, at the museum. For a brochure listing available events and locations call 212-HI5-TKTS, or visit the Web site at http://www.high5tix.com.

A few of the smaller to mid-size Manhattan theaters (generally off-

Broadway and off-off Broadway) will exchange admission for volunteer ushering, a boon to the theater devotee who is light of wallet. Call around for participating theaters.

An indispensable aid for the dedicated theater goer, sports fan or classical music enthusiast is **STUBS**, a paperback which publishes the seating plan of every concert hall, opera house, stadium, arena and theater in town. STUBS in hand, you can immediately locate the seats being offered by TKTS booths, brokers, Ticketmaster outlets and others who have no seating diagrams available for ticket purchasers.

Subscriptions

Common practice dictates that new subscriptions to any series—symphonic, operatic, dance, theatrical—must wait to be filled until the previous season's subscribers are given an opportunity to renew. Once the renewal deadline is past, new subscriptions are processed on a first-come, first-served basis. The initial announcement of each new season's schedule is sent to everyone on the mailing list anywhere from six weeks to six months before performances are scheduled to begin. To assure a position near the beginning of the line, call whatever institution interests you well in advance of its season and ask to be put on the mailing list. Upon receipt of the announcement schedule, choose your series and return the coupon and a check quickly. Full-page ads in The New York Times Sunday Arts and Leisure section herald symphonic, operatic and dance seasons five to six months before performances begin, but usually a week or two after the first public subscription mailers have been sent out.

Incidentally, certain nights are traditionally more popular than others. If good seats are more important than sitting next to the right people, find out which night or series has the best tickets available.

Grand Opera

Metropolitan Opera, Metropolitan Opera House, Lincoln Center, NYC 10023; Subscriptions, 212-362-2080; Met Ticket Service for current sales, 212-362-6000. Subscriptions range from $144 for an eight-opera series high up in the Family Circle to $1,160 for an eight-opera series in the Center Orchestra. The Met charges $20 per subscription for handling. Renewal notices are mailed to current subscribers, and once these orders are processed in the spring, new subscriptions are filled.

The Met's season is broken into three periods for the sale of individual seats: fall, winter and spring. Subscribers are given first crack, then seats for single performances are offered to the public, first through a mailing, then via newspaper ads about a month and a half before each of the three seasons begins. Standing room goes on sale the Sunday before performance.

New York City Opera, New York State Theater, Lincoln Center, NYC 10023, Subscriptions, 212-496-0600; Box Office, 212-870-5570. The

New York City Opera offers about 48 two- to four-opera series for performances between mid-July and mid-November. The cheapest seats for a three-performance series cost $45; the most expensive for four performances, $278. With a top ticket price of $82, City Opera performances are a grand bargain.

Classical Music

New York Philharmonic, Avery Fisher Hall, Lincoln Center, NYC 10023, Subscriptions, 212-875-5656; Center Charge for current sales, 212-721-6500. Fifteen different series are available for a September through June season. Easiest to obtain are subscriptions to the three-concert mini-series. Prices run from $36 in the Third Tier Box with partial view for the three-concert series to a top of $500 for concerts down front in the Center Orchestra. Fall schedules are announced in late February/early March.

Carnegie Hall, 57th Street and Seventh Avenue, NYC 10019, Subscriptions, 212-903-9700; current sales, 212-247-7800. One hundred years old and still counting, Carnegie is still the concert hall preferred by many performers, and it continues to host programs by a variety of virtuosos and orchestras (to say nothing of popular superstars) with age-given grace. The Philadelphia, Cleveland and Boston Symphony Orchestras all hold their New York concert series here. Call Carnegie Hall for subscriber information. A series can cost anywhere between $37 and $430.

Chamber Music

Several halls traditionally host the extraordinarily popular chamber music groups that perform here regularly. The Guarneri Quartet, the Juilliard Quartet and the Beaux Arts Trio might give two or three New York series during any given year, each at a different location. Only the Lincoln Center Chamber Music Society has a hall—Alice Tully Hall in Lincoln Center—which it can call home. Good seats go fast once the *Times* advertisements appear, so it's important to get on each group's mailing list. The following spaces are most likely to host chamber music performances. Call them or keep your eyes on the Arts and Leisure section of the Sunday *New York Times* in late spring and summer.

- **Abraham Goodman House**, Merkin Concert Hall, 129 West 67th Street between Broadway and Amsterdam Avenue, NYC 10023, 212-362-8719.

- **Alice Tully Hall**, Lincoln Center, NYC 10023, Subscriptions, 212-875-5050; Center Charge for current sales, 212-721-6500. Concerts by the Lincoln Center Chamber Music Society as well as other groups.

- **Carnegie Hall**, 57th Street and Seventh Avenue, NYC 10019, Subscriptions, 212-903-9700; current sales, 212-247-7800.

- **Metropolitan Museum of Art**, Grace Rainey Rogers Auditorium,

83rd Street and Fifth Avenue, NYC 10028, 212-570-3949.

• **92nd Street Y** (YM-YWHA), Kaufmann Concert Hall, 1395 Lexington Avenue, NYC 10028, 212-427-6000.

Dance

American Ballet Theater, Metropolitan Opera House, Lincoln Center, NYC 10023, Subscriptions, 212-799-3100; Met Ticket Service for current sales, 212-496-0600 Seventeen series are offered, each with four ballets, for the ABT's nine-week season April through June. The first announcement, mailed to friends in late December, is followed by a new subscriber mailing towards the end of the month and then a week or so later by the traditional January *New York Times* ad. Subscriptions for seats high up in the Family Circle cost $54, while way down in the Orchestra they command $260.

Individual tickets at the Box Office and by phone from the Met Ticket Service go on sale in March.

New York City Ballet, New York State Theater, Lincoln Center, NYC 10023. Subscriptions and current sale information, 212-496-0600. Two seasons provide balletomanes the opportunity of feasting on dancing by Balanchine's company. Both the Winter Season, November through February, and the Spring Season, April through June, have sixteen four-performance series, and good seats are easiest to come by for weekend matinees. First announcements go out nine weeks before the season begins. A tip for *Nutcracker* ballet fanciers: first orders for single, non-subscription performances of the *Nutcracker* are accepted in late October. Call 212-870-5500 for prices and dates, and if certain seats for special performances are important, make your order several weeks before that time.

The City Center Theater, 131 West 55th Street, NYC 10019, 212-581-1212. Dance companies dominate City Center's performance schedule. The house, open from mid-September through June, is in fact almost totally given over to productions of modern dance and modern ballet. The following are among the major groups performing regularly here:

• **Martha Graham**, 316 East 63rd Street, 212-833-5886.

• **Alvin Ailey American Dance Theater**, 211 West 61st Street, 212-767-0590.

• **Paul Taylor Dance Company**, 552 Broadway, 212-431-5562.

• **Dance Theatre of Harlem**, 466 West 152nd Street, 212-690-2800.

As with the chamber music ensembles, it is best to get on each particular company's mailing list. Call the company direct or City Center's Subscription Department. Prices vary for each series. Single tickets average $15 to $45.

The Joyce Theater, 175 Eighth Avenue at 19th Street, NYC 10011, 212-242-0800. Celebrating dance of all kinds—the Joffrey II and Erick Hawkins Company dance here, and the Joyce is practically the Feld Ballet's home—the Joyce is an elegantly revamped former Art Deco movie house in Chelsea. Your reward for buying tickets to performances by four different dance groups during the fall or spring season is a membership that entitles you to 40% off on all tickets purchased subsequently. Your membership card also entitles you to priority seating and various discounts at fifteen Chelsea restaurants located between 14th and 23rd Streets and Sixth and Tenth Avenues.

Theater

A high percentage of the most critically acclaimed plays produced in any given year originate off-Broadway, more often than not in theaters that offer subscriptions as a means of financing productions. Season tickets not only ensure exposure to new artists, playwrights and directors, but in most cases save money as well. A few of the most established groups are mentioned here, but please don't be limited by this list. Many more experimental but no less rewarding companies exist and should be explored.

Circle in the Square, 1633 Broadway at 50th Street, NYC 10019-6795, 212-581-6371. Plays by Tennessee Williams and Eugene O'Neill premiered at Circle in the Square with such young actors as Jason Robards and George C. Scott beginning in the 1950s in the Village. Uptown now, the theater continues to stage some of the best contemporary drama and comedy with first rate actors and directors. A $40 membership gives the owner one year's access to each production for only $10 each. Nonmembers pay $45 a seat to any of the three-four yearly presentations.

CSC Repertory Theater, 136 East 13th Street, NYC 10003, 212-677-4210. Founded in 1967, CSC has been performing Ibsen, Strindberg, Brecht and other mostly-contemporary classics in this comfortably intimate theater since then. It's not a resident company, but three or four plays are performed in repertory throughout the season, with an occasional lecture bonus. The season is announced in August, but you can subscribe anytime for $45 to $250 (for opening night performances).

Joseph Papp Public Theater, 425 Lafayette Street south of East 8th Street, NYC 10003, 212-260-2400. Joseph Papp was perhaps the single most important figure in the post-WWII American theater. With his death in 1992, and after 40 years of his leadership, it was not surprising that the Public experienced some turmoil as it sought its way through a difficult transition. With the appointment of George Wolfe (acclaimed director of *Angels in America*) as its artistic director, the renamed New

York Shakespeare Festival's Public Theater appears once again to be on firm ground, offering events that are hailed for their diversity as well as their excellence.

A membership package plan allows the public inexpensive access to productions and flexibility in choosing which of the season's productions one wishes to see. Packages start at $90 for three productions. Seats are not pre-assigned at The Public, so members simply call the members' hotline to order tickets, which are then mailed or held at the box office. A small allotment of the seats for any performance at The Public are held for same-day sale at a discount. The tickets, called Quicktix (see Discounts section), go on sale at 6 p.m. for about half the price of regular tickets.

Lincoln Center Theater, 150 West 65th Street, Attention: Members Department, NYC 10023, 212-239-6277. Members in this innovative theater program have access, at $20 a ticket, to a potpourri of presentations from Shakespeare to Mamet, with an occasional first-rate musical thrown in, be it at Lincoln Center, on Broadway or off-off-Broadway at the experimental LaMama. The $35 membership fee buys one year's access to Lincoln Center Theater plays already in progress around town and first crack at six new productions a year as they come up. Popular productions with outstanding casts have included *Our Town, Sarafina, Waiting for Godot* and *Anything Goes.*

Manhattan Theater Club, 321 East 73rd Street, NYC 10021, 212-645-5848. Upper East Siders don't have to go downtown for good theater. The Manhattan Theater Club's critically acclaimed plays have been produced here since 1972. However, productions have proven so popular that the traditional five-play September-through-May series now takes place at The Space, a 299-seat theater at City Center, 131 West 55th Street, while the four-play "Special Events" season occupies the Downstage Theater at the Manhattan Theater Club proper. A five-play series starts at $190.

National Actors Theatre, Lyceum Theatre, 45th Street (East of Broadway), NYC 239-6280. Despite the ignominy of less than supportive critics, Tony Randall has persisted in his dream of a theater of American actors performing the classics of the world stage. The former Felix Ungar now presents plays by Chekov, Ibsen, Gogol, Shakespeare and Shaw with actors who have made their careers in America's repertory theaters as well as those best known for their work on television. The ingredients seem unlikely but the intent is sincere and the results have begun to pay off. Subscriptions for the four-play series begin at around $120.

Roundabout Theater Company, 1530 Broadway (at 45th Street), 212-719-9393. With a subscription base second only to the Metropolitan Opera, the Roundabout is obviously doing something right. What that involves is presenting plays such as Pinter's *Old Times* and O'Neill's *Anna Christie* and musicals such as *She Loves Me* with such stars as

Natasha Richardson, Jason Robards, Christopher Plummer and Kelly McGillis. A five-play series starts at around $185, a bargain considering the Roundabout is a Broadway house. The Roundabout has also pioneered special subscriptions for singles (straight and gay) that are a good way for fellow theater lovers to meet.

All of the Above

Brooklyn Academy of Music, 30 Lafayette Avenue, Brooklyn 11217, 718-636-4100, is a center for all the performing arts. Best known for its Next Wave Festival, which takes place September to December, BAM (as it is popularly known) is the premier New York showcase for cutting-edge dance, theater, music and opera. From the intimate LeClerq Space to the magnificent Opera House and the newly renovated Majestic Theater, BAM presents everything from small chamber performances like Eiko and Komo to Peter Brook and Arianne Mnouchkine epics. With several series taking place year-round, it is best to call and get on the mailing list in order to have a shot at getting tickets.

Queens Theatre in the Park, Flushing Meadow Corona Park, Flushing 11368, 718-760-0064, brings major dance companies, Off-Broadway plays and children's theater to its two theaters located in the Philip Johnson-designed New York Pavilion of the I964-65 World's Fair. Subscriptions are $67.50 for four theater productions or four dance programs. A foreign film series, featuring golden oldies as well as contemporary film is being planned. Call for details.

Film

New York is a movie buff's paradise. **The Museum of Modern Art**, 11 West 53rd Street, 212-708-9480, is famous for its carefully planned retrospectives. Screening of new filmmakers' works are a constant at the **Whitney Museum of American Art**, 945 Madison Avenue, 212-570-3617, as well as at most of those all-encompassing, art-encouraging alternative spaces sprinkled throughout New York. **The New School for Social Research**, 66 West 12th Street, 212-229-5600, and the Cinema Department of **New York University**, 721 Broadway, 6th floor, 212-998-1600, explore movies in depth through numerous seminars and courses and, almost every semester, sponsor a film series or two as well.

Some of Manhattan's remaining revival and art film showcases include: **Angelika Film Center**, 18 West Houston Street, NYC 10003, 212-995-2000; **Anthology Film Archives**, 32 Second Avenue at Second Street, NYC 10003, 505-5110; **Cinema Village**, 12th Street east of Fifth Avenue, NYC 10003, 212-924-3363; **Film Forum**, 209 West Houston, NYC, 212-727-8110; the **Paris Theater** at 4 West 58th Street; the **Public Theater**, 425 Lafayette Street, NYC 10003, 212-598-7171; and the **Walter Reade Theater**, 165 West 65th Street at Broadway, NYC 10023, 875-5600. Weekly schedules for these theaters, as well as first and rerun houses, are found in the "Arts and Leisure" section of the Sunday *Times* and *The New Yorker.*

- **The American Museum of the Moving Image**, 36-01 35th Avenue at 36th Street, Astoria 11106, 718-784-0077, is a continuous movie, animation and video art retrospective with exhibits, speaker series, symposia, celebrity appearances and film series throughout the year to quicken the pulse of the true movie maven. Membership, $50 for individual, $60 for family, gives you admission, reservation privileges for screenings, a subscription to the *Quarterly Guide,* a 15% discount at the museum shop, and reduced admission to special programs and celebrity appearances.

- **The Film Society of Lincoln Center**, 140 West 65th Street, NYC 10023, 212-875-5600, presents the New York Film Festival each fall (late September through October) as well as the New Directors/New Films series in conjunction with the Museum of Modern Art each spring. Established in 1963, the Film Festival presents some 20 films during its annual run. A $50 membership in the Film Society ($35 for students) provides the following perks: right to buy two twelve-film subscriptions to the New York Film Festival and first crack at certain other Festival tickets, discounts on tickets for New Directors/New Films at the Museum of Modern Art, and a free subscription to the society's bi-monthly magazine *Film Comment.*

   If you're not interested in membership, it's a good idea to get on the society's mailing list before the Film Festival's program is announced the last week in August, in order to obtain the schedule before it appears in the papers. The Box Office for performances at Alice Tully Hall is at 1941 Broadway at 65th Street, NYC 10023, 212-875-5050. It opens the Sunday after Labor Day for single ticket sales to the public.

Broadcasting

The Museum of Television and Radio, 23 West 52nd Street, 212-621-6600, shouldn't be missed as a chance to have a lot of fun experiencing American culture in video and audio tape form. Call for schedule listings of special screening events. Annual memberships begin at $35 for students, $50 for the general public, and allow you free admission to the museum's theaters and screening and listening rooms. The museum offers 96 video monitors for individual viewing of any television program in their collection. Membership also gives you a discount on museum seminars and magazines as well as all gift shop items. For more membership information, call 212-621-6600.

Memberships

The benefits that can be reaped by joining any of the city's myriad non-profit institutions are really quite amazing. There seem to be museums and societies for every possible interest, and if you're an avid aficionado of a certain discipline, seek out the institution which best reflects your avocation and join. You'll be inundated with free literature, offered perquisites of many kinds and probably be invited to teas, cocktail parties and even banquets if your contribution is big enough. For the generalist, membership in one or two of the city's established cultural citadels is a wonderful way of obtaining well-researched information on any number of subjects. For those who want to keep up with the latest in museum happenings, there's a colorful bimonthly magazine, *Museums of New York*, that will inform you of all the museum news and events in town. Call 800-NYC-MUSE for a subscription. As an indication of the kind of benefits memberships provide, we've noted below details for a few of New York's major institutions.

Metropolitan Museum of Art, Fifth Avenue at 82nd Street, NYC 10028, 212-879-5500. The sumptuous Bulletin published quarterly by the Met, filled with high-quality color photographs and illuminating texts of catalog caliber, comes free with the museum's $70 Individual Membership. Other bonuses include the bi-monthly *Calendar News,* free admission to the museum and the Cloisters, invitations to previews and private viewings of two exhibitions a year, and copies of the Met's Christmas and Spring Catalogues illustrating the museum's publications and glamorous reproductions of everything from Chinese scarves to early American pewter pitchers, which, as a member, you can buy for a 10% discount. But probably the biggest bonus you'll receive is the program and exhibition information, which will impel you to get over to the Met more often than you might otherwise.

American Museum of Natural History, Central Park West at 79th Street, NYC 10024, 212-769-5100. A $30 Associate Membership here entitles you to as many visits to the dinosaurs as you wish, to say nothing of the Hall of Meteorites, a subscription to *Natural History* magazine and a 10% discount in the store; a $50 family membership provides as well a monthly newsletter and calendar, 25% discount on Planetarium tickets and invitations to previews of the exhibitions. You also receive a 10% discount on most educational programs at the museum and a 40% discount at the Naturemax Theater, a thoroughly modern revamping of the old auditorium with an oversized retractable screen and a dizzying IMAX projector.

The Museum of Modern Art, 11 West 53rd Street, NYC 10019, 212-708-9480. With the ambitious expansion program complete, gallery space for the museum's unparalleled collection of 20th century art has been doubled and MoMA now has two theaters for films and a new glass-enclosed garden hall overlooking the sculpture garden. Those who pay $75 for an entry level membership can lunch in the new members' restaurant, receive 25% discounts at the enlarged museum store and on catalog merchandise (10% on non-museum merchandise), free admission to the galleries and daily film programs, discounted admission for guests, reduced subscription rates on major art magazines, invitations to exhibition previews and special events as well as free subscriptions to the monthly *Members' Calendar* and to *MoMA*, the quarterly newsletter.

Guggenheim Museum, 1071 Fifth Avenue, NYC 10128, downtown at 575 Broadway at Prince, NYC 10012, 423-3500. Even the basic individual membership at $60 confers an architectural bonus, providing free admission to the justifiably famous Frank LLoyd Wright spiral uptown, the handsome brick and cast iron SoHo museum downtown and the Peggy Guggenheim Collection in her palazzo on the Grand Canal in Venice. In addition members get an invitation to one gala preview, to private viewings, subscription to the museum newsletter, 10% off at all museum stores, at the Dean and DeLuca Cafe uptown and discounts on guest admission and on parking uptown. Fellow Associates, at $250 per, also attend special openings, and receive one major show catalogue, a private reception and tour of the permanent collection (mostly Impressionists), and free guest privileges.

Whitney Museum of American Art, 945 Madison Avenue, NYC 10021, 212-570-3676. An Individual Membership costs $65 and benefits its holder with free museum admission for two, 20% discount on museum publications, two invitations to exhibition opening receptions and a free museum publication, as well as calendars of events. If American art or experimental film interests you particularly, it is worth belonging to the Whitney to have ready access to its excellent series of large and small exhibitions and also to the works presented by the museum's New American Filmmakers series in some 25 or 30 different programs every year.

South Street Seaport Museum, 207 Front Street, NYC 10038, 212-748-8600. Despite the commercial redevelopment of the Seaport's facilities by the Rouse Corporation—in main part the construction of a glimmering glass Pier Pavilion over the East River—Phase I, encompassing the new Fulton Market with its intriguing stores and jolly restaurants, the restoration of Schermerhorn Row's handsome brick houses, and the Museum Block with old shops and new walkways, continues to attract crowds.

For $35, the cost of an Individual Seaport Membership ($25 for students), you become involved with conserving an historically valuable part of downtown and preserving New York's maritime traditions while receiving discounts and free admissions in a vibrant entertainment area. Museum members tend to be a youngish crowd, drawn as much by the ambiance and the idea of the museum as by the perks, which include free admission to the ships and the Seaport Gallery on Water Street, quarterly copies of *Seaport* magazine and the museum's bulletin, as well as reduced admission to the South Street Venture multimedia show and other special events. Furthermore, you get first shot at seats for the free Summerpier jazz concerts and special member rates on the Pioneer's two-and three-hour sails of New York Harbor.

The Bronx Zoo (its new official name: **New York Zoological Society's International Wildlife Conservation Park**), Fordham Road and Bronx River Parkway, Bronx, 718-367-1010, is the largest zoo in the five boroughs and, stretching over 265 acres, the largest urban zoo in the world. An annual membership costs $41, $58 for a family membership, and gives you free admission to this zoo as well as to the **Central Park Zoo**, Central Park, East 64th Street and Fifth Avenue, 212-861-6030; **the New York Aquarium**, Surf Avenue and West 8th Street, Coney Island, Brooklyn, 718-265-3400; and the **Queens Zoo** and **Children's Farm**, 111th Street at 54th Avenue, Corona Park, Flushing, Queens. Bronx Zoo membership also includes three free parking passes and tickets to seven seasonal attractions. Call 718-220-5111 for membership information.

For the record, the comprehensive *New York City Culture Catalog* ($16.55), compiled and published by the Alliance for the Arts, 330 West 42nd Street, NYC 10036, 212-947-6340, briefly describes and gives directions to scores of local institutions and attractions—from historic houses and botanical gardens to alternative spaces and zoos. Call for further details.

Colleges and Universities

Manhattan

- **Bank Street College of Education**, 610 West 112th Street, NYC 10025, 875-4400

- **Barnard College**, 3009 Broadway, NYC 10027-6598, 854-5262

- **Baruch College of Adult and Continuing Education**, 48 East 26th Street, 10010, 477-3020

- **City College, CUNY, 138th Street and Convent Avenue**, NYC 10031, 650-7000

- **City University of N.Y. Graduate School and University Center**, 33 West 42nd Street, NYC 10018, 642-1600

- **Columbia University**, Broadway at 116th Street, NYC 10027, 854-1754

- **Fordham University**, 113 West 60th Street, NYC 10023, 800-FORDHAM

- **Hebrew-Union College-Jewish Institute of Religion**, One West 4th Street, NYC 10012, 674-5300.

- **Hunter College**, 695 Park Avenue at 68th Street, NYC 10021, 772-4000

- **Jewish Theological Seminary**, 3080 Broadway, NYC 10027, 678-8000

- **Manhattan College**, Riverdale 10471, 800-MC2-XCEL
- **Marymount Manhattan College**, 221 East 71st Street, NYC 10021, 517-0400
- **New School**, 66 West 12th Street, NYC 10011, 229-5600
- **New York University**, 50 West 4th Street, NYC 10003, 800-771-4NYU
- **Pace University**, 1 Pace Plaza, NYC 10038-1598, 346-1200
- **Parsons School of Design**, 66 Fifth Avenue, NYC 10011, 229-8900
- **Pratt Manhattan**, 295 Lafayette Street, NYC 10012, 925-8481
- **Union Theological Seminary**, Broadway and 120th Street, NYC 10027, 662-7100
- **Yeshiva University**, 500 West 185th Street, NYC 10033, 960-5400

Brooklyn

- **Brooklyn College,** 2900 Bedford Avenue, Brooklyn 11210, 718-951-5000
- **Pratt Institute**, 200 Willoughby Avenue, Brooklyn 11205, 718-636-3600
- **St. Joseph's College**, 245 Clinton Avenue, Brooklyn 11205, 718-636-6800

Queens

- **Queen's College**, 65-30 Kissena Blvd., Flushing 11367, 718-997-5411
- **St. John's University**, Grand Central and Utopia Parkways, Jamaica 11439, 718-990-6161

Staten Island

- **College of Staten Island**, CUNY, 130 Stuyvesant Place, Staten Island 10301, 718-390-7733
- **St. John's University**, 300 Howard Avenue, Staten Island 10301, 718-390-4000
- **Wagner College**, 631 Howard Avenue, Staten Island 10201, 718-390-3100

DESPITE the city's rapid pace and anonymity, or perhaps because of it, New Yorkers by the thousands volunteer their services to hundreds of worthy causes. Motivations are as varied as the tasks. So are the rewards.

A mind-boggling array of public, private and non-profit organizations will gladly put to use whatever talents or interests you have. Experience is not necessarily required; most institutions provide training. What kinds of jobs are available where? Read on. We've also listed the names of agencies which refer volunteers to other organizations and included a few alternative suggestions as well.

How You Can Help

The Hungry and the Homeless

Scores of volunteers concern themselves with shelter for the city's homeless. Jobs include: monitoring and organizing the shelters, providing legal help, ministering to psychiatric, medical and social needs, raising money, manning phones, and caring for children in the shelters. Many people solicit, organize, cook and serve food to the destitute at sites throughout the city. Still others deliver meals to the homeless and the home-bound.

Children

If involvement with children is especially appealing you can: tutor in and out of schools, cuddle a foundling, be a big brother or sister, teach music and sports in shelters, parks and hospitals, and accompany kids on weekend outings.

Hospitals

The need for volunteers in both city-run and private hospitals is manifold: chaplain's aides, interpreters, laboratory personnel, admitting and nursing aides are required; assistants in crisis medical areas—emergency rooms, intensive care units and the like—are wanted; so are ambulance drivers, and volunteers to work with victims of sexual abuse.

The Disabled and the Elderly

You can read to the blind, help teach the deaf, work to prevent birth defects, help the retarded and developmentally disabled, among others. You can also make regular visits to the homebound elderly, deliver them hot meals, and teach everything from nutrition to arts and crafts in senior centers and nursing homes.

Extreme Care Situations

Helping with cancer, suicide prevention, Alzheimer's and AIDS patients, rape victims and abused children is a special category demanding a high level of commitment—not to mention emotional reserves.

The Culture Scene

Unpaid stamp-lickers and benefit chairmen keep the city's cultural institutions afloat. Consider guiding tours, raising funds or assisting the staff at your favorite museum, library or ballet company.

The Community

Work in your neighborhood. Block associations and community gardens are run strictly by volunteers. You can help out at the local school, nursing home, settlement house or animal shelter.

Where You Can Help

Specific-Need Organizations

The organizations in New York City that address a major disease, disability or social problem are legion. For example, there's the Memorial Sloan-Kettering Cancer Center, The Coalition for the Homeless, Volunteer Services for Children, New York Association for the Blind (The Lighthouse), Literacy Volunteers of New York, Volunteers in the Schools, the Gay Men's Health Alliance, Women in Need, and City Harvest, which collects and distributes food to the hungry.

Institutions

New York's health, education and, some would say, its very civilization rest upon the city's institutions. Hospitals, museums, libraries, schools, animal shelters, opera and ballet companies are mostly under-funded and rely on a veritable army of volunteers to survive.

The Religious Connection

Individual churches and synagogues (in particular, those serving the homeless and the needy) and church federations such as the Federation of Protestant Welfare Agencies, the Catholic Charities and the UJA-Federation of Jewish Philanthropies use volunteers for a variety of activities.

The Community

More than 5,000 block associations and neighborhood-wide organizations, such as Greenwich House in the Village and Yorkville's Civic Council (see below), can use your talents. Citywide there is a need for volunteers in the schools, parks, shelters and in consumer affairs.

Multi-Service Organizations

Don't forget such well-known groups as the Salvation Army, American Red Cross and the Visiting Nurse Service (it's not just nurses).

The Corporate Connection

Corporations encourage employee voluntarism through company-supported projects such as literacy programs, pro bono work and management aid to non-profit groups. Check with the company personnel or public relations department to see if your firm is involved in any specific project. Many corporations have set up programs with the help of Corporation Volunteers of New York, 17 John Street, NYC 10007, 212-696-2442.

Referral Services

If you don't know which way to turn, try one of several umbrella organizations which find volunteers for affiliated agencies. At these referral services, staff members will help you determine the tasks you would be interested in doing, where and when. Your interviewer will make specific suggestions and appointments at the places that sound appealing. Interview at several sites if you wish, and return to the referral agency until you find something you want to undertake.

- **Catholic Charities of New York**, 1011 First Avenue, 212-371-1000, are affiliated with more than 100 different agencies dealing with shelters, food kitchens and the homeless. An interview may be requested.

- **The Federation of Protestant Welfare Agencies**, 281 Park Avenue South, 212-777-4800, open 8:30 to 6 Monday through Friday. This ecumenical group, with connections to some 800 agencies in the metropolitan area, finds jobs for volunteers of any religious persuasion.

- **The Mayor's Voluntary Action Center**, 250 Broadway, 212-566-5950, open 10 to 3 Tuesday and Thursday, to 7 Wednesday. The city's largest referral agency has 10,000 job openings in nearly 5,000 public and private non-profit organizations. This enormous clearing house can place just about anyone in a useful job, especially in the human services and cultural areas.

- **New York Cares**, 116 East 16th Street, NYC 10011, 212-228-5000 is a favorite volunteer organization among young professionals. It was founded in 1986 by people anxious to volunteer but discouraged by other organizations' long waiting lists and required time commitments. New York Cares lets its 8,000 volunteers choose from a monthly calendar of events set up with the more than fifty not-for-profit organizations they serve. These projects include reading with homeless children, serving brunch at soup kitchens, cleaning public parks and visiting elderly homebound. "Joining a volunteer team within a month after my move to New York gave me an immediate sense of belonging to the city. It's also been a great place to meet people," says a two-year New York Cares volunteer. He adds, "The funny thing is, most of the volunteers I meet here are somewhat new to New York themselves." Call to attend one of two weekly orientation meetings.

- **The United Jewish Appeal-Federation of Jewish Philanthropies**, 130 East 59th Street, NYC 10022, 212-980-1000 open 9 to 5 Monday-Friday. The Jewish Information Referral Service sends callers a catalog describing nearly 200 agencies and projects. Programs include revitalizing old neighborhoods and synagogues as well as working with children, immigrants, the elderly and the homeless.

- **The Volunteer Referral Center**, 161 Madison Avenue, NYC 10016, 212-889-4805, 212-745-8249, interviews by appointment, 11 to 3 Tuesday through Thursday, and 5:30 to 7 Tuesday and Wednesday. The Center can place adult and student volunteers at some 350 not-for-profit agencies throughout Manhattan.

Other Connections

Check bulletin boards at your office, church, neighborhood grocery store, Laundromat and school.

- **WBAI-FM** (99.5 FM) discusses, and occasionally stimulates, volunteer projects, especially those involving the homeless and the hungry.

- *The Yellow Pages*, under "Social and Human Services," contains more than five pages of organizations and institutions—in categories from Abortion Alternatives Counseling to Youth Services—many of which welcome volunteers. It's a great source of ideas, as well as a tool for follow-through.

- *Volunteering in New York City* by Richard Mintzer is a useful reference. Published by Walker & Company.

I N NEW YORK you can root, root, root for the home team, canter along Central Park's cinder track, join a pickup basketball game, work up a water ballet, or sit spellbound at the US Open Tennis Championships. The city hosts events for every season and activities for every appetite. As an aid to sorting out the teams you wish to follow and the activities you wish to pursue, ticket information and other details about the area's major teams are listed below followed by a section devoted to **Participant Sports**. For specifics about ticket sales see also **Tickets** in the chapter on **Cultural Life**.

Professional Sports

For weekly specifics on leading amateur and professional sporting events check "This Week in Sports," a box in the Sports section of the Sunday *New York Times*, and *The New Yorker* magazine's Sports section.

Baseball

The season begins in late March and lasts until early October. General admission costs $6 at Yankee Stadium in The Bronx. Single tickets for Yankee games are $20 to $30 for box seats, $12 and $18 for reserved seats; Mets tickets cost $7, $18 and $19; there is no general admission to Shea Stadium in Queens, the Mets' home base. Reserve seats for Yankee games through Ticketmaster, 212-307-7171; you can charge tickets to a credit card and have them sent or pick them up at one of 20 locations in Manhattan. The Mets use Ticketmaster, 212-307-7171, for phone orders and for direct sales.

- **New York Mets** (National League), Shea Stadium, 126th Street and Roosevelt Avenue, Flushing, NY 11368, 718-507-8499. The Mets have innumerable subscription plans ranging in cost in 1997 from $169 for 13 Saturday games to $1,458 for the full plan of box seats. Call Shea for everything in between. Availability is generally good, and applications for new subscriptions are filled around January.

- **New York Yankees** (American League), Yankee Stadium, 161st Street and River Avenue, Bronx, NY 10451, 718-293-6000. Season tickets at Yankee Stadium run from $80.50 for a reserved seat for seven games to $2,835 for a full season's box seat. For a chance at the most desirable location, get on the mailing list by November.

Basketball

Basketball begins when baseball leaves off, around late October, and continues through mid-April. Home games are played in Madison Square Garden and at the Meadowlands, the huge sports complex in New Jersey that each year seems to have attracted yet another New York City team across the Hudson and into the marshlands. Single seats for the Nets and the Knicks range between $20 and $1,000 each and go on sale late October. Call Ticketmaster, 212-307-7171, for mail orders; visit an outlet to pick up your tickets.

- **New Jersey Nets** (NBA) play in the multi-million-dollar Byrne Meadowlands Arena, East Rutherford, NJ 07073, six miles west of the Lincoln Tunnel; call 201-935-8888 for ticket information. Season tickets for the 41-games start at $410 and reach a top of $3,075 for first row (which you'll never get!). They go on sale at the end of the previous season.

- **New York Knickerbockers** (NBA), Madison Square Garden, 33rd Street between Seventh and Eighth Avenues, NYC 10001, 212-465-5867. Individual tickets for all games go on sale in early September and can be purchased through Ticketmaster outlets, 212-307-7171, as well as at the Garden Box Office. There is a three-year waiting list for season tickets.

Football

The popularity of Jets and Giants games during the pro football season, September through December, is clearly demonstrated by ticket scarcity. Business contacts or generous friends are about the only ticket sources for Giants games; chances of buying Jets tickets are slightly better.

- **Giants** (NFL), Giants Stadium, Meadowlands, East Rutherford, NJ 07073, 201-935-8111. Regular season tickets, $350 to $400 for ten home games, are sold out about thirty years in advance at this point. Individual tickets, $35 and $40 each, are also sold out for next season.

- **New York Jets** (AFL) play at the Giants Stadium in the Meadowlands too. Call 516-560-8200 for ticket information. Renewals for season tickets to the eight home-game season are filled by May 15. New subscriptions ($200 a seat) are then issued from the fairly long waiting list on a first-come, first-served basis in early June.

Hockey

The New York Rangers play their home games at Madison Square Garden between late September and early April. An alternative to the Rangers is the Islanders, considered a local team by many New Yorkers. Call the Nassau Coliseum, the Islanders' home rink in Uniondale, Long Island, NY 11553, 516-587-9222, for information and tickets.

- **New York Rangers** (NHL), Madison Square Garden, 33rd Street between Seventh and Eighth Avenues, NYC 10001, 212-465-6471. Rangers management must be overjoyed with the team's present "sold out" state. Waiting list requests are accepted only for seats in the Blue and Green sections near the Garden's ceiling. Individual tickets, again available only in the Blue and Green sections, go on sale in early September.

Racing: Harness and Thoroughbred

All the local tracks are easily reached by public transportation. Call the numbers listed below for directions.

- **Aqueduct**, Jamaica, Queens, 718-641-4700. The track is open from October until May for thoroughbred races starting at 1 p.m. daily.

- **Belmont Park**, Elmont, Long Island, 718-641-4700. Thoroughbred races May through July and again, after the Saratoga meet, August through October begin at 1 p.m. every day (1:05 p.m. Sunday) except Tuesday.

- **Meadowlands Racetrack**, East Rutherford, NJ, 201-935-8500. Harness racing every day but Monday at 6 p.m., January through mid-August. Thoroughbreds run September through December.

- **Monmouth Park**, Oceanport, NJ, 201-222-5100. Thoroughbred races daily except Sunday at 1:30 p.m., June through late August.

- **Yonkers Raceway**, Yonkers, NY, 914-968-4200. The season's dates for the trotting races at Yonkers are determined by the New York State Racing Board. The post time is 8 p.m., and the track is closed Sundays.

Tennis

The two biggest tournaments held in the New York area are listed below. The West Side Tennis Club at Forest Hills, once the site of the US Open, now hosts the Tournament of Champions for men in May.

- **United States Open Tennis Championships**, United States Tennis Center, Flushing Park, Queens, NY 11365, 718-760-6200. The US Open consists of 13 days of afternoon and evening matches held in late August and early September. The finals take place the weekend after Labor Day. Individual tickets for the finals and semifinals are sold as soon as the first mailing goes out in late March or early April and cost $15 to $45. Tickets for matches earlier in the tournament aren't so hard to come by and are sold at Ticketmaster outlets, 212-307-7171, as well as the Tennis Center.

- **Virginia Slims Tennis Championships**, Madison Square Garden, 33rd Street between Seventh and Eighth Avenues, NYC 10001, 212-465-6000. Box seats for the five-day women's tournament, held in the Garden annually in November, sell out fast. Individual tickets usually go on sale at Ticketmaster and the Garden in mid-December and cost between $12 and $30.

Participant Sports

Swimming pools, tennis, squash and racquetball courts, bowling alleys and billiard parlors as well as roller and ice skating rinks dot the island for your sporting pleasure, and practically any outdoor recreation you want can be found in Central Park. It's not just a super place to ride bikes or listen to classical performances of a summer evening. You can also schedule football and baseball games, play tennis or row a boat around The Lake. Flanked by Central Park West and Fifth Avenue to the east, the park covers some 750 acres between 59th and 110th Streets and is Manhattan's prime outdoor recreation area. So, before listing information about sports citywide, as well as multipurpose facilities such as health clubs and Ys, we've detailed opportunities to be found in the park, sport by sport.

Central Park

The park's Visitor's Information Center run by the Department of Parks and Recreation is located at the Dairy, 65th Street between the Zoo and the Carousel. Call 212-360-8146 for event information. The Arsenal, 830 Fifth Avenue at East 64th Street in front of the Zoo, is the park's administrative hub. For Parks Information call 212-360-8236 or the switchboard at 212-360-3456 for general information.

- **Baseball, Softball, Football, Rugby and Soccer** Fields are located in the North Meadow, at the Great Lawn and Heckscher Playground. Call 212-408-0209 for permits.

- **Bicycling** Cycling is encouraged when the park drives (but not the sunken cross-town transverses) are closed to motorized traffic on weekends from 7 p.m. Friday to 6 a.m. Monday (all day on holidays), and from 10 a.m. to 3 p.m. and 7 p.m. to 10 p.m. weekdays from April through October as well. For rentals, see Bicycles under Participant Sports for names of bicycle shops near the park.

- **Boating** The Loeb Boathouse, near East 74th Street, 212-517-2233, rents rowboats at $10 per hour for sorties onto The Lake between 9 a.m. and 5 p.m. daily in season. For $35 per half hour you can glide beneath Bow Bridge in a black Venetian gondola, complete with (not necessarily Venetian) gondolier. Armchair sailors can enjoy the comfort and cuisine of the glass-enclosed Boathouse Cafe March 21st through Thanksgiving. Fast food is available year round.

• **Horseback Riding** The Claremont Riding Academy, 175 West 89th Street, 212-724-5100, rents mounts to experienced riders for rides along the six miles of bridle paths that circle the park. You must reserve in advance.

• **Ice Skating** The park boasts two beautiful rinks: Wollman Memorial on the East Side near 62nd Street, 212-396-1010, and Lasker Memorial at Lenox Avenue at 110th Street, 212-534-7639. Wollman is open September through April, 10 a.m. to 5 Monday, to 9:30 Tuesday through Thursday and Sunday, to 11 p.m. Friday and Saturday. Admission is $6.50 for adults, $3.25 for children under l2, and skate rentals are $3.25. Besides being less crowded, Lasker is a bargain, with admission at $3, $1.75 for children, and rentals at $2.25. Lasker is open November l5 through March 15, Sunday through Thursday 10 a.m. to 9:30 p.m., Friday and Saturday to 11. In either case mornings and weekdays offer the best ice time: i.e., fewer skaters.

• **Ice Hockey** Every Saturday and Sunday morning between 7:30 and 9 a.m., ice hockey games are played at the Lasker Rink. The fee is $4 and anyone can join in the mayhem. Call the rink for more information.

• **Paddleball and Handball** You can use the ten courts located near the North Meadow at 97th Street and Transverse Road on a first-come, first-served basis. Watch the all-City and Budweiser Championships on the park courts or join the informal round robin tournaments held during the summer. Call the Department of Parks and Recreation, 212-477-4430, for more information.

• **Roller Blading/Roller Skating** In-line skaters and old-fashioned roller skaters can be found strutting their stuff (or falling down) throughout the park, but the road west of the Sheep Meadow near 69th Street is designated specifically for blading and skating. Skates can be rented for use at Wollman Memorial (see above) April through November. Hours and admission are the same as for ice skating.

• **Running** Joggers traditionally work out on the 1.58 mile cinder track girdling the Reservoir between 85th and 96th Streets, but running isn't limited to that patch. The New York Road Runners Club, 9 East 89th Street, 212-860-4455, sponsors races and clinics during the season. The 97th Street Field House houses lockers and showers for men and women.

• **Sledding** The park has hills for all kinds of sledders, from the beginner to the more advanced. For children or timid sledders, a perfect spot is Pilgrim Hill by the 72nd Street and Fifth Avenue entrance closest to the pilgrim statue. For more of a challenge, try Cedar Hill close to the Belvedere Castle at the 77th Street entrance off Central Park West.

• **Tennis** 26 clay and four all-weather courts, open from 7 a.m. to dusk, are located on the west side of the park near 95th Street. In the summer, play necessitates tennis permits, which in turn require a 1 1/2" x 1 1/2" photo (there's a photograph machine in the Arsenal), a completed application blank and $50 (no personal checks). Permits can be obtained by mail or in person at the Arsenal Building, Fifth Avenue and 64th Street, NYC 10021, 212-360-3456, between 9 and 4 weekdays. Permit holders can reserve a court for $3 by going to the Tennis House adjacent to the 95th Street Courts, 212-280-0206. Single play tennis tickets cost $4 for one hour of court time and are issued at the Arsenal on a first-come, first-served basis.

Basketball

The Department of Parks and Recreation maintains over 1,000 courts throughout the city in gyms (see **Swimming** below) as well as in city parks, large and small. Call 212-408-0209 for the location nearest you. Some of the health clubs and YMCAs have basketball courts, and the Chelsea Piers Sports and Entertainment complex includes two new courts with electronic scoreboards for league basketball, open to players of all skill levels.

Baseball

Most of Manhattan's 26 diamonds, seven of which are located in Central Park, are under the aegis of the DPR. Call 212-408-0209 for information.

Bicycling

• **American Youth Hostels**, 891 Amsterdam Avenue, 212-932-2300, the city's largest cycling organization, sponsors the Five Borough Bicycle Race which bumps and winds its way through New York each spring. AYH also promotes a number of day rides as well as weekend trips for enthusiasts.

If you don't own a bike, you may well want to rent one on a beamish spring day. At least half of Manhattan's bike dealers rent both three-and ten-speed bicycles. Rates average $4 an hour for a three-speed, $7.50 an hour or $25 per day for a hybrid, an 18-speed cross between a mountain bike and a road bike. You'll have to leave money, or a driver's license or major credit card behind as a rental deposit. A handful of the many bike rental outfits include (all telephone numbers are Area Code 212):

- **Bicycles Plus**, 1690 Second Avenue at 87th Street, 722-2201.
- **Fourteenth Street Bicycle Discount House**, 332 East 14th Street at First Avenue, 228-4344.
- **Metro Bicycles**, 1311 Lexington Avenue at 88th Street, 427-4450; 360 West 47th Street, 581-4500; 231 West 96th Street, 663-7531; 332 East 14th Street, 228-4344; 417 Canal Street, 334-8000; and 546 Avenue of the Americas at 15th Street, 255-5100.
- **Midtown Bicycles**, 360 West 47th Street at Ninth Avenue, 581-4500.
- **Pedal Pusher Bike Shop**, 1306 Second Avenue at 69th Street, 288-5592.

Billiards

There are 29 pool halls in New York City at last count, and no doubt Minnesota Fats would still be comfortable at many of them. Others, with a clubby ambiance rather than the smoke-filled hustler hangouts of yore, have attracted women to the traditionally male pastimes of pocket pool, billiards and snooker and have brightened the sport's image in the process.

- **Amsterdam Billiard Club**, 344 Amsterdam Avenue at 76th Street, 496-8180, open 11 a.m. to 3 a.m., 4 on weekends. Some 350 enthusiasts participate in league billiards here, where you can also throw a pool party without water—or liquor either, it's illegal in NY pool halls—improve your skills in private or group instruction and take a cafe-style break. The fare ranges from $5 to $15 an hour, depending on the day and time, and there are special rates for groups.
- **The Billiard Club**, 220 West 19th Street between Seventh and Eighth Avenues, 212-206-7665, open 10 a.m. to 3 a.m., Friday and Saturday until 5 a.m. It's $5 an hour to shoot pool here, $10 after 7, on two floors of a converted warehouse with 33 tables beneath brass chandeliers, two private rooms and a snack bar with waitresses. In fact, you can rent the whole place for a party, or rack 'em up with the lunch crowd.
- **Brownstone Billiards**, 308 Flatbush Avenue at Seventh Avenue, Brooklyn, (718) 857-5555, open noon to 1 a.m., to 4 a.m. Friday and Saturday. With 32 tables, including one snooker and one billiard, six ping pong tables, air hockey and video games, Brownstone has positioned itself to be a family entertainment center. The rate is a flat $3.95 per hour for pool. There's a concession stand with coffee and snack food and a Wednesday night pool class at 8, registration required. Available for children's parties.
- **Chelsea Billiards**, 54 West 21st Street west of Fifth Avenue, 212-989-0096, open 24 hours, is the biggest in the country at this writing,

with 44 Brunswick pool tables, four antique snooker tables and two billiard tables on two floors of a converted printing plant. Yet you might have to wait for a table, Friday nights especially. Best times are mornings and Sunday daytime. The tariff is $6 per hour 9 a.m. to 5 p.m., $8 per hour 5 p.m. to 9 a.m. and $10 on weekends, $2 per hour each additional person. Snooker costs $10 and $12 per hour, $2 for each additional person. There is a private room with two tables for private parties.

- **Corner Billiards**, 11th Street and 4th Avenue, 995-1314, open 11 to 2 a.m., Friday to 3, Sunday noon to 2 a.m., Saturday to 3 a.m. This is the only pool hall in Manhattan with a license to sell beer, but you can also get cappuccino in the cafe. A fairly collegiate crowd patronizes the 28 tables here at $7 per hour weekdays, $9 after 6 p.m. and daytime weekends, $12 Friday and Saturday after 6. Each additional player, up to four, costs $2 per hour. Special rates for students and seniors.

- **East Side Billiard Club**, 163 East 86th Street between Lexington and Third Avenues, 831-7665, open daily from noon to 3:30 or 4 a.m. A little jazz plays in the background, the ambiance is cozy, despite 18 regulation tables in 50,000 square feet, and, well, upscale. You take a break at the cappuccino bar. Early evening after the high school kids have left it's relaxed before the crowds arrive. There's tournament and league billiards. It costs $6 to $l4 a hour to play here, depending on the time. Monday night is ladies' night; they play half-fare.

- **Julian's Famous Poolroom**, 138 East 14th Street between Third and Fourth Avenues, 598-9884, open weekdays and Sunday 11 to 2 a.m., Friday and Saturday to 4 a.m. They shot "The Hustler" here, and the clientele hasn't changed much. Forget Cappuccino. The location upstairs over the Palladium maintains its gritty realism, and Mini-skirt Wednesday means women in minis play free after 7. Despite the ping pong tables, it's serious pool at the 29 mostly-pool tables. The rate is $8 for unlimited play weekdays, Thursday through Saturday $10 for three hours. For private parties or location shoots, call Randy or Andy.

Bird Watching

"Oh! A winter wren," warbles naturalist Sarah Elliott as she leads a group of bird-watching enthusiasts through the Ramble in Central Park. Unlikely as it may seem, Central Park is a mecca for birders because it is a magnet for migrating birds; encircled in concrete, from the sky it appears as an oasis in which to land, rest and refuel. The city's outer parks also offer prime sites for the city's dedicated birders. Below, a few organized groups and walks.

- **The American Museum of Natural History,** 212-769-5000; the **Brooklyn Botanical Garden,** 718-622-4433; and the **New York Botanical Garden** (Bronx Park), 718-817-8705, make the guidebooks as good bird-watching areas. Rare Bird Alert, 212-979-3070, provides recorded information on interesting sightings in the New York City area.

- **Central Park Conservancy**, 315-0385, sponsors a Family Bird Watching Club, which meets every Saturday from l1 a.m. to 1 p.m. April through June and September through December at the Charles A. Dana Discovery Center at 110th Street near Fifth Avenue, where Urban Park Rangers teach participants to identify birds by their song.

- **Linnaean Society of New York**, 15 West 77 Street, NYC 10024, holds its meetings at the American Museum of Natural History and is open to amateurs and professionals interested in ornithology. The organization does not list a phone number; for more information, write to the address above.

- **New York City Audubon Society** naturalists lead a walk around the Harlem Meer and surrounding woodlands every Saturday from 9 to 11 a.m., April through June and September through December. The walk leaves from the Dana Center. Call 691-7483.

- **Sarah Elliott** has become a noted fixture, a movable one, in Central Park, with her Wednesday and Sunday morning walks, spring and fall. She teaches bird-watching basics and leads her pack on their quest for the indigo bunting, the grackle and the pileated woodpecker. The walks leave at 9 a.m., Wednesdays from Fifth Avenue and 76th Street, Sundays from the Loeb Boat House. Call 689-2763 to sign up for five sessions at $35.

- **The Urban Park Rangers** sponsor a variety of bird walks, such as the fall hawk watch, in all five boroughs. For times and meeting places call 800-201-PARK.

Bowling

- **Bowlmor Bowling**, 110 University Place, between 12th and 13th Streets, 212-255-8188, 44 lanes, open 10 a.m. to 1 a.m. Sunday to Thursday, 10 a.m. to 4 a.m. Friday and Saturday, call for lane availability.

- **Gil Hodges Lanes**, 6161 Strickland Avenue, Brooklyn 718-763-6800, named after the famed Brooklyn Dodgers first baseman. This 68-lane alley is the biggest in the five boroughs, open 9 a.m.- midnight Sunday to Tuesday, 9 a.m. to 2:30 a.m. Friday, 9 a.m. to 2 a.m. Saturday.

- **Leisure Time Bowling**, 625 Eighth Avenue (in the Port Authority Building), 212-268-6909, 30 lanes, open 10 a.m. to 11 p.m. Sunday to Thursday, 10 a.m. to 2 a.m. Friday and Saturday.

Fencing

- **The New York Fencers Club**, 154 West 71st Street, 212-874-9800 (after 4:30 p.m.), offers duelists a place to parry and thrust, as well as a space for lessons to better foil their opponents. Dues for this membership organization cost an average of $650 a year.

- **Blade**, 212 West 15th Street, 212-620-0114, teaches fencing to beginners, intermediate and advanced students, supplying equipment if necessary. Four group lessons cost $65, plus a $10 registration fee. Private sessions are more expensive.

Football

Most playing fields fall under the Department of Parks and Recreation, call 212-408-0220 for information and permits. Eighteen football fields, some of which are suitable also for soccer, are located in Manhattan.

Games

- **The Mayfair Club**, 51 East 25th Street, 212-779-1750, is not a casino or a gambling house, says its owner. "It's a place to play games." Poker is the game mostly played, but there's bridge and backgammon too.

- **Hackers, Hitters and Hoops**, 123 West 18th Street, 212-929-7482, offers 23,000 square feet of miniature golf courses, each hole a replica of a famous course. You'll also find batting cages, ping pong tables, and basketball courts as well as an amusement park space ride called Orbitron.

Golf

Manhattan boasts no 18-hole golf courses, though a 17-acre course is in the planning stages for Randall's Island, but the American Golf Corporation operates seven city-owned public courses in the outer boroughs. Manhattanites seem to favor the two courses at Pelham/Split Rock, 870 Shore Road in the Bronx, 718-885-1258, both of which are handsomely located, Split Rock being the more challenging of the two; the Van Cortlandt Golf Course, the oldest public course in the country, at Van Cortlandt Avenue South and Bailey Avenue, 718-543-4595, also has its partisans. Fees, uniform for the seven courses, are $19.50 for daytime play on weekends and holidays, $17.50 during the week, with special twilight rates. Reservations, recommended, especially on weekends, are $2 per player with a resident card (costing $6 one time at the course). Call 718-225-GOLF to reserve at any of these American Golf courses, all of which are listed under "Golf" in the Manhattan Yellow Pages.

Plenty of slightly tonier public clubs surround the metropolitan area. Higher fees, averaging $37 Monday to Friday and $47 on weekends, are the norm at suburban courses. Typical of the county-run golf links is Mohansic Golf Club, 914-962-4065, in Yorktown Heights. Rental equipment is available here, just as it is at other clubs found in New Jersey, Long Island and Connecticut, but balls must be purchased. The city-bound golfer isn't entirely without recourse, however. Miniature golf courses abound, and now there are two driving ranges from which to tune up that swing.

- **The Golf Club at Chelsea Piers,** Hudson River at 17th Street, 212-336-6400, open 7 a.m. to 11 p.m., to midnight during summer months. This membership golf club with its white shingled clubhouse entrance, pro shop, putting green and golf academy has, as its *piece de resistance*, 52 heated, weather-protected driving stalls with Japanese-designed computerized automatic ball returns and tee-ups in four tiers fronting on a 200-yard, net-enclosed artificial turf fairway with four target greens. Non-members pay $10-15 per half-hour, $20-25 per hour, depending on the season and time of day. Microbrewery restaurant next door.

- **Golfport**, next door to Tennisport at 51-24 Second Street, Long Island City (opposite Manhattan on the east River near Midtown Tunnel exit), 718-472-4653, open Tuesday-Friday 9 to 9, Monday noon to 8, Saturday and Sunday 10 to 8. $5 gets you a bucket of balls to drive off a covered, heated deck 65 yards down a netted fairway. There's a golf shop, club rentals and a coffee shop. Private lessons, videotaped swings and analysis are extra.

Horseback Riding

Care to canter Central Park bridle trails, or brush up on your dressage in the ring? Manhattan has one stable. In the outer boroughs and near New Jersey the trail rides meander woods and seaside, and you can practice your jumping outdoors.

- **Claremont Riding Academy**, 175 West 89th Street corner Amsterdam Avenue, 212-724-5100 for reservations, essential weekends. Open 6:30 a.m. to 10 p.m., 6:30 to 5 on weekends. They stable about 100 horses here, some 70 for rental, English saddle only, at $33 an hour either in Central Park or in the ring. Private lessons cost $35 per half hour, group lessons $35 per hour.

- **Lynne's Riding School**, 88-03 70th Road, Forest Hills, 718-261-7679. Open daily 8 to 4. You can take public transportation—the F train and then the Q23 bus—to Queens where Lynne's offers riders a choice between Eastern or Western tack. Private lessons cost $30 a half hour, $45 an hour, and renting a horse costs $17 an hour English, $20 Western.

- **Kensington Stables**, 51 Caton Place at Coney Island Avenue, Brooklyn, (718) 972-4588, open daily 10 a.m. to sunset, operates guided trail rides, English or Western, in lovely Prospect Park for $20 an hour. Private lessons, indoors or out, are $40 an hour, $25 a half hour; $30 an hour in a group. Call ahead. Take the F train to Ft. Hamilton Parkway.

• **Jamaica Bay Riding Academy**, Belt Parkway East between Exits 11 (King's Plaza) and 13 (Rockaway Parkway), Marine Park, Brooklyn, (718)531-8949. Open daily 9 to 5. You need no appointment for a guided trail ride along Jamaica Bay beach, 45-minutes for $23. Lessons cost $45 an hour, $25 a half hour, private; $40 an hour in a group. Bring your own helmet.

• **Riverdale Equestrian Centre**, West 254th Street and Broadway, inside Van Cortlandt Park, 718-543-3344. Open 9 to 5, Saturday and Sunday 8:30 to 6 or 6:30. Rabbits, raccoons and other wildlife are a bonus on the guided trail rides in this large city park. Tack is English, and the cost, after a one-time half-hour evaluation lesson, is $60 per hour, $35 per half hour, private; $35 per hour in a group. Lessons in or out of doors are $50 per semi-private hour, $60 per hour and $35 per half hour for a private lesson. Pony rides for children are $5 and pony parties can be arranged. All rides by appointment. To get there by public transportation take the #1 train to 242nd Street (last stop) and the #9 bus (262nd Street) from there; ask to get off at the stables. Or take the Liberty Line Bx-M3 bus, which goes up Fifth Avenue, stopping every 10 blocks, and drops you at the stable door, 20 minutes from the Upper East Side.

• **Pelham Bay Riding**, 9 Shore Road, City Island/Orchard Beach, (718) 885-0551. Open daily 8 a.m. til dusk, but call ahead for a guided trail ride, Western only, through woods by the Split Rock Golf Course and Pelham Bay, $20 for one hour, $40 for a two-hour loop. Lessons, English or Western, are $50 for one hour, $45 for 45 minutes, $35 for a half hour, private; a group lesson is $25 an hour. Reachable by car from the New England Thruway; or take the #6 train to the last stop and walk east or take the Bx29 City Island bus, which stops across the street from the stable.

• **Overpeck Riding Center**, 40 Fort Lee Road, Leonia, NJ 07605, 201-944-7111. Open 9 to 5, Saturday and Sunday to 6 p.m., by appointment. By #4 Red and Tan Lines or #166 New Jersey Transit bus from the Port Authority Terminal, have the driver let you off at Overpeck Park. By car, take Route 80 off the George Washington Bridge, off at the first exit ("70—Leonia"). A quarter mile south on the right are the stables, which are run by Claremont, offering private lessons at $33 a half hour, $66 an hour, and group lessons for $33 an hour. There are riding clinics, shows and competitions in the indoor and outdoor rings. Boarding is also available. Bergen County residents are offered discounts.

Ice Skating

Besides the Wollman and Lasker rinks (and the Sailboat Pond at 73rd Street when it freezes) in Central Park, Manhattan boasts six other fine places to skate. In Queens try the Flushing Meadow rink.

- **The Ice Studio,** 1034 Lexington Avenue at 73rd, 212-535-0304, this intimate rink in a brownstone offers a measure of privacy at your lessons. Skate rentals available; call for hours.

- **Riverbank State Park**, 145th Street and Riverside Drive, 212-694-3642. Skate outdoors just above the Hudson River Monday through Wednesday 12:30 to 1:30 p.m., Tuesday and Thursday 8:30 to 10 p.m., Friday 5 to 6 and 8:30 to 10 p.m., Saturday and Sunday noon to 1 and 5:15 to 6:15. Private and group lessons at other times. Skate rentals.

- **Rivergate Ice Rink**, First Avenue and East 34th Street (next to the Rivergate apartment complex), 212-689-0035. This outdoor rink is open daily through March.

- **Rockefeller Center Rink**, 50th Street off Fifth Avenue, 212-332-7654. Open daily and evenings in season; skate rentals.

- **Skyrink at Chelsea Piers**, Pier 61 at Hudson River and 22nd Street, 212-336-6100, open for general skating Monday and Tuesday noon to 6:20, and 8 to 9:20 p.m. Monday, Wednesday through Friday noon to 9:20, Saturday 11:45 to 4:45 and 8 to 10:20 p.m., Sunday 12:30 to 4:45 p.m. With two indoor rinks in use some 20 hours a day, this facility offers public skating, figure skating and hockey instruction for adults and children, league hockey, a skating club and ice theater. Rentals and a skate shop are on site, as well as audience seating for 1,600, including two sky boxes for special events, and a snack bar.

- **Kate Wollman Rink**, sister to Central Park's Wollman Rink, is located on the east side of Prospect Park, off the Parkside and Ocean Avenue entrance, in Brooklyn, 718-287-6431. Open 10 to 5:30 Wednesday, 10 to 9 Thursday and Friday, 10 to 10 Saturday and 10 to 8 Sunday, to 6 on holidays. Closed Monday and Tuesday.

- **World's Fair Skating Rink**, 111th Street, Corona, Queens, in Flushing Meadow Park, 718-271-1996. You can walk to this large, indoor rink from the Shea Stadium—111th Street stop on the #7 train. Open Monday, Wednesday, Friday, Saturday and Sunday, call for hours and prices; skate rentals.

Lacrosse

- **New York Lacrosse Club**. This dues-paying amateur group fields both an A and B team and competes against members of an Eastern Seaboard league of lacrosse clubs. New York City is their home base but the home field is on Long Island. Write Dr. Bernard Schoenbaum, 21 Ridge Road, Little Falls, NJ 07424 for information.

- **Chelsea Piers Field House,** 23rd Street and the Hudson River, 212-336-6500, call for hours. Registration is open to individuals and complete teams, men and women, for indoor adult lacrosse league play on a variety of skill levels. Teams play one night a week for a season of 8 to 12 games and league playoffs. Games consist of two 25-minute halves.

Racquetball

Devotees of this popular sport can burn off calories at two of the Ys we mention below—the West Side YMCA at 5 West 63rd Street and the 92nd Street YMHA at Lexington Avenue (three practice courts only)—as well as:

- **Club La Raquette**, 119 West 56th Street at Avenue of the Americas (Hotel Meridien), 212-245-1144. Buried beneath the hotel are four racquetball courts and two squash courts which are open to the public by reservation. Membership is $15, plus $15 per hour of court time.

- **Manhattan Plaza Racquet Club**, 450 West 43rd Street, 212-594-0554, a tennis club with two regulation courts. Use does not require membership but costs $28-38 per hour, plus $10 per person guest fee.

Roller Blading/Skating

For exhilarating outdoor fun, try **Central Park** blade action. Roller disco, though passé, still has followers here also. Other in-line skating (its official moniker) hot-spots: **Union Square, Battery Park City** and Brooklyn's **Prospect Park.** In fact, now you can skate (walk or bike) along the Hudson from Gansevoort Street to Battery Park City. If you plan on renting, bring a credit card for a deposit on the equipment.

- **Blades East and West Skate and Sport**, 160 East 86th Street, 212-996-1644; 105 West 72nd Street, 212-787-3911; open 10 to 8 weekdays and Saturday, 10 to 6 Sunday. With the help of the friendly staffers at either of these locations, you too can join the fun (and risk your neck) by in-line skating. Rollerblades, the best-known brand, can be rented for two hours ($16, weekends,) or the whole day ($25), wrist guards and knee pads included. And if you want to join the growing army of neon-clad bladers permanently, you can also buy skates, equipment, and gear here ($95-$350).

- **Chelsea Piers Roller Rinks**, 23rd Street and Hudson River, 212-336-6200, open for general skating Monday, Tuesday, Thursday

10:30 to 7, Wednesday to 6:30, Friday to 8, Saturday and Sunday noon to 6, DJ parties Friday and Saturday 8 to 11 p.m. Besides general skating in two outdoor, regulation-sized in-line and roller rinks, there are classes at various levels from basic technique to hip-hop to aggressive and league hockey games for adults and youths. Or you can just watch. BLADES operates a board and skate pro shop and rental outlet, and there's a snack bar. Admission is $3.50 for adults, $2.50 for children. DJ parties are $8, and classes cost $15, including skate and gear rental.

• **Lezly Dance and Skate School**, 622 Broadway between Bleecker and Houston Streets, 212-777-3232, holds classes for every level; skate rentals available for classes only.

• **Manhattan Sports**, 2188 Broadway (at 78th Street), 580-4753 and 2901 Broadway (at 113th Street), 749-1454; blades rent for a reasonable $10 per day weekdays, $15 per day weekends. Also sell and repair in-line skates.

• **Skate Key Roller Rink**, 2424 White Plains Road, near Pelham Parkway, Morris Park, the Bronx, 718-547-0700, open for general skating Wednesday and Thursday 8 to midnight, Friday 4:30 to 7:30 and 8 to 1 a.m., Sunday 12:30 to 12:30. Parties Monday and Tuesday are open to the public, with variable hours. Special nights for reggae, women, adults only and house music.

• **Village Wheels**, 63-73 East Eighth Street between Mercer and Broadway, 505-6753, will apply the price of rental, $15 a day with pads, shields and helmet, $20 on weekends, toward purchase of their skates. The new bike/skate path along the Hudson means you can skate west to the river with smooth sailing down to Battery Park City, a prime blading site.

Rugby

• **Gaelic Park**, 718-548-9566, in The Bronx is the center of rugby play in New York City. The park is located at Broadway and West 240th Street.

Running

• **The New York Road Runners Club,** with over 25,000 members "the world's largest running club," maintains an "International Running Center" at 9 East 89th Street, NYC 10128, 212-860-4455. Road Runners sponsors the New York Marathon and more than 150 other races a year. Regular annual membership costs $25.

Sailing

If you want to bound over Long Island Sound, City Island in The Bronx is an accessible starting point. Take the #2 (Seventh Avenue) or #6 (Lexington Avenue) train to Pelham Parkway and transfer to the Bronx #12 City Island bus.

- **Great Hudson Sailing Center**, Chelsea Piers, 23rd Street and Hudson River, 212-741-SAIL, call for hours. Learn to sail a 22' Beneteau sailboat at the beginner, intermediate or coastal cruising level in weekend classes, four four-hour lessons for $425. Private lessons also available, as are rentals of one of the center's six 22- to 40-foot Beneteaus.

- **Manhattan Sailing School**, 393 South End Avenue in Battery Park City, NYC 10280-1003, 212-786-0400. Sail out of classy North Cove Yacht Harbor in front of the World Financial Center. Beginners take a 20-hour basic sailing course and continue on to basic coastal cruising, also 20 hours, in J-24 sailboats, each course for $460. Private lessons as well, and rentals at $150 per half day. Affiliated with the Manhattan Yacht Club.

- **New York City Community Sailing Association**, 545 West 111th Street, NYC 10025, 222-1405. Operating with five 22'-24' keel sloops out of the 79th Street Boat Basin on the Hudson, this non-profit organization was founded in 1996 with the idea that sailing ought to be easy and viable all over the city. Call it "Not the Yacht Club." Lessons cost $250 for 16 hours, taught over two week-end days or four half-days over two weeks. High school students learn free. There are no rentals, but a $150 membership entitles qualified sailors to five week-end or summer evening sailing sessions, two-hour minimum; the same sessions on weekdays before 3 p.m. cost $75. Renew for more sessions.

- **North Cove Sailing School and Club**, 393 South End Avenue in Battery Park City, NYC 10280, 800-532-5552, just down the pier from the Manhattan Sailing School, teaches basic keelboat sailing and basic coastal cruising in a J-24 for $425 each. Membership in the club, with access to their boats, is a bit less expensive than at the Manhattan Yacht Club.

- **The New York Sailing School**, 697 Bridge Street, City Island, The Bronx 10464, 718-885-3103, offers a 28-hour sailing course for $470 on board one of its Solings, Sonars, Merit 25s or J-22s. You can also rent boats here for $70 to $185 a day, depending on the size of the boat, day of the week and whether or not you are a Sailing School graduate. (1995 rates.)

- **Offshore Sailing School,** locations in Jersey City, NJ and

Greenwich, CT, 800-221-4326, has a fleet of 27' to 43' boats on which they teach beginning three-day courses for $375 weekdays, $495 weekends. Advanced courses available for slightly more (1995 rates). There is a $50 discount for each person in groups of two or more.

Scuba

While no one's suggesting dives to the murky depths of the Hudson, you can take certification courses in local pools preparatory to plunging into the Caribbean's turquoise waters.

- **PanAqua Diving**, 166 West 75th Street, 212-496-2267, is the only dive shop with a compressor on site. In addition to selling and repairing equipment, they organize group and individual diving travel and run certification courses of six evening sessions each, over a two-week period at the West Side Y and the Vanderbilt Y, over three weeks at Manhattan Plaza, and Sunday evenings over five weeks at the 92nd Street Y. The cost for each is $235 to $270.

Sea Kayaking

That's right—sea kayaking. For those who seek watery adventure in *and* out of the city, the **Metropolitan Association of Sea Kayakers** unites groups of paddlers who plan trips up and down the East Coast as well as to locations as far north as Greenland and Alaska. Two or three trips around the island of Manhattan each summer, light and currents permitting, start and end in Liberty State Park (NJ) and take about 11 hours. B.Y.O. kayak. Membership, $20, includes a published schedule, a quarterly newsletter, and a guide to coastal launch sites along the East Coast. Contact Al Ysaguirre, 212-260-5185 or 718-783-2306. You can store your kayak at the **Downtown Boathouse** at Pier 26 on the Hudson, near North Moore Street; call 966-1852. Membership in the non-profit organization costs $50 a year, and storage is $200 per boat.

Skiing

You won't schuss downhill in New York City, but cross country skiers take to the gentle slopes of Central Park and, in the boroughs, Van Courtland Park, Split Rock Golf Course in Pelham Bay Park, The Bronx, Prospect Park in Brooklyn and Flushing Meadow Park in Queens.

The **New York-New Jersey Trail Conference**, 232 Madison Avenue, 212-685-9699, can provide ski touring information by phone.

Soccer

The Cosmopolitan Soccer League, 201-861-6606, represents amateur and semi-pro clubs from New York, New Jersey and Connecticut. The League has one semi-pro and two amateur divisions consisting of about

20 clubs each. You don't have to join a club to play on a team, but club facilities are limited to members. Coaches are available for training; all age groups are welcome.

Indoor league play is available now in the field house at **Chelsea Piers**, 23rd Street at the Hudson River, 212-336-6500. Teams accommodating men and women at various skill levels play one night a week on an Astroturf indoor field. A season consists of eight or 12 games, consisting of two 25-minute halves, and league playoffs.

Squash

When you consider that a tennis court takes up about ten times as much space as a squash court, it is easy to understand the great attraction squash holds for sports club operators as well as for a population determined to exercise, but at the lowest cost possible. See **Health Clubs** and **Ys** for other locations with courts.

- **New York Sports Clubs**, 404 Fifth Avenue at 37th Street, 212-594-3120, four courts; 61 West 62nd Street, 212-265-0995, four courts; and 151 East 86th Street, 212-860-8630, eight courts; 49th Street and Lexington Avenue, 212-838-2102, three courts; and 110 Boerum Place (Cobble Hill), 718-643-4400, two courts.

- **Park Avenue Athletic Complex**, 3 Park Avenue at 34th Street, 212-686-1085; one squash court.

- **City Hall Squash Club**, 25 Park Place at Church Street;212-964-2677, five courts.

Swimming—Beaches

City strands traditionally open on Memorial Day and close the day after Labor Day. Managed by national, state and city park departments, all the beaches mentioned below are staffed with life guards. For information on beaches open to the general public, as opposed to residents with permits, in Nassau and Suffolk Counties, call the Long Island Tourism and Convention Commission, 516-951-3440.

- **Jones Beach State Park**, 516-785-1600. No car? Take a bus from the Port Authority Terminal, 42nd Street and Eighth Avenue, or the Long Island Railroad from Penn Station as far as Freeport, and change to a bus for the ride direct to the beach.

- **Riis Park**, managed by the Gateway National Recreation Area, 718-318-4300, can be reached by taking the #2 (Seventh Avenue) or #5 (Lexington Avenue) train to Flatbush Avenue and changing to the Q35 Queens Green Line bus.

Call the Transit Authority, 718-330-1234, for directions on how to reach the following beaches managed by the city Parks Department: **Brighton**

Beach and contiguous **Coney Island Beach,** two of Brooklyn's Atlantic Ocean beaches; **Orchard Beach** on Long Island Sound in The Bronx; **Rockaway Beach** (near Riis Park) on the Atlantic in Queens; and **Great Kills Beach, South Beach** and **Wolf's Pond Park** on Staten Island.

Swimming—Pools

The Department of Parks and Recreation maintains a number of indoor and outdoor pools with inexpensive admission. In the heat of summer, the outdoor pools are more for play and cooling off than serious lap swimming. The swimming's easier during off hours in winter. Note that gyms are attached to the three city pools listed. Winter indoor pool hours are generally 3 p.m. to 10 p.m. weekdays, 10 a.m. to 5 p.m. Saturday, closed Sunday. Summer hours for the outdoor pools are 11 a.m. to 7 p.m. daily. The indoor pools are closed in summer.

- **Asser Levy Pool,** 23rd Street between First Avenue and FDR Drive, 212-447-2020. Built in 1906 as a public bath modeled on the Roman baths, this granite gem with a marble lobby and 20-foot ceilings reopened in 1990 after extensive renovations. A $25 membership donation ($10 for seniors) gives you a year's entree to the 21' by 65' indoor pool and the very popular workout room, which is used from 7:15 a.m. until 10 p.m., including some 60 classes from aerobics to yoga. The 50 by 125 foot outdoor pool is free.

- **Carmine Street Gymnasium and Pool,** Clarkson Street and Seventh Avenue South (Greenwich Village), 212-242-5228. 20' by 70' indoor pool; 50' by 100' outdoor pool. Two upstairs gyms and a running track.

- **East 54th Street Gymnasium and Pool,** 348 East 54th Street between First and Second Avenues, 212-397-3154. 50 by 54 foot indoor pool (open year round). Upstairs gym and running track. $25 annual membership donation.

- **Hansborough Recreational Center,** 35 West 134th Street, 212-234-9603, in Harlem has an indoor pool and gym with dance and aerobic classes. Membership is $25 annually.

- **West 59th Street Gymnasium and Pool,** West 59th Street and West End Avenue, 212-397-3166. 34 by 60 foot indoor pool; 75 by 100 foot outdoor pool. Gym has basketball and paddleball courts. $25 annual registration fee.

Health clubs and Ys with pools are described at the end of this chapter. Dedicated swimmers might wish also to check out other swimming situations such as:

- **Jerome Coles Sports and Recreation Center,** Mercer and Houston Streets, 998-2020. New York University's sports facility, with racquet ball and squash courts, a weight room and 25-meter pool with six lanes beneath frosted glass windows, is available to residents from 14th to Canal Streets, Fourth to Eleventh Avenues. After a three to six-month wait to register you may purchase a punch card good for l2 weekend admissions between 9 a.m. and 2 p.m. for $58, which is renewable. NYU alumni can join for $375 a year.

- **Manhattan Plaza Swim and Health Club**, 482 West 43rd Street at Tenth Avenue, 212-563-7001. The handsome, verdant, glass-enclosed 40' by 75' pool with four lap lanes is the main lure here, but there is also a gym and sauna. Annual membership costs $850, renewal is $700.

- **Riverbank State Park**, 679 Riverside Drive at 145th Street, 694-3666. This glorious new facility atop a waste treatment plant over the Hudson River is a treasure for uptowners. Recreational swim sessions in the 50-meter indoor pool cost $1 for evening and weekend sessions; daytime and evening lap swim sessions cost $2. There are a host of water classes and activities between sessions, and the outdoor pool is open in the summer. Call for hours.

- **Trinity School Swim Club**, 91st Street between Columbus and Amsterdam Avenues, 212-873-1650. The Olympic-sized 45' by 75' pool is available to members for swimming six nights a week. Membership is for a summer session and for a winter session that corresponds to the academic year (and therefore includes fall and spring). Currently, there's a long waiting list.

If a dip for a day is all you require, try the **Asphalt Green Aqua Center**, under **Health Clubs**, or one of these two West Side hotel pools:

- **Days Inn**, Eighth Avenue at 48th Street, 212-581-7000. 20' by 30' outdoor rooftop pool, call for seasonally changing hours, $25 a day weekends, $20 weekdays.

- **Sheraton City Squire**, 790 Seventh Avenue at 52nd Street, 212-581-3300. Covered 20' by 40' pool with outdoor sunning area, open 7:30 a.m. to 8 p.m., $20 a day.

Tennis

The Department of Parks Permit Office in each borough issues tennis permits for city courts. Manhattan permit particulars are detailed under Central Park—Tennis. Of the city's 535 public courts, more than 100 are located in Manhattan at nine sites. The largest single concentration, 30 courts, is in Central Park off 96th Street. Seven of the other locations are north of 96th Street, and the eighth is at East River Park at Broome Street on the Lower East Side.

In Brooklyn, permits are sold at the Brooklyn Borough Parks

Department office in Litchtfield Mansion, 95 Prospect Park West off Fifth Street, 718-965-8900, Monday through Friday 9 to 4. The ten city courts located at the Parade Grounds, Coney Island and Parkside Avenues, open from April through November, are probably those most popular with tennis permit holders. The same courts are covered with a bubble and run as a concession in the winter. Call 718-236-7045 for hours and rates.

Eight private clubs with four or more courts in Manhattan, Roosevelt Island and across the East River in Queens are listed below. Check the Yellow Pages for other facilities near you.

- **Crosstown Tennis**, 14 West 31st Street, 212-947-5780. Four indoor courts; hourly and seasonal rates.

- **East River Tennis Club**, 44-02 Vernon Boulevard, Long Island City (located on the East River; courtesy minibus service leaves hourly on the half-hour from 57th Street and Third Avenue), 718-937-2381. 20 courts, under bubble in winter; membership.

- **Manhattan Plaza Racquet Club**, 450 West 43rd Street, 212-594-0554. Five courts, two racquetball courts and swimming pool privileges; membership, hourly and seasonal rates.

- **Midtown Tennis Club**, 341 Eighth Avenue at 27th Street, 212-989-8572. Eight courts; hourly and seasonal rates.

- **Roosevelt Island Racquet Club**, 281 Main Street, Roosevelt Island, 212-935-0250. Twelve clay courts indoors, league play, a Seniors' Club and babysitting; membership, hourly rates.

- **Tennisport**, Borden Avenue and Second Street, Long Island City (opposite Manhattan on the East River near Midtown Tunnel exit), 718-392-1880. 16 indoor, 13 outdoor courts; membership.

- **Trinity School**, 91st Street between Columbus and Amsterdam Avenues, 212-873-1650, has two outdoor courts open April 1 through December 1 and one indoor court open September thru May; seasonal memberships.

Windsurfing

- **Island Windsurfing**, 1623 York Avenue, 212-744-2000. This full-service shop provides everything from boards to wetsuits. They can arrange lessons at and transportation to either of their two Long Island locations for $65 for three hours. In summer they run day trips to both; call for current rates. The Manhattan store is open year round and has ski gear and snowboards as well.

- **Olympic Windsurfing**, 475 Port Washington Boulevard, Port Washington, Long Island, 516-883-8207. Call during the season for information.

Health Clubs, YMCAs, YWCAs and YMHAs

Health and fitness clubs have proliferated in the city at an astonishing rate. Newest are clubs applying a scientific approach to physical health, clubs featuring cardiovascular and "health enhancement" facilities where fitness regimes are custom-designed after a thorough physical and where a trainer is assigned to supervise progress. More traditional are those ubiquitous all-purpose spas where you set your own pace using the most appealing facilities. These often include a pool (varying from postage stamp to Olympic in size), exercise equipment, steam rooms, whirlpools and saunas, as well as exercise, yoga and calisthenics classes. Hospitals have gotten into the act as well by offering low-key but well-equipped exercise facilties for patients and others affiliated with a hospital; contact the hospital nearest you to find out what may be available. To indicate the amenities offered, a few of the dozens of health facilities located here are described.

- **Asphalt Green,** 1750 York Avenue at 90th Street, 369-8890. Two gyms, indoor and outdoor running tracks, state-of-the-art cardiovascular and weight-training equipment at this community-oriented, not-for-profit 5.5-acre sports and fitness complex. But the centerpiece is its AquaCenter, a spectacular 50-meter Olympic-standard pool. Membership is on a monthly, semi-annual or annual basis. Non-members can purchase a day pass for $14 for use of the pool, $25 for full access to the facility.

- **Bally's Jack LaLanne Fitness Center**. This fitness mass merchant has five locations in Manhattan: Broadway at 75th Street, 212-877-1111; Lexington Avenue at 86th Street, 212-722-7371; Fifth Avenue at 53rd Street (women only); Madison Avenue and 55th Street, 212-688-6630; 233 Broadway near Wall Street, 212-227-5977; three locations in Brooklyn; three locations in Queens; one Bronx location. Bally's is one of the few New York City clubs that does not require a full year's payment up front but allows you to pay on a monthly basis. Includes Universal and Lifecycle exercise machines, free weights and daily aerobics classes. Warning: the Wall Street location is cramped and sweaty. Some membership packages provide for use of other Bally centers throughout the country.

- **Battery Park Swim & Fitness Club**, 375 South End Avenue, 321-1117. Swim in a glass-enclosed pool with a patio which opens out onto the Hudson River in summer. Swim classes and aquacize are offered, as well as free weights, Cybex and Nautilus, StairMasters, treadmills and Lifecycles. A host of classes, whirlpool, saunas and steam rooms complete the facility.

- **Cardio-Fitness Centers** at 79 Maiden Lane, 943-1510; 345 Park Avenue at 53rd Street, 838-4570; 1221 Sixth Avenue at 48th Street,

840-8240; 200 Park Avenue at 45th Street, 682-4440; and 9 West 57th Street, 753-3980. (All Area Code 212.) Some corporations pay part or all of their employees' fees for the individualized, instructor-designed exercise programs at the Cardio-Fitness Centers (members can use the clubs interchangeably). Saunas are in place, as are exercise machines, bikes and treadmills. A medical history is required and a stress test as well for those over 35.

• **Downtown Athletic Club**, 19 West Street, 212-425-7000, occupies a 35-story building housing numerous dining rooms, hotel rooms on 15 floors, and sports and fitness facilities on 13 floors. These include a 30' by 75' pool, two handball and/or racquetball courts, ten squash courts, a basketball court, Nautilus and Universal exercise machines, saunas, steambaths and a whirlpool. You must be proposed by a current member.

• **Equinox Fitness Club**, 897 Broadway at West 19th Street, 780-9300; 344 Amsterdam Avenue at West 76th Street, 721-4200; Broadway at 92nd Street, 799-1818; and 205 East 85th street, 439-8500. Certified personal trainers, 75 of them at the downtown club, characterize this three-story operation. Some 200 classes, from high and low impact to Aerobox to pre- and post-natal exercise to yoga and meditation fill out the day. Besides up-to-date equipment, the club boasts a boxing circuit training room, one-on-one boxing (for women too) and cardio/theater television with the cardiovascular workout equipment. A nutritionist supervises personal weight-loss programs. At the Amsterdam Avenue location a physiology lab offers comprehensive metabolic testing for a fee, to non-members as well as members. No boxing uptown.

• **New York Health and Racquet Club**, 212-797-1500, has six locations. Rates go down considerably in the summer (watch for ads offering discounts, and ask about corporate discounts). Membership includes use (for a fee) of the club's tennis court in the Village and admission to any of its locations: 20 East 50th Street, 18' by 50' pool; 1433 York Avenue at 76th Street, 30' by 35' pool; 24 East 13th Street, 20' by 35' pool; 132 East 45th Street, 18' by 50' pool; 110 West 56th Street, 20' by 60' pool; and 39 Whitehall Street, Olympic-sized pool. Other facilities include tennis courts downtown, a yacht and the midtown Kimberly Hotel.

• **New York Sports Clubs**, 18 locations, among them: 30 Cliff Street (Seaport), 212-349-7700; 541 Lexington Avenue at 50th, 212-838-2102; 404 Fifth Avenue at 37th, 212-549-3120; Madison Avenue at 46th, 212-983-0303; 61 West 62nd Street, 212-265-0995; 151 East 86th Street, 212-860-8630; 614 Second Avenue, 212-213-5999; 110 Boerum Place, Brooklyn, 718-643-4400; 151 Reade Street (Tribeca), 212-571-1000. Eagle and Nautilus circuits, Lifecycles,

StairMasters, Gravitron and other equipment are available in all clubs. Most have one-on-one training, pools, squash courts, whirlpools and saunas. Membership includes entrance to all clubs and access to tennis courts (additional court fee) in Brooklyn. Fees vary with locations. This is one of the few clubs that does not require payment for a full year up front but will bill you monthly.

- **The Printing House Fitness and Racquetball Center**, 421 Hudson Street at Leroy, 212-243-7600. On the first Floor are five racquetball and four squash courts; on the ninth floor four kinds of gym machines, treadmills, locker rooms and a sauna, a steam room and whirlpool as well as a cardiovascular fitness center, two dance studios and a full-service salon. On the roof above is a seasonal 20' by 30' heated outdoor pool. There are three different membership rates here, depending on whether you want to use just the racquetball and squash courts, just the gym, or everything. Call for specifics.

- **Reebok Sports Club/NY**, 160 Columbus Avenue at 67th Street, 212-362-6800. An upscale, landscaped urban country club, this 140,000-square foot facility on six floors features a 45-foot climbing wall, a rooftop in-line skating and running track, swimming pool with underwater sound, a virtual reality sports simulator for skiing, windsurfing and golf, spa cosseting, a bar, health food cafe and a bistro.

- **Sports Center at Chelsea Piers**, 23rd Street and Hudson River, 212-336-6000. The 150,000 square foot pier houses a 4-lane, 1/4-mile running track, competition track, three basketball courts, a 100-foot climbing wall and a bouldering wall, a six-lane, 25-yard swimming pool with an outdoor sunning deck, cardiovascular, circuit and strength training equipment, a boxing ring, aerobic studios and an infield for volleyball, sand volleyball and touch football. Also training, sports medicine, spa facilities and a physiology lab. Members have the use of all the other Pier facilities at a 10% discount. Day passes for non-members cost $25.

- **The Sports Training Institute**, 239 East 49th Street, 212-752-7111, specializes in one-on-one, personalized training on Nautilus, Universal, Orthotron and Cybex machines. Besides their strengthening regime, one that has kept numerous sports personalities in the very best of health, the institute offers aerobic equipment, including Nordic skis, Sitron bicycles and rowing machines, a mat-covered area and a stretch class every 15 minutes.

- **The Vertical Club**, 330 East 61st Street, 212-355-5100, is that glamorous seven-story building you see when entering Manhattan on the 59th Street Bridge from Queens: lots of tinted glass, gleaming chrome and lithe-looking figures back-lit and working out. The big club accommodates a 20' by 40' pool, exercise machines, squash and racquetball courts, an indoor track, sun deck, restaurant and juice bar, among other amenities, and is slick and classy. Other locations: 335 West Madison Avenue, 983-5320; 139 West 32nd Street, 466-1750; 351 West 49th Street, 265-9400. A two-year minimum membership is $1399.

- **Brooklyn YWCA**, 30 Third Avenue between State Street and Atlantic Avenue, Brooklyn, 718-875-1190. For a reasonably priced $395 Athletic Membership plus a $35 Y membership, both men and women can work out on the Universal machines, punching bags, the large basketball court, jogging track and in the 20' by 60' swimming pool, as well as relax in the sauna.

- **Harlem YMCA**, 135th Street and Lenox Avenue, 281-4100, offers two pools (for adults and children); Nautilus and weights; a track; basketball courts; table tennis; aerobics, yoga and karate classes; athletic membership (for men and women) costs $350 per year plus $125 initiation fee.

- **McBurney YMCA**, 215 West 23rd Street, 212-741-9210. This Y has a carefully developed children's after-school program as well as adult gymnastics, adult lap and recreational swimming, full-court basketball, indoor jogging track, fencing, handball, volleyball and weight lifting room. Annual adult membership costs $708 for those over eighteen, with a $125 joiner's fee for the first year.

- **92nd Street YMHA**, 1395 Lexington Avenue, 212-427-6000. The cost of Athletic Memberships are determined by the member's sex (men are charged more because their locker facilities are better): $625 or $992 for men; $625 or $884 for women. If you know a member, the Y takes $150 off the price; your friend receives one month free. The program provides indoor jogging, weight training, volleyball and handball as well as fitness programs and use of the 50' by 75' pool.

- **Vanderbilt YMCA**, 224 East 47th Street, 212-756-9600, offers yoga, handball and paddleball, along with swimming, basketball, volleyball, indoor jogging, Nautilus and aerobics. Regular memberships cost $708, with a joiner's fee of $125, and include use of the gym, 20' by 60' swimming pool, a 40' by 75' lap pool and other sports facilities. Annual dues for the Businessman's Club and the men's Athletic Club are higher.

- **The West Side YMCA**, 5 West 63rd Street, 212-787-1301, is justifiably proud of its Sports Fitness Department, which keeps both men and women members in the very best of shape. The seven-story building houses two pools, a wrestling room, indoor running track, handball, squash and racquetball courts, Universal exercise machines and numerous other facilities. Annual adult membership is $684, plus a $75 initiation fee.

Subways

The subway is still the quickest way to get around New York City. All city subway lines are administered by the New York City Transit Authority, and recently they've been considerably improved. Subway crime is down, the graffiti plague has been all but eradicated, and many stations have been handsomely renovated. Call 718-330-1234 for train information or stop by one of the authority's Information Booths, open from 7 a.m. to 11 p.m. at Pennsylvania or Grand Central Station. Subway and bus maps for all five boroughs are readily available there. In theory, token sellers at the subway stops also distribute maps, but in practice they are often out of stock. The cyber inclined may want to visit the excellent Metropolitan Transit Authority web site (www.mta.nyc.ny.us/) which offers a complete subway map as well as information on local bridges and tunnels and more.

Subway tokens currently cost $1.50, but the new MetroCard is the way to go. The plastic debit card, available at token booths and neighborhood stores for $6 or $15, can be used in most stations and on all city buses. Swipe it through the turnstile slot, and one fare is subtracted. When the card is empty it can be refilled by up to $80 and is good for one year. Seniors and persons with disabilities are eligible for half-fare cards (call 212-878-7294). Two-zone transfers means riders with the MetroCard can move from subway to a bus (and vice versa) without paying another fare.

Subway trains operate 24 hours a day, but service slows appreciably after 11 p.m., when it is generally best to take a cab or bus anyway. Subway entrances with red lights have no token booths; avoid them.

PATH

The PATH (for Port Authority Trans-Hudson) tubes provide clean and efficient service connecting Manhattan with Hoboken, Jersey City and Newark for $1 round the clock. Trains leaving 33rd Street at Avenue of the Americas (Sixth Avenue) go to Hoboken or Jersey City, with stops along the way at 23rd, 14th, 9th and Christopher Streets. From the World Trade Center in Lower Manhattan trains leave for Hoboken and for Newark by way of Jersey City. Schedules are available in most stations, or call 800-234-7284.

Buses

Independent bus lines found mainly in boroughs other than Manhattan co-exist with those run by the New York City Transit Authority. Call 718-330-1234 for Transit Authority information as well as telephone numbers for the independents. Also, you can now get up to date NYC Transit information on the MTA web site: www.mta.nyc.ny.us/.

Maps are sometimes available from drivers but are always stocked at the Information Booths mentioned under Subways above.

Buses cost $1.50. Transfers are free. Exact change is required for buses, but the MetroCard and tokens are also accepted.

Ferries

Time was, before the advent of the auto, when some 125 passenger boats plied 50 different routes across the Hudson and East Rivers. With the closing of the Hoboken Ferry in 1967, only the Staten Island Ferry remained, both a commuter necessity for Staten Islanders and an excursion delight for Manhattanites and tourists alike.

The water commute is once again a reality on more than a dozen privately operated routes connecting Manhattan with New Jersey, Brooklyn and Queens. And the Hoboken Ferry is back, faster than ever and landing this time at a floating terminal with a canvas marquee at the World Financial Center in Battery Park City. The new ferries cruise at 35 miles per hour, twice as fast as the Staten Island Ferry. In increasing numbers commuters are choosing this alternative to gridlock, exorbitant parking fees and expressway dementia, especially during the oppressive heat of summer. As more passengers take to the water, increased service comes on line.

- **Staten Island Ferry**, at 50¢ still New York's best transportation (and entertainment) buy, leaves the South Ferry Terminal at Whitehall in Battery Park for St. George, Staten Island, every half hour between 6:30 a.m. and 11:30 p.m. and every hour between 11:30 p.m. and 6:30 a.m. Car service, suspended in 1991 after a fire in Whitehall, runs between 6 a.m. and 11 p.m. and costs $3.50, plus 50¢ for each passenger in the car. Call 718-390-5253 or 718-815-BOAT for information.

- **Staten Island/Midtown Ferry**, the privately operated up-scale Staten Island ferry between St. George and East 34th Street, with four free shuttle bus loops around Midtown, operates weekdays every half hour between 6:35 and 9:35 a.m. and between 4 and 7:30 p.m. The fare is $5. Call N.Y. Fast Ferry, 1-800-NYFF or 718-815-6942.

- **Mariners Harbor/Bayonne Ferry**, operated weekdays by Harbor Shuttle, 888-254-RIDE, departs from Mariners Harbor, Staten Island and from Brady's Dock at East First Avenue, Bayonne, N.J., hourly between 6 and 8 a.m., and between 4:30 and 7:30 p.m. in return. Arrival is at Pier 11 on the East River at Wall Street. The fare is $5.

- **New Jersey passenger ferries** are dominated now by NY Waterway 800-533-3779, which operates the Hoboken Ferry, running weekdays every 5 minutes during rush hours between 6:50 a.m. and 10 p.m., every 15 minutes off peak. The fare is $2 each way. Service is every half hour on weekends, 10 to 10, with stops at Liberty State Park in New Jersey as well for a $5 round trip fare.

    The firm also operates service between Port Imperial, Weehawken, and Pier 78 at 38th Street and Twelfth Avenue and to Whitehall next to the Staten Island Ferry in Battery Park. Boats run every 15 minutes from 6:45 a.m. to midnight, Friday and Saturday from 8 a.m. to 1 a.m., Sunday 9 a.m. to midnight. The five-minute ride costs $4.50 each way to midtown and $5 to Whitehall, including mini-bus service in Manhattan. Parking on the Jersey side is extra ($5 per day).

    Their weekday ferry between the World Financial Center and Exchange Place beneath the Colgate clock in Jersey City runs every 15 minutes between 7 a.m. and 10 p.m. The five-minute ride costs $4 round trip. Weekends, the ferry travels a triangular route from Hoboken to Jersey City to the World Financial Center and back to Hoboken. Same fare.

    Express Navigation operates commuter ferries from Highlands to Pier 11 at the foot of Wall Street on the East River, Monday through Friday during commuter hours (call 800-B-O-A-T-R-I-D-E for times). The fare is $28 round trip for the 55-minute ride.

- **Yankee Stadium Ferry**, operated by NY Waterway, 800-53-FERRY, departs South Street Seaport, East 34th Street, and East 90th Street for night games Monday through Friday; departures from Port Imperial, Weehawken, N.J. are for weekend day games. Round trip on either route is $10.

- **Long Island City passenger ferries** are operated by NY Waterway, 800-533-3779. between Borden Avenue on Hunters Point and East 34th Street at FDR Drive Monday through Friday every 15 minutes from 7 to 9:45 a.m. and 4 to 8 p.m. The fare is $3 each way.

- **LaGuardia Airport** service is described below under Airport Transportation.

Taxis and Car Services

All car services in New York City, unlicensed as well as licensed, come under the jurisdiction of the Taxi and Limousine Commission (TLC: 212-221-8294 for questions or complaints; 212-302-8294 for lost and found).

Licensed cabs in New York City tend to be reliable and safe, although in 1994, for the first time, the TLC required licensed cabs to install Plexiglas shields between driver and passenger. This is intended more for the driver's safety, however. The TLC licenses chauffeur-driven stretch limos as well as three types of cabs:

- **Yellow cabs,** or "medallion"—for the emblem affixed to the hood—cabs, are the only taxis authorized to pick up passengers on the street. There are 12,187 of these charging $2 for the first 1/5th of a mile, 30¢ for each additional 1/5th of a mile, and 30¢ for each 90 seconds waiting time. A 50¢ surcharge is collected between 8 p.m. and 6 a.m. No legal surcharge for luggage. Tips in the 15% to 20% range are expected. If you're going cross-town, especially mid-day in the crush of midtown traffic, it pays to take a cross-town bus. Better yet, walk; it's faster.

- **Black cars,** the trade term for those high-quality (somewhat limousine-like), radio-dispatched fleet cars you see around, aren't licensed to stop for street hails. Corporations, and private charges, account for most of the "black car" business. That's why shiny Oldsmobiles and Buicks with quivering radio antennas, discretely lettered fleet plates and the official blue decal of the Taxi and Limousine Commission affixed to the passenger side of the windshield blanket Wall Street. In theory, these meterless "voucher cabs" (which charge by zone or by mileage registered on the odometer) will respond to telephone requests from charge-accountless individuals; in practice few do.

- **Car services** are licensed to work only from a telephone base and can't legally pick up passengers on the street. The vehicles, of which there are some 36,000 licensed, range from the less-than-lovely to the pristine-upscale, but they are never yellow. Each vehicle, as proof of licensing, must display the blue decal of the Taxi and Limousine Commission on the passenger side of the front windshield. Especially useful to residents of the outer boroughs, where cabs rarely cruise, and to baggage-laden wayfarers, these for-hire vehicles charge flat rates per trip, sometimes less than the cost of a metered cab. In fact, with two or three sharing a car, it may be cheaper and more pleasant to go out of town, to Washington or Philadelphia, say, by car service than to fly.

It pays to shop around by phone. Some rides can be reserved 20 minutes before departure, others require a day's notice. Rates and features vary: you may wish to pay a few dollars extra for a station wagon or for a Lincoln Town Car, and you may wish to arrange to have the car wait for you for the return trip from out of town, for which some services charge only half fare. In any case, be sure the service is licensed, and don't hesitate to ask how much liability insurance they carry for passenger injury; they should carry a minimum of $1 million.

The car lurching to your side looks a wreck, and there's no decal? Then it's probably an unlicensed **gypsy cab**, in which you'll ride at your own risk without recourse in case of bad service.

Limousines

For those occasions when you wish to ride in style or have a car and driver at your beck and call, consider hiring a limousine. Many car services also operate limousines; rates are usually on a per hour basis, although some firms set flat rates for trips to airports or for dinner-and-theater evenings. White, 40-foot-long strrrretches such as those operated by Amex Limousine Service, 212-696-4088, are the current ultimate. These block-long beauties carry 14 people including two in the rumble seat; the garden-variety stretch limos offer stereos, color TV and a stocked bar with ice for five or six. One day's notice is usually required, though cars (but not necessarily your first choice) are sometimes available on short notice. Most firms accept major credit cards, but check when you call. Below are some representative rates. Add 15% gratuity for the driver.

- **All-State Car and Limousine Service, Inc.**, 446 Hudson Street, 212-333-3333. This service requires a two-hour minimum plus gratuity when you rent a sedan at $20 an hour or stretch limo at $45 an hour plus 20% gratuity. All-State also offers good rates to LaGuardia ($20 plus toll and gratuity), JFK ($30 plus toll and gratuity) and Newark ($32 plus toll and gratuity). A stretch to LaGuardia is $75, to Newark or JFK $90, each plus tolls and a 20% gratuity.

- **Carey Limousine**, 62-07 Woodside Avenue, Woodside, Queens, 212-599-1122. Cadillac sedans cost $46 per hour, limousines $65 per hour, starting from the time the car leaves the garage on 34th Street, Manhattan, until it returns. You pay tolls or parking fees plus 10% service charge.

- **Communicar Ltd.**, 129-02 Northern Boulevard, Corona, Queens 11368, 718-418-1500. Call 15 minutes ahead of time to have an unmetered maroon Oldsmobile at your door. Flat rates depend on pickup point and destination (fees are listed in a book). East Side to LaGuardia Airport is $25, to JFK $39. Cars are available hourly at $30 per and can be reserved one day in advance at an additional $4.

- **Dav-El Livery**, Pier 62, North River at 23rd Street, 212-645-4242. Sedans cost $46 per hour or $1.45 per mile and stretch limos cost $59 per hour or $1.95 per mile, beginning when the car leaves the garage. Add a 15% gratuity for sedans, 20% for limos. A trip to or from all airports is charged at the two-hour rate. There is a one-and-a-half-hour minimum before 6 p.m., two-hour minimum after 6.

- **Fugazy International Corp.**, 212-661-0100. Sedan town cars for $38 per hour, beginning at the scheduled pickup time. Stretch limos at $50 per hour, $75 for super-stretch, with a two-hour minimum, from the time of prearranged pickup.

Airlines

The Port Authority of New York and New Jersey manages John F. Kennedy, LaGuardia and Newark Airports and strives mightily to upgrade airport transportation and services and to disseminate information to the public about the facilities. To this end, they distribute particularly helpful materials and staff several telephone information numbers.

Since deregulation, the 90-plus airlines serving the three airports seem to be perpetually changing flight schedules, destinations and names, to say nothing of fares. To order this chaos, the Port Authority publishes the *International and Domestic Consolidated Airline Schedule,* a pocket-sized quarterly useful for finding the flight to fit one's needs.

The Port Authority also publishes the *Airport Map/Guides*—one each for JFK, LaGuardia and Newark—illustrating the locations of parking lots, airlines, access routes and other services. Call the 800 number listed below or write or phone the Aviation Public Service Division, Room 65N, One World Trade Center, NYC 10048, 212-435-7000, for copies of either series.

Call **800-A-I-R-R-I-D-E** 9 to 5 weekdays for a menu of recorded information.

Airport Transportation

The easiest, fastest, and most expensive way to reach JFK is by helicopter. **New York Helicopter**, 800-645-3494, charges $299 for up to five passengers for a ten-minute chartered flight between JFK and the 34th Street Heliport

At $1.50, the cheapest and one of the slowest methods is to take the A train (destination Rockaways, *not* Lefferts Blvd.) to the Howard Beach station, from which a free yellow, white and blue shuttle bus leaves for all stops at JFK. Allow an hour and a half or more. Between these two extremes are other possibilities.

First, a word about airport parking. You can, of course, drive to the airport and park there for up to 30 days at Kennedy International or Newark (tab: $150). LaGuardia has no long-term parking. Short-term parking at all airports is closer to the terminal and more expensive, $48 per day after the first day, for example, at Newark. Only LaGuardia accepts credit cards for parking. Remember that Fridays and holiday periods most lots are full. Business travelers fill short-term lots on Wednesdays. Arrive at the lot before 3 p.m. most days to be sure of a parking spot, and don't expect to find a space at LaGuardia Sunday night.

John F. Kennedy International Airport

Call 718-244-4444 for information, lost and found, and for parking.

- Taxis from midtown cost about $35 to $40 not including tolls and tip. From JFK to Manhattan there is a flat rate of $30 plus tolls and tip; if there is a second person going beyond the first stop in Manhattan, the meter is started after the first stop and this passenger pays the metered rate.

- **Carey Transportation**, call 718-632-0500 for exact schedules, leave approximately every half hour from four different locations: East Side, 125 Park Avenue, across from Grand Central between 40th and 41st Streets; West Side, Air Trans Center located in the Eighth Avenue and 42nd Street wing of the Port Authority Bus Terminal, and the New York Hilton and Marriott Hotels. Fares are $13 one way, and the trip takes about a hour, more in bad traffic.

- **Shared minibus service**, call 212-757-6840 for information. Gray Line Air Shuttle provides minibus service every 15 minutes to major Manhattan hotels from 6 a.m. to 7 p.m. for $16.50 per person.

- **Bus** If you're frugal and subway-phobic, take the Q60 bus (get a transfer) from 60th Street and Second Avenue to the last stop in Kew Gardens and transfer there to the Q10 to Kennedy, where it circles the airport, stopping at each airline terminal. One fare.

LaGuardia Airport

Call 718-533-3400 for information; 718-476-5000 for lost and found and for parking.

- **Taxis** to and from midtown cost about $16 to $26, plus tolls and tip. If you can find a friendly fellow Manhattan (or wherever you are going) bound traveler you can split the fare.

- **Carey Transportation**, call 718-632-0500 for exact schedules, leave approximately every 15 minutes from four different locations: East Side, 125 Park Avenue, across from Grand Central between 40th and 41st Streets; West Side, New York Hilton at 53rd Street, Sheraton City Squire at 50th Street, and Marriott Hotel at 48th Street. Fares are $10 one way, $20 round trip.

- **Shared minibus service**, call 212-757-6840 for information. Gray Line Air Shuttle provides minibus service to major Manhattan hotels every 15 minutes from 7 a.m. to 11 p.m. for $13.50 per person.

- **Public Subway and Bus** Call the **Transit Authority**, 718-330-1234, and Triborough Coast Line, 718-335-1000, for information. Take the E or F train to the Roosevelt station in Queens and change to the Q33 bus, which runs to LaGuardia every 15 minutes 24 hours a day. Total cost $3 one way.

  If you're leaving from the Upper West Side and have 45-60 minutes to spare, take the M60 bus from Broadway and 106th Street or anywhere along Broadway north to 125th Street to Second Avenue before midnight. It goes to LaGuardia for one fare.

- The **LaGuardia "Q.T."** (Quick Trip) leaves from all LaGuardia terminals and the Marine Air Terminal every 20 minutes from 6:35 a.m. to

11 p.m. The express bus leaves you at 21st Street and 41st Avenue in Long Island City, where you can catch the B or Q into Manhattan. Total cost is $5 in exact change or tokens.

- **Delta Water Shuttle**, 800-54-F-E-R-R-Y, operates a regularly scheduled launch shuttle between LaGuardia and East 34th Street and Pier 11 at the foot of Wall Street Monday through Friday. The trip takes 25 minutes from East 34th Street, 40 minutes from Pier 11 and costs $15 one way, $20 round trip.

Newark International Airport

Call 201-961-6000 for information; 201-961-6230 for lost and found; 201-961-4755 for parking.

The Port Authority, which runs all three NYC area airports, supervises efficient, inexpensive transportation to and from Newark.

- **Taxis** can legally add $10 to the meter rate, and the trip from midtown to Newark Airport costs about $40 without tolls and tips. Returning to Manhattan, New Jersey cabs are limited to fixed fares determined by location, for example $30 to the West Side between the Battery and 59th Street. Share and Save rates for groups of up to four passengers cut costs by almost half and are available between 8 a.m. and midnight. Check with the dispatcher at the terminal's hack stand.

- **Bus Service** by New Jersey Transit to and from the Port Authority Bus Terminal, 212-564-8484, uses a special air-conditioned airport departure lounge, the Air Trans Center, in the North Wing of the terminal at 42nd Street and Eighth Avenue. Buses leave every 15 minutes from 6:45 a.m. to midnight and cost $7 one way ($3.50 for seniors), $12 round trip.

- **Olympia Trails Bus Company**, call 212-964-6233 for information, runs a bus about every 30 minutes during rush hours that stops first at 125 Park Avenue, between 40th and 41st Streets across from Grand Central, then at One World Trade Center before arriving at Newark Airport some 25 minutes later. The cost is $7 one way.

- **Shared minibus service**, call 212-757-6840 for information. Gray Line Air Shuttle provides minibus service every 15 minutes to major Manhattan hotels from 6 a.m. to 7 p.m. for $18.50 per person.

Inter-Airport Service

Every half hour between 6:30 a.m. and 11:30 p.m. **Carey**, at 718-632-0513, runs a shuttle bus that loops between the passenger terminals at **Kennedy and LaGuardia Airports**. The fare is $11 one way. If you are traveling with a companion, or can find someone to share with, it is probably worth taking a taxi. The fare is about $12 to $15 without tip.

As described above, Carey also provides transportation from these airports to the Air Trans Center at the Port Authority Bus Terminal. Because New Jersey Transit, 212-564-8484, also uses the Air Trans Center as a depot for Newark Airport service, a direct bus link has been forged between **Newark, LaGuardia and Kennedy Airports**. Just change at the Air Trans Center from Carey to New Jersey Transit or vice versa. The fares remain the same: $11 from Newark to New York, $11 from New York to LaGuardia, $11 to Kennedy.

Satellite Airports

Three airports outside the city offer an attractive alternative to the JFK-LaGuardia-Newark axis: uncrowded access roads, easy parking and fewer delays all around for domestic flights.

- **Long Island MacArthur** in Islip, Long Island, is served by American Airlines and USAir, plus the commuter lines of Continental, Delta, Northwest and United, with direct flights to ten cities in the East. Call 516-467-3210 for information.

- **Stewart Airport**, a former Air Force base 60 miles north of the city in Newburgh, NY, at the juncture of I-87 and I-84, opened for commercial service in 1990 and offers flights by American and USAir and the commuter lines American Eagle and United Express to five cities and Kennedy Airport. Call 914-564-2100 for information.

- **Westchester County Airport** in White Plains, 914-285-4860, is served by American, Carnival, Northwest, USAir, and United as well as by commuter service of the same lines and Delta. The airport boasts a new terminal, completed in 1995, and ample parking in a three-story lot. Lacking a car, take the Harlem Line out of Grand Central to White Plains, and the Bee Line #12 bus to the airport.

Commuter and National Rail Service

Pennsylvania Station, between 31st and 33rd Streets and Seventh and Eighth Avenues, with the Long Island Railroad Station adjacent between 33rd and 34th Streets, and Grand Central Station at 42nd Street between Vanderbilt and Lexington Avenues at Park are the railroad hubs in New York City. The waiting room at Grand Central has recently been renovated in celebration of the grand old station's 75th birthday and is once again habitable. The Oyster Bar downstairs, unbelievably, is one of New York's best restaurants.

- Amtrak trains, call 212-582-6875 for information and reservations, leave Pennsylvania Station for the Northeast Corridor between Washington and Boston and for destinations throughout most of the country and to Canada. For Metroliner service between New York and Washington call 800-872-7245 for information and reservations and for the internet-inclined, go to www.amtrak.com.

- **Metro-North trains**, 212-532-4900, leave from Grand Central Station and include the Hudson Line to Poughkeepsie, New York; the Harlem Line to Brewster, New York; and the New Haven Line to New Haven, Connecticut. Find up to date Metro-North information on the MTA web site: www.mta.nyc.ny.us/.

- **The New Jersey Transit Information Center**, 201-762-5100 and 800-772-2222, is the place to call for Pennsylvania Station-New Jersey train schedules.

- **Long Island Railroad trains**, 718-217-5477, leave from their own station next to Penn Station. Find up to date LIRR information on the MTA web site: www.mta.nyc.ny.us/.

Commuter and National Bus Service

The Port Authority Bus Terminal, between 40th and 42nd Streets and Eighth and Ninth Avenues, 212-564-8484, strikingly modernized and enlarged, is the center for almost all inter-city bus traffic. The exceptions are inter-borough expresses, which have designated pickup points at certain Manhattan intersections, and buses, mostly from New Jersey, that arrive and leave from the Port Authority Bus Station at the George Washington Bridge, 212-568-5323.

- **Greyhound Bus Lines**, 800-231-2222, has its principal ticket offices in the Port Authority Terminal, and their buses arrive and depart from the Lower Level of the North Wing with entrances on both 41st and 42nd Streets.

- **Peter Pan Trailways**, 800-237-8747, uses Adirondack Trailways as its local ticket agent in the Port Authority Terminal. Its buses also arrive at and depart from the Lower Level of the North Wing.

Car Rentals

If you let your fingers do the walking through the 19 Yellow Pages of car rental firms in the *Manhattan Telephone Directory,* you will undoubtedly come up with the best rate for your particular needs. National and local companies rent everything from the latest model cars in all sizes to subcompacts, station wagons, vans and "oldies." Prices vary widely from firm to firm, and special rates (for a weekend, say, or midweek) are common; call around for cost comparisons. Keep in mind that companies located just outside the city may have low enough rates to more than compensate for the lack of convenience.

Be sure to ask if there is a charge for leaving the car at another location, if that is your plan. Some other helpful hints: Manhattan car rental companies run out of availability quickly, especially before summer and holiday weekends. *Do not wait until the last minute!* Calling early may also get you a better discount. You may be able to get discount packages through your employer's company policy. When you to book your reservation, ask for a confirmation number so you can be sure to get the rate you were quoted when you reserved the car.

Finally, becoming a member of New York City's AAA, 212-757-2000, even if you do not own a car, is a good idea. Aside from access to good discount rental rates, you're guaranteed the protection you might not otherwise get from a small rental company.

Here are some of the largest companies. All of them accept major credit cards.

- **Avis** In New York City call 212-308-2727 for information and reservations; elsewhere call 800-331-2847. Eleven locations in Manhattan; cars available at John F. Kennedy International Airport, LaGuardia Airport and Newark International Airport.

- **Budget** 800-527-0700. Nine locations in Manhattan and at all three airports.

- **Dollar** 800-800-4000. Three locations in Manhattan and at all three airports.

- **Hertz** 800-654-3131 anytime. Eleven locations in Manhattan and at all three airports.

- **National** 800-227-7368. Nine locations in Manhattan and at all three airports.

SUMMER accommodations in university dorms, Ys, church-run women's residences, hotels and even B & Bs provide temporary shelter en route to a permanent living situation. Later, there may be the occasional visiting aunt and uncle whom you can not squeeze into your cramped one bedroom. Descriptions of these varied lodgings are furnished, together with a selection of hotels categorized by price and location.

A couple of generalizations: rates are often negotiable (up as well as down), weekends and the summer months offer the best opportunity for lodging bargains, holidays and the fall months are usually the priciest times to stay in the city.

The rates quoted are from 1997. Increases during the year are a good bet, particularly in the case of hotels, which traditionally hike prices in April or September. To avoid check-out shock, note that New York hotel rooms are subject to 13.25% tax, plus a flat $2 room tax. Prices quoted in this chapter do not include tax.

Summer Only

Dorm accommodations and other special situations include (all Area Code 212):

- **Barnard College**, contact Ms. Jean McCurry, Director, Summer Program, 2009 Broadway, NYC 10027, 854-8021. During the summer, Barnard opens the doors of its dorm and student apartment rooms to men and women students both, as long as they have jobs, an internship or are attending an accredited school. 1997 rates: an air-conditioned room is $112 to $168 per person per week, two-week minimum. Meal plans are extra. (Closed for renovations 1997 and part of 1998)

- **Columbia University's Intern Housing**, c/o Conference Housing Office, 116 Wallach Hall, Columbia University, NYC 10027, 854-2946. Columbia's traditional summer hostel is open to anyone, including June graduates, with a current student ID and a paying or non-paying internship. There is a one-month minimum stay payable in advance. Rates run about $171 a week, depending on the amenities.

- **International House** (near Columbia University), 500 Riverside Drive at 123rd Street, NYC 10027, 316-8400. You don't have to matriculate at Columbia to be eligible for one of the approximately 700 dorm rooms and suites available to students, interns and other visitors from late May to mid-August on a first-come, first-served basis. Rates are $500 to $600 a month, depending on amenities; for short stays, $30 a night. Write or call for information or to reserve. These bargain accommodations are sometimes available during the school year as well.

- **New York University Dormitories**, c/o New York University, Office of Summer Housing, 14A Washington Place, NYC 10003, 998-4621. There is a three-week minimum stay requirement at the NYU dorms, which are open to other students, age 17 or older, and June graduates from early May through early August. However, priority is given to enrolled summer students. Room rates range from $155 a week for a double or triple room without air conditioning to $210 per week for an air-conditioned single, meals included. All rooms are contained within shared suites; halls are co-ed, rooms and suites are single sex. Apply early.

See also **Sublets** and **Sharing** in the chapter on **Apartment Hunting.**

Transient YMCAs

All of the three Ys in Manhattan offering accommodations house both men and women; all rent rooms on a daily basis only and all subscribe to the "Y's Way" central booking office. Anyone (member or no) can write or call the "Y's Way" booking office located at the Vanderbilt YMCA, 224 East 47th Street, NYC 10017, 212-308-2899, to obtain confirmed reservations at the three YMCAs listed below. "Y's Way" rates range from $45 to $50 single and $54 to $61 double. Rates vary if you book direct at a specific Y. In all cases the room rate includes use of all athletic facilities on the premises (see YMCAs under Participant Sports).

- **McBurney YMCA**, 206 West 24th Street, NYC 10011, 212-741-9226. Co-ed. 279 single rooms, $43 to $50 per day ($2 less if you're an out-of-state Y member), plus $5 refundable key deposit.

- **Vanderbilt YMCA**, 224 East 47th Street, NYC 10017, 212-756-9600. Coed. 370 rooms, $53 single, $66 double.

- **West Side YMCA**, 5 West 63rd Street, NYC 10023, 212-787-4400. Coed. 550 single rooms with shared bath, $55 single, $65 double.

Residences

Daily transients are not accepted by any of the residences noted below, which, with the exception of the 92nd Street Y and the Pennington, are for women only. Weekly rates are the norm and many include two meals a day in the price. Full occupancy is the rule at most of these places, as is the requirement for a personal interview, and you should therefore make arrangements for a room well in advance of arrival. Some have special house rules, such as curfews, so inquire about these before booking. For further listings, call or write for *A Temporary Place to Live* published by the Open Housing Center, 594 Broadway, Suite 608, NYC 10012, 212-941-6101. The cost at this writing was $4.

- **92nd Street YM-YWHA**, 1395 Lexington Avenue, NYC 10128, 212-415-5650. Co-ed, for men and women ages 18 and older. 400 rooms, $550 to $685 a month for a minimum (by application only) stay of two months. Weekly rates: $294 single, and $200 per person in a double. Daily rates (3 day minimum): $49 single, $35 in a shared room.

- **Brandon Residence for Women**, 340 West 85th Street between Riverside Drive and West End Avenue, NYC 10024, 212-496-6901. 120 single rooms with shared baths, a handsome lobby and 24-hour security. Applicants who will be working or students must apply in advance, with approval pending an interview. Rates: $579-$692 per month single, shared bathrooms, includes breakfast and dinner.

- **Katherine House** (Ladies Christian Union), 118 West 13th Street, NYC 10014, 212-242-6566. 82 rooms, $143 a week includes two meals a day; three-month minimum stay for women 18-25 with an income less $25,000 per year.

- **Markle Residence** (Salvation Army), 123 West 13th Street, NYC 10014, 212-242-2400. $210 a week for private room and bath includes two meals a day. Four week minimum stay.

- **Parkside Evangeline Residence** (Salvation Army), 18 Gramercy Park South, NYC 10003, 212-677-6200. About 200 rooms, $170-184 a week including two meals a day. Require $680 refundable security deposit and a $15 non-refundable registration fee. Three months minimum.

- **Roberts House** (Ladies Christian Union), 151 East 36th Street, NYC 10016, 212-683-6865. $143 a week including two meals a day; three-month minimum. Ages 18 to 25.

- **St. Mary's Residence** (Daughters of the Divine Charity), 225 East 72nd Street, NYC 10021, 212-249-6850. $135 a week for private rooms with shared baths and facilities, with a three month minimum, no meals.

- **Webster Apartments**, 419 West 34th Street between Ninth and Tenth Avenues, NYC 10001, 212-967-9000. Call well in advance to reserve for a minimum of four weeks at this attractive establishment, which features gardens, a library and maid service in its 373 rooms. An interview is required of applicants in the area; out-of-towners write directly for an application. Current weekly rates: interns/trainees, $168; students, $190; working residents, $142-$187, depending on your weekly gross income. You must provide proof of enrollment in a school, a letter of proof of internship or four consecutive pay stubs with application.

Bed and Breakfast

In Manhattan? Yes! Many a resourceful New Yorker has let out that extra room and thrown a Continental breakfast into the bargain. It's even possible to have the whole apartment, in a charming brownstone or a high tech high rise, to yourself, which is to say unhosted. In any case, it will be cheaper than comparable digs in a hotel, but the visitor may give up something in privacy, service or convenience. However, don't look for hand lettered shingles advertising availability because owners require anonymity and an agency acts as intermediary.

This cottage industry is unregulated, though reputable agencies inspect the properties they represent and attempt to monitor the quality of service and accommodations on an ongoing basis through visitor critique cards. Shop around by phone; be as specific as you can be about preferred location, likes and dislikes, allergies and other restrictions. There is usually a two-night minimum stay, but there may be exceptions off-season. For the best choice, book well in advance (reasonable B&Bs have gotten as scarce as affordable hotel rooms) and expect to pay a 25% deposit or more. The commission is included in the fee. Many accept credit cards. Expect to pay 8.25% sales tax above the given room price. Unless stated otherwise, all telephone numbers are Area Code 212.

- **Abode Bed and Breakfast**, P.O. Box 20022, NYC 10021, 472-2000 (800-835-8880 for out-of-state callers only), represents about 200 hosted and unhosted apartments, mostly in Manhattan, a few in Brooklyn, and some long-term locations. They request business references from guests. Three—night minimum, $135 - $325 a night for a studio. AE

- **B&B Registry**, operated by Manhattan Lodgings, Inc., 70 East 10th Street, NYC 10003, 475-2090 or email info@manhattan lodgings. com, offers 200 furnished,luxury short-stay apartments in Manhattan. Three-night minimum; 2 week advance notice required, $75 - $300 per night.

- **Bed, Breakfast and Books**, 35 West 92nd Street, NYC 10025, 865-8740, so named because the owners also operate a book business, attracts a fairly bookish clientele, not surprisingly. One of the more established agencies, they handle about 35 apartments, mostly hosted, all over Manhattan and a couple in Brooklyn. In telephone interviews they attempt to match the visitors' background, age and preferences to the location. Prices range from $90 for a hosted single, to $130-plus for an unhosted one-bedroom apartment. Two-night minimum; some long-term stays.

- **Bed and Breakfast Network**, 130 Barrow Street, NYC 10014, 645-8134, lists 700 places, hosted and unhosted, and suggests a few weeks' advance notice. Rates range from $60 to $90 single, $90 to $120 double, and $100 to $325 for an unhosted apartment. There is a two-night minimum in most cases.

- **City Lights Bed and Breakfast**, P.O. Box 20355, Cherokee Station, NYC 10021, 737-7049, lists several hundred rooms and apartments, hosted and unhosted, all in Manhattan. Rates are $75 to $300 per night, depending on the accommodation, with a two-night minimum. V, MC, DC.

- **New World Bed and Breakfast**, 150 Fifth Avenue, Suite 711, NYC 10011, 675-5600, or 800-443-3800 from out of town, represents about 120 apartments, all in Manhattan. Perhaps because the owner is a woman, the agency tends to attract working women. Rates for hosted rooms range from $65 to $70 single, $80 to $90 double with a two-night minimum. Furnished apartments with kitchens start at $110 per night. Discounts for longer stays. AE, MC, V.

Residential Hotels

A number of hotels, particularly smaller neighborhood properties equipped with kitchenettes, quote weekly and monthly, as well as daily, rates. You'll find several listed under Inexpensive Hotels below. There is also a group that offers monthly rates in eight apartment hotels located in some of New York's nicest neighborhoods:

- **Manhattan East Hotels**, call 800-637-8483, represents the Shelburne (Murray Hill), Eastgate Tower (fringes of Murray Hill), Beekman Tower (near Sutton Place), Plaza 50 and Lyden/53 (Midtown East), The Surrey and Lyden/64 (Upper East Side) and Southgate Tower (Penn Station area). The least expensive rental, a studio in Southgate Tower, costs $3,600 a month, a one-bedroom apartment in the more prestigious Beekman Tower goes for $5,500 and up.

- **Hotel Olcott**, 27 West 72nd Street, NYC 10023, 877-4200, nicely located between Lincoln Center and Central Park, tends to attract musicians and actors to its homey confines. Rates by the week are $590 plus tax for a studio, $770 for one bedroom.

- **The Phillips Club**, 1965 Broadway at 67th Street, NYC 10023, 835-8800, at the high end and designed for the corporate traveler, is discreetly tucked into four floors of a sleek 32-floor building just north of Lincoln Center. Decor in the 96 furnished suites, ranging from studio to two-bedroom apartments in soothing beige, cream and taupe, is somewhat corporate, and a minimum stay of one month ranges from $4,950 to $11,000.

Hotels

Prices and occupancy rates fluctuate seasonally depending on location. The friendly, and sometimes frenetic, first-class commercial establishments along Central Park West and Lexington and Park Avenues in the East 40s and 50s are impossibly full weekdays in the fall, winter and spring, but both occupancy and prices languish during the summer dog days. This is the season, however, when the comparatively feisty West Side tourist class hotels sprinkled around the Broadway theaters in the West 40s cost the most and are the fullest. Low rates are never in season at the town's justifiably famous deluxe hotels, be they large and extravagant, quietly posh or smoothly contemporary—but many do have weekend plans.

Anyone who wants to lessen the blow of oppressive hotel prices should know where to find the lower rates at various times of the year (or week), and some generalizations are included here. *The rates quoted are for two people in a room, week nights, not including tax.* All Manhattan hotels are Area Code 212.

Weekend Rates are almost always lower than prices charged during the week. However, flossy "weekend packages" with champagne, flowers and free brunches for two don't represent the best values. Ask about the no-frills prices available Friday, Saturday and sometimes Sunday nights. Weekend rates are, in effect, contingency plans to fill the house. If full occupancy looms, off they go.

Unadvertised Discounts Even with the surge of tourists visiting New York City, the occupancy rate of some hotels is erratic, with the result that accommodating, unadvertised prices are occasionally available. After you've been quoted the standard rates, ask for information about any special deals.

Hotel Discounters buy blocks of rooms from hotels at volume discounts and pass savings, some as high as 60%, on to consumers. Visit their web site or call to have their lists mailed or faxed to you, then you call for rates and to reserve. You must give a credit card number to hold your room, and payment is at the hotel when you check out. There is no fee for the service. **Express Reservations**, 800-356-1123 (http://www. express.—res.com), for example, books into 25 hotels in mid-town Manhattan and one in Soho at rates generally ranging from $105 to $250 a night. At **Quikbook**, 800-789-9887 (http://www.quikbook.com), you are connected with a reservation agent who can reserve rooms at dozens of moderate to deluxe hotels all over Manhattan (as well as Chicago, LA and four other cities). Prices are discounted from the hotel's regularly quoted rates.

Inexpensive Hotels

Doubles for $75 to $185 not including tax may not seem cheap, but that's the range separating New York's hotel bargain category from the rest of the flock this year. All telephone numbers are Area Code 212.

- **Allerton Hotel for Women**, 130 East 57th Street, NYC 10022, 753-8841. The commendable location of this somewhat spartan hotel keeps the place full to overflowing in spite of the fact the rooms are small and occasionally unkempt. $75 double with private bath ($50 single without bath), taxes included.

- **Best Western Seaport Inn**, 33 Peck Slip, NYC 10038, 766-6600. A pleasingly restored 19th century building one block from the waterfront at the very lower tip of Manhattan. Doubles start at $175 per weeknight, a bargain if you get one of the upper floor rooms with great views of the Brooklyn Bridge.

- **Excelsior**, 45 West 81st Street, NYC 10024, 362-9200. A great location facing the Museum of Natural History and Central Park compensates for occasionally grungy rooms. $149 single, $169 double, $169-$189 for a one-bedroom suite, $249 for a two-bedroom suite.

- **Gorham**, 136 West 55th Street, NYC 10019, 245-1800. All 116 rooms in the narrow, 17-story Gorham just off Sixth Avenue have kitchenettes and dining tables; a 1993 renovation resulted in the addition of a fitness center among other amenities. $180 to $320 for a double.

- **Herald Square**, 19 West 31st Street, NYC 10001, 279-4017. Recently renovated, its Beaux Arts facade cleaned up, this tourist hotel is a favorite with European travelers looking for value. Rates begin at the bargain-price of $50 for a small, one-person room and run up to $125 for four.

- **Off Soho Suites**, 11 Rivington Street, off the Bowery, NYC 10002, 800-OFF-SOHO, is technically on the edge of the old Lower East Side, a short walk from Soho and Chinatown and a location which may not be for everybody. But the accommodations are clean and comfortable, and a bargain especially for a family or a group of four. The economy suites for two include kitchen and marble bath, which may be shared, for $92.50; suites for four, with private kitchen and bath, are $159. There is a cafe on site and 24-hour parking for $8.

- **Paramount**, 235 West 46th Street, NYC 10036, 764-5500. The designer of the avant-garde Royalton, Philippe Starck, turned his charms on a lower-priced venue. This whimsical effort aimed at the young, hip and financially strapped offers amenities including a $1 screening room with penny candy, a 24-hour day-care center designed by the Pee Wee Playhouse people, and a Dean & Deluca store. Rates are between $220 for a double, with special weekend rates from $140 to $185.

- **Pickwick Arms**, 230 East 51st Street, NYC 10022, 355-0300. Bits of peeling paint, randomly-sized rooms, some without baths, don't deter fans from this slightly flaky place with its East 50s location and doubles for $105 with shower.

- **Quality Hotel on Fifth**, 3 East 40th Street between Fifth and Madison Avenues, NYC 10016, 447-1500. Reasonably priced and centrally located, this midtown newcomer offers spacious, no-frills comfort. You can walk to Grand Central Station and the glorious Morgan Library. But don't walk to Times Square at night, when this area is a bit eerie. Single: $195; double: $210; weekend rate: $119.

- **Radisson Empire**, 44 West 63rd Street, NYC 10023, 265-7400. The major selling point for the basic but cheerfully furnished 507-room Empire is its location next to Lincoln Center and near Columbus Circle. $155 to $600 double.

- **Westpark**, 308 West 58th Street, NYC 10019, 246-6440. With a grand location facing Columbus Circle and Central Park and tidily-renovated rooms—those 16 (out of 99) with park views are especially nice. La Place on the Park, a jazz and rhythm and blues club with bistro food on the lobby level, is another draw. At $95, the Westpark is an especially good buy for a single, doubles $110, $180 for a suite.

West Side Tourist Hotels

The cheapest rates for reliable, if far from classy, rooms are found in the tourist hotels along Eighth Avenue and in the West 40s surrounding the theater district. Better deals are offered here in the winter than in the summer.

- **Hotel Edison**, 228 West 47th Street, NYC 10036, 840-5000. A thousand rooms convenient to the theater and reasonable: $105 single, $115 double.

- **Howard Johnson's Motor Lodge**, Eighth Avenue and 51st Street, NYC 10019, 581-4100. A HoJo's is a HoJo's, even in New York: clean, decent and about $128 to $156 for two, with parking at a rate of $11 for every 24 hours.

- **Ramada Milford Plaza**, Eighth Avenue and 45th Street, NYC 10036, 869-3600. Big, basic and sometimes exceedingly reasonable. Rates: $130 to $190 single, $142-$202 double.

- **Days Hotel**, Eighth Avenue and 48th Street, NYC 10019, 581-7000. Recently refurbished, and as a result, the nicest motel in town. Pool makes this a good buy for $152-$166 double, high season. Parking is $11 per day.

First-class Commercial or Deluxe Hotels

Manhattan is known for its grand and luxurious hotels, among which a handful are legendary: the Pierre, the Plaza, the Carlyle, the Plaza Athenee, the Ritz Carlton, the Waldorf Astoria. To these have recently been added I.M. Pei's marble Four Seasons, the Righa and the Peninsula. Deluxe hotels all. We've chosen to list a few which are perhaps less well-known, on the basis of glamour and singularity, as well as fair prices, when they can be found. As said, discounts and good weekend values in these hotels are generally available only in the summertime.

- **Omni Berkshire Place**, 21 East 52nd Street at Madison Avenue, NYC 10022, 753-5800. Carefully created bouquets frame the elegant marble lobby and provide a backdrop for the toney (in a low key) tea and cocktail area on the far side of the flowers. An accommodating concierge caters to clients with dispatch in this bijou hotel, where the only major drawbacks are the smallish rooms and higher than average prices: $359 to $429.

- **Doral Court**, 130 East 39th Street between Park and Lexington Avenues, NYC 10011, 685-1100, or 800-223-6725 from out of town. The rooms are large and sunny, the youthful staff delightful and the dining al fresco in the Courtyard Cafe and Bar of this quietly elegant hotel. A double here runs from $259 to $289.

- **Doral Inn**, Lexington Avenue between 49th and 50th Streets, NYC 10022, 755-1200. Flight crews compete for space with Latinos laden with shopping bags in the relatively spacious lobby of this popular, mildly chaotic commercial hotel, where the small yet tidy rooms are a good value for this location at $159 single and $194 double. Special rates are available for government and non-profit employees.

- **The Drake**, 440 Park Avenue at 56th Street, NYC 10022, 421-0900. Glowingly updated in the Continental manner complete with attractive lobby bar, the Drake is now owned by Swissair's hotel division. Doubles cost $265 to $385 weekdays. Summer rates are lower.

- **Grand Hyatt New York**, 42nd Street and Lexington Avenue at Grand Central Station, NYC 10017, 883-1234. Fast paced and glitzy with a terrific lobby, especially when the fountains are splashing, and a dramatic bar cantilevered over 42nd Street. Rooms, 1407 of them updated in 1996, with a penthouse health club and other features to appeal to business travelers, $199 to $325 for two. Weekends are cheaper: $199 per night.

- **The Mark**, 25 East 77th Street at Madison Avenue, NYC 10021, 744-4300, or 800-T-H-E-M-A-R-K from out of town. Your Frette linens are tended to twice daily in this handsome, sophisticated late arrival in Carlyle country. Dining is on a par with its "glorious" rooms, which run $355 to $2,500 for the Presidential Suite, $285 weekends.

- **Michelangelo**, at the Equitable Center, 152 West 51st Street at Seventh Avenue, NYC 10019, 765-1900. Most recently known as the Park 51, this is the old Taft Hotel resurrected in Eurostyle "neoclassical" elegance with well-designed rooms and great baths attracts a glitzy crowd. Bring the kids, but avoid the slow, overpriced room service. Doubles run $295 to $575 for a suite. Corporate rates available.

- **Middletowne Helmsley**, 148 East 48th Street near Third Avenue, NYC 10017, 755-3000. One-, two-and three-room suites all with kitchenettes and cheerful flowered decor. A favorite of UN personnel when the General Assembly's in session. Weekdays a double is $200, $250 for a suite.

- **The Millenium**, 55 Church Street, NYC 10007, 693-2001. Easily the classiest and most elegant of the downtown hotels. Modern and convenient (if you're visiting Wall Street), the Millenium offers stunning views as well as first-class amenities such as computers and a health club with an attractive pool. Service too is top-notch. Singles can be had here for $350, doubles start at $380 per night. Weekends all rooms are discounted.

- **Morgan's**, 237 Madison Avenue between 37th and 38th Streets, NYC 10016, 686-0300. An upstart on New York's rather traditional hotel scene, this narrow, vertical little place around the corner from the staid Morgan Library, has been re-decorated and toned down from its original sleek and swinging look to a softer, earth-toned feel. There are still stereo cassette players in every (small) room and VCRs for rent ($6.50 a night). Rates have come down at this once-trendy spot to $195 single and $220-265 for a weekday double.

- **Royalton**, 44 West 44th Street off Fifth Avenue, NYC 10036, 869-4400. With mahogany beds, Danish faucets, French and Italian furniture, Ian Schrager (see Morgan's) has fashioned a swinging silk purse out of a sow's ear. You can have a gym, a computer and a fireplace too in your room, which will run about $295 to $400 for a double, singles for $275 - $375

- **SoHo Grand**, 310 West Broadway between Grand and Canal Streets, NYC 10013, 965-3000, at this writing the only hotel in Soho, offers 367 rooms with amenities to suit the businessman as well as tourists in the midst of the art galleries, boutiques and cafes which fill the formerly industrial buildings of this landmarked cast-iron district. Doubles $209 - $369.

- **San Carlos**, 150 East 50th Street, between Lexington and Third Avenues, NYC 10022, 755-1800. Quiet, small hotel with pleasantly spacious rooms and kitchenettes. $170 to $190 for a single, $180 to $195 for a double.

- **St. Regis**, 2 East 55th Street at Fifth Avenue, NYC 10022, 753-4500. This grande dame of Fifth Avenue reopened in all her Beaux

Arts glory, and then some, after a multi-million dollar restoration in 1991. A continental hotel in the old style with no modern convenience overlooked. And, yes, you can still dance on the St. Regis Roof. Doubles $455 to $565.

• **The Stanhope**, 995 Fifth Avenue at 81st Street, NYC 10028, 288-5800, or 800-828-1123 from out of town. Quiet, discrete, Old World luxury is what the Stanhope achieved with its $30-million facelift. It's all French antiques, crystal ashtrays, Egyptian cotton sheets, fresh flowers, that sort of thing, not to mention unrivaled views of Central Park and the Metropolitan Museum. Superb food and impeccable service gild the lily at $350 -$850 for a large suite.

• **United Nations Plaza**, 44th Street and First Avenue, NYC 10017, 758-1234. Superior service and sensational views from every room because they begin on the 28th Floor. A good-sized pool, health club, tennis court and free limousine rides to Wall Street make this classically modern hotel unique. Doubles start at $300, $199 weekends.

Six Favorites

Small, charming, personal hotels are not the city's forte, but there are seven fairly priced, medium-sized hotels *in other Manhattan* areas that deserve special mention.

• **Algonquin**, 59 West 44th Street, NYC 10036, 840-6800. Little has changed under Japanese ownership. All muted rose, green and burnished wood, the famous lobby bar combines with anachronistic elevators and smallish, genteel rooms to make you feel welcome, secure and part of a pleasantly elite and talented group. Singles: $270; doubles: $290; suites from $350 to $525.

• **Doubletree Guest Suites**, 1568 Broadway, NYC 719-1600. Overlooking Times Square, this recently renovated hotel rents suites (sitting room and bedroom) rather than single rooms, at the reasonable rate of $199 to $359 for a double. Corporate accounts available.

• **Lowell**, 28 East 63rd Street, NYC 10021, 838-1400. Once the haunt of independent parents come to visit their well-established Upper East Side children, the Lowell has been totally refurbished and now lets only a quarter of its 60 rooms to transients. But the more-attractive-than-ever Art Deco hotel remains intimate and friendly. Doubles start at $385.

• **Salisbury**, 123 West 57th Street, NYC 10019, 246-1300, or 800-223-0680 from out of town. Pleasant, pastel rooms in a relatively intimate setting attract a high percentage of women travelers. $189 - $209 for a single, $209 - $229 for a double.

- **Sheraton Park Avenue**, 45 Park Avenue at 37th Street, NYC 10016, 685-7676. The wood-paneled, book-lined lobby (perfect for tea after 3) and the agreeable welcome complement carefully decorated rooms, and the incomparable Morgan Library is just around the corner. Don't miss it. Singles $330; doubles $360. Weekends lower.

- **Wales**, 1295 Madison Avenue corner of 92nd Street, NYC 10028, 876-6000. Long an annex for guests of Upper East Siders with too-small apartments, the recently renovated Wales is clean, cheerful and a good value for $189 double a night, including breakfast and an evening dessert buffet to a harp accompaniment. Chamber music Sunday evenings is a nice touch. Suites are $229 to $279.

- **Wyndham**, 42 West 58th Street, NYC 10019, 753-3500. Small, attentively managed and nicely furnished, the Wyndham is home to numerous theatrical luminaries whenever they're in town and is one of the very best buys around at $120 to $135 for a single, $135 to $150 for a double, and $180 to $210 for a one-bedroom suite.

The hotels mentioned here reflect a purely personal taste and are not meant to be an all-city catalog of lodgings. For a free comprehensive compilation, get *Hotels in New York City* published by the **New York Convention and Visitors Bureau**, 2 Columbus Circle, NYC 10019, 212-397-8200. The Bureau's New York City Tour Package Directory lists bargain weekend rates.

NEW YORK CITY fairly crackles with events: parades, festivals, celebrations, ethnic holidays, shows, feasts, and tournaments. Imperceptible at first to the newcomer, there is, in fact, a rhythm to this endless round of activity: many of these events occur annually at about the same time, and New Yorkers look forward to them. The calendar below lists them by month. Watch the *Times, New York* magazine, or *The New Yorker* for specific dates and details. Or stop by the New York Convention & Visitors Bureau at 2 Columbus Circle to pick up brochures and a complete seasonal calendar of events.

January

Big Apple Circus, Lincoln Center
Three Kings Parade, 5th Ave., 104th to 116th Streets
Winter Festival, Central Park

February

Chinese New Year celebrations
Westminster Kennel Club Dog Show, Madison Square Garden

March

International Cat Show, Madison Square Garden
St. Patrick's Day Parade, Fifth Ave., 44th to 86th Streets
Circus Animal Walk to Madison Square Garden

April

Easter Parade, Fifth Ave. near 50th Street
Spring Flower Show, Brooklyn International Botanic Garden
Mets and Yankees baseball season
Rockefeller Center Flower and Garden Show
Cherry Blossom Festival, Brooklyn International Botanic Garden

May

Prospect Park Carousel opening
9th Ave. International Food Festival, 37th to 57th Sts.
You Gotta Have Park celebration, Central Park

Washington Square Outdoor Art Exhibit
Promenade Art Show, Brooklyn Heights

June

Summer Stage concerts, Central Park
Puerto Rican Day Parade, 5th Ave., 44th to 86th Streets
Welcome Back to Brooklyn festival, Grand Army Plaza
Museum Mile Festival, 5th Ave., 82nd to 102nd Streets
Queens Festival, Flushing Meadows Corona Park
Feast of St. Anthony of Padua, Sullivan St. below Houston

July

Mostly Mozart Festival, Lincoln Center
Free Shakespeare in Central Park, Delacorte Theatre
Macy's Fireworks, Lower Hudson River
Summergarden free concerts, Museum of Modern Art

August

N.Y. Philharmonic free parks concerts, all boroughs
U.S. Open Tennis Tournament, Flushing, Queens

September

Metropolitan Opera season begins, Lincoln Center
Washington Square Outdoor Art Exhibit,
N.Y. Film Festival, Lincoln Center
San Gennaro Festival, Mulberry Street, Little Italy

October

Ice Skating, Rockefeller Center and Central Park
Next Wave Festival, Brooklyn Academy of Music
Promenade Art Show, Brooklyn Heights
Greenwich Village Halloween Parade, 6th Ave., Spring to 23rd Streets

November

New York City Marathon
N.Y. City Ballet, winter season, Lincoln Center
Virginia Slims Tennis Tournament, Madison Square Garden
Christmas Spectacular stage show, Radio City Music Hall
Thanksgiving Day Parade, 77th St. to Herald Square
N.Y. Knicks basketball season, Madison Square Garden

December

Christmas Tree Lighting, Rockefeller Center
New Year's Eve Celebration, Times Square
Fireworks, South Street Seaport; Grand Army Plaza, Brooklyn
Midnight Run, Central Park
First Night events throughout city
New Year's Eve concert, N.Y. Philharmonic, Lincoln Center

Call 911 for Police, Fire and Ambulance Emergencies

All numbers are Area Code 212 unless otherwise indicated. All numbers listed below are answered 9 to 5 weekdays unless otherwise indicated.

An asterisk (*) indicates a recorded message.

Animals

ASPCA, American Society For The Prevention
of Cruelty to Animals 876-7700
Animal Bites

Bureau of Animal Affairs, NYC Dept. of Health 566-2068
Animal Emergency Care

Animal Medical Center 838-7053
Open 24 hours; phone calls 9 a.m. to 11 p.m.
Nuisance Complaints

Bureau of Animal Affairs, NYC Dept. of Health 442-1999

Consumer Complaints and Services

Better Business Bureau *533-6200
Cable Television Complaints

NYC Office of Telecommunications 800-342-3330
Consumer Complaints

NYC Dept. of Consumer Affairs 487-4444

NY State Consumer Frauds and Protection Bureau 416-8345
Moving and Storage Complaints

Interstate Commerce Commission 264-1072

New York State Dept. of Transportation 718-482-4816

Crime

Crime Victim Hotline

Non-profit Metropolitan Assistance Corp. 417-5160
24 hours a day

Police Emergency Number 911

Police Headquarters 374-5000
24 hour number for precinct referrals

Sex Crime Hotline

Sex Crimes Unit, Police Dept. 267-7273
24 hour service staffed by female NYPD detectives

Discrimination

Complaints

State Commission on Human Rights .417-5041

NYC Commission on Human Rights 360-7640

Dow Jones Report *976-4141
24 hour number

Education, Board of 718-935-2000

Elections, Board of 886-3800

Entertainment

Broadway Show Line 563-BWAY

Cultural Affairs Department Hotline 841-4100

NYC/OnStage 768-1818

Parks and Recreation Department

Special events 360-8146

Summer Stage *360-2777

Fire

Emergency Number 911

Health and Medical Care

Ambulance Emergency Number 911

Animal Bites

Bureau of Animal Affairs, NYC Dept. of Health
24 hour service: 9 to 5 weekdays 788-4204
Evenings, weekends and holidays .340-4494

Dental Emergencies

First District Dental Society
Names of members on call *679-3966
Department of Health Central Complaint Bureau *442-1999

Doctor Referrals

New York County Medical Society, AMA 684-4670

Doctors on Call .212-737-2333, 718-238-2100

Drug Store

Kaufman Drugstore, 557 Lexington Avenue corner 50th 755-2266
Open 24 hours a day

Medical Help

Doctors-on-Call, private group 718-745-5900
24 hour house-call service

New York Doctor Line

Referrals to St. Luke's-Roosevelt Hospital physicians 876-5432

Poison Control Center

NYC Dept. of Health 764-7667

24 hour service 340-4494

Suicide Prevention 718-389-9608

24 hours a day 532-2400

24 hours a day 673-3000

After 6 p.m. 718-389-9608

Housing

Electrical and Steam Emergencies

Consolidated Edison 683-0862
24 hour service

Gas Leaks

Consolidated Edison 683-8830
24 hour service

Heat Complaints

NYC Housing Preservation and Development 960-4800
24 hour service of the Central Complaint Bureau

Housing Complaints

(In general) 960-4800
See "Heat" above

Rent Stabilization Information

Rent Stabilization Assn. (Owners) 214-9200
Rent Stabilization Assn. (Tenants) 961-8930
Division of Housing and Community Renewal 240-6010
Rent Administration Info line 718-739-6400

Income Tax

Federal Tax Information 800-829-1040
Federal Tax Forms 800-829-3676
24 hour number
New York City and State Information 718-935-6000
New York City and State Tax Forms 800-462-8100
24 hour number

Legal

Association of the Bar of the City of New York

Legal Referral Service 626-7373

Library

New York Public Library Information .340-0849
Bronx Reference Service 718-579-4257
Brooklyn Reference Service 718-780-7700
Manhattan Reference Service 340-0849
Queens Reference Service 718-990-0714
Staten Island 340-0849

Marriage Licenses

NYC Marriage License Bureau *669-2400

Motor Vehicles

Alternate Side of the Street Parking Regulations

NYC Bureau of Traffic Operations *442-7080

Highway Emergencies

NYC Dept. of Highways 442-7094
24 hour service; calls tow trucks for highway (not street) breakdowns
Motor Vehicle Department, New York State
Licenses and Registration Information 645-5550
7:30 a.m. to 4 p.m.

Parking Violations Help Hotline
NYC Dept. of Transportation 477-4430
Property damage claim forms
NYC Controller 669-8750
Towed Away Cars
NYC Bureau of Traffic Operations 971-0770
7 a.m. to 10 p.m. daily

Ombudsman

Complaints, City Agencies
Office of City Council President 788-7100
Complaints, State Agencies
New York Dept. of State 417-5760
Information 417-4000
Consumer Frauds
NY State 416-8345

Post Office

General Information 967-8585
8 a.m. to 8 p.m., Saturday 8 to 4, closed Sunday

Sanitation and Garbage

Complaints
NYC Department of Sanitation 219-8090
Environmental Action Coalition
Recycling 677-1601

Sports Phone

Schedules, scores *976-1313
Supplemental information *976-2525

Street Maintenance

Potholes
NYC Bureau of Highways 768-4653
After 4:30 p.m. and weekends 442-7097
Streetlights
NYC Bureau of Electrical Control 669-8353

Water Mains, Sewers

NYC Dept. of Environmental Protection 718-699-9811
24 hour service

Telephone

Credit Card, Special Services

AT&T 800-C-A-L-L-A-T-T

Equipment Sales and Leasing

AT&T 800-555-8111

Residential Equipment Service and Complaints

AT&T Repairs 800-526-2000
Service complaint 908-582-8500
Federal Communications Commission 620-3436
Advice on any interference in television, radio, and telephone reception

Information

Nynex/Bell Atlantic 411
24 hour service

Repairs

Nynex/Bell Atlantic 611
24 hour service

Residential Installation and Information

Nynex/Bell Atlantic
To order service 890-1550
Payment 890-2100

MCI NYC Residential Service .888-624-5622

Wiring Service and Complaints

AT&T Service and Information 800-222-0300
MCI Customer Service 800-727-5555

Time /Temperature *976-1616

Tourism and Travel

New York City Information

New York Convention and Visitors Bureau 397-8222

New York State Information

New York State Dept. of Commerce 803-2200
Vacation Information 800-225-5697
Recording after 5 p.m.

Passports

US Passport Agency 399-5290

Traveler's Aid Services

Metropolitan Assistance Bureau 944-0013

Transportation - Airports

Airports

Port Authority of NY & NJ 800-A-I-R-R-I-D-E

John F. Kennedy International

Information 718-244-4444

Lost and Found/Airport Police 718-244-4225

Parking Information and Conditions 718-656-5699

LaGuardia

Information 718-533-3400

Lost and Found/Airport Police 718-539-3900

Parking Information *718-533-3850

Newark

Information 201-961-6000

Lost and Found/Airport Police 201-961-6230

Parking Information and Conditions *201-961-4751

Transportation - Buses

Lost and Found (NYC Transit Authority) 718-625-6200

Bus Schedules (NYC Transit Authority) 718-330-1234

Port Authority Bus Terminal Information 564-8484

George Washington Bridge Bus Terminal Information 564-1114

Greyhound/Trailways Bus Lines .800-231-2222

Transportation - Ferry

Staten Island Ferry 806-6940

Transportation - PATH (Hudson Tubes)

Travel Information 800-234-7284

Transportation - Railroads

Staten Island Rapid Transit 718-966-7478

Amtrak (Penn Station and Grand Central) 582-6875

Amtrak/Metroliner Reservations and Information 800-872-7245

Metro-North (Grand Central) 532-4900

Long Island Railroad (Penn Station) 718-217-5477

New Jersey Transit (Penn Station) 201-762-5100

Transportation - Subways

Lost & Found (NYC Transit Authority) 718-625-6200

Subway Schedules (NYC Transit Authority) 718-330-1234

Transportation - Taxis

Complaints (NYC Taxi and Limousine Commission) 221-8294

Lost & Found (NYC Taxi and Limousine Commission) 302-8294

Transit Authority Customer Service Office

Complaints about service 718-330-3322

Weather *976-1212

A Newcomer's Reading List

Below, we list a few books, four of which have already been mentioned in this Handbook, which the newcomer may find helpful.

- *Away for the Weekend, New York,* by Eleanor Berman, with 52 weekend excursions less than 250 miles from New York, some possible without a car.

- *The Dog's Guide to New York City, with Jack, the City Dog*, by Jan Rohman.

- *Don't Even Think of Parking Here*, by Paul Trapido and Barbara Ensor. Keeping a car in the city; it's not all parking.

- *Glanton's Guide to the African American New York*, by Latrice Glanton-Chandler.

- *The Great New York Dog Book*, by Deborah Loven.

- *How to Find the Best Doctors*, New York Metropolitan Area, by John Castle and John Connolly.

- *Mr. Cheap's New York, by Mark Waldstein,* with cheap eats and things to do, bargains, factory outlets, off-price and discount stores, interesting things to do in the city for little or nothing.

- *The New York Parents' Book*, by Lois Gilman.

- *The Parents' Guide to the Best Public Elementary Schools in N.Y. City*, by Clara Hemphill.

- *Where to Go: A Guide to Manhattan's Toilets*, by Vicki Rovere. Don't laugh. In a city with a dearth of public toilets this can be a life-saver…well, a dignity saver.

Belden Randolph Merims was a newcomer to New York longer ago than she wants to remember. A researcher at Newsweek then, she married a native and stayed to raise a family in Greenwich Village. After some 30 years here as an occasional editor and writer, she still finds the city endlessly fascinating, exciting and, yes, beautiful.

Do you think you know New York City better than we do? Please, tell us!

If you are the first to offer any new information about
New York City that is subsequently used in the next
Newcomer's Handbook® for New York City,
we'll send you a free copy of our next edition.

SUGGESTIONS:

_____

_____

_____

_____

_____

YOUR NAME: _____

YOUR ADDRESS (PLEASE INCLUDE TELEPHONE NUMBER): _____

_____

_____

Help keep this guide current. If a listing has changed, let us know.

UPDATES:

_____

_____

_____

_____

_____

Send to: First Books, Inc.
P. O. Box 578147, Chicago, IL 60657

The original, always updated, absolutely invaluable guides for people *moving* to a city!

Find out about neigborhoods, apartment hunting, money matters, deposits/leases, getting settled, helpful services, shopping for the home, places of worship, belonging, sports/recreation, volunteering, green space, transportation, temporary lodgings and useful telephone numbers!

	#/COPIES		TOTAL
Newcomer's Handbook™ for Atlanta	_____	x $13.95	$_____
Newcomer's Handbook™ for Boston	_____	x $13.95	$_____
Newcomer's Handbook™ for Chicago	_____	x $13.95	$_____
Newcomer's Handbook™ for Los Angeles	_____	x $13.95	$_____
Newcomer's Handbook™ for Minneapolis-St. Paul	_____	x $14.95	$_____
Newcomer's Handbook™ for New York City	_____	x $17.95	$_____
Newcomer's Handbook™ for San Francisco	_____	x $13.95	$_____
Newcomer's Handbook™ for Washington, DC	_____	x $13.95	$_____

SUBTOTAL $_____

TAX (IL residents add 8.75% sales tax) $_____

POSTAGE & HANDLING ($5.00 first book, $.75 each add'l) $_____

TOTAL $_____

SHIP TO:

_____
Name

_____
Title

_____
Company

_____
Address

_____   _____   _____
City   State   Zip

_____
Phone Number

Send this order form and a check or money order
payable to: First Books, Inc.

First Books, Inc., Mail Order Department
P. O. Box 578147, Chicago, IL 60657
773-276-5911

Allow 2-3 weeks for delivery.

NOTES:

NOTES:

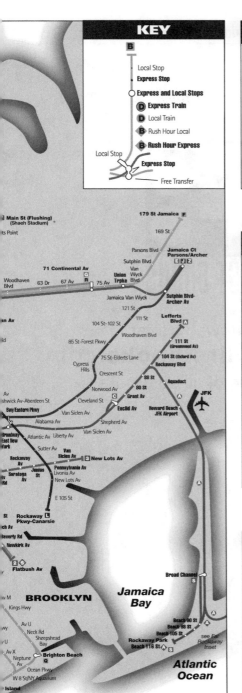

KEY

B

Local Stop
Express Stop

○ Express and Local Stops

D Express Train

D Local Train

B Rush Hour Local

B Rush Hour Express

Local Stop

Express Stop

Free Transfer

Express Trains

IRT	② ③ ④ ⑤
IND	Ⓐ Ⓔ Queens
BMT	Ⓑ Manhattan & Bklyn eves
	Ⓓ Manhattan
	Ⓙ Ⓩ Queens Myrtle-Marcy Av, Manhattan
	Ⓠ No service after 9pm, Queens use B train, Brooklyn use d train

---

Local Trains

IRT	① ⑨ ⑥ ⑦
IND	Ⓐ Brooklyn after 9 pm & weekends Ⓒ
	Ⓔ Manhattan Ⓢ
BMT	Ⓑ Brooklyn 36 St - Coney Island late night
	Ⓖ
	Ⓓ Brooklyn & The Bronx
	Ⓕ Manhattan & Brooklyn
	Ⓙ evenings Ⓜ
	Ⓝ
	Ⓡ
	Ⓢ
Canarsie	Ⓛ

Rush Hour Trains

IRT	⬥ Brooklyn & The Bronx
IND	◆ Rockaway ◆ The Bronx
BMT	◈ Manhattan 59 St - Brooklyn 36 St
	◈ Manhattan 59 St - 168 St
	◈ Manhattan & Bronx ◈ Brooklyn
	◈ Queens 71 Av -Queens Plaza
	◈ Brooklyn
	◈ Queens & Manhattan

Map labels

Main St (Flushing) (Shaeh Stadium)

ts Point

179 St Jamaica F

169 St

71 Continental Av

Woodhaven Blvd

63 Dr 67 Av 75 Av Ⓖ Ⓡ

Parsons Blvd
Sutphin Blvd
Van Wyck
Union Blvd
Trpke

Jamaica Ct Parsons/Archer Ⓔ Ⓙ Ⓩ

Jamaica Van Wyck

Sutphin Blvd-Archer Av

an Av

121 St

104 St-102 St

111 St

Lefferts Blvd Ⓐ

id

85 St-Forest Pkwy

Woodhaven Blvd

111 St (Greenwood Av)

Cypress Hills

75 St-Elderts Lane

104 St (Oxford Av)
Rockaway Blvd

Crescent St

88 St

Av

Norwood Av

80 St

Aquaduct

ashwick Av-Aberdeen St

Cleveland St

Ⓒ Grant Av

JFK

Bwy/Eastern Pkwy

Euclid Av

Howard Beach JFK Airport

Alabama Av

Shepherd Av

Van Siclen Av

Broadway East New York

Atlantic Av Liberty Av

Van Siclen Av

Sutter Av

Rockaway Av

Van Siclen Av Ⓛ New Lots Av

Saratoga Av

Junius St

Pennsylvania Av
Livonia Av
New Lots Av

v Rd

E 105 St

St Rockaway Ⓛ Pkwy-Canarsie

ch Av

everly Rd

Broad Channel Ⓢ

Newkirk Av

Ⓩ ◇ Flatbush Av

BROOKLYN

Kings Hwy

w M

Ⓐ

Jamaica Bay

Av U

wy

Neck Rd
Sheepshead Bay

y U

Av X

Beach 90 St
Beach 98 St
Beach 105 St

see Far Rockaway Inset

Neptune Av

Rockaway Park
Beach 116 St Ⓐ Ⓢ

Brighton Beach Ⓠ

Ocean Pkwy

W 8 St/NY Aquarium

Atlantic Ocean

Island